Six Sigma
Financial Tracking
and Reporting

Other Books in the Six Sigma Operational Methods Series

Parveen S. Goel, Rajeev Jain, and Praveen Gupta • *Six Sigma for Transactions and Service*

Praveen Gupta • *The Six Sigma Performance Handbook*

Thomas McCarty, Lorraine Daniels, Michael Bremer, and Praveen Gupta • *The Six Sigma Black Belt Handbook*

Alastair Muir • *Lean Six Sigma Statistics*

Andrew Sleeper • *Design for Six Sigma*

Kai Yang • *Design for Six Sigma for Service*

Six Sigma Financial Tracking and Reporting

Michael Bremer
President
The Cumberland Group
Chicago, Illinois

Brian McKibben
Partner and Vice President
The Cumberland Group
Chicago, Illinois

Thomas McCarty
Jones Lang LaSalle Americas, Inc.
Chicago, Illinois

McGraw-Hill

New York   Chicago   San Francisco   Lisbon   London   Madrid
Mexico City   Milan   New Delhi   San Juan   Seoul
Singapore   Sydney   Toronto

The *McGraw·Hill* Companies

Cataloging-in-Publication Data is on file with the Library of Congress

1 2 3 4 5 6 7 8 9 0   DOC/DOC   0 1 0 9 8 7 6 5

ISBN 0-07-145891-3

The sponsoring editor for this book was Kenneth P. McCombs and the production supervisor was Pamela A. Pelton. It was set in Times by International Typesetting and Composition. The art director for the cover was Handel Low.

Printed and bound by RR Donnelley.

This book is printed on recycled, acid-free paper containing a minimum of 50% recycled, de-inked fiber.

McGraw-Hill books are available at special quantity discounts to use as premiums and sales promotions, or for use in corporate training programs. For more information, please write to the Director of Special Sales, McGraw-Hill Professional, Two Penn Plaza, New York, NY 10121-2298. Or contact your local bookstore.

CONTENTS

PREFACE

In the 1980s the late Bill Smith, a senior field engineer at Motorola, coined the expression "Six Sigma" as a more rigorous approach to reducing defects in Motorola's business processes. His approach quickly demonstrated the power of establishing common metrics, setting outrageous goals, and applying analytical rigor to achieve those goals. Motorola University was created to foster implementation of this Six Sigma methodology. Their charter was to build employee capability globally, with a special emphasis on both technical skills and the leadership skills required to achieve the highest levels of business performance, and customer loyalty.

Six Sigma as a management system evolved out of benchmarking conducted by Motorola University at organizations like General Electric, Dow, DuPont, Citibank, and Caterpillar. It has become a powerful tool for driving break-through change inside a business, integrating performance improvement and key business strategies with focused execution.

This book grew out of the *Six Sigma Black Belt Handbook* published in November, 2004. One chapter in the book, "Financial and Performance Measurement," discussed the problem of reported savings, not seeming to make their way to the P&L. Hence our fun title for this book, *I Had a Million Dollars in Savings, But My P&L Did Not Change. Where Did They Go?* Ken McCombs, our editor for the last book, liked this chapter so much he asked us to write a new book based on this subject.

This book provides insights for Black Belts, trying to capture "real" savings, Six Sigma leaders, as well as, performance improvement practitioners using lean manufacturing, lean enterprise, or other business improvement methodologies. It can help engineers talk to accountants about savings, and it provides a number of different ways to ensure that more savings actually make their way to the P&L.

Written by experienced instructors from Motorola University and the Cumberland Group, Chicago, this book is inspired by years of teaching and coaching focused on helping countless aspiring Six Sigma and Lean practitioners to understand and apply these powerful improvement methodologies. These instructors and coaches know from experience what Black Belts and senior leaders need to know to be more successful in their Six Sigma and Lean implementations.

This book avoids the theoretical and focuses instead on practical insights that will drive success at both a project level and an organization-wide implementation. The makings of this book actually emerged over almost 30 years. It took about that long to acquire a reasonably complete view of how organizations *really* work.

The original concept seemed somewhat narrow. But subsequent discussions clarified that the only way to fully explain how Lean-Sigma-CI project results get to the bottom line is by tracking the upstream business process metrics that lead downstream to the financial statement. This is a much broader view that will be valuable to anyone wrestling with the role of Lean-Sigma-CI efforts in their business.

This book provides structure, practical mental models, and some implementation outlines. Hopefully, it emphasizes the importance of "the careful journey," versus "just do it" wishful thinking, i.e., the "whats" of tracking Lean-Sigma-CI results into the financial statement. To fully explain the "hows," we may have to follow later with an in-depth discussion of how four things interplay through all of this: visionary business goals, detailed journey roadmaps, technical processes, and people processes.

If nothing else, this should help explain why measurement is a key to organizational success. The clock and sports scoreboards are basic examples of the impact metrics have on the effectiveness of people working together. It's tempting to say that measurement is the most important of the "fundamentals of high-performance business processes." But I have to stop short of that because I believe that structured "involvement" of the entire workforce is a more fundamental root cause that makes use of measurement and the other fundamentals.

Michael Bremer

Brian McKibben

Thomas McCarty

ACKNOWLEDGMENTS

Michael Bremer: Man, this is hard work! First, I have to thank my coauthors: Tom McCarty, formerly with Motorola and now EVP and Six Sigma Practice Leader at Jones Lang LaSalle, because I never would have had an opportunity to write a second book, if he had not invited me to the party in writing *The Six Sigma Black Belt Handbook*; and Brian McKibben, who is also my partner in Cumberland. Brian has put up with me for close to 20 years, allowing me to bounce new ideas off of the wall and then even more importantly, try them. Brian adds much needed structure to my thought process.

My first partner though is Lynn Sieben. After 30 years of marriage, I still get excited when I see her. She has been a constant source of encouragement and support throughout the writing of both books and in my life. My mother, Mary, was proud of the first book; I'm sorry that she is not with us to see the second.

Finally, I wish to thank you, the reader. We wrote these stories for you. If you read this material and use it to improve performance, to better understand and probe, learning what financial numbers truly represent, and if your organization becomes more competitive and a better place to work, then all of our hard work was not hard work.

When Tom McCarty encouraged me to become a Six Sigma Black Belt, I really did not look forward to the ordeal. Having worked with organizations over 30 years on process improvement, I just did not feel, I had that much more to learn. Surprisingly (to me anyway) is the higher energy level, enthusiasm, and excitement I again have for something I love doing.

Six Sigma as a management system has the power to transform organizations. I am not saying other improvement methodologies could not do the same. But the structure of the DMAIC (if you don't understand it … you must read the inside) problem-solving process with its spotlight on measurement, and the management system's focus on strategic priorities are very powerful. When I first started doing this type of work in the early 1980s, I wanted a tool like this. In some ways, it is so simple; I can't believe it took me so long to find it. I am very much appreciative of my learning and experiences with Motorola University, as well as all of my other client relationships, where we have been able to explore better ways of doing work.

Brian McKibben: I have to thank several people who helped make the book possible. Michael Bremer, my business partner for many years, has been a tremendous help because of his eclectic way of looking at the world. That provides balance for my structural view that needs a defined process for predictability, but can get bogged down in the details along the way. The results of collaboration are absolute proof that one plus one can add up to three or more.

To an old friend and one-time boss, Jim Nolan, I have to say thanks for being a role model for the way I view both the business management process and the change management process. They seemed to be instinct with Jim, but were always hard work for me. It was reflection on how Jim managed the organizational Support Systems that influenced the Business Process Model as it's shown several times in the book. That provided the explanation for how dramatic business changes can be made seemingly overnight if you have a clear view of which levers need to be repositioned for the changes at hand. I hope you notice where measurement fits in that model.

And to my wife Joanne and sons Jason and Greg, I have to say thank you for putting up with my 24/7 preoccupation with business. I have badly shortchanged them of my time, which I am now vowing to change. One consolation is that they are all doing wonderful things in their chosen fields and I hope that just a little bit of that was due to the little time I spent in seed planting or tilling.

Lastly, I want to thank the many people I've worked with over the years, who have offered feedback and ideas that shaped my views of the work world. And special thanks to those of you who noticed my subtle (hopefully) efforts contributed to their team's success. I suspect these are the compliments that keep coaches going.

Six Sigma
Financial Tracking
and Reporting

Introduction

We are here to make another world.
W. EDWARDS DEMING

1.1 Overview

How many people inside your organization would say, "We have the best performance measurement system; we learn so much from it!" Or, "This performance improvement initiative is really great! Our customers, employees, and shareholders all benefited from it." Or might they say something else?

What would they say about leadership? Would they be able to describe the three most important things executive leadership plans to accomplish? Would they have any idea of leadership's role in governing and providing active support for improvement activities beyond listening to a PowerPoint presentation heard with hundreds of other employees?

If they worked for General Electric, Allied Signal, or a handful of other organizations, they probably know what the leadership believes is truly important. But leadership teams in many other organizations tend to have general statements about what is important: We need to innovate, we need to improve customer satisfaction, and so forth. How different those statements are from "We need to be number one or two in our industries," or "We need to promote boundarylessness across our lines of business," which were two GE key statements in the 1990s. Both were backed up with very specific performance metrics.

The title for this book could have been *I Had a Million Dollars in Savings, But My Bottom Line Did Not Change? Where Did Those Savings Go?* Questions one might ask: Were those savings real? Did they make any difference to the business? Did they increase or decrease credibility between people in the organization? In the world of business performance improvement, these questions have been asked many times over the years. The historical record of most improvement initiatives shows a failure to transform improvements into visible financial results. This is not a new problem. It has been a major issue in business performance improvement initiatives over the last 20 years. However, organizations often improved more than they realized.

There are many Six Sigma Black Belt and Lean Manufacturing books on the market that describe the Control phase of the DMAIC model, or where "lean accounting" texts touch on the simplification of financial reporting, and where the Balanced Scorecard emphasizes the importance of leading indicators and the use of an overall improvement index. Project management books may also describe techniques for sustaining the gains. But none of these texts provide executives with a convenient tool they can use to manage the current year earnings and make certain that savings from improvement efforts actually reach the bottom line, or to understand why, when they don't. This text addresses these issues.

1.2   Numbers Paradox

This book is about measurement, yet at the same time this story has a paradox. How can an organization be numbers driven, yet *not be* numbers driven? What is an appropriate balance between stretch and unrealistic goals? How can leadership governance of performance improvement initiatives move an organization from average performance (which by definition is where most companies and people operate) to great performance? What actions move people from going through the motions, but largely gaming the system, to true commitment? Every organization faces these challenges, whether for-profit or nonprofit, business or government. Unfortunately we have not discovered a "magic pill" to fix these problems. But the answers are not complex. As you read through these chapters you will discover simple steps you can take. Simple does not equal easy, but they are practical, doable actions—one pathway to higher-level performance.

A famous quote attributed to numerous people runs along the lines of "What gets measured is what gets done." A corollary to that expression could also be, "What gets measured is what gets reported." Dr. W. Edwards Deming said many things about measurement in numerous presentations, in *Out of the Crisis,* and in the three-ring notebook that traveled everywhere by his side. Two quotes that influenced the writing of this book are:

1. "95% of all troubles in an organization are the result of the system (processes) and only 5% are the fault of people."
2. "Over 97% of the circumstances that affect an organization's results are immeasurable, and that a disproportionate amount of management's time is spent on the 3%."

Consider the second quote for a moment from the perspective of a healthy person. There is not a one number that tells you if a person is healthy. And if "healthy" includes a mentaly well-balanced or a fulfilling life, then metrics become even more difficult. Consider a few: pulse, wealth, and maybe sickness. With sickness you may know it when you see it, but sometimes it takes years to become noticeable. This is certainly true of many types of cancers. Wealth, you could count it. But have you ever met an unhappy, wealthy person, or seen an artist who (from your perspective) is bubbling with talent, only to see him or her commit suicide? There is a lot going on inside of a person that is not measurable. Measures for any one of the above items, or even for all three, would still not tell you about the whole person.

That does not mean that meaningful metrics don't exist—many do. Pulse rate, cholesterol levels, temperature, smile counts, observing people serving others, marriages that last more than 50 years, number of good friends, number of promotions, and the like. Some of these are easier to measure than others. But no one metric tells it all.

The same is true of organizations. No one number does it. Balanced Scorecards attempt to bring these multiple perspectives together. And they are certainly better than just one number. Just like with a person, the real depth, the real power is the story behind the numbers, not the number. The number is simply a point-in-time indicator. To know what is really going on, you have to think, and learn the story behind the numbers. Unfortunately, if you look at the way many organizations implement this, they appear to have read Norton and Kaplan's "The Balanced Scorecard—Measures that Drive Performance," in the *Harvard Business Review,* 1992. And then took the four categories suggested by Norton and Kaplan and said, "Well, we need one of these, and one of these, and presto! We have a Balanced Scorecard." That was not the intention of the authors. The metrics on most Balanced Scorecards seem to come from what we *can* measure versus what we *should* measure.

Deming once said, "Most troubles result from process/system problems, not from a person's fault." This was extremely profound thinking, when he said it.

There were not very many people thinking from a process perspective in the 1970s and 1980s. This is still a difficult concept for many people to understand today. Here are two short stories that might better explain this hypothesis.

Story One. A new product development team is asked to develop a blockbuster new product. The team begins its assignment using a set of requirements, constraints, and customer needs provided by marketing and senior management. Halfway through the project, senior management comes to the team and says, "Here are several *other* things we would like this product to do." The company had already committed to tooling, had purchased some equipment, and the team was working pretty effectively. Later, when the product is launched, customers are less than impressed; parts of the design look like an afterthought, and sales only hit 50 percent of targeted levels. Who is at fault? One could point a finger at several candidates, but it would probably be more beneficial for this organization to address these issues from a process perspective. What should the rules be for changing foundation elements of a new design? Should the organization have a series of simple, rapid prototypes to get customer feedback during the design stage? How were the original requirements developed? And so forth. In this story, from the details provided, it is impossible to know the right answer; but more gain would most likely come from fixing the processes, not from beating on the new product development team.

Story Two. Picture a customer service call center. Employee turnover runs around 30 percent per year. When customers call, they are routed to the next available representative. A record exists on when the last call was made, but the screen takes several seconds to load and the representatives are supposed to be resolving their calls within 45 seconds. Policy information is also spread over several screens and in order to answer questions, customer service representatives typically need to go through four or five computer screens. Customer's satisfaction with the process is OK. There is no segmentation of phone calls by customer type. Are you starting to get the idea? Problems in this unit are most likely not employee-fault-type problems. The business processes in the organization are making it difficult for employees to do anything more than average level work. If this unit is going to excel, it is not by telling people to work harder or smarter.

And in today's world, it is harder, not easier, to design and implement "great" business processes due to the complexity of the environment and the fast pace of change.

Organizations also need a language people can understand. Engineers and accountants often encounter difficulties when trying to communicate and cooperate on measuring improvement. They speak in totally different languages when they look at the world of improvement. Today, lean accounting efforts are helping to bridge that gap, but the chasm is still wide and many organizations still struggle with this language barrier. Engineers look at the physical world. Accountants tend to look at how the macro pieces go together. Then, they try to tell a story about the business by looking at the numbers; but they don't have all the pieces of the puzzle to fully describe what is happening in the business from a numbers perspective. The Financial Bridge Model will shed some light on this problem.

1.3   Performance Improvement Initiatives: Were They Failures?

Many performance improvement initiatives have come and gone over the last 20 years (See Exhibit 1.1).

In the eyes of many executives, these initiatives failed to meet their expectations. Studies by A. T. Kearney, McKinsey, and Bain & Company, among others, have shown that 70 percent of executives stated their performance improvement initiatives failed to meet their expectations. While there was a 5-year period in the early 1990s where winners of the Malcolm Baldrige Quality Award experienced significant stock appreciation (more than the

Exhibit 1.1   Performance Improvement Initiatives

growth experienced by their respective industries) they, too, fell by the wayside as the stock market experienced dramatic losses after the year 2000.

So is it true that these programs are not worth while? Or was something else happening? Let's first consider why companies embark on these initiatives:

- Improve competitive position.
- Improve customer satisfaction.
- Address a major organizational issue (quality, timeliness, and the like).
- Increase sales (revenues).
- Improve profitability.
- Decrease costs.
- Improve employee/management relationships.
- Identify major innovation opportunities.
- And the list goes on.

Often when senior executives are interviewed at the beginning of a major organizational improvement initiative they will state, "… this initiative will help us leap ahead of the competition." So their expectations might graph as follows:

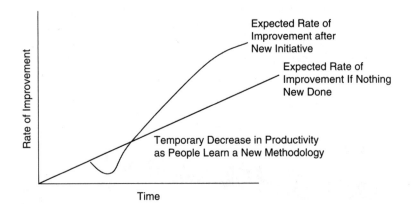

There is actually a temporary drop in performance/productivity when organizations implement a major new improvement initiative. This was discovered in research done by General Electric and DuPont in the 1950s. The time invested in training and in learning new skills and how to apply them to work results in a temporary drop in performance. This is true for large-scale change initiatives in the use of new software and in the use of new equipment to do work. It simply takes people a while to figure out the new methods. This drop-off in performance is called the "J" curve effect. It is also called the "learning curve" to understanding new methods.

After the learning curve is absorbed, managers typically expected to see a great leap ahead of the competition. But think about it. What is the competition most likely doing at roughly the same time? Most likely they are implementing a similar improvement initiative. The good thing is they are probably also doing a mediocre job of implementing it, so at the end of the day when leadership looks around to see what has changed, at least the situation hasn't gotten worse. From a competitive perspective, fortunately, very few organizations that implement these change initiatives realize the maximum potential benefits they could get from it.

Now consider the question: Were these performance improvement initiatives worthwhile? Let's answer this question with another question: Would you rather buy a car for driving everyday made new from any manufacturer? But it is a 1971 car using 1971 processes and procedures. Or would you rather buy a car that was made by any manufacturer yesterday?

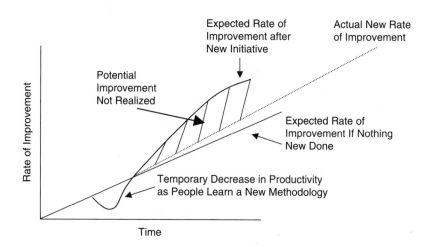

Most people say, "I would buy the car made yesterday." So there really have been major improvements made across the board. But relative to competition, most organizations did not accomplish the great leap forward in front of everyone they were anticipating. Unfortunately, many organizations could have made far more improvement happen than they actually realized. This shortfall results in many of the frustrations expressed.

The Toyota Motor Company might be one of the few exceptions to this experience. For over 50 years they have plugged away at one pretty consistent theme, "Eliminate Waste," in all its forms, and practiced learning to see waste in new ways. Other companies try to copy the Toyota Production System (TPS) or the Toyota Development System (TDS) for new product development, but they miss the essence. They look at the tools and figure if they simply toss those tools in their tool box, their organization will be like Toyota—perhaps a slight oversimplification. But Toyota has been misinterpreted by many people over the years. Atsushi Niimi, president of Toyota Motors Manufacturing North America once said, "Many people have tried to capture what we do in a book. At Toyota we do not have a 'book.' This is the way we live. What we do is simple, it could be summarized on three pages, but what we do is not easy."

Later during the course of an informal conversation at an AME* national meeting, Mr. Niimi went on to say, "Of course now we are giving some thought to writing three pages for our American managers. They tend to try to do too much. Our American managers don't seem to have the same patience to let people learn and to figure it out in order to obtain 'real' knowledge." This touches on a subject we will come back to again and again in this book: Open dialog, a willingness to listen, and creative tension.

1.4   Purpose of This Book

This book is about making the metric systems more dynamic and the governance of improvement initiatives more meaningful. It provides several templates for understanding why all savings may not reach the bottom line. And also addresses why it is so difficult for accounting, engineering, and other people involved in business performance improvement to be on the same page, when the end goals of "better, faster, cheaper" should be common to all.

The book uses the Six Sigma DMAIC problem-solving methodology: Define, Measure, Analyze, Improve, and Control to tell a measurement and governance story (See Exhibit 1.2).

People around the world, from many different cultural backgrounds, have said the following. "The people who get promoted in our organization are very good at identifying the problem and then quickly coming up with a solution to fix it." So, rather than follow the steps of the DMAIC model

---

*Association of Manufacturing Excellence; www.ame.org.

1.0 Define Opportunities	2.0 Measure Performance	3.0 Analyze Opportunity	4.0 Improve Performance	5.0 Control Performance
What is important?	How are we doing?	What is wrong?	What needs to be done?	How do we guarantee performance?

Exhibit 1.2   DMAIC Problem-Solving Steps

outlined above, they jump from "identify what is important to fix" to "improve it." It sounds great, but we live in a world of complexity. (See Exhibit 1.3).

Most business processes are too complicated. Over time a process gets modified to handle exceptions. Pretty soon all transactions get run through this extremely complicated process, just in case an exception takes place. Even though 80 percent of the time most of the checks and adjustments are not needed. A quick example: a manufacturing company on the south side of Chicago that makes a custom and a standard product runs all customer orders through engineering. They check the drawings, do a series of calculations, and then, without making adjustments to 75 percent of the orders, hand them off to operations for manufacture. Or a health care foundation that funds research projects checks the tax status of major universities and hospitals, just in case their tax status changed since the last time that organization received a grant. The number of times this problem surfaced in 20 years is zero!

Parts of this book will stress the need for speed. Much about speed is good; speed can drive out a lot of process waste. But in the extreme, speed can

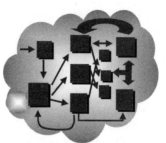

Most organization processes are too complex; they may be world class but no one understand them!

Exhibit 1.3   Complexity Diagram

drive goofy (*scientific term*) behaviors. Managers may know how to do it best because of their experience; it will take the subordinate more time. But "time" is an investment in future knowledge and in ownership of our workspace. Sometimes in haste to get something accomplished, they overlook the power of this investment. When people own their workspace, they have a greater feeling of responsibility and accountability. This feeling of responsibility and accountability gets torn down when other people are telling you what to do and how to do it, which happens way more often in organizations than is necessary.

1.4.1   Problems with the "Quick Fix"

Sustaining the gains is a major problem in any improvement project. Things that allow gains to slip away just happen. So when a fix gets made, it does not stay fixed. Sooner or later the problem resurfaces again, or the fix causes a disruption someplace else. We have probably all heard the expression, "Some how there is never time to do things the right way, but we always have time to do something over again."

There is nothing magic about the DMAIC problem solving process, but it does emphasize measurement more than most other performance improvement methodologies. The DMAIC model from Six Sigma, if followed rigorously, will help organizations to sustain the gains. The whole idea of actually gathering some evidence to measure the significance of a problem to have some objective data, and then to actually take time to analyze the problem before jumping to a quick fix, could be an innovation in many organizations.

Each chapter in this book strives to go from an organizational governance or leadership level down to a project team and department level. It covers leadership governance responsibilities because they are such a critical component of making improvements happen. The way executives lead an improvement initiative is a major factor in the types of savings that get reported, the actual improvement realized, and the number of improvements that get left on the table, never to be realized within the organization.

A major short fall of most lean improvement initiatives is also metrics. Engineers tend to like "lean" because of its very physical orientation toward improvement. But leaders that do not frequently venture out into the operational area of their business, be it manufacturing or transaction processing, typically do not "see" the physical improvements that engineers involved in improvement projects tout! It takes a while for those improvements to work their way through the system, especially if they are not focused on the ideal projects from a customer and P&L oriented perspective.

1.5   Chaos and Fractals

A few points in this book touch on *chaos theory*. Chaos in many ways is the opposite of what you might expect. It does not mean disorder, it means nonlinear. Chaos theory predicts that complex nonlinear systems are inherently unpredictable using linear thinking. Chaos theory is the study of forever-changing complex systems. Organizations tend to be complex, unpredictable systems, in that you cannot take the past, and always predict the future. Many times looking at the past works, so we may think it's a truth. But using linear mathematics and linear thinking in that environment sometimes results in misleading conclusions.

When one considers behaviors, or rules that people follow, very much of the behavior in an organization is predictable when looking at groups, but this is not true when you look at individual behaviors or pieces of the organization. Often, the way to best understand such an unpredictable system lies not in exact equations, but in representations of the behaviors of the system—in plots of strange attractors or in fractals. Fractals represent one way to begin to pierce this veil of invisibility and apparent disorder. Fractals exist in the world of mathematics and in nature. So even the most unstable system can have predictive qualities, if people understand the patterns and rules.

Benoit Mandelbrot, a research scientist at IBM, defined a fractal as a geometric object which can be divided into parts, each of which is similar to the original object. Fractals are said to possess infinite detail, and are generally independent of scale. In many cases a fractal can be generated by a repeating pattern, typically a recursive or iterative process.

Now consider a simple example in an organization. In a "do it now" culture, where decisive action is generally a top-ranked trait, people may be conditioned to act quickly because that is more likely to receive positive recognition than other behaviors. In some instances this is totally appropriate behavior. Time spent in "preaction analysis" in this type of environment can easily be construed as "analysis paralysis" in an impatient business world. So a repeating behavior pattern can emerge in this type of environment. When other behaviors are needed people are less likely to do them, even when they know the facts. These patterns trap organizations into certain behavioral modes that make it difficult for people to do the right thing.

They happen when:

- People get into trouble when they don't react according to the expected norm.
- The data are too complex or too numerous to easily use.
- The process metrics in use do not truly reflect reality.
- There is little accountability over the long term for decision making, because of the complexity of the organization.

Using the knowledge/approaches used in chaos theory (fractals being one of them) we can better understand the underlying rules that cause the resultant behaviors and then investigate what changes can be made with expected results.

Here is an example of how rules-based behavior differs from control-based methods. A few years ago Gregg Ekberg, a young engineer at a GM automotive plant, was struggling with the problem of paint booth utilization and changeover cost. He kept trying to develop traditional control-based scheduling algorithms that would send the ideal mix through the booths, but nothing seemed to work. He worked with a crazy guy named Dick Morley— inventor of the PLC and a leading thinker in manufacturing and automation. They had been doing some research in the application of chaos theories to practical manufacturing problems.

They decided to experiment with the paint booth. Ultimately they developed a three-rules model that they called a *bidding system.* A paint booth would look at the cars coming down the line and place a bid based on three questions. If the answer to any one of the questions was "yes," that car belonged to that paint booth:

1. Is one of the next three cars in line the same color I'm currently painting? If no, then ask—
2. Is one of the cars coming down the line a rush job? If no, then ask—
3. Is the next car in line unclaimed by the other booths? If no, just keep going down the line for the next unclaimed vehicle.

What were the results? Ernest Vahala began testing Morley's chaos computer system at the General Motors assembly plant in Fort Wayne, Indiana. At the time, Vahala was director of manufacturing engineering for

GM's worldwide truck group, so he had the clout to try an experiment that even he regarded as a trifle bizarre. More importantly, the chaos-based approach "reduced the software we required by nearly 100 times" says Vahala—no small matter given the enormous cost of software engineering. "It ran beautifully" says Vahala. "It saved $1 million a year in paint alone. You don't have to be a rocket scientist to say 'Holy damn!' I became a complete believer."[*]

Now for the depressing part. This system increased throughput, decreased toxic waste (excess paint waste), significantly reduced cost and complexity. So what did GM do with this breakthrough idea? They dismantled the computer system. Vahala explains that the company is replacing its hydraulic paint robots with electric ones, an overhaul that requires the installation of new software. He says, "GM will drop the chaos approach," and admits, "There continues to be resistance to chaos because people don't understand it. It defies traditional logic."[†]

If your organization is going to move from average performance to great performance, people's beliefs and behaviors will need to change. Most people don't believe they can be great. And there is comfort in being average.

In our hearts, we believe "greatness" is obtainable. We have tried to share ideas and practical actions you can take. They are sprinkled throughout this book. Your challenge is to unearth them, understand them, and use them in a way that makes sense to your organization, to your customers, and to the challenges that you face.

1.6   People Side of Measurement/Change

Much of the magic in the world comes from interactions between people: love, relationships, joy of discovery, high-performing teams, learning about different cultures, friends, and the like. At the same time, much of the misery in the world comes from the way people interact: wars, dysfunctional teams, crime, cruelty, and the like. While metrics may not cause behaviors as extreme as those two polar opposites, metrics can drive positive or negative behaviors.

---

[*]*The Man from Chaos,* William Green; Fast Company; November, 1995 (first issue).
[†]Ibid.

Deming talked about companies that manage through fear. While a little bit of fear can sometimes be a good thing; fear drives goofy behavior when it comes to performance measurement. People like to stay out of trouble, so in many organizations there is a tendency to take actions that make the numbers look good. Even if people realize those actions may not make sense from an overall business perspective. If this book stimulates an idea for action, that is a wonderful thing. But before we act we should think. We are really trying to guide organizations toward a greater sense of profound knowledge about their organization, a level of deeper thinking. Actions taken merely to make the numbers look good are not a good thing. People with courage and intelligence can find a better way.

In a *Fortune* magazine article, Jim Collins (author of *Good to Great*) was asked, "Why are people decisions so important?" He responded,

> I look at my research notes and I look at interview transcripts from the executives we've interviewed, one theme that comes through is that their greatest decisions were not "what" but "who." They were people decisions.... Let's take the story of a company heading into a very uncertain world: Wells Fargo in the late 1970s. Everybody knows the storm of deregulation is going to hit. But nobody knows precisely how it's going to shake out. When is it going to hit? What exact form is it going to take? What impact is it going to have on the banking industry? Dick Cooley, chief executive of Wells Fargo at that time, was very clear with us when we did our research. He said, in essence, I did not know what we were going to have to do to prevail through deregulation, because it was an uncertain set of contingencies. Too many of them. But I did know that if I spent the 1970s building a team of the most capable executives possible, they would figure out what to do when deregulation hit. He couldn't lay down a plan for what was going to happen, because he didn't know what was going to happen. So his decision was actually a bunch of decisions about getting the people who could deal with whatever deregulation turned out to be.[*]

1.6.1 Digging Deeper to Increase Knowledge

In the May 2005 issue of *Harvard Business Review*, Richard Tanner Pascale and Jerry Sternin wrote an article titled, "Your Company's Secret Change Agents." In this article they talk about people working at half of their

---

[*]"Collins on Tough Call," Jerry Useem; *Fortune Magazine,* June 27, 2005.

potential and the tyranny of averages, which is also a strong theme in this text. Assume for the moment that half of the people in your organization were below average (some might say that is a mathematical fact by the way); that means that half of your people are also above average. But the average company's approach to solving problems is to look at the under-achievers and try to fix them. Pascale and Sternin suggest an alternative approach. The next few paragraphs paraphrase one of their stories. This story also relates to examples used in later this text from Nissan, Allied Signal, and Toyota USA.

They suggest six steps that provide an alternative model to traditional perceptions about how change works. You can read the article if you have an interest; it's very good. One of the six steps states "reframe through facts." This nest very well with the second step of the DMAIC model "Measure: Determine how well we are doing; gather some evidence." They describe the importance of reframing a problem to get a different perspective on the situation. Look for exceptions to the problem. If most people are struggling, who is doing well?

They share an example of an elementary school in the rural province of Misiones, Argentina, where student dropout rates were extremely high. The classic definition of the problem (commonly given around the world in poor districts) was: teachers were not paid enough, parents did not care, the facilities were lousy, and so forth. Most participants believed this to be the "truth." Then someone asked if any schools in the same district had a better track record. Most of the 120 schools were clustered near the median, but one school had a near 100 percent retention of its students through the sixth grade and nearly 90 percent through the tenth grade.

The first thought was these people are playing a numbers game. But a group went to investigate.

> They discovered the differentiating factor had little to do with what was happening in the classroom. The teachers there were negotiating "learning contracts" with rural parents before the beginning of each school year. In effect, the teachers were enrolling illiterate parents as partners in their children's education. As the children learned to read, add and subtract, they could help their parents take advantage of government subsidies and compute the amount earned from crops or owed at the village store. With parents as partners, students showed up at school and did their assignments.

> The teachers and principals who had participated in the workshop began negotiating similar contracts with families of at-risk

children. One year later, dropout rates in Misiones had reportedly decreased by half.[*]

This is a powerful change tool. Rather than leadership telling people what to do, they are allowed to discover a solution on their own. This learning experience is powerful and emotional. Obviously there is also power in removing the filters (biases) we all carry and learning new "truths" which fit with the idea of profound knowledge.

1.7   Profound Knowledge

Dr. W. Edwards Deming coined the expression, or certainly made the words "profound knowledge" more famous. Deming's management theory is centered on thinking of an organization, its suppliers and customers as a system. He called this *profound knowledge*—a system designed and managed to yield maximum value to all involved. Deming identified four interacting parts to this system of knowledge:

- Appreciation for a system
- Knowledge about variation
- Theory of knowledge
- Theory of psychology

1.7.1   Appreciation for a System

Appreciation for a system means that parts of an organization are always considered in relationship to the other parts. Every process is connected to another process. When a change gets made, it has ripple effects beyond the borders of the process being worked. Recognition of the interdependencies within and between organizations, and the potential of these relationships is crucial in order to maximize value. Simply speaking, the whole is greater than the sum of the parts.

An example of failure to appreciate a system would be setting up divisions or departments within an organization that compete with each other. While it divides the whole into bite-size pieces, if managed incorrectly it inhibits the optimization of value. When divisions or departments are thoughtfully managed as a whole system, greater benefits will be realized.

---

[*]"Your Company's Secret Change Agents," Richard Tanner Pascale and Jerry Sternin; *Harvard Business Review,* May, 2005.

Deming suggested that key parties involved with the organization (including shareholders, personnel, customers, suppliers, and the broader society) should be better off than they would be if the organization did not exist. Think about it. This is a different philosophy than "win-lose;" following this philosophy everyone gains. It is impossible to maximize every component part of a system. There needs to be a sense of balance (creative tension) between the parts. If each component tries to maximize its individual piece, the overall system flow will break down. One component part may maximize its piece of the pie for a period of time, but it will not be sustained over the long term. This is a major problem in U.S. manufacturing today with the excessive attention paid to shareholders.

1.7.2   Knowledge about Variation

The second part of Deming's theory of profound knowledge deals with understanding variation; it requires separating common-cause and special-cause variation. All processes experience variation. Over the long term, variation is responsible for evolution. On a shorter time frame, variation takes place for all sorts of reasons. A 6-foot, 250-pound man working on an automotive assembly line is going to do his job differently than a 110-pound, 5-foot-tall woman doing the same job.

Deming emphasized the importance of understanding (through proper statistical methods) the degree of common cause variation that is a natural part of a repeating process and special cause variation. Common cause variation comes from the environment, processes, equipment, material, and people. Too often, managers tamper with systems that are in control, which is just a likely to make something worse as it is to make a temporary improvement. Or they blame people when actually 95 percent of the results are actually attributable to the process. Those actions undermine credibility and destroy relationships between managers and employees. For example: Common cause variation takes place when service times are longer at the busy lunch hour and 7:00 pm when a restaurant experiences maximum capacity utilization.

Special cause variation represents extraneous phenomena or the existence of external issues that should be addressed. This type of variation demands a different response than common cause. Special cause variation takes place in a restaurant when a new server is working, when there was a recipe change in the kitchen, or when a stove breaks down.

Knowledge about variation allows managers to make better decisions regarding what variation should be reduced, and what variation should be left alone. Without this understanding, the system cannot be managed or improved. Common cause variation is only improved through changing or fixing the process. Optimization of the component parts does not optimize the whole; it usually makes the system worse.

1.7.3 Theory of Knowledge

The third part of Deming's system of profound knowledge concerns understanding how knowledge is created and used (i.e., how people learn). Information is not knowledge. Deming defined knowledge as a rational prediction (or theory) about a relationship between phenomena that are separate in time. A rational prediction conforms faithfully to observations that have been made in the past.

Much of what Deming believed fits with the way people talk today about learning organizations and continuous improvement. Simply speaking, a theory must change when new observations refute previous theory. Knowledge is built through cycles of theory, experience, and then corroboration or revisions of the theory. These improvements create new value in a system. New knowledge typically comes from outside the system. That is one of the reasons it takes cross-functional project teams to implement meaningful improvement to complex processes.

Knowledge, or good theory, is essential for creating value in a system. Knowledge must be extracted from experience, and sought from outside the system. Deming encouraged us to see knowledge in terms of useful models (theories) that can always be improved. Copying or following tradition for its own sake does not lead to knowledge, actions need to be based on a sound theory and then corroborated over time, because change is always happening.

1.7.4 Theory of Psychology

The fourth part of Deming's system of profound knowledge deals with knowledge about people. Understanding what people do and why they do it. Some people get upset over the use of the word "psychology." Psychology simply helps us to understand human behavior and the way people interact, i.e., interactions between customers and suppliers or between managers and their people, and the way people do things.

Deming was especially concerned with effective and ineffective uses of motivation. He emphasized the power of the joy, satisfaction, and pride that occurs when one contributes to an effective system. If you have ever been part of a high-performing team, you know much of the joy comes from accomplishment. Team members may work very hard, but the goals they accomplish and the trust they have in their teammates makes for a wonderful lifetime experience.

Deming noted how many typical employee reward programs run contrary to appreciation or understanding of the overall system. Many motivational programs do more harm than good. They hurt, rather than help, morale with their win-lose philosophies, or with the emphasis on just one component part of the overall system. Deming was also concerned about organizational cultures based on fear, which are destructive to both the system and to individuals.

At the root level most projects, most work, and most decisions get done by people. Therefore leadership's understanding of psychology is essential to success.

1.8   Measurement

The chapters in this book share actions, stories from successful and not-so-successful organizations and provide examples you can use to address similar issues in your organization. We have drawn on experiences from a variety of industries, including nonprofit enterprises. Measurement is relatively simple, but selecting the right metrics is not easy. It's very much like a puzzle. Place the right pieces in place and a picture emerges. Place the wrong pieces in place, and they don't exactly fit, the picture (if you can see one) looks disjointed and distorted.

Consider *Fortune* magazine's "Most Admired Companies." They measure their top 100 against eight criteria:

1. Innovation
2. Employee talent
3. Use of corporate assets
4. Social responsibility
5. Quality of management
6. Financial soundness
7. Long-term investment
8. Quality of products and services

At least five of the items on that list have a fundamental "people" component:

- *Innovation:* Does the organization use its knowledge capital to help grow the business?
- *Employee talent:* Are people bright? Does the organization foster an idea of teamness? Are people permitted to fully use their talents?
- *Social responsibility:* Does the organization look beyond its walls to the communities and societies in which it operates?
- *Quality of management:* Do they make wise decisions?
- *Quality of products and services:* Does the organization have high standards and hold itself accountable for that level of performance?

This list differs somewhat from the Baldrige Criteria (U.S. National Quality Award) or the Shingo Prize (manufacturing award), but it has a similar feel. If organizations are looking for key metrics to use, any one of these could provide useful perspectives and insights into the business. The other thing this list offers is a sense of balance. Balance not so much in terms of equilibrium. Most companies would not see equilibrium (calmness) as necessarily a good thing. There are internal and external factors on the list. While the individual scores (numbers) may not be critically important; the creative tension and interplay between the numbers is extremely important. It takes depth of understanding knowing what is behind the numbers to make this information most useful. Simply reacting to a number is like being a puppet. Understanding what is behind a number is profound.

1.9   Executive Summary (Cliff Notes* Version of this Book)

There is a wonderful sport metaphor that can be used to summarize this entire book. Michael Lewis wrote a book called *Moneyball.*† Baseball is an industry driven by statistics.

If you do not understand how baseball is played, here is a very simple explanation. It's a sport in which teams have nine players on a side and there are four bases. One team takes the field and plays defense against the other side. The team on offense takes turns batting, one at a time. The goal of the game is to score more runs than the other team.

A pitcher on the defensive team throws a ball. The pitcher's goal is to throw the ball over or near a 17-inch-wide plate. The batter standing next to the

---

*A summary version of a book that some high school students in the 1960s and 1970s read instead of the real book, then used to write their book report. One of the authors can attest to the fact that most teachers were wise to this practice.

†*Moneyball: The Act of Winning an Unfair Game,* Michael Lewies; W.W. Norton, 2005.

plate tries to hit the ball into play. If a defensive player catches the ball on the fly, the batter is out. If the ball is caught and thrown to first base before the batter can get there, the batter is also out.

Also, if the batter swings and misses the ball, it is a strike. Three strikes and the batter loses his turn; he is out. Three outs and the teams switch their offense and defense positions. If a batter advances around all four bases to home plate, his team scores one run.

All sorts of data have been pulled together, published, and used to manage baseball teams. Two statisticians independently asked, "Is there any correlation between the statistics collected by baseball teams and the number of wins that a team could be predicted to win during the course of a season?" (See Exhibit 1.4.)

Neither statistician could predict the number of wins a team should experience based on the performance statistics being tracked. The book tells a story about the search for data that did correlate to number of wins and the ultimate use of that information by one team to develop the equivalent of a new business model. It turns out that baseball teams were not tracking the correct information.

Baseball's Right "Ys"

So what is the Big "Y" in the game of baseball?

➢ Review the list of metrics that are routinely tracked in major league baseball.

➢ Individually identify the one or two that qualify as the Big Y.

➢ Then describe why you selected these data points above the other possibilities.

➢ As a team, consolidate most critical ideas and report back.

Hits	Runs	Errors	Home Runs	Triples	Walks	Saves	Left on Base	On Base Percentage
Doubles	Singles	Innings Pitched	Sacrifice Bunts	Ground Outs	Total Bases	Lead Off Hits	Full Counts	Slugging Percentage
Sacrifice Fly's	Fly Outs	Extra Base Hits	Strikes	Balls	Total At Bats	Complete Games	Pitches Thrown	Fielding Percentage
Team Batting Average	Team Pitching Average	Stolen Bases	Walks to Hits Ratio	Strikes to Balls Ratio	Night vs Day Record	Won-Loss Record	Strike Outs	

intelligence ⓜ everywhere™

Exhibit 1.4   Baseball Statistics Example

Several data items were tracked but not really used by teams. One of them was the number of walks versus the number of hits by batters. A walk happens when the pitcher misses the plate four times. The batter then gets to go to first base. Traditionally, batters would rather hit the ball and go to first base, as everyone knows "real baseball players" hit the ball. So using traditional metrics, teams are less likely to recruit players who get on base by walking, nor are players managed in a way to encourage more walks.

Billy Beane, the manager of the Oakland Athletics, began to use these metrics for managing his ball club and for recruiting new talent. With a team payroll at the low end of the league the athletics were able to consistently make the play-offs at the end of the season and did win one championship. One of the biggest differences between this ball club and the rest of the league was the fact that this team had identified and used process metrics that were more predictive of winning games. See Exhibit 1.5.

Other business models exist in major league baseball. The New York Yankees hire the most powerful hitters in baseball, have player salaries higher than most other teams, and have won a number of championships based on talent. The team in Atlanta for many years had the best pitchers in baseball and used this strength to win a number of league championships. Multiple business models exist. Most teams could not afford the New York Yankee's business model because their local markets are smaller and they could not generate the same number of advertising and TV revenue dollars.

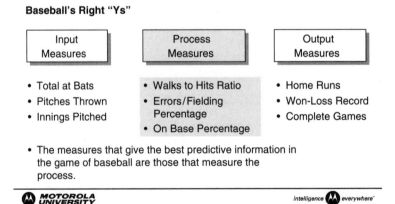

Baseball's Right "Ys"

Input Measures	Process Measures	Output Measures
• Total at Bats	• Walks to Hits Ratio	• Home Runs
• Pitches Thrown	• Errors/Fielding	• Won-Loss Record
• Innings Pitched	Percentage	• Complete Games
	• On Base Percentage	

• The measures that give the best predictive information in the game of baseball are those that measure the process.

MOTOROLA UNIVERSITY   intelligence everywhere™

Exhibit 1.5   Predictive Metrics Example

This story relates to this book in that you had an industry more than 100 years old, which was metric driven. But they were collecting metrics based on tradition and gut feel. And the metrics turned out to be wrong! They did not have a high correlation with the number of wins a team could expect to experience over the course of an entire season. This situation mirrors the experiences of many companies and organizations. People think they are measuring the right factors, but in fact their metrics could be causing dysfunctional behaviors and in some instances, actually suboptimize business results. The governance, management systems, and beliefs actually drive average performance, not excellence. Not to carry the metaphor too far, but leadership in baseball teams also resisted looking at their "business" using these new metrics. They did not ask, "Why might this apply?" Instead they said, "We know what we are doing and don't need any information from outsiders." Not exactly open minds.

1.10   A Team Sponsor's Role and Responsibilities

The DMAIC model that teams apply is really iterative. It is like a continuous loop of concentric circles that lie next to one another. Once you have gone through the loop one time, a team goes back through it again, at a deeper level. The leadership team of an organization does its own version of an iterative DMAIC loop just to define each candidate project and launch a team. The Measurement step of the DMAIC model exists in other problem-solving methodologies, but it has a much stronger spotlight in this model. Part of the emphasis is on process metrics and part on financial management. The sponsor along with a project team has accountability for hitting financial improvement targets.

Just like the team members are expected to spend time working on their project, the team's sponsor must also spend time sponsoring. When an improvement team is working on their project, the sponsor should be engaged enough to know what is happening. In the case of longer-term projects this requires one-on-one meetings with the project lead, and meeting with team members on a weekly or biweekly basis. Strategic breakthrough projects require direct involvement from the sponsor, or executive lead.

A key thing to consider is that the sponsor really has three different responsibility channels that often operate in parallel:

1. *Project governance:* Guiding, getting started, making certain solutions align with business (financial) and customer objectives,

reviewing projects regularly, ensuring the methodology is followed appropriately, and providing reasonable protection for team members to do their tasks.

2. *Change management:* Providing resources, helping to address conflict on an as-needed basis, preparing the organization for change, providing assistance as needed, encouraging team performance, and gaining support from peers.

3. *Advocacy:* Supporting the team, making certain communications are active and relevant, aligning other people in the organization that have the "clout" to support or resist proposed changes, removing roadblocks, identifying and rallying key players, and challenging the status quo.

Motorola uses the DMAIC phase chart shown in Exhibit 1.6 to highlight the sponsor's responsibilities.

1.11   Excellent versus Average Performance

In *Good to Great,* Jim Collins and his team near the University of Colorado in Boulder researched to learn if an organization could move from average performance to great performance for an extended period of time (in excess of 15 years). Applying a fairly rigorous set of criteria they identified 11 out of 1500 organizations that met their conditions. In Jim's book he outlines several common traits that the 11 companies appeared to have in common. The research team concluded that companies moved from a sustained period of average performance to sustained period of great performance:[*]

1. First they got the right people on the bus, in the right seats, the wrong people off the bus, and the right people in the right seats—*then* they figured out where to drive it. You need the *right* people, in the right seats.

2. Maintain unwavering faith that you can and will prevail in the end, regardless of the difficulties, and *at the same time* have the discipline to confront the most brutal facts of your current reality, whatever they might be.

3. Have a clear understanding of what your organization can be best in the world at, and equally important what it cannot be the best at—not what it "wants" to be the best at. It is not the same as having a goal, a strategy or intention; it is understanding:

---

[*]*Good to Great: Why Some Companies Make the Leap...and Others Don't,* Jim Collins; Harper Collins, 2001.

Role of the Six Sigma Champion

	1.0 Define Opportunities	2.0 Measure Performance	3.0 Analyze Opportunity	4.0 Improve Performance	5.0 Control Performance
Project Governance	• Choose a team leader. • Review Charter and project scope for focus, clarity. • Share the business case.	• Assure the business relevance of the project metrics. • Evaluate the data gathering plan. • Review baseline results.	• Probe for the completeness of the data. • Assess the analysis approach. • Constructively challenge the team conclusions.	• Assess the practicality of the proposed approach. • Revisit the cost/benefit analysis. • Oversee implementation and deployment plans.	• Validate the improvement. • Evaluate the financial impact. • Assure disciplined follow-through of the proposed approach. • Assess Black Belt performance. • Celebrate and reward.
Change Mgmt.	• Budget and provide resources for team. • Reallocate work to allow for team member participation. • Assure adequate multi-disciplinary representation on the team. • Establish empowerment guidelines for team.			• Build organizational consensus in support of the team's approach. • Influence decision makers to implement changes.	• Facilitate transfer of improved process to the Process Owner.

Advocacy & Culture (arrow spanning):
• Retain alignment (at BB level, at Champion level).
• Conduct weekly project review meetings (30-60 min).
• Identify the right BB and GB projects.
• Assure an adequate number of MBBs, BBs and GBs.
• Make data driven decisions.
• Act quickly and decisively on issues and obstacles.
• Model and communicate Six Sigma.
• Apply consequences.

MOTOROLA UNIVERSITY

intelligence **M** *everywhere*

Exhibit 1.6   Team Sponsor/Champion's Role and Responsibilities

25

a. What you are deeply *passionate* about
b. What you can be the *best in the world* at
c. What drives your *economic engine*
4. Have a culture of discipline. When you have disciplined people, you don't need hierarchy or excessive controls. When you combine a *culture of discipline* with an ethic of entrepreneurship, you get the magical alchemy of great performance.
5. Never use technology as the primary means of igniting a transformation. Yet paradoxically, they are pioneers in the selected application of *carefully selected* technologies.
6. The transformation from good to greatness did not happen as the result of a revolution or in one fell swoop. The process resembled a *relentless push* on a large flywheel, turn upon turn, building momentum until a point of breakthrough, and beyond.
7. The leaders of these organizations practiced what Collins called, "Level 5 Leadership." They did not stand in the spotlight, they were able to subordinate their egos to the greater good of the organization with a paradoxical blend of personal humility and professional will.

In our opinion, this is an excellent business book, one of our top 10. We kept going back to this Collins text because we found that we were also confronting paradoxes in the story of this book. *Six Sigma Financial Tracking and Reporting* is obviously about numbers, but as we state and restate several times throughout this text, *it is not about the numbers*. It is about understanding what they represent. We also had conclusions about what makes a great company versus an average performer. While our wording may differ, we believe our conclusions parallel those of the Boulder Colorado Good to Great Team.

Goodness is the enemy of greatness. There is great comfort in average. You're better than 50 percent. But for organizations to truly accomplish their potential, they need to be willing to let go of things they should not be doing and to focus on what Jack Welch called #1 or #2 in your marketplace. In your niche, no matter how large or how small, what can you do to be the number one or number two provider of those services or products? If the alignment is right and if the people are right, the financial results will follow.

Throughout the rest of the book, we share industry examples and try to describe actions you can take to move your organization toward greatness. We hope you embark on a challenging, exciting, and rewarding journey to move beyond … good.

1.12   Summary

At the end of the day, organizations are trying to get three things done. It does not matter if it is a for-profit enterprise, an office, a governmental unit, or a manufacturing company. These organizations need to improve three metrics over time:

1. Get the same amount of work done, using fewer assets.
2. Get the same amount of work done with less waste.
3. Experience profitable (meaningful) growth (this does not always mean getting bigger).

A for-profit business might measure the above three items through:

1. Net working capital.
2. Net gross margins.
3. Percent of revenues and profits from new products or new markets.

A not-for-profit organization or a governmental unit may not measure these factors exactly the same way but the concepts still apply. A not-for-profit business might measure:

1. Net working capital (still need to pay the bills).
2. Net intellectual capital (perhaps this is volunteers or specific skills).
3. Net gross margins (how much money is being lost on each transaction?).
4. Net funding revenues or new sources of funding.

There are certainly more metrics, many more. But the above items tend to be base level keys to success. One might also argue that more meaning in work is a natural goal that all organizations should be trying to accomplish. Certainly decreasing waste is intended to increase meaningful work, but that won't happen automatically.

At different points in times any one of these metrics may be far more important than the others. But over the long term, in an excellent enterprise, they will all come into play. Certainly different organizations pursue these metrics with varying levels of rigor. Average is average for a reason; it is in the middle. At any given point in time, by definition, one-half of all organizations are below average. Many of those will go out of business, but many will also continue to limp along, getting by, and doing just enough to survive.

If an organization is going to have positive energy, if it is truly going to make a difference for customers and the people who work for the enterprise, if it is going to strive for greatness, then much of what we discuss in this book applies. A reader's challenge is to find one or two ideas you can use. What will move your organization toward greatness? What will increase the meaning of work? What will build for the future? What will make it more fun for you to go to work and more enjoyable for your colleagues, customers, and suppliers? That is our search, and that is your challenge in using this material.

2

Financial Bridge P&L Model

*Two roads diverged in a wood, and I . . . I
took the one less traveled by, and that has
made all the difference.*

ROBERT FROST

2.1   Overview

There are two models used in the book to provide an overall framework:
The Financial Bridge Model and the Six Sigma DMAIC model outlined in
the Overview chapter and explained in more detail on subsequent pages.

This Financial Bridge Model (FBM) tells the story of what happened to
earnings on a period-to-period basis. How much did changes in unit volume,
product mix (margins), selling price or materials cost, project savings or
other significant events contribute or take away from earnings? Perhaps the
organization did actually realize savings from their improvement activities,
but they were offset by other changes in the business. Or perhaps the reverse
is true. The FBM simply makes understanding what happened to earnings
on a year-to-year basis a little more easy. Throughout this book several
different versions of a Financial Bridge Model are shown. The reason for
this is there are multiple ways to do it. At the highest level this model will
serve as a bridge to reconcile last year's earnings to the current year. This is
the model shown below. This same model could also be used to reconcile
savings as is shown in the Measure chapter.

Calculations exist for shareholder value, economic value, and even customer
value. But none of those really answer the question, "Why is this year's
earnings number different from last year?" What happened in the business to
cause the number to go up or down? When the organization reports millions
of dollars in savings or for that matter, increased unit sales, why don't the
earnings numbers reflect that fact? It's a mystery, but not all that difficult to

solve. While the numbers themselves will not totally answer these questions, they do begin to tell the story of "why?" More probing is needed to go below the surface of the numbers to gain further understanding.

2.1.1   Understanding Earnings Changes

Organizations have struggled over the last 20 years with having the savings from improvement initiatives actually and visibly hit their bottom line. Often there seems little correlation between reported savings and net P&L results, thus undermining the credibility of improvement activities. And very little has been written about understanding the changes in P&L earnings on a year-to-year basis. The DuPont RONA (return on net assets) model has existed for many years as a tool for identification of high-leverage financial improvement opportunities, although few people are aware of it today (Exhibit 2.1).

Balanced Scorecards have helped to broaden the way leadership looks at the business, but a Balanced Scorecard does not tell the story of *earnings changes*. While some numbers on the scorecard have a direct correlation to earnings changes, executives cannot usually explain how much each factor individually contributed. Currently, companies that are adopting Six Sigma and lean manufacturing improvement initiatives both experience similar problems in this arena—the numbers don't tell the story well enough to keep people interested in the improvement process.

At the end of the day, organizations are measured on their ability to grow and to improve profitability. Management positions exist, from a shareholder perspective, to make this happen. A Balanced Scorecard is one tool managers use to find leading indicators that, if done correctly, will ultimately result in growth and increased profitability. For more information refer to "Six Sigma Business Scorecard;" P. Gupta and A. W. Wiggenhorn; McGraw-Hill, 2004.

But businesses seem to lack a comprehensive model for the cause-and-effect links between business performance improvements and converting improvements into financial results. Business improvement efforts are severely hampered by that shortfall. It plays out as a chill on human inter-actions that instead should be ignited by obvious apparent opportunities. But, if there is not an effective way to describe the expected base-level results of a proposed improvement, then it is difficult to muster broad-based support and commitment for its accomplishment. And if the results of enacted improvements just seem to disappear, with little visibility of their

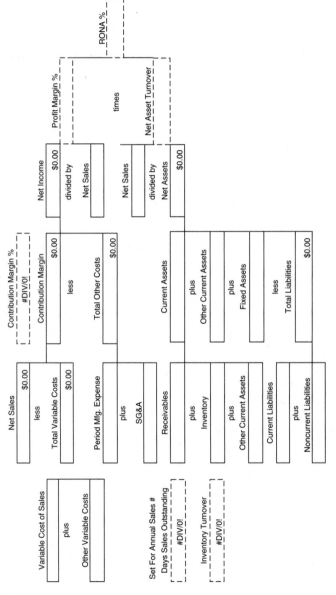

Exhibit 2.1 DuPont RONA (Return on Net Assets) Model

final benefits, then countless opportunities are lost to reinforce employee contributions to business improvement efforts.

The Financial Bridge P&L Model is an additional tool for the leader's toolbox. It offers a different, but complimentary picture to the information contained on the Balanced Scorecard. The model addresses two sides of the problem: technical process design and human involvement. The technical side will be easier to see since it builds on common financial and operational models already in use. The human side will be more difficult to explain because it has more dimensions to it and must deal with the complexity and range of human interactions in the workplace in order to make sense of the sustainability issues involved in the problem. We are confident that the Financial Bridge P&L Model can become a powerful new tool for the business community.

2.1.2   The Financial Bridge P&L Model

This model builds a bridge from last year's earnings to the current year's earnings. It provides executives with a tool they can use to manage the current year earnings and make certain that savings from improvement efforts actually have the impact intended on the current year's performance (Exhibit 2.2).

What are these key elements that increase or decrease earnings on a year-to-year basis?

They include foundation columns such as:

- Changes in unit volume
- Changes in prices

■ Need to understand what happened between last year and this year
    ■ Savings from improvement activities
    ■ Unit volume changes
    ■ Material cost changes
    ■ Mix of products change (gross margins)
    ■ Windfalls or catastrophes
    ■ Other

Exhibit 2.2   Financial Bridge

- Changes in product mix
- Changes in performance from improvement projects (there is an array here of timing, real or potential savings)
- Changes in cost of quality
- Changes from disasters and windfalls

One of the interesting things is most of this information already exists inside any publicly held company. It is covered to one degree or another in most management reports at the end of an annual report's financial statements "Management's Statement of Operations and Earnings.". But this information is typically pulled together after the fact (too late to impact actual improvement actions) by the accounting department, and not used or disseminated in a very powerful way. The model pierces this fog of invisibility.

Reading and understanding the elements of business financial reports (P&L and balance sheet) is a basic management skill. But even the most astute managers often have difficulty communicating with their workforce about the upstream operating factors controlled by employees that have major downstream result consequences. So maintaining a consensus view of "where an organization is headed and how it's going to get there"—in metrics that coordinate the operational and financial views—is a frustrating dilemma in most businesses. See Exhibit 2.3.

While parts of this book have been touched upon previously, very little has been written about understanding, and equally important, communicating the changes in P&L results on a year-to-year basis. Conversely, much has been written about tools that address parts of this subject.

2.2   Six Sigma Financial Tracking and Reporting

At Motorola, Six Sigma transformed from a focus on defect reduction to "Six Sigma as a management system" because of what was learned—that improvement teams be focused on top-down business results, not on simply launching teams to improve projects. In 1998 Motorola had a chance to do benchmarking of what is working at other corporations: Dow, GE, Allied Signal, and Caterpillar. Motorola actually introduced the Six Sigma system to GE, but GE quickly turned into a mentor in many ways as they transformed this project improvement methodology into a system for managing a business.

Exhibit 2.4 shows the evolution of Six Sigma at Motorola. It evolved from a track-and-eliminate-defects (3, 4 parts per million), to a problem-solving

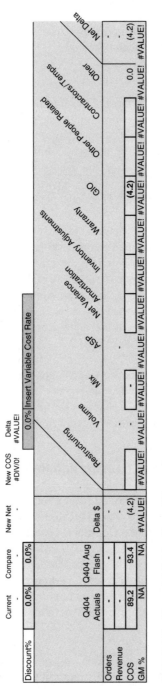

Exhibit 2.3   Financial Bridge Report Example

methodology (DMAIC), to a management system. Six Sigma was actually dying off within Motorola as an improvement methodology and then had a rebirth as a result of this transformation. Business unit leadership could see a clearer connection to business results.

So many organizations launch improvement initiatives by asking, "What can we improve?" Rather than asking, "What is the most important thing we need to be working on in our business right now?" As a matter of fact, most leadership teams don't have Six Sigma or lean enterprise concepts on the radar screen when they discuss this second question. So improvement activities get launched working on items that are important, but they are not typically the *most* important issues facing a business. At the start of an improvement initiative, this is not a critical difference. But later, when it comes to resource allocation, to competing inside the business for people to be on teams, to sustaining leadership's interest over time, and to making a meaningful difference to a business, they are critically different.

Businesses and people need to begin improvement activities somewhere. And they almost never has as much leadership support as they would like at the start. So it is unfair to say, "don't start without this leadership focus on business results." At the beginning it may be impossible to get. But it has to ultimately happen if an improvement initiative is going to transform from an improvement team thing to a strategic tool.

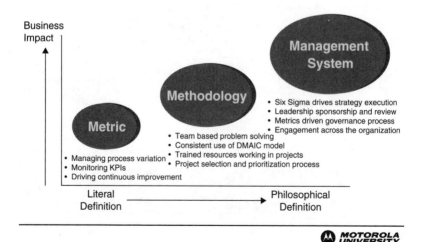

Exhibit 2.4   The Six Sigma Maturity Model

2.2.1 Business Results

As was mentioned earlier, Motorola has gone through several transformations using Six Sigma thinking. Here is a short story that might illustrate a focus on meaningful business results. During a tumultuous time in the technology industry (of course one might argue that every year is a tumultuous time in this industry) the new COO of what we will call Global Tech noted that everyone was planning to grow their business unit, and that net cash usage was going to be in excess (let's say, using round numbers) of $3 billion. This was during a time of excess capacity and falling prices (again, what's new about that?).

Being a prudent business guy and also looking at checking account balances, the new COO decided that perhaps some leadership guidance was needed. So he quickly informed the leadership team that perhaps they wanted to reconsider their plans. His statement was simple, "Don't come back to me with a business plan that does not generate cash!"

This target focused on a clear meaningful business result. The executive team did not simply ask people to improve, they had a very focused area where they were looking for improvements to happen. The "Big Y" target caused several changes in the organization. (See Exhibit 2.5).

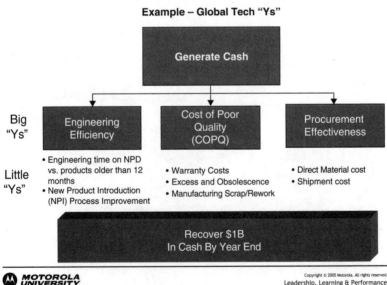

Exhibit 2.5   Generate Cash—Big Y

Design engineers are very much like "sacred cows" in Global Tech. They are pretty much left alone to do great work. Everyone expects this group to develop the next generation of great, new Global Tech projects. They operated very much like the Jim Croce song, "You don't mess around with Jim." Well, the popular belief was that these engineers spent 70 percent of their time designing new products and 30 percent of their time supporting existing products. Someone asked the question, "If the design engineers spend 70 percent of their time designing new products, then why are we having so many problems getting new products out the door, and why are they failing to meet our customers' expectations?"

This question opened the door to looking at where design engineering time went. As it turned out, reality was 180° different from popular beliefs. The design engineers were actually spending 70 percent of their time on existing products and only 30 percent on new product development and understanding customer requirements. Once these data were gathered and people saw reality for what it is, the organization was able to make changes that previously would have run into considerable resistance. Over the next three years Global Tech did a much better job of hitting new product performance targets. Think Razr!

The Big Y (cash) also unearthed a second major improvement opportunity. Global Tech, like many other firms, has outsourced manufacturing to Asia. As a result its business units were constantly filling up boats with products and shipping them across the Pacific to the United States. Someone asked a related question, "Why does each business unit fill up its own boat from a different carrier and ship so much inventory at one time?" A project team worked this issue. The organization realized they could reduce inventory levels by more than 50 percent, reduce cost in the millions, and simplify logistics, simply by combining their orders with the other business units. The total additional cost involved was three people assigned to coordinate boat traffic and order management. Each business unit received weekly replenishments of stock rather than 30 days worth of product, so warehouse costs were also reduced. Global Tech saved more than $40 million annually as a result of this improvement. This was in a well-managed business to begin with. People say we have plucked all of the low hanging fruit, but if questions are asked in a different way, additional low hanging fruits can usually be found.

As the late Senator Everett Dirksen used to say, "A billion here, a billion there and soon you are talking real money." You put enough zeros on there, and an organization is definitely talking "real money." Once an organization focuses on real money, tracking and reporting is not all that difficult.

In Six Sigma parlance, Big Ys targeted on important business results provide a clear sense of focus. They provide focus on a real business need. And everyone understands what needs to be accomplished. All businesses have these Big Ys but surprisingly or even shockingly, the leadership teams in many businesses do not always concur on the Big Ys. Differing interpretations of the Big Y prevent an organization moving from average to great performance. If each functional department or unit pursues its own version of the Big Y, major improvement opportunities get missed.

2.2.2 More Than One Master

Governance is discussed in more detail in the Control and Leadership and Governance chapters. But here are a few things to consider. Leadership cannot serve just one master. There are multiple voices to service: customers, regulators, employees, suppliers, and, of course, shareholders.

If one of these voices continually dominates all of the other key stakeholders over a long period of time, an organization is likely to operate with a major imbalance and skewed view of the world. We believe an organization is unlikely to remain healthy if it only serves one master. Which seems to be taking place in many U.S. companies today, as shareholders trump all other perspectives. Shareholders are certainly important, but if the organization does not periodically take into account the views of other key stakeholders, it loses its sense of balance.

Leadership needs to understand the priorities between these important stakeholders and clearly communicate them to employees in the enterprise. They need to track key results using some type of a scorecard. It should be noted here that most teams believe that they already have an effective business planning/strategy development process. The reality is most organizations have strategy and tactics at a business unit or functional level, but very often the strategy is little more than a thick strategy document, developed once a year, or the strategies are too complicated to drive focused action. In average organizations the leadership team has not taken the time to align and agree upon strategies across functions and business units. People walk out of a room and sort of agreed, but they don't have a clear, specific commitment. Then, functional groups fall back to focusing on departmental goals rather than clear strategic priorities. That is why it is useful and indeed essential to bring the leadership team together for a session in which they clearly agree as a team on their strategies, key initiatives, and performance measures. At Motorola, this is called a "Leadership Jumpstart."

The Cornerstone of a Six Sigma Business Improvement

STRATEGIC DIRECTION		PERFORMANCE MEASUREMENT	
Strategies and Objectives	Current Year Initiatives	Business Processes	Business Results
Vision: Our overriding purpose—how we will deliver value to customers. **Mission:** Who we serve, what services we provide, and how we achieve competitive advantage **Strategic Objectives:** Goals we must accomplish to achieve of vision.	**Make or Break Initiatives:** What we need to do to be able to be successful today. **Breakaway Initiatives:** What we need to do to be successful in the future	What we need to do to build the capability to achieve our strategic objectives.	**Customer and Market** Metric Goal: Actual: **Financial** Metric Goal: Actual: **Internal Business** Metric Goal: Actual: **Learning and Growth** Metric Goal: Actual:

MOTOROLA UNIVERSITY

Exhibit 2.6   Business Unit Scorecard

At Motorola we have found that an effective way to articulate leadership agreement on strategies, key initiatives, and performance measures is the four-column scorecard shown in Exhibit 2.6.

Once the scorecards are in place, the charters are approved and the teams are launched; success of the campaign is ensured through rigorous, ongoing integrated business reviews.

- Governance is key to sustained improvement.
- Ensures that executives own the success of the projects.
- Visibly makes senior leaders accountable for projects and project reviews.
- Provides early warning signs for removing barriers or providing support.
- Provides insight into quick win opportunities.

2.2.3   Governance Model Overview

Picture the governance process as a flow using a series of structured posters. The structure and the posters might send a signal to a leadership team that they will follow a focused process which is an integral part of their overall Six Sigma business improvement effort. The poster sequence is as follows:

1. Updated team scorecard
2. Updated team dashboard
3. New project selection matrix
4. Action tracking

The key objective with this activity is to get leadership commitment to the topics, allowing the leadership team to add topics and then get commitment to the time frames for each topic.

Updated Team Scorecard

A governance session begins with a review of the scorecard. The leadership team checks their strategic objectives and the key initiatives to determine if they still reflect the direction and priorities of the team. This only needs to be a poster if the scorecard is still a rough work in progress.

The Dashboard Concept

Once the leadership team confirms the scorecard, they discuss their key performance metrics (their Big Ys). Mature leadership teams will have data on hand showing the tracking and trends for their metrics. However, teams that are early in their development will still be struggling with data collection. They should work with whatever level of data they have, including the team's consensus or gut feel, regarding where they stand. The goal is to determine, from a stop light perspective, whether the team feels that the metric status is red, yellow, or green and to determine what direction the team believes the metric is trending—up, down, or flat.

Purpose: The dashboard is a management tool that helps clarify and monitor the measures in the organization that drive accountability and behavior and improve business results. See Exhibit 2.7.

Organizations tend to either narrowly focus on single measures like revenue or profit, or track and measure dozens of activities. Leadership alignment on a small set of measurements, that are the most important strategic improvement targets, positions an organization to move from average to great performance. Leaders have a responsibility to monitor progress toward goals, while simultaneously causing the organization to balance its efforts across four dimensions:

- Improving internal processes
- Achieving financial goals
- Growing the customer base
- Building employee capability

Corporate Dashboard Results Status Report – Q1 '02

Click on color bar 1st, then click on the 'color fill' icon below to select the color to indicate overall status of Business Result.

Select arrow to indicate status of metric – copy, paste, and drag to metric.

1.0 CUSTOMER & MARKET

1.1 CUSTOMER SATISFACTION

Goal: 10% quarterly improvement in survey gap. # 1 in customer satisfaction in key accounts.

Current:

1.2 MARKET SHARE

Goal: 50% larger than #2 competitor; annual gain 20% top share.

Current:

2.0 FINANCIAL

2.1 EBIT

Goal: 20% operating profit over 3-year period.

Current:

2.2 REVENUE

Goal: 25% CAGR over 3-year period.

Current:

2.3 CASH FLOW

Goal:

Current:

3.0 INTERNAL

3.1 PRODUCT QUALITY

Goal: 70% improvement per year.

Current:

3.2 PLC PERFORMANCE

Goal: Right tool at the right time on time.

Current:

4.0 LEARNING & GROWING

4.1 EMPLOYEE SATISFACTION

Goal: Employer of choice.

Current:

4.2 TECHNICAL EXCELLENCE

Goal: 10% increase of technical papers/patents over baseline.

Current:

MOTOROLA UNIVERSITY

Exhibit 2.7 Corporate Dashboard

Through discussion and debate, the senior team identifies and agrees on metrics for each area, as well as stretch goals. These performance metrics and goals provide the basis for the dashboard. Ultimately the metrics will most likely roll up through some type of an electronic reporting process. (See Exhibit 2.8).

The dashboard activity is based on the Malcolm Baldrige Balanced Scorecard process, which states that success is achieved by balancing performance in multiple categories simultaneously. There may be resistance in assigning measures and stretch goals because of a fear of not meeting them. There may also be resistance in narrowing down measures due to industry nuances, complexity of business, and the like.

The push back is that if you can't get really clear and focused on what's important and narrow that down to a one-page dashboard, your chances of meeting targets in time to make a difference are seriously diminished. (See Exhibit 2.9).

New Project Selection Matrix

Many organizations have active leadership involvement when a major new improvement initiative is launched. This was true of TQM, reengineering, and a myriad of other improvement programs that have come and gone over the years. After the initial launch, though, executive attention often shifts elsewhere. Leadership teams seem to assume the improvement programs will focus on important issues; meanwhile they have to run the business. This model isn't completely bad. A critical mass of an organization can learn the methodology. Some improvements happen, but, and we will come back to this theme again and again in this text, this is not strategic use of improvement methodologies.

A quick example: A very common and strategic use of improvement methodologies is to go after the new product development process. Unfortunately, companies usually go after one product, not the product development process. Sometimes this works. When Palm rolled out their first Palm Pilot, they just needed to get it out. It was a new start-up and the process was not critical, at the moment. But for a Xerox, to focus on getting one new product out, and to avoid addressing the underlying issues that hinder new product development is simply not good use of company resources.

All too often we have talked with leadership teams that are using Six Sigma, lean and other methodologies after they return from the mountain top, or mountain retreat, conducting a strategy session. When asked about how much time was spent discussing lean, Six Sigma, or whatever, I (breaking tense for the moment) can count on two hands the number of times an

Dashboard Example

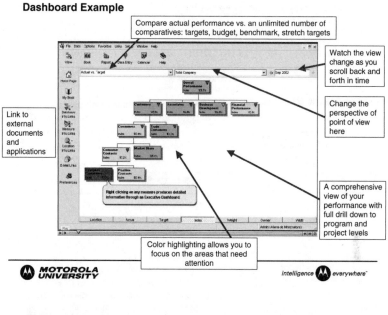

Compare actual performance vs. an unlimited number of comparatives: targets, budget, benchmark, stretch targets

Watch the view change as you scroll back and forth in time

Change the perspective of point of view here

Link to external documents and applications

A comprehensive view of your performance with full drill down to program and project levels

Color highlighting allows you to focus on the areas that need attention

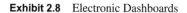

MOTOROLA UNIVERSITY

intelligence everywhere™

Drill Down on Vital X

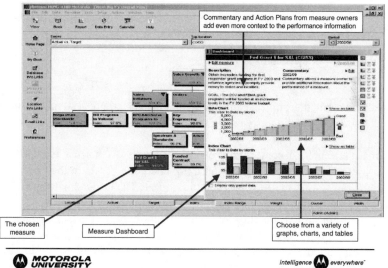

Commentary and Action Plans from measure owners add even more context to the performance information

The chosen measure

Measure Dashboard

Choose from a variety of graphs, charts, and tables

MOTOROLA UNIVERSITY

intelligence everywhere™

Exhibit 2.8   Electronic Dashboards

**The Leadership Challenge—Keeping a
Focus on the Big "Ys"**

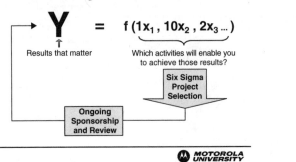

$$Y = f(1x_1, 10x_2, 2x_3 \ldots)$$

Results that matter

Which activities will enable you
to achieve those results?

Six Sigma
Project
Selection

Ongoing
Sponsorship
and Review

**MOTOROLA
UNIVERSITY**

Understanding what the Big "Y" is? What
is it we're trying to accomplish?
What results are important?
What activities will have the most impact
on those results?
Any outcome we are trying to achieve is
the function of a certain set of variables.
Our end outcome is a function of the
factors that drive improvement results.
Getting very clear on what you are trying
to improve and which critical actions will
get you there is the key to simplifying the
game.

Exhibit 2.9   Leadership's Big Ys

executive said that subject came up in their conversations. And half of those
companies on my fingers were units of GE.

Project selection can come from a sophisticated matrix as shown in Exhibit 2.10,
or it could come from Post-its on a flip chart sheet, where the executive
team brainstorms, clarifies, and combines ideas. The leadership team knows
what is important. These tools are used more to clarify commitments, and
most importantly, cement clear agreements across functional lines of
authority on the organization's key priorities (i.e., those priorities that
preempt functional goals). When everyone knows and agrees on the top
three priorities, there is power in that agreement.

Action Tracking

At the start, this can be simple where the leadership team tracks a handful of
key projects. Not a long laundry list of every project is underway in a

Project Selection Matrix

	Criteria #1	Criteria #2	Criteria #3	Criteria #4	Criteria #5	Criteria #6	Total
	Is the project tied to a scorecard strategy or a core process?	Can statistical tools be applied to the project?	Is there a major customer with significant pain involved?	Will the project result in desired annualized returns?	Can the project be completed in time to make a difference?	Cross Sector, Cross-Group?	
Weight	15	10	10	30	30	5	100
Rating	2	3	3	3	5	3	81%
Rating Criteria:	Rating Criteria:	Rating Criteria:	Rating Criteria:	Rating Criteria:	Rating Criteria:	Rating Criteria:	Selection Criteria
	0 - No, not tied to scorecard or core business process.	0 - No	0 - No customer or no pain	0 - No Financial Impact	0 - Unlikely to be completed in time to accomplish goal	0 - Limited to one deparment	All categories must be a minimum of 2 to be considered for a Six Sigma Project.
	1 - Yes, Project is tied to scorecard.	1 - Very basic tools: Paretos/histograms, flowcharts	1- Internal business issue causing internal business problems (e.g. HR)	1 - < $50,000	1 - Very risky - small chance that it could be completed on time	1 - Process spans a group	50–59%: Weak Six Sigma Project: Action Workout or Empowered Team
	2 - Yes, KPI are tied to strategy/core process and are defined.	2 - Very basic tools: Attribute data, cause and effect diagrams	2 - Customer complaints about problem	2 - $50,000– $100,000	2 - Risky, but could be completed on time	2 - Process spans business unit and at least two functional areas (e.g. HR and Finance)	60–69%: Moderate Six Sigma Project: Action Workout or Green Belt
	3 - Yes, KPI are tied to strategy/core process, KPI are defined and data is available.	3 - Descriptive data (mean, standard deviation), distribution analysis, run charts, scatter plots, box plots.	3 - Unfavorable financial consequences (e.g. paid penalties; reduced order volume) due to	3 - $100,000– $249,000	3 Likely to be completed on time	3 - Process spans functions within an entire sector	70–79%: Solid Six Sigma Project: Green Belt Project

Exhibit 2.10 Project Selection Matrix

Vital X Project	Big Y	Sub Y	Estimated $ Savings	Actual $ Value	Champion	Black Belt	DMAIC Phase	Target End Date

Exhibit 2.11   Project/Action Tracking Matrix

business. This can obviously become way more sophisticated than the simple Excel spreadsheet headers shown in Exhibit 2.11. Integrated dashboards with all of this information sound kind of cool, but don't get carried away with the idea. Project reviews typically flow along a standard pathway:

- Champions (operational managers closest to projects) receive weekly feedback from the Black Belts on project progress, and projects do not move to the next stage of completion until the champion has signed off on the project.
- On a monthly basis, in a more strategic review the project champions or team sponsors, along with Black Belts, present project results to senior leadership. Progress is demonstrated, possible solutions are tested, and a case is made for additional support and resources when necessary.

More detailed information is covered on this topic in the Improve and Control chapters.

2.3   Savings Analytical Guidelines

2.3.1   Purpose

Effective performance improvement is about more than just cost savings. So while savings rules or guidelines are outlined in the section "Savings Rules," leadership needs to be careful not to make their performance improvement activities just a numbers-driven exercise. At the same time, if the performance improvements are going to be meaningful, they ultimately need to result in some type of financial benefits to the organization. This is another paradox: how do leadership teams look at the numbers, but avoid making improvement activities simply a numbers-driven exercise? We have tried to highlight and focus on a myriad of ways to broaden the focus through out this book.

Effective financial measurement will both serve as an indicator on how well the organization is doing and will also contribute to shared learning across a business. The importance of "integrity" cannot be overstated. It is better to foster the building of "quality" results, rather than quantity (i.e., How large can the number be?). The rules and guidelines outlined in the section "Savings Rules" are actually repeated again in the "Improve" chapter, where savings reporting is discussed.

2.3.2 Savings Rules

To avoid a non-value-adding numbers exercise, it is important to track only meaningful projects. Stay away from a too-low level of detail. One large global manufacturer only tracks projects that yield $100,000 or more in net savings over a 12-month period. And in the Financial Bridge Model they only report numbers in excess of $250,000 impact. Twenty percent of improvement projects are most likely to yield 80 percent of benefits. So those are the ones that should be tracked most closely and get very specific with improvement targets and metrics.

Another way to decide what level to report is materiality. In public financial reporting a general rule of thumb has always been ±5 percent. If a number is greater than that, it is determined to be material. In the case of savings reporting, this is an internal information guide, a ±5 percent level is probably too granular. If these savings numbers are ±20 percent, that is probably sufficient for reporting purposes. Especially if people don't go crazy over the number, but instead focus on the story behind the number.

Reported Six Sigma savings could be classified into four categories.

Hard Dollar

Savings are directly traceable to the bottom line and should primarily be attributable to one of the following:

"Hard Savings" Revenue Growth

Recognize hard revenue improvement savings to the extent that they provide measurable, incremental benefits to the current base business. Improvements could be from margin growth or increased volumes from specific sources— existing customers, existing products or new products, and new customers. Projects should indicate which groups are targeted and how much revenue is expected. *Be certain not to duplicate margin growth with the cost savings recorded next.* Examples include:

1. Higher volume
   - New customers
   - New products
   - New product category
   - Over quota for a focused program
2. Accelerate customer acceptance time (time value of money)
   - New product development (faster cycle times…)
   - More sales person or engineer time with customers versus administrative or fix-it work

3. More throughput out the door (lean manufacturing...)
4. New customer acquisition (due to improvement projects)
5. Additional sales to existing customers of existing or new products (due to improvement projects)
6. Changing net price (negotiated term with indirect sales)

Revenue savings may take longer than costs savings projects to see the benefits. Earnings contributions from new revenues are typically gross profit margins, less any direct overhead expenses associated with the product or service, or in the case of accelerated sales the savings would be the time value of money.

(Net) Hard Cost Savings

Demonstrate a clear and direct impact by quarter (traceable) of changes in the financial results. Hard cost savings come from a net reduction in resources used (materials, people, outside contractors, transportation cost, and so forth) or an increase in outputs that result in revenue. Savings can also revolve around a specific customer or customer group. Time is not necessarily a "hard" business cost savings. It is only a hard savings if the time is productively used for some new activity. Examples include:

a. Net direct labor/direct material savings.
b. Many Six Sigma projects focus on the cost of poor quality (CoPQ). CoPQ improvements will often yield direct savings from scrap reduction, reduced defects, or warranty costs.
c. Elimination or reduction of net overhead and other indirect costs: operations, production, transaction, storage, outsourcing, subcontractors, energy, and the like.
d. Productivity can also yield measurable direct savings improvements, where the same resources are generating more output. However, if it does not decrease resources or increase throughput, then it is probably not a direct business cost savings. Productivity improvements upstream of a bottleneck operation or process step will usually not yield measurable bottom line improvement.
e. Other period costs, possibly including the elimination of unprofitable customers or products.

Show timing of incremental investment and savings by month or by quarter. Trace benefits to actual financial results. Report any benefits *net* of incremental investment cost.

Reported Hard or Soft Savings	Measure	Factors
Revenue	Revenue – (variable mfg costs + variable field selling costs)	All before tax
Cost	Cost	Cost of sales, operating costs all before tax impact

Soft Dollar

Savings come from projects that are not directly traceable to the bottom line, but that over time should yield a business benefit. It's important for the leadership teams to be aware of "soft dollar" savings. They will most likely require actions from leadership if they are ever to be converted into "hard dollar" savings. Soft dollar savings come from the following:

Faster Cycle Times

Projects that yield a time or capacity savings, where one cannot trace this time to a measurable reduction in resources used or revenue increase. An indirect or soft cost savings can be recognized for this. For example, setup time reduction. If we can't say for certain the freed-up time is being used to produce product going out the door (which would be a direct savings) the savings calculation might be number of hours or minutes saved times cost/hour of production for that product. This savings could be turned into a direct savings if, for example, "reduce cycle time with the 'X' automotive products in order to increase sales with these customers by XX percent" was the original goal, and metrics tracked to see if it happened.

Freed-up Engineering or Sales Time (Resources)

Projects that reduce the amount of engineering or sales person time might be tracked. One way to do this is to determine the costs per engineering or sales hour and show this as a soft dollar savings (assuming these resources were deployed elsewhere). From a business perspective, these resources are key to increased revenues. We would expect to see increased revenues in the following quarters as a result of freeing up these resources. If a direct linkage can be made between the freed time and increased revenue, this could be a hard savings.

Freed-up Indirect Time (Resources)

Projects that reduce the amount of indirect time or overhead resources (e.g., less material handling, less time spent bill processing, and less time expediting orders). This is a fairly straightforward calculation. Cost of the indirect time multiplied by hours saved, but it is typically not traceable to the bottom line.

Common soft savings include:

- Faster cycle, lead or other time savings, without a clear increase in revenues, or reduction in cost
- Capacity enhancements, w/o a P&L connection
- Reductions in rework, w/o a P&L connection
- Improvements to process steps that are not the constraining station/operation (bottleneck)

Projects that yield cycle time improvement or help to get work done faster need to be looked at beyond just the simple project. For example, reducing changeover time yields a process improvement savings. It does not necessarily yield a business or bottom line savings. The bottom line only benefits if the organization uses that time to make more products or provide more services that are going out the door to customers. Until the organization actually gets additional revenue or actually reduces "net" inputs, it realizes no real dollars from soft savings; in fact the company may actually incur additional cost because some cost were moved from direct to indirect or shifted from one overhead category to another.

Reductions in Invested Capital

Include improvements (typically reductions) to invested capital that are measurable and incremental in absolute dollars. These savings come from

- Reductions specific to a project (i.e., specific part number, specific region)
- Sustainable asset "dollar" reductions, working capital improvements could be counted as savings.

These savings are normally counted one time in the year that they are realized.

Invested capital	Change in invested capital × groups' annual cost of capital	Adjust according to length of savings (e.g., % of year −18% COC for 2 quarters would be 9%)

Cost Avoidance

These savings are tough to quantify. For example, if the organization develops a series of improvements that permit it to avoid a major capital expenditure, it may have an avoidance savings, but they are costs never actually incurred.

It's usually not a good idea to capture or track these savings. If a project team feels they have an important savings to report, they may do so but it should not be reported as a savings in the overall company savings totals. If a disagreement arises as to whether or not something is an avoidance or a hard cost savings, it is really the call of the appropriate manager responsible for the P&L of that unit to decide. If avoidance savings is recognized as "hard," one would expect to see a measurable impact at some point in the P&L.

If this category is abused from a savings perspective, the company could save its way into bankruptcy, so use common sense when reporting this type of savings.

This is not saying that avoidance benefits are not important. They are simply hard to objectively quantify, they lend themselves to very strong emotional arguments (more so that any other category for some reason) and most importantly, they tend to foster gaming of the reporting system.

Real avoidance benefits could include, avoiding:

- Safety problems
- Losing a customer (customer retention)
- Environmental disasters
- Business disasters (e.g., information system disaster recovery programs)
- Governmental compliance problems

In a few instances "avoidance savings" can be traced to the financials. For example, risk mitigation (clean rooms, earthquake mitigation, ergonomic improvements, and so forth) might actually translate to a hard savings due to lower insurance premiums, higher employee retention, or lower worker's compensation counts.

A savings reporting form is shown in Exhibit 2.12.

More information is provided on the project reporting and the Bridge Report in the "Improve and Control" (governance) chapters.

2.3.3   Where Do These Savings Come From?

In the case of a project team, savings begin with their charter. This happens well before any savings are actually realized. If the charter is a general

Six Sigma Financial Benefits Calculation Worksheet

Project Name: _____
Black Belt: _____
Project Type: _____
Division: _____
Financial Benefit Type: _____
Process Owner: _____
Date of Calculation: _____

Project #: _____
Project Start Date: _____
Savings Start Date: _____
Completion Date: _____
Savings reporting not to exceed 12 month period
All dollars ($000)
FY

Six Sigma Savings Calculation (show savings by quarter)	Hard or Soft Savings (H or S) By Quarter	Projected Savings (000)			Actual Pilot Project Net Savings	Actual Savings (after implementation)			
		Projected Savings (list by quarter, show TY, NY)	Annualized 12 Month Projected Net Savings	Projected Pilot Project Net Savings		By Quarter	Cumulative Fiscal Y-T-D	2nd Fiscal Y-T-D (when overlaps to second year)	Total 12 Month Actual Savings
Total Reported Hard Dollar Savings		0	0	0	0	0	0	0	0
Potential Soft Savings									
	Soft Savings								
	Soft Savings								
	Soft Savings								
	Soft Savings								
Total Soft Savings		0				0	0	0	0

Calculation working notes:

Exhibit 2.12 Sample Project Reporting Form

statement with no specific way to measure results, then the overall savings the organization is trying to achieve will be lost. The team's champion, Black Belt facilitator, and project lead should all seek to get Six Sigma or other performance improvement projects launched with appropriate goals that relate in a measurable way to key business objectives.

As a project team goes through the steps of the DMAIC problem-solving model, or whatever problem-solving methodology is being used, they should be able to ascertain the degree and types of savings. See Exhibit 2.13.

Typically the team's champion and/or the team's Black Belt works with a financial person to verify savings calculations assumptions and to make certain that the project's estimated savings will flow to appropriate summary reports. As was stressed earlier, the point of this exercise is not to inflate savings numbers. The organization should be seeking savings that will first help the business to survive, then seek savings that will allow the business to grow.

Merely focusing on cost reduction rarely allows an organization to grow. Sometimes that must happen, but organizations that only focus on reducing cost, risk giving away core competencies and missed opportunities. Consider General Motors. Every year GM reports major cost savings, while their market value declines. And many key industry suppliers have said they take their new designs elsewhere, because they are not dealt with fairly. This major stakeholder group has been alienated. While GM has developed a

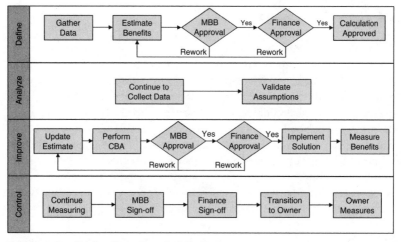

Exhibit 2.13 Project Team Benefit Life Cycle

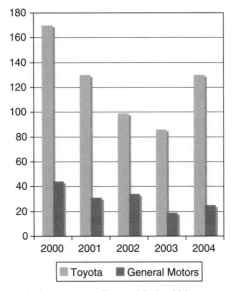

Exhibit 2.14   General Motors versus Toyota Market Value

couple of new products recently that are doing well in the marketplace, it has continued to lose market share against Toyota. Though Toyota has less sales than GM, its market value is more than twice GM's value, as shown in Exhibit 2.14.

2.4   Lean Accounting

Traditional accounting system logic was developed and implemented years ago for use in a competitive environment that does not resemble today's realities. Fifty to seventy-five years ago most companies' cost structures consisted of 60 percent direct labor, 30 percent materials, and 10 percent overhead. These costs could be easily traced to individual products that made their way through a plant. An overhead allocation at 10 percent of total costs was not a big deal, and simple formulas worked just fine. In today's environment, labor is largely fixed and overhead has become 50 percent or more of total cost. Since there has been a 180° turnaround in the percentages of labor, materials, and overhead as a percent of total cost, it is highly likely that the accounting concepts of 50 to 75 years ago no longer apply.

Traditional accounting also focuses on complex metrics that are long on variance reports and short on meaningful measures that drive the business.

Traditional accounting does not look at things customers care about. The apparent objective of traditional accounting measurement is to keep every person and every machine busy all the time, so that efficiencies look good. Unfortunately, much of what is being made following those strategies has little to do with customer demand. Or if that is a slight overstatement, then today tools are available that get more alignment between accounting and customers.

Lean companies emphasize the elimination of waste, increasing inventory turnover, and reducing inventory levels. The focus is on achieving the shortest possible production cycle and making what the customer needs, when the customer needs it. The benefits generally are lower costs, higher product quality, and shorter lead times. While people call this "lean" today, 20 years ago a Motorola vice president said, "If I could only focus on one improvement driver, it would be cycle time. Finding ways to get faster cycle times would incorporate all of the other improvement initiatives we have launched." So lean is not a new concept.

When companies adopt lean methods, their financial statements often show a temporary hit to the bottom line as deferred labor and overhead move from the inventory account on the balance sheet to the expense section of the income statement, thus lowering profits. So sometimes accountants will argue with engineers and operations about lean philosophies. It can also cause a short-sighted executive group to resist moving in a positive direction for their business.

2.4.1   What Is the Problem?

So if traditional accounting is providing misleading information, what is the problem? And what is the solution? Call it what you like, but the idea is to move to a more realistic picture of financial performance.

Traditional accounting was designed to support mass production; today manufacturing companies operate in a much more fluid environment. Many of traditional accounting assumptions contradict lean manufacturing thinking. Under lean manufacturing some nonfinancial measures including lead times, scrap rates, and on-time deliveries show significant improvements, yet these benefits are not easily seen using traditional accounting. Companies typically allocate overhead costs to products as a percentage of direct labor. Since overhead is a much bigger percentage of total cost, this can result in misleading or down-right wrong cost information.

The variance reporting based on standard costs, standard material usage, standard labor rates, and the like that show up in traditional financial statements (all based on someone's assumption of reality) make them nearly impossible for most nonfinancial people to understand. Variance reporting typically includes material, price or purchasing, usage, labor rate, labor efficiency, overhead, and volumes. Traditional financial statements are generated by standard cost-based assumptions. They show what the margins would be if the standards were achieved, then the variances are applied against these numbers. You may have difficulty simply understanding those two sentences, let alone the financial numbers in traditional statements.

One example of misguided behavior the above reporting generates is "earned hours." In an attempt to avoid unfavorable overhead or labor variances, factory managers learn that labor hours absorb overhead (it goes into the balance sheet with the created inventories), so creating hours is a good thing. Even if the products that labor is producing are not needed by customers. This results in excess inventory that may later be written down, discounted in order to move it, or damaged as it is moved around the factory.

2.4.2   Lean Accounting

Lean accounting seeks to organize costs by value stream, change inventory valuation techniques, modify management financial reports, and make more use of nonfinancial information. As a result, a growing number of companies are implementing lean accounting concepts to better capture the performance of their operations.

So, if standard cost accounting doesn't make sense in a lean operation, what does? Lean advocates propose a new way of looking at the numbers. Rather than categorize costs by department, organize them by value stream. A value stream includes everything done to create value for a customer that can reasonably be associated with a product, a product line, or a product family. Costs are still going to be allocated to some degree, but this is something an organization should do only once a year, or after a major change. If a group of products tends to use 30 percent of engineering's time, and a specific subset of engineers cannot be assigned full time to those products, then just use the allocation for a period of time. Coming back once a year, perhaps to make certain the assumptions are still valid.

Value stream expenses include costs to design, engineer, sell, market, promote, and ship a product—all of which are easily traceable to product families. Expenses might also include costs related to servicing the customer, purchasing materials, and collecting payments on product sales. These latter costs would most likely be an allocation estimate.

Think of a value stream as a minibusiness or profit center inside an organization. Ideally, the value stream has its own employees and own customers for its products/services. Value streams go across functional department boundaries. So one value stream would most likely include sales, marketing, promotional discounts, material, labor, design, and cash collection costs. Ideally, each employee is assigned to a single value stream, rather than being split among several, but that can't always be done. Once a value stream is defined, gather the related revenue and expenses to produce an income statement. All other corporate overhead costs that cannot specifically be traced to a value stream or product family are accounted for below the line on internal financial reports, because employees working in the value stream can't directly control those costs. The value steam's net operating margins calculation is

Sales – discounts – directly traceable cost = value stream contribution margin to the remaining overhead

Traditional accounting looks at the cost for each piece or work order and then adds an overhead allocation. This is a made-up number, no matter how many decimal points you carry it out. It's not real! Once a company moves to value stream reporting they can track costs at the product line level, as defined above, subtract those costs from revenues, and then they have a much better understanding of profitability. With this information, managers easily can see whether material use, scrap rates (if those are still being tracked), and labor costs for a product line are moving up or down. This number may still have some estimation in it, but it is much closer to "real."

Inventory valuation may also change under lean accounting. Inventories tend to be much lower than in traditional manufacturing operations, so at the end of a quarter, the company can simply add an overhead number back to the inventory values to get a number for external reporting.

Note in Exhibit 2.15 a couple of alternatives. Some people would just show the total manufacturing cost on that sheet. An argument could also be made not to include scrap (that it should be dealt with on the floor and with visual controls), and that other direct costs (if they are an allocation) should not be shown. The cleanest number possible would be as shown in Exhibit 2.16.

Nonfinancial data in the statements become much more important in this type of an environment. After all, the language of the shop floor is things, not cost.[*] Nonfinancial data may show sales leads, deals lost, a sales pipeline, and the like.

---

[*]Paraphrased from a Michel Baudin quote.

Lean Accounting Statement

Net Sales		$100,000
Value Stream Direct Cost:		
Materials Costs:		
Purchases	$23,000	
Net Change in Inventory (+ or –)	$2,000	
Total Material Costs	$25,000	
Processing Costs:		
Factory labor	$10,000	
Factory salaries	$3,000	
Factory benefits	$7,000	
Supplies	$2,000	
Equipment	$1,500	
Scrap	$1,000	
Total Processing Cost	$24,500	
Occupancy Cost:		
Building depreciation	$300	
Building services	$1,500	
Energy costs	$700	
Total Occupancy Cost	$2,500	
Other Direct Costs:		
Engineering	$3,000	
Sales salaries	$7,000	
Promotions	$2,500	
Total Other Direct	$12,500	
Total Value-Stream Direct Costs	$64,500	
Gross Profit		$35,500
Gross Profit %		35.50%
Other Indirect Costs		$20,000
Net Profitability		$15,500
Net Margins		15.50%

Exhibit 2.15   Lean Accounting Statement of Earnings

Accountants worry that by not including overhead as part of cost, that sales and operating people will begin selling products or services at a net loss for the business. To prevent this problem from happening, a company needs to determine whether the new product/service will beat a "hurdle" rate that covers both direct value stream costs and the desired contribution rate against "remaining overhead costs." A hurdle rate refers to the return the company requires before it will invest in a product or operation. Ideally, it exceeds the company's cost of capital rate. Actually, in total they had better exceed the cost of capital.

Alternate Lean Accounting Statement

Net Sales		$100,000
Cost of Goods Sold		
Materials Costs:		
	Purchases	$23,000
Net Change in Inventory (+ or –)		$2,000
Total Material Costs		$25,000
Processing Costs:		
	Factory labor	$10,000
	Factory salaries	$3,000
	Factory benefits	$7,000
	Supplies	$2,000
	Equipment	$1,500
	Scrap	$1,000
Total Processing Cost		$24,500
Occupancy cost:		
	Building depreciation	$300
	Building services	$1,500
	Energy costs	$700
Total Occupancy Cost		$2,500
Total Manufacturing Cost		$52,000
Inventory poriton of overhead increase or decrease*		$4,000
Gross Profit		$48,000
Gross Profit %		48.00%

* This converts numbers back to
full-absorption accounting

Exhibit 2.16   Alternate Lean Accounting Statement

In some ways this is simply a return to accounting at the turn of the twentieth century. At that time manufacturing companies were not highly diversified. All costs went to just a handful of products and the products for the most part absorbed a similar amount of materials, human resources, and indirect cost. The "remaining overhead costs" number should be a much smaller part of total costs so that when it is ultimately allocated to the value streams through the contribution margin percentage it is not a significant number.

Now we are trying to return to what accountants called *direct costing,* which had a brief period of fame in the 1960s and 1970s. Like everything else, a sense of balance is needed. If lean accounting were practiced too rigorously, it could emphasize speed and quality almost to the exclusion of cost concerns. For more information on this subject, read:

- *Real Numbers: Management Accounting in a Lean Organization,* Jean Cunningham and Orest Fiume; Managing Times Press, 2003.
- *Making the Numbers Count,* Brian Maskell; Productivity Press, 1996.
- *Profit Beyond Measure,* Thomas Johnson and Anders Bröms; Free Press, 2000.
- *Relevance Lost: The Rise and Fall of Management Accounting,* T. Johnson and R. Kaplan; Harvard Business School Press, 1991.

2.4.3   Bridge Financial Model Close

The Bridge Financial Model helps to tell a story about what is happening with earnings. It can lift some of the fog that hides where savings go or when savings are shown when they are not real. If the organization is truly making meaningful cost reductions that the marketplace cares about, it should see increased revenues over time. If reported savings are mostly soft dollars, then the leadership team needs to focus on actions that will turn those savings into real dollars. This is a key part of lean enterprise or lean manufacturing initiatives. For example, if the organization increases capacity and capability to make more, it has a soft dollar savings, it needs to sell more product or services if those dollars are going to be realized and converted into hard dollar savings.

If lean accounting concepts are adopted along with the Bridge Model, the organization can also simplify its reporting. The high number of nonvalue adding transactions will be significantly reduced and financial statements will be easier to comprehend.

This is what one senior country manager of a global restaurant chain said about the Bridge Model the first time he saw it (see Exhibit 2.2),

> This is exactly what we were running into in our company when I was in global purchasing. We were involved in identifying global sourcing opportunities for the food and packaging needs of each country. We found millions of dollars in savings opportunities, executed many of the strategies, but had difficulty in tracking those savings to the bottom line. The main issue was isolating the other factors that affected the bottom line in addition to the cost of individual raw materials. In our case they were primarily sales volume, menu pricing, and product mix. We did not have a model

to take into account all of the competing factors and enable the isolation of the variable we were trying to measure. The Bridge Model was exactly what we needed.

The key contribution of these methodologies should be to contribute to the organization's intellectual capital, to create new profound knowledge, and to help an organization do a better job of accomplishing key strategic change, key strategic improvement. If an organization is expanding overseas, reorganizing, complying with Sarbanes-Oxley, or figuring out how to comply with new environmental regulations coming from Europe, these are the types of issues senior leadership should consider for project selection. Areas where an organization must change to survive, must change to grow, are areas where, if this is done well, the organization may, in fact, get that leap over the competition.

Chapter 3

Define—Defining What Is Important

3.1   Overview

Someone once asked in a workshop, "Where do we start our improvement activities?" They were upset when the answer came across, "Pick someplace." It's a little bit like the NIKE commercial, "Just do it!" You have to get started somewhere. If the people making this choice have some experience in the industry, it's highly likely they have some idea of what is important. The problems typically come into play with what happens next. People around the world, from many different cultural backgrounds, have said the following: "The people who get promoted in our organization are very good at identifying the problem and then quickly coming up with a solution to fix it." Sounds great! Unfortunately the fix is often not "the fix!" and a short time later the problem is being fixed once more, following a repeating pattern.

Metric systems are very much like these problem-solving methodologies. Organizations pick something reasonable to measure and then assume that it must be the right metric, with little analysis of the metric and little machinery to validate that the metric is the correct measure for what they are trying to understand. Sometimes the metrics even cause dysfunctional behaviors to take place in the organization as people "game" the metric system.

"Pick some place" does not mean just go fix something. It means define something important that needs to be fixed, and begin the process of gathering evidence (measurement) about the degree of the problem. Then analyze the opportunity so that an implemented fix is a meaningful fix. A company with a series of project-improvement teams working on issues, selected by people in the middle of the organization, may be working on important actions. This is a critical component of continuous improvement. However, the leadership team needs to recognize the difference between fixing things that are broken or not working well and improving something strategic, if they hope to meaningfully impact their P&L.

A team working to solve a production line changeover problem or looking for faster cycle times in transaction processing is working on important, but probably not strategic, problems. Sir Howard, the new CEO of Sony, addresses strategic issues when he says, "We need better integration between our services and our device (hardware) portfolios."[*] That is a much different problem than a line changeover. Many executives do not appear to realize they can take the improvement methodologies in which their businesses have already invested and use them to address strategic problems. In this chapter, we try to distinguish between those two perspectives: project team improvement versus strategic problem solutions.

3.2 Purpose of Define

The primary purpose of the Define phase is to ensure the organization, department, or team is focusing on the right things. The Define phase answers the question: What is important? The organization should have a clear focus and agree on key priorities for the business. As one goes down into the organization working on improvement activities, one should be in alignment with the key priorities set at a higher level and focused on accomplishing meaningful results. This chapter defines key steps organizations should take to provide more meaningful direction for their improvement activities.

If you read Sec. 1.5, "Chaos and Fractals" in Chap. 1, you will realize that the issues and actions described at an organizational level play out again at a department or team level. The organization needs clear direction and priorities. It needs to take the voice of the customer and the voice of the business into consideration. The same is true of smaller units inside the business. Repeating patterns! That is one of the reasons why clear priorities

---

[*]"Sony's Sudden Samurai," Brian Bremner, Cliff Edwards, Ronald Grover, Tom Lowry & Emily Thornton; *Business Week,* March 21, 2005.

are so critical. If they are understood, believable, and meaningful, it is easier for the rest of the organization to move more into alignment.

The better the job is done to set the direction, the easier it will be to measure the results. Leadership has a major challenge in setting a clear direction. First they must have one—it is impossible to set clear priorities if the direction is not clear. As the Cheshire Cat said to Alice, "If you don't know where you are going, then it doesn't matter what road you take."* While most organizations are not that loose, it is surprising how often the direction is not clear and the activities inside the business are not in alignment with the stated direction.

After leadership sets the direction, they need to stop and listen. Did associates in the organization hear the message? Are there other considerations that the leadership team missed? Active listening to customers and employees can have a powerful impact on getting the direction right!

3.3 Define Phase Organizational Level

Most organizations are familiar with basic strategic planning: understand your strengths, weaknesses, opportunities, and marketplace threats (SWOT analysis). Based on an assessment of the organization's situation, set clear, meaningful goals. Sounds simple—and in many ways it is. But many businesses seem to simply go through the motions during these steps. There is little emotional investment and the leadership team does not hold itself or people inside the organization accountable for the results. At the end of the day, people take care of their functional responsibility areas first. Typically, little thought or commitment is given to those initiatives that cross functional responsibility lines of authority. Thus things go along normally and at the end of the year, the business has most likely performed in an average fashion. Nothing terrible happened, but nothing great happened either.

Many of the businesses at Motorola use a "Leadership Jumpstart" to focus their improvement activities. A key outcome from this event is for the leadership to agree on organizational priorities. But it goes one step further than the scenario outlined above. If you need to support a key business priority, it preempts any functional priorities you might have. General Electric did a form of this when Jack Welch decreed the boundarylessness concept. In this example, if one of its businesses fell upon hard times due to marketplace realities, GE did not lower its overall goals. When this happened

---

*Alice in Wonderland, Lewis Carroll (paraphrased, slightly).

the other businesses needed to make up the shortfall. Or if one business was having major problems, the other businesses should step up to assist by providing resources, contacts, or whatever other action was needed.

It can be very energizing when the executive groups aggressively debate key organizational priorities, actions, goals, objectives, and issues. And absolutely amazing when the discussion is finished and the leadership team takes the next step to reach a clear agreement on which of those factors are the most important. This agreement means that the key organizational priorities preempt functional priorities. When leadership teams do this well, everyone clearly understands the key priorities. If a department needs to support another group's improvement activities or strategies, a means to hold them accountable exists, as in the GE example above. Otherwise, people sort of agree to these actions in a meeting, then run off with the best of intentions, while ultimately doing their own thing (meeting the needs for their department first), instead of implementing the action needed by the overall business.

For an organization, "defining what is important" begins with a clear understanding of the voice of the customer and the voice of the business.

3.4   Voice of the Customer

Clearly defined customer needs create opportunities for business growth. Isn't that insightful? This is like "Sales 101." Any great sales person understands this concept. Unfortunately, many organizations do not clearly define these voices, and thus they fail to develop a true understanding of the context in which customers use their products and services. They do not understand why their customers buy, nor what problems they are trying to solve. True customer needs are left open and subject to a wide variety of assumptions, interpretations, and variation within the organization, rather than a clear understanding of the value provided. Some pockets of the organization may have an understanding of "true" customer needs, but this view is not understood across functional departmental lines of authority. These differing views cause conflict, as debate rages on inside the company.

This debate leads to a focus on how products perform rather than on which elements of an offering combine to create value for the customer. Incomplete and often vague value propositions do not allow an enterprise to differentiate its offerings from the competition.

Undiscovered customer needs go unmet and opportunities are created for competitors to displace you as a supplier. Customer voices need to be listened to and translated into prioritized *critical to quality* (CTQ) and *critical to process* (CTP) metrics. Then the organization can state the most important of these metrics, which would make it far easier for people inside the business to cooperate. Amazingly, this shortsightedness also happens inside the organization. People serving other people inside a business typically do not have a clear understanding of the true needs of internal customers for most business processes. This leads (you guessed it) to a wide variety of assumptions, interpretations, and variation in terms of the value provided inside as well as outside. Talk about a depressing "repeating pattern."

In the Define stage the organization or project team may first simply identify the customer and business voices (Exhibit 3.1). These voices may be further translated to key issues. In the Measurement stage then these issues would be translated into actual CTQ and CTP metrics (Exhibit 3.2).

3.4.1   Defining the Voice of the Customer

Leadership needs to agree on what is important. There are many ways this can be done. One way is to go through a SWOT assessment exercise and select key priorities. Leadership can also consider the voice of the customer (VOC) and voice of the process (VOP) following the method outlined in

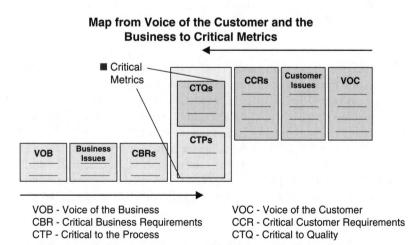

Map from Voice of the Customer and the Business to Critical Metrics

VOB - Voice of the Business
CBR - Critical Business Requirements
CTP - Critical to the Process

VOC - Voice of the Customer
CCR - Critical Customer Requirements
CTQ - Critical to Quality

Exhibit 3.1   Voice of the Customer/Voice of the Business Metrics

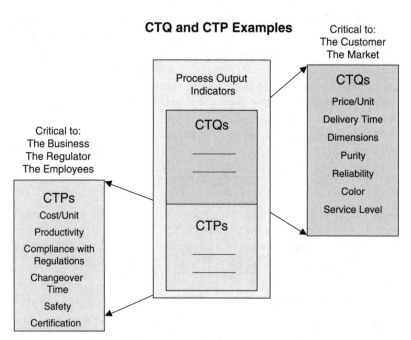

Exhibit 3.2 Example of Critical Metrics

this chapter. Defining the VOC is a leadership responsibility. It is critical to alignment; starting with the customers is most important, because they preempt all other parties. If the business does not at least do a good job serving customers, none of the other constituencies will fare very well over the long term.

Different businesses will have different customer needs. In the electronics business the focus is on invention. Hewlett Packard actually has the word "invent" as one of its trademarks. Motorola, Sony, Matsushita, and any other business that expects to survive in this competitive environment will have a steady stream of new product line extensions and new products. If organizations get the voice of the customer right, powerful changes can be made. Consider Apple Computer and the success of its iPod in the early twenty-first century. Apple took the success with iPod in the music market and used that momentum to open new lines of business with iTunes, iPhoto, and iMovie.

Consider the automotive industry. Some people might say, "It is a competitive industry." Their VOC might emphasize design, quality, performance (for some groups of customers), and comfort (which would also have differing meanings depending on the customer group). Hyundai was a Korean manufacturer of poor quality and poorly designed cars in the 1990s. They turned around their business with significant quality and performance improvements, a 10-year warranty to add credibility to their quality claims, and new designs. They made major market share inroads against European and U.S. automotive manufacturers in the early 2000s.

A person commenting in a lean manufacturing discussion list said

> We are trading our Ford Taurus wagon in for a Nissan Quest. The Ford was recalled five times, and I can't take it anymore. Nissan had problems with their redesigned 2004 Quest model, but they proactively recalled the affected vehicles and extended warranties on the minivans. By the way, it was fit and finish problems, no power train problems. So far, the 2005 Nissans have had zero recalls, so it seems that Nissan worked out the bugs within a short time span. How long did it take Dodge to fix the transmission problems with the new Caravan? We looked at Dodge, Chrysler, Ford and Chevy minivans for our growing family, and were not only unimpressed with the performance and styling. I also think the resale value comparisons between imported versus domestic says it all. Consumers directly affect that resale value level, and I think that is one of the more telling Lean Metrics in the automobile world.

Look at the success Hyundai has had over the 10-year period 1996 to 2005. It truly shows the sad state of traditional U.S. car manufacturing with the market share they lost over the same time frame.

The overall business results metrics for these strategic changes were easy to see, because Apple and Hyundai generated a tremendous amount of new sales. From a strategic perspective you also saw a decline in market share at Ford and GM, which would indicate something is not right. Hyundai implemented a host of cost savings and quality improvement metrics during their period of transformation. Hyundai did not change overnight! Over a 3-year period the organization focused on quality issues from a customer perspective and design issues from a customer acceptance per-spective. Their designs are not "Wow;" they are very simple. But from a price and quality standpoint, they were able to fulfill customer requirements. The end result of those changes to the outside public was "Wow, what happened here? This is not my grandmother's Hyundai!" When done in the right way this is a powerful driver of change.

Meanwhile, the U.S. automotive industry largely continues to lose market share, maintains an inward focus, provides mediocre product designs, and—like the airline industry—whines about legacy union costs. This does not mean costs are not an issue, but beyond a few pockets of excellence, management and union leadership do not seem to understand they need to work together. They need to begin with a "real" customer focus. Just look at Delphi. Once spun off from General Motors, this dying division became a powerful global competitor. Product innovation, low cost, and largely the same workforce excelled, where previously mediocrity was the norm. At the moment Delphi is facing some major business problems, hopefully they will overcome them.

Different Customer Voices

Different customer voices also need consideration. American Express divides its customers into regular, Gold, Platinum, and Optima. There are separate organizations with differently trained employees to serve each of those markets. In the early 1980s all departments were meeting their performance objectives right on schedule, but customers were not happy. "Customers don't care about how well internal operations perform; they are only interested in getting the service they want." So, instead of looking at how well each department performed, AMEX-TRS started looking at their business processes. One of the first ones they examined was the process of replacing lost cards—customers care about timeliness, accuracy, and AMEX employees' ability to act knowledgeably, with care, and courtesy. AMEX developed a new process to replace lost cards in 24 hours, versus their old standard of 2 days.

Customers weigh the quality attributes of service differently depending on their expectations. Cardholders may expect more from AMEX than they do VISA or MasterCard. AMEX's services may in fact even be superior, but not meet customer expectations.

After the customer voice is synthesized, consideration needs to be given to the voice of the business and the financial impact on the organization from both of these views.

3.4.2 Sources of Customer Information

There are many sources of customer information. At the start a leadership team might rely on its internal view. But the conclusions drawn should be validated during the measurement and analysis cycles. Customer service records, internal and external databases, external surveys, and the like all provide potential sources for defining key customer metrics. At the end of the day the organization needs to boil down key customer information to measurable factors.

The voice of the customer is a little bit different than the voice of the business in that these requirements regularly change over time. Organizations that successfully provide new "delighters" to customers see those requirements melt away from being a delighter to being an expected service over time. When people say customers become more demanding over time, they aren't kidding. Occasionally demand may exceed supply, as recently happened in steel, or with successful new product offerings, or in novelty items like Beanie Babies, Cabbage Patch Dolls, and so forth. But as time goes by, and capacity exceeds demand, the tables turn in the customers' favor. So the delighter of today becomes the expected practice of tomorrow. Successful delighters can even jump to new industries. Federal Express was one of the first organizations to be able to tell you where your package was at any point in the delivery cycle; that whole practice has now spread to many other industries.

Jeff Immelt, CEO of General Electric, stated, "I want the company to be more innovative, more global, and more focused on the customer. Twice every month I do town hall meetings with several hundred customers to share ideas on GE's direction and to listen to their thoughts on what we can do better. And we are doing what I call 'dreaming sessions' with key customer groups, trying to think about where their business and our business will be in 5 or 10 years. We will define four or five key conditions, and I will ask," 'If you had $200 million to $400 million to spend on R&D at GE, where would you spend it?' Customers, though, tend to focus on immediate problems; they look to solve issues they are grappling with today. "Customers always pay our bills. But they will never pick our people or set our strategies."[*] GE starts with a customer's voice; then they plan their business strategies, taking into account additional perspectives.

3.4.3   Requirements Setting Guidelines—Voice of the Customer

Clarifying and understanding the requirements for a product or service is a critical step in improving it. The guidelines below outline a process to achieve clarification. You can be either a customer or a supplier in a relationship to apply these principles.

---

[*]"Interview with Jeff Immelt," John Byrne; Fast Company; July, 2005.

Requirements are agreements between customers and suppliers as to what is needed to perform a job properly. The requirements must be:

- Mutually agreed upon
- Attainable
- Well communicated
- Measurable
- Changed officially if they need to be changed

3.4.4   Requirements Setting Process—Leadership Team Level

An executive leadership team is not going to dig into this as deeply as the requirements guidelines outlined for project teams. Ideally, someone at the executive level has deep knowledge about the business, process, or opportunity being discussed. Without what Deming called "profound knowledge," the leadership team is highly likely to make critical decisions without sufficient depth of knowing. But this knowledge is needed when coming into an executive session for priority setting. An entire leadership team is highly unlikely to dig this deeply.

The other thing helpful to a leadership team is data. Many teams operate without data, because they are overwhelmed by data sources, and the data they do see have little credibility. Much more discussion is given to making data "credible" in the measurement and analysis sections of this book. Suffice it to say that:

Reasonable people

Equally well-informed

Will seldom disagree

Of course the challenge here is getting everyone equally well-informed and decreasing time wasted arguing over whose data are right. Ultimately, the leadership team needs to agree on *critical customer requirements* (CCRs), further described in the section, "Determine Critical Customer Requirements."

3.4.5   Requirements Setting Process—Project Team, Department or Product Level

Each of the steps outlined in the process is very important. This outline really speaks to a team level, a department level, a process level, or for an organization's product or service families. The whole is incomplete if any of the steps are overlooked or superficially tackled at those levels of the

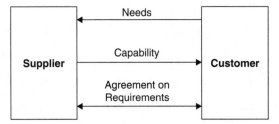

Exhibit 3.3   Customer Supplier Model

business. This model shows the relationship between a customer and supplier regarding their requirements (Exhibit 3.3).

For an effective relationship, customers and suppliers must be honest with each other. "Real" needs and "real" capabilities must be expressed. Once those are on the table, an agreement can be reached. (See Exhibit 3.4.)

Select Product or Service

 Think of the product or service for which you want to clarify requirements. This is typically one which is giving the organization a lot of "pain," either in terms of the rework when requirements are missed, the cost of not conforming to requirements, or simply those about which there are complaints. Some customer/supplier dialog is helpful in this step. It is important to be specific—if the product is an engineering drawing, are you setting requirements for all engineering drawings or just this one? Which departments or levels of management would be affected by changed requirements? Be specific.

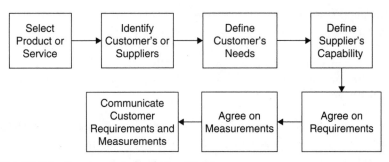

Exhibit 3.4   Requirements for Setting Model

Identify Customers or Suppliers

Identify Customers or Suppliers

Who shares this product or service with you? Be sure to include all customers who receive it and all suppliers you get it from. It is important to identify everyone involved because requirements may be different for each person.

Define Customer's Needs

Define Customer's Needs

When going through the process of defining possible customer needs, keep some perspective. Gather information from those customer employees on what the most important problems are, or where the requirements are missed most often. These are the areas where you want to begin the process of setting requirements.

When defining customer needs, consider the following areas: accuracy, format, schedule, legibility, consistency, cost, and any other issues unique to your business. Customer needs can take many forms. A complicating factor is that, in order to stay competitive, you must *anticipate* customer needs. The supplier and customer should discuss this openly so that both can plan based on the same assumptions.

Define Supplier's Capability

Define Supplier's Capability

The supplier's capability must be defined in response to the customer's needs. The fundamental question to ask for each of the expressed needs is: Can we meet that need? This is not always an easy yes or no answer. It may depend on how much the customer is willing to spend, how much additional training is required, or some other factor.

It's important to realize that in order to define capability, the process of production must be controlled. You must understand and be aware of the critical variables that affect that process. You must also understand what is not within your control in that process. In some situations, you may require statistical process control to define what a supplier's capabilities actually are.

In either case, it is crucial that those employees closest to the actual work be involved in defining exactly what the supplier is capable of producing.

Agree on Requirements

Agree on Requirements

This can come down to a give-and-take negotiation. The goal is to reach consensus on what the mutual definition of requirements will be. Mutual definition involves an open discussion between customer and supplier around such questions as:

- How is the product or service used?
- What happens when this product or service fails to conform to requirements?
- Are the customer needs realistic?
- If the supplier cannot meet these needs, how much will it cost to start meeting them?
- What can be done by either the customer or supplier to better meet the requirements?
- Are there any improvements that could be made to simplify the product or service, making it easier to conform to requirements?

The result must be that the customer and supplier reach a consensus on acceptable requirements for the product or service.

At this stage, it is also important to acknowledge that there will be times when the supplier will fail to conform to requirements. Although this is considered unacceptable, it is still helpful to discuss what the supplier and/or customer can do if this happens. For example:

- Should the supplier call the customer to inform him or her of the problem ahead of time?
- Should the supplier send the product or service to the customer anyway, hold it for customer inspection, or not send it until the requirements are met?
- What should the customer do if he or she encounters a special situation where a slightly different requirement is present?

Again, these discussions should not be interpreted as acceptance of the failure to conform to requirements. Rather, they should be considered opportunities for the customer and supplier to better understand one another and to continue the dialog around mutual requirements.

Agree on Measurements

Agree on Measurements

After the requirements have been agreed to, the customer and supplier should reflect on measurements that would show how well conformance is being met. Address the following issues:

- Where the data will come from.
- Who will do the actual measurements.
- How the measurements will be presented (table, graph, and so forth).
- How often the measurement will be done.
- Who the measurement results will be distributed to.

Don't try to measure everything. A few good measurements are the best policy.

Communicate Requirements and Measurements

| Communicate Customer Requirements & Measurements |

One of the key characteristics of good requirements is that they be well communicated. Consider all the discussions between the customer and supplier and decide who needs to know what the requirements are.

The importance of communicating the requirements cannot be stressed enough, especially if negotiations resulted in requirements that are significantly different than a party's expectations at the beginning of this process.

The format and type of communication must also be decided. Besides choosing whether to communicate the new requirements formally or informally, verbally or written, there are other possibilities:

- The requirement is very stable and simply needs to be communicated in writing.
- The requirements vary from product to product and should be communicated with a specification sheet or transmittal memo each time.
- The requirements are complex and a standard operating procedure must be written.

It is critical that the rationale behind the requirements and measurements also be communicated. People are much more likely to accept changes if they understand why they are important and what they will achieve.

As a final note, remember that requirements change over time. Customers and suppliers should maintain a dialog and be sensitive to the need to review requirements. When requirements change, change them officially. This will mean applying the principles of setting requirements all over again.

Most Six Sigma teams are trained in a similar technique to the above, called Kano analysis, named after Noriaki Kano (see Exhibit 3.5). He classified customer requirements into three categories: must-be's, primary satisfiers, and delighters. A must-be requirement is a basic requirement the customer

Category	Hotel Example
Must-be	Clean room, king-sized bed, room away from highway...
Primary satisfier	High-speed Internet connection, someone available at front desk, ability to check in/out early/late...
Delighter	Your choice of newspaper at the door, greeting by name, basket of fruit in your room...

Exhibit 3.5   Sample Kano Analysis of Hotel Industry

will not do without—they must have it. A must-be requirement can dissatisfy, but will not increase satisfaction. A primary satisfier is one where the more these requirements are met, the more the customer is satisfied, at least up to a point. A delighter will not cause dissatisfaction, but will delight customers if they are done well.

3.4.6   Determine Critical Customer Requirements

The voice of the customer needs to be synthesized down into critical customer requirements. Different customer voices exist: buyers, users, designers, and so forth. Organizations may deal with an industry customer at one level and a consumer at another for products or services they sell. At the end of the day, after all of the customer groups are considered, the CCR should ultimately be measurable with a target and an allowable range of performance. At a leadership, department, or team level a filtration should take place that gives consideration to the customer's voice, filters the key messages into key issues, and then defines the critical customer requirement (See Exhibit 3.6). Typically, if the right requirements are identified, they will apply to multiple customer groupings.

3.5   Voice of the Business

If the voice of the customer represents the paying public, the external voice, then the voice of the business represents all other stakeholders: shareholders, management, employee associates, suppliers, regulators, and so forth. All of these voices need consideration. At any given point in time, one

Industry	Voice of Customer	Key Customer Issue	Critical Customer Requirement
Home delivery	Make me feel safe in my home	Safety	Delivery personnel wear a uniform, they are clean shaven, and no body piercings are permitted

Exhibit 3.6   Translating VOC to Critical Customer Requirements

voice may outrank the others. It depends on the competitive climate, regulatory situation, and shareholder needs. The voice of the customer needs to be balanced against these other views. The financial impact on the organization also needs consideration at this point. This was a problem in many previous organizational improvement initiatives, like Total Quality Management. The financial side was not always considered.

There is power in doing this analysis. There is a tendency in many organizations to determine what information is available about a problem, and then begin building solutions based on that information, rather than first determining what information is needed, gathering that information, and then developing solutions. Organizations and teams that follow the former or latter path will end up in different places. Under time pressure, people tend to say, we just don't have time to follow the latter path, but then somehow time is always found to do it over again, when things were not done right the first time. In a global market, an organization does not always get a second opportunity.

Remember the Apple Newton? This was one of the first personal digital assistants. John Sculley, the former CEO of Apple Computer, bet the success of the organization on this product. They kept everything pretty secret when it was under development; there was very little customer input. When they rolled out the product it failed. It was not powerful enough to be a computer. It was bigger than a Daytimer and was initially a little bit difficult to use. Palm Computing was actually developing a similar concept. When they saw the market's reaction to the Apple Newton, Palm went back to the drawing board. They simplified the electronics in the Palm Pilot and determined that it had to be as small as a pack of cigarettes. The Palm was one of the most successful electronic products ever. Apple came close to going out of business until Steve Jobs came back and refocused the organization.

3.5.1   Critical Metrics

Metrics are a key part of "Define" and critical metrics start with the voice of the customer in mind. That voice kicked off the Six Sigma process in Motorola. In the mid-1980s one of Motorola's large divisions was celebrating their new products' successes. Engineering and management were very struck by the beauty of their new products. Then Art, the national sales manager, gave a presentation that pretty much poured cold water on the party when he said, "We are proud of our innovations, but I want you to know our customers are about to start leaving us in droves if we do not do something about our quality." Talk about a wake-up call. Bob Galvin, the chairman of Motorola at the time, was at this session. He changed his calendar and visited the top 50 customers over the next 2 months, where they reinforced Art's message. They said, "We love your products, but we would invest three times as much in your business if the quality was better."

Once this external voice was recognized and accepted, all sorts of improvement activities began to be guided by that view at Motorola. There was also a translation into the voice of the business. Motorola cycle times were too slow, quality was obviously an issue, a better understanding of customer requirements in new product development was needed—all driven by this clear customer need. It's not clear if this was a "learning" insight, but it's obvious that customer voices are powerful change drivers. And in many ways a clear customer voice makes it much easier for businesses to cut through the myriad of noise to identify more quickly which voices of the business need to be heard.

At Pitney Bowes they have radically redefined their metrics, given their changing business situation. They used to ask, "How many meters (postage) did they have in place and how many customers do they have?" Now they ask, "How many pieces of mail are we participating in and how many pennies do we get per piece?"[*] Currently they are at 30 billion pieces of mail touched per year and 8.7 cents per piece. They continue to add new services to deal with mail before and after their traditional meter business.

3.5.2   Voice of the Business—Don't Go Crazy with It!

The voice of the business (VOB) must be translated, just like the voice of the customer. But the VOB needs to be kept in perspective. Many companies

---

[*]"Back Where We Belong," Michael Critelli; *Harvard Business Review,* May 2005.

today, especially in the United States, overreact to one voice—that of the shareholder. Whenever one constituency vastly outweighs all others over the long term, goofy things will happen. The organization and the people within it lose their sense of balance and perspective. If the organization is seen only through shareholder eyes, then other voices important to long-term success remain unseen and unheard.

Harold Geenen, the late former CEO of ITT was famous for his ability to run the business by the numbers. For many years, before *economic value added* and *shareholder value added* were commonly known terms, those concepts were discussed under different labels. ITT provided high returns for many years. Harold stated simply that, "At the end of the day, it's all about performance." Although this was true to a degree, shortly after he left the house of cards fell apart. In addition to Geenen's mental ability to run the business by the numbers, he had also personally participated in most of the organization's major acquisitions. He oversaw a period of rapid growth and through his experiences he had much more than just the numbers to guide him. Unfortunately, he did not perceive that part of his responsibility was to leave a legacy, nor that he needed to groom a replacement. In addition, much of the internal reaction to his "run the business by the numbers" mentality was low loyalty, high turnover of talented managers, strained employee relationships, and a litany of problems hidden by people who did not want to get into trouble with the boss. Geenen was famous and took great pride in his ability to dress down executives in front of their peers when they failed to meet his expectations.

While ITT was still running strong when he left, his successor(s) were not able to maintain his momentum. It is also highly likely that his style would not have worked well during the 1980s and 1990s when international competition began to intensify. While performance is important, it's also about balance. One might argue that this is still performance, but the point remains that multiple perspectives are needed, not just the numbers.

3.5.3 Defining the Voice of the Business

Just like the voice of the customer, leadership needs to agree on what is important from a business perspective. This view really takes into account all other key stakeholders outside of paying customers.

An organization needs to start somewhere. When Chung Mong Koo became CEO of Hyundai Motor Company in March 1999, the industry yawned.

Chung, the eldest living son of Chung Ju Yung, Hyundai's late founder, was widely deemed a colorless executive who would promote the status quo.[*]

Days after he took over, Chung visited Hyundai's sprawling plant at Ulsan on the southeastern tip of the Korean peninsula. To the shock of his employees, who had rarely set eyes on a CEO, Chung strode onto the factory floor and demanded a peek under the hood of a Sonata sedan. He didn't like what he saw: loose wires, tangled hoses, bolts painted four different colors—the kind of sloppiness you'd never see in a Japanese car. On the spot, he instructed the plant chief to paint all bolts and screws black and ordered workers not to release any car unless all was orderly under the hood. The plant chief recalls Chung fuming: "You've got to go back to basics. The only way we can survive is to raise our quality to Toyota's level." In this instance the CEO made a visible statement. Other actions were also taken, but nothing unusual to begin this organization's turnaround. Market value of Hyundai Motor Company increased from approximately US$6 billion in 1998 to over US$14 billion in 2004. Hyundai's goal is to become the Number 5 global automotive manufacturer by 2010.

There is no mystery here. Chung Mong Koo began with a view of what customers wanted in terms of quality, "Toyota's level." Quality at Hyundai at the time was horrid, it did not take a major engineering study to understand this. Pretty clear goal, pretty long stretch for Hyundai at that point in time.

Taking a lead from customers, leadership needs to identify what the business voice is saying, then filter the voices to key issues. They in turn are filtered to critical business requirements and then to critical to process metrics, which are typically process-output related (Exhibit 3.1).

3.5.4 Identifying the Leverage Points—Voice of the Business

These are typically more well known than the voice of the customer. Most organizations do some type of strategic planning, so issues that typically surface through that medium will not be covered here.

Nor does this book speak to regulatory issues in any great depth. If an organization is having them, they would clearly be important issues to address. Some of the pharmaceutical companies today, given the litigious environment

---

[*]By Moon Ihlwan in Seoul, with Larry Armstrong in Los Angeles and Katie Kerwin in Detroit, *Business Week,* December 17, 2001.

in the United States, should be regularly screening potential issues. This is far more easily done when looking at the past than looking at the future so it is a constant challenge. Perhaps some type of a prioritization method similar to the evaluation criteria we describe in the following sections could apply.

Identify Key Stakeholders

The leadership team needs to give some thought to key stakeholders in the business. They include shareholders, suppliers, employees, management, communities, regulators, and the like. Identify key groups, outside of the customer realm, that could significantly influence the organization's future. Out of this list, no more than three of them are normally most important at any given point in time. So first identify which groups need attention at this point in the life of the organization.

Determine What is Important—Leadership Team Level

Determine what is important. At an executive level this can often be done by focusing on one or two core issues. Chung Mong Koo focused on quality at Hyundai; Carlos Goshen, at Nissan, focused on new product designs and excessive costs. In Jim Collins' book *Good to Great,* he describes how 11 organizations moved from being average to truly being "great" based on a number of selective criteria. One of the common traits was all 11 companies identified one metric that was supreme above all others. Walgreen's moved from "profitability per store" to "profitability per customer visit"—in some ways a small change, but a major move on a cultural front. Not unlike Chung's focus on quality several years ago, Jack Welch said, "We will only keep businesses that are number one or two in their industry." If people are held accountable, and if they will think beyond just the simple numbers, great changes can take place. Organizations can move from average performance to great performance.

Organizations try to make this much more complicated than it truly is. And the concepts apply to not-for-profit as well as for-profit enterprises. Consider this short story.

The Association of Manufacturing Excellence is headquartered in the Chicago, IL area. The headquarters, which has a small office staff of less than 10 people, largely survives based on the revenues generated from an annual conference held for organizations around the world and intended to draw global attendance. This organization exists to share best practices and to promote learning. Its current vision is: "Inspire a Commitment to Global Enterprise Excellence through Shared Learning."

When the volunteers come together to plan a new conference for the following year, a discussion takes place. Does this conference exist to generate cash to fund the small headquarters staff and to promote research? Or does this conference exist to promote shared learning? Well, the answer is "Yes! We need to do both of those things. It is not one or the other." But the primary driver of both desires is to put together a program that is interesting to potential attendees. And the competitive climate for doing this has changed for AME over the years. Five years ago very few people were talking about lean manufacturing and the lean enterprise. Today, many other organizations are operating in this space. So from a business standpoint, AME has been forced to redesign its business model over the last several years. This same story applies to just about any organization, anywhere on earth. They have standardized their processes, improved the quality of their programs and site tours, and outsourced some administrative support functions.

So what is important? Where is most money spent ("follow the money")? What is difficult to do? Where does cooperation break down or disagreements take place between different functional units? Where is the blood on the floor, the big hurt?

Determine What is Important—Project Team, Department, or Product Level

It is similar to the leadership team level, but at a more detailed level. Focus on a specific process, product, or service. Products and services can often be grouped into families with a common set of issues. What metrics exist, or should exist, to provide more objective information about people's opinions? (That can be crucial.) How common is the understanding of associates in the business of these key requirements? Amazingly, when you synthesize this down and go talk to people they will say, "Of course." But in reality, until some objective data are pulled together, people don't really see or understand the depth or degree of a problem.

Team Charter

If a team is being commissioned to work on a problem, their definition begins with the charter. The team's Sponsor or Champion, typically along with a Six Sigma Black Belt, creates the charter draft. *The Six Sigma Black Belt Handbook*[*] goes into more explanation of the actions necessary for successful process improvement. This book primarily focuses on the metric components for success. Team metrics begin with the charter; they include:

---

[*]McCarty, Daniels, Bremer and Gupta; McGraw-Hill, 2005.

- *Business case:* This contains a description of the "Big Y," which is the reason for the project. It explains usually using narrative and metric information, why it makes strategic sense to do this project.
- *Goal statement:* What are the objectives and improvement targets? What does success look like? The goal statement should contain the metric(s) the team is trying to improve and indicate a target performance level.
- *Project scope:* This not really a metric, but it defines the boundaries the metrics need to consider. What are the start and stop steps of the process under consideration?

3.6   Pulling the Voices Together

Remember, the leadership group or process improvement team is trying to identify the leverage factors. Everything may be important, but everything does not offer the same degree of leverage for performance improvement. When the prioritization happens, a leadership team is depending on the diversity of the group to take into account the different perspectives, trade-offs, and views of the key stakeholders.

A visual way to do this is to create a wall chart for each major stakeholder group. Charts might include customers (maybe even split groups), shareholders/finance, regulators, and the like. Usually there are no more than four key stakeholder groups that need active consideration at any given point. The team is not trying to come up with every stakeholder group, it is trying to identify which groups need consideration at a given point in time, relative to organizational or process performance improvement.

3.6.1   Setting Priorities

It's usually worthwhile to have the entire leadership team (if less than 12 people) consider customer requirements. From a customer perspective the question is asked: In order to meet my expectations, you must ___ *(fill in the blank [Exhibit 3.7])*.

Then have the leadership team split into subteams to address each selected voice. Assign each subteam one stakeholder to further refine. Label each group's poster with the stakeholder group they have been assigned. The idea here is to identify what this stakeholder group expects from the company. Make sure that the teams express their ideas in "must do" statements, as this keeps the discussion on the level of action (things they can actually do).

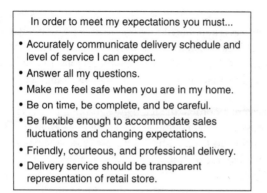

Exhibit 3.7   Voice of the Customer

Answer one of two questions: In order to meet my expectations you must
____. Or in order to meet my key requirements this process must _____.

3.6.2   Brainstorm Using Post-Its

Capture the key requirements on post-it notes, and paste them on flip-chart
sheets hung on the wall. Post-its are easy to move around, so when it comes
time to clarify and combine ideas it is easy to move the post-its into
groupings. See Exhibit 3.8.

The leadership team can use a round-robin (one person at a time shares one
idea) session to identify key requirements. It's best to start this process with
each participant quietly (without discussion) taking a few minutes to write

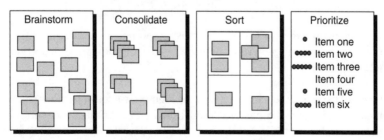

Exhibit 3.8   Brainstorming and Prioritizing Requirements

down their ideas (one idea per post-it), and then take turns going around the table or room, each person sharing one idea per round. (Passing is okay.) The quantity of ideas is not important. It is far better to give in-depth thought to a few meaningful insights than to capture a long list of irrelevant ideas. So this is a slight variation from normal brainstorming methods.

After all ideas are recorded, the team goes through a clarification and combination discussion. When combining like items, a good rule to follow is if one person wishes to keep an item separate it stays separate and does not get combined. The team should be careful not to create too many "super categories" where so many ideas are combined that the team is actually looking at a super project. At this point, the team also needs to remain focused on key expectations, and attempt to stay away from solutions.

3.6.3   Weighted Voting

Once all items on the list have been clarified and combined, the team can prioritize the list. There are a number of ways to do this. One way is "weighted voting," where each team member is given one vote for every seven to 10 items on the combined list. For example, if there are 50 items on the combined list, each team member might get five votes. In this example they would take five 1×1-inch post-its and write down the numbers one to five (one number per post-it).

A team member's most powerful vote is the number 5 vote. It's worth five points. The second-most powerful vote is the number 4 vote, worth four points, then the 3 vote, the 2 vote, and the 1 vote (Exhibit 3.9). Team members should individually review the list of opportunities, and decide where they wish to put their votes.

Team members can write the line items, or opportunity numbers, on their post-its. From the list of 50 opportunities, say one team member selects these and records opportunities, as shown in Exhibit 3.10.

This team member is giving the most important vote (five points) to opportunity #9, the next most powerful vote (four points) to opportunity #21, and so on.

Once all team members have determined their prioritized votes, they can put their post-its on the flip-chart sheets. (The reason for writing the opportunity number on the post-it is that the post-its will cover the opportunities on the flip chart.) After everyone has put their post-its on the list, the leader should

Exhibit 3.9   Weighted Votes

tally the point totals. This produces a prioritized list of opportunities. This technique is called the Nominal Group Technique (weighted voting).

It does not matter a whole lot whether weighted votes, colored dots, or checkmarks get used for voting. Weighted voting might be a little more useful if risks are high. Once all of the votes are cast, there should be a few clear priorities. If the votes are spread evenly throughout the overall list, and the difference between high and middle is just two or three votes, perhaps more discussion is needed or possibly what is really important, for some reason, has still not been added to the list. Remember—the team is searching for leverage factors. See Exhibit 3.7.

3.6.4   Examples of Customer Requirements

Story One.

This business is about 5 years old. They did home deliveries for large national retailers. Overall, they probably had 10 flip-chart pages of voice of the customer and voice of the business. They synthesized their list down to three key issues. Two were strategic in nature and the other operational.

1. Develop a policy manual and guidelines for starting up a new distribution facility in a new city—in order to have a new site start-up process, rather than being totally dependent on one experienced employee to get the new sites started.
2. Broaden the customer base, to lessen the impact (percent of sales) their largest customer represented as a percent of sales.
3. Develop an Operational Policy Manual for site managers, along with a training plan with a clear focus on several business issues (which will go unnamed here).

Exhibit 3.10   Weighted Votes Coded to Opportunities

Story Two.

Pitney Bowes is an organization in transition. Michael Critelli, Pitney Bowes' CEO describes their situation as, "…first class transaction mail, which has been our sweet spot…is declining. To use the most ominous metaphor, 'In a world of e-mail and electronic transactions, we are the buggy whip to the postal service's buggy.' "[*]

As Pitney Bowes' leadership team redefines the future of their business, they needed to understand the realities about their business and to find new "profit zones."[†] In doing this, they defined several new business opportunities such as: presorting mail, which helps organizations handle the large workloads and save substantial postage costs; moving to digital postage equipment, allowing PB to move into the replenishment of inks and printer supplies business.

3.7   Actions to Avoid Metric Problems

First, business performance improvement metrics need to start with the customer in mind. No real surprise here. The surprising thing is how often this does not happen. The voice of the customer is a basic element of most Six Sigma initiatives. The improvement opportunities here are so large that this does not typically require an exhaustive or expensive customer study to identify meaningful issues. Just using a few metrics focused on meaningful customer issues can drive behavioral change and reallocation of resources. Second, metrics need to focus more on "process" drivers, if they are going to influence early corrective action. Consider the model:

$$\text{Inputs} \Rightarrow \text{Process} \Rightarrow \text{Outputs}$$

Most business performance metrics focus on process outputs, not the actual process itself. For example, late deliveries is an output metric for the delivery process. An item is either delivered late or on time (assuming early is not a factor). But the final delivery time is the result of many upstream in-process actions, some of which can cause considerable delivery variability if they are not monitored and controlled. Those key controls are sometimes called *process drivers* because they literally drive the process in a particular direction—hopefully, on the right road—so both the drivers and the roadmap had better be clear to everyone involved.

---

[*]"Back Where We Belong," Michael Critelli; *Harvard Business Review,* May 2005.
[†]*The Profit Zone and Profit Patterns;* Adrian Slywotzky

It's important to identify the drivers with causal relationships to output results. A helpful tool for that is the cause-and-effect (fishbone) diagram. Start with a question like: What are the possible causes of late deliveries? Identify a few categories for the main "bones" in the diagram and work down each of them to identify as many causes as possible. Asking "Why?" five times is also a good way to get farther down each of the bones in the diagram.

At different times certain drivers will impact a process more than others that currently have only minor impact on the outputs. Consider the 80/20 Rule: twenty percent of the process performance drivers probably have the major impact at any given point in time.

Output metrics are not going to go away. They are the easiest to compare on a period-to-period basis. Give thought ahead of time to the key performance drivers that impact the critical output metrics. If something begins to slip out of alignment, simply dig down to the next level of detail to provide more useful information for addressing the key process issues.

Organizations need to realize that process metrics are iterative and that the organization needs to focus on what is important to improve given the current situation. An effective measurement system should be dynamic enough to rotate different drivers onto the radar screen to monitor process health. The drivers may be looked at for a 3-, 6-, or 12-month period. After the process has stabilized the process driver metrics on the radar screen may change as new issues emerge.

While it may feel comforting to say that all metrics need to be maximized, it is simply not the real world. Trade-offs exist—customer service levels versus inventory levels; on-time delivery versus resources to make it happen; responding to customer needs to customize offerings versus process capabilities or resources to accomplish the task. Measurement is relatively simple, but selecting the right metrics is not easy. And depending on the level of the organization and the ultimate connections between processes, the definitions of output versus process can change. Just look at the above example of late deliveries. In the delivery process, this is a process output, with a related set of process drivers sitting underneath. From a customer satisfaction perspective, on-time deliver may itself be a process performance driver. This is why it is so important for the leadership team to agree on what is most important to improve. This has a profound impact on the proper or improper allocation of resources focused on improvement.

3.8   What Is Great versus Average?

This paragraph was added near the end of our writing. We mention great versus average throughout the book, so we really should define our terms. In Jim Collins' *Good to Great*, the first couple of paragraphs in Chap. 1 state, "Good is the enemy of great. And that is one of the key reasons why we have so little that becomes great. We don't have great schools, principally because we have good schools. We don't have great government, principally because we have good government. Few people attain great lives, in large part because it is just so easy to settle for a good life...."

Most organizations with whom we have an opportunity to consult are very good. They do many things in the right way. But at the same time vast opportunities to improve exist. The leadership team knows this; that is why they embark on change programs and their expectations for improvement soar at the outset, as was described in the Introduction chapter. See Exhibit 3.11.

Part of the problem with greatness, which Collins so clearly addresses, is that many people believe greatness is simply not obtainable. "Who, me? Great? Come on!" Some organizations make it to great, only to lose it for a period of time. If you look at some of the organizations listed in *Good to Great* or Jim's earlier book *Built to Last* many of them would not make your list of greatness today. Perhaps this is inevitable, because like most things that are worthwhile in life, this is a journey, not a destination.

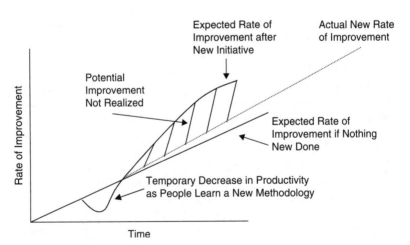

Exhibit 3.11   Performance Improvement Expectations

Here is how we look at greatness.

Rule One

Your organization outperforms its peers and its industry. Collins' research team did not define a specific number but the average cumulative stock returns of their 11 final cut organizations was stock appreciation in excess of 6.9 times the general market. That is pretty great! So for our metric let's just say *Over 5-year periods, the stock appreciation of an organization is in excess of five times the general stock market* (pick your country; Japanese firms could rate against a U.S. or Japanese market set). Average? Pretty easy, appreciation the same rate as the overall market or your overall industry.

Rule Two

The organization brings its people up; it does not tear them down. A few simple questions might clarify. Do you want to work for this place? Does it attract the type of people with whom you want to work? Do the star performers bring up the rest of the pack, or do they shine on their own. The Chicago Bulls basketball team won a number of championships. But they did not win any, nor could they defeat their nemesis opponent, the Detroit Pistons, until the Bulls' star performer, Michael Jordan, brought up the skills of his fellow teammates. The metric here is a soft one, but it is very clear, "you feel challenged to your limits, and you are excited about going to work....every day." The environment is open, people can say what is really going on without negative consequences. Average? Again a soft metric, but easy to see. It's a job. Not terribly exciting, the people you work with are OK, but no one is busting their butt or overly excited about what they do. Going to work is OK; there are worse things in life. You may see problems, but it is safer to not rock the boat.

Rule Three

When you are in attendance, you are expected to have your head in the game, and execute your responsibilities with integrity and with personal accountability for your actions. Johnson & Johnson is the poster child organization for integrity and accountability. They are the benchmark in terms of acting honorably in a way that benefits society overall. The metric here is accountability. "People are expected to do what they say they are going to do. But not just hit a number, they are expected to think about their actions in a holistic way." Average organizations have the exact same goals as great ones, but they are a little more less defined, and people are not held accountable for execution in quite the same way.

3.9   Define—Team Sponsor's Role and Responsibilities

An actively involved Sponsor working with a Black Belt Team Leader sets the stage for good measurement right at the outset of a project. A good Sponsor or team Champion is likely to do all of the following to get a team launched into the Define phase.

- Draft a project description that includes a team charter (i.e., why work on this).
- Select a strong team leader, someone with knowledge of the process being worked. Often this is a manager or supervisor, since they typically have responsibility for sustaining the improved process.
- State a clear business case. This is most likely one of the things the team will need to measure before and after.
- Reallocate work to allow for team member participation on a project team. Any organization wants good people on a team like this; it's only fair to give team members some small degree of relief from some other activity (transferring a responsibility elsewhere or giving more time to get something else done, and so forth).
- Compile information that may be useful to the team. However, the Sponsor must be careful not to overwhelm them with paperwork and must guard against generating improvement ideas (i.e., ways to do it better), that are more appropriately left to the team members.
- Establishing a clear project scope or boundaries that define the team's world of work. How far upstream or downstream does the team go? What is included in the team's scope and what is outside? Many teams have wasted considerable time getting started when they were not presented with a clear project scope.

Exhibit 3.12 shows a project team Sponsor's key responsibilities when launching a Six Sigma team. Actually those responsibilities are pretty much the same when launching any type of improvement team.

There are also a number of questions to address from a management perspective for each phase. While the team Sponsor and the leadership team may give initial thought to these questions before launching a team, given the iterative nature of DMAIC the same questions can be used as an indicator of how effectively the team completed this phase of the project.

3.9.1   Define Phase Questions—Management Perspective

Preproject Launch

1. Who is the customer and how will this project benefit the customer?
2. What is the impact on the business?

Six Sigma Sponsor—Key Project Activities

1.0 Define Opportunities	2.0 Measure Performance	3.0 Analyze Opportunity	4.0 Improve Performance	5.0 Control Performance

Project Governance
- Choose a team leader.
- Review Charter and project scope for focus, clarity.
- Share the business case.
- Budget and provide resources for team.

Change Mgmt.
- Reallocate work to allow for team member participation.
- Assure adequate multidisciplinary representation on the team.
- Establish empowerment guidelines for team.

Advocacy and Culture
- Retain alignment (at BB level, at Sponsor level).
- Conduct weekly project review meetings (30–60 min).

2.0 Measure Performance
- Assure the business relevance of the project metrics.
- Evaluate the data gathering plan.
- Review baseline results.

Key Project Activities
- Choose a team leader.
- Review Charter and project scope for focus, clarity.
- Share the business case.
- Budget and provide resources for team.
- Reallocate work to allow for team member participation.
- Assure adequate multidisciplinary representation on the team.
- Establish empowerment guidelines for team.

- Ide...
  and
- Ass...
  num...
  and

4.0 Improve Performance
- Assess the practicality of the proposed approach.
- Revisit the cost/benefit analysis.
- Oversee implementation and deployment plans.
- Build organizational consensus in support of the team's approach.
- Influence decision makers to implement changes.

5.0 Control Performance
- Validate the improvement.
- Evaluate the financial impact.
- Assure disciplined follow-through of the proposed approach.
- Assess Black Belt performance.
- Celebrate and reward.
- Facilitate transfer of improved process to the Process Owner.

- ...ke data driven ...cisions.
- ...t quickly and ...cisively on issues ...d obstacles.
- Model and communicate Six Sigma.
- Apply consequences.

Exhibit 3.12 Sponsor's Responsibilities—1.0 Define Opportunities

3. What is your problem or opportunity statement—what are you trying to fix or avoid?
4. How will this project help the business?
5. Has the project focus been sufficiently narrowed to complete in an appropriate time frame (different for each team type)?
6. Are there sufficient resources in place to ensure project success?
7. Taking into account the opportunity statement, goals, and scope outlined above, what is the team's charter?

Postproject Launch

8. Describe what you learned from the as-is process mapping.
9. What are the critical to customer requirements?
   a. How did you determine them?
   b. How are you measuring them?
   c. How good is the measurement system?
   d. Have you verified them with the customer?
   e. Do the current specifications reflect them?
10. What are the critical to business requirements?
11. What are the "quick wins?"
12. Has the team put together a communications plan to let relevant people in the organization know what is happening to regularly solicit (appropriate) inputs?
13. What are the next steps?

3.10   Technical Business Unit Case Study

This case study is based on a business similar to Motorola. It is a global enterprise, engineering-driven culture, with success determined by the speed and relevance (acceptance by customers) of new technical products and services. The organization was in the process of rolling out a Six Sigma initiative in each of its global business units.

One of the units was getting ready to release nine new products. When the sales force went out to get customer orders, only one customer placed an order for the new products. This was a painful wake-up call to the executive team. They realized they were out of step with their customers.

At that point the Technical Business Unit (TBU) executives took a new look at their global markets; they realized they were not selling to some of the companies they wanted as customers. TBUs were not in dire straits, their numbers were OK, but they had lost four points of market share during the last 12 months.

In many ways TBU was at the leading edge of technology development. But when they took a hard look, they learned customers were buying 15-year-old technology from their competitors. The older technology was simpler to understand, easier to install, and much easier to maintain. TBU delivered technical products, but did not deliver customer solutions to problems. They had no clear agreement across functional lines of authority on what a solution needed to be. So TBU was often its own worst enemy as different functional groups lobbied for their view of the world during product development. Without a clear set of guidelines, unnecessary features would creep in, and features truly important to customers would get overlooked.

After a healthy dose of reality, talking with customers and employees, leadership develops two key goals:

- Grow market share by 5 points.
- Obtain 70 percent of revenues from products developed in the last 3 years.

Neither one of these goals was earth shattering or terribly profound. The difference between these goals and similar statements in the past was the across-the-board commitment of the leadership team to the numbers. In the past, the revenue goal might have been seen as more of a sales goal and perhaps engineering product development. But the new goals applied to all functional departments. If the company did not hit the targets, everyone's compensation suffered. They had a new sense of commitment across the board from the leadership team to these numbers.

3.11   Tollgate Questions

As a team progresses through the Define phase, the leadership team should schedule meetings with the Sponsor/Champion and Master Black Belt to review all that has been accomplished. The following are a list of questions, called "tollgate questions," which apply to an organizational level or project teams. The wording may need to be changed slightly depending on the perspective. A Sponsor/Champion or Master Black Belt can use these questions to prompt discussion in these meetings. Also, a team can use these questions as they progress through the Define phase to be sure that they have completed all the important items.

1. What is the Big Y that will be influenced by this project?
2. How does the project link to organizational key business strategies?

3. What voice of customer data were used to establish critical customer requirements? How were the data validated?
4. What voice of business data were used to establish critical business requirements? How were the data validated?
5. Have clear priorities been established for the VOC/VOB?
6. What are the boundaries of the process to be improved?
7. What is the specific problem being addressed?
8. Has this problem been tackled before? What was learned from that attempt?
9. How do the little ys directly or indirectly influence the Big Y?
10. What are the goals, in measurable terms, of the project? Are they achievable in the timeframe established?
11. How were the members chosen for the team? How did the Black Belt ensure that the members understood their roles and responsibilities?
12. Were team guidelines (norms) established? How are violations of the guidelines handled?
13. Has the team created a detailed project plan with milestones and associated activities?
14. How detailed were the process maps? How were the maps validated? Did the team ensure that they were "as-is" maps showing the actual state of the process (not the desired state)?
15. Who are the stakeholders that will be affected by this project? What level of communication or involvement is necessary for each stakeholder group?
16. What concerns may the stakeholders have? How will the team prevent these concerns from becoming obstacles?
17. What quick wins have been identified? What is the plan for implementing quick wins? What are the plans for ensuring that the quick wins work? What effect will the quick wins have on the goal?
18. How well did the leadership team stick to the key VOC/VOB priorities as a team and avoid preempting the overall business priorities with their functional goals?

At the completion of the Define phase, the team members, team leader, Master Black Belt, and Champion should feel comfortable with the answers to all these questions and any others that might be specific to the organization.

4

Measure—Developing and Tracking Bridge Metrics

"Measure" in DMAIC

Far and away the best prize that life offers is the chance to work hard at work worth doing.
THEODORE ROOSEVELT

4.1 Purpose

This chapter describes how part of the solution for continuously improving business performance involves establishing clear baseline metrics that spotlight the cause-and-effect relationships to be managed. And it illustrates why Measurement—the springboard to improvement—may be the *most fundamental* of the fundamentals of high-performance business processes.

It will also show how Six Sigma DMAIC methods provide a convenient framework for two aspects of the Financial Bridge Model:

• Organizing the project work for efficient application of the Financial Bridge Process.
• Using Six Sigma statistical process analysis to identify key correlations between downstream process results with their upstream causal factors.

4.2 Introduction

This chapter is about three facets of how business process metrics are positioned to lead as directly as possible to the bottom line.

- *Complexity:* How to make simple and practical
- *Causality:* Focusing on the few most important process metrics
- *Communication:* Of timely information for continuous improvement

Complexity

The challenge here is to put the broad range of business process metrics in a framework that simplifies the process of developing and maintaining an appropriate set of them for a particular business and its specific processes. The Financial Bridge Process is the main framework for that purpose. In addition, a number of metrics tools are discussed that are useful—first to give you a broader perspective on the types of metrics for consideration in the Bridge Process, and second, as organized ways to handle the detailed development work involved in creating a coherent Bridge Process and metrics.

Causality

The main hurdles in developing effective business process performance measures are the identification and validation of upstream, causal metrics that are strongly correlated with the targeted downstream results goals. Some cause-and-effect relationships are obvious, as for example, on-time performance of upstream steps to ensure on-time delivery of orders. But some are less obvious, like a safety-stock nonconformance metric as a predictor of dependable on-time shipments. The Business Metrics Roadmap is a visual model for looking at the full range of upstream metrics that need to be examined in the search for the few metrics with best leverage for day-to-day process control and predictability of downstream results.

Communications

Lastly, the Measure phase is focused on communicating timely data about current process status that is useful for the operating team in assessing process performance relative to targeted performance. That amounts to development of a process design that puts the right data in front of the people who are in a position to take action to make continuous improvement of the process operations, and thereby cause the process to produce improved overall performance.

In summary, this is about development of high-leverage routine process metrics and a process to put them in front of the eyeballs that can take timely improvement actions based on them.

4.3   Overview and Background

Numbers make us sleepy. Business people, especially those who have been successful with an "action-oriented" style, are not interested in detailed, numeric (quantitative) performance reporting methods. Sometimes, when participating in the creation of a "reporting system" they approach the task half-heartedly, hoping that enough can be done to satisfy "the boss's need for metrics," so she or he will "go away and leave me to do real work." There is limited acknowledgement of the rational purpose for business performance reporting—that it's necessary to keep score on all efforts to make a business more effective and competitive in the contest for survival in the marketplace.

Sociologists might explain the "number phobia" of business managers in terms of their conditioning in a "do it now" culture where decisive action is generally a top-ranked trait. So people in that environment may be conditioned to act quickly because that is more likely to receive positive recognition than other behaviors. Certainly, time spent in preaction analysis can easily be construed as "analysis paralysis" in the impatient business world. So business culture expectations may cause a drag on measurement-oriented management behaviors.

But there's more to it. Under time pressure, people make rational choices about how to spend their time in dealing with urgent business problems. If it will take too much time to interpret the available data in performance reports, then one is likely to skip the report and make a decision based on "gut feel." That's the likely behavior when experience is that the data available are too complex to use easily, not adequately indicative of the process to be managed—therefore, not useful for process management decisions, or both. And, we would argue that too-complex performance data reporting is no more useful than bad data, because it's unlikely to be used in routine operations.

In any case, if the data available for process management decisions aren't a good return on manager time, then they won't be used. And simplification is a necessary design criterion for the model we're describing here.

4.3.1   Importance of Communications for Organization Alignment

Speaking of sociologists, they have periodically looked at civilization and asked questions like: What has been man's greatest invention? A common answer has been the clock, since the timed coordination of human activity is crucial for organized productivity. It allowed geometric increases in human prosperity. Today, the information technologies of personal computer, the Internet, and cell phones might rank high on the great-inventions list.

But in business organizations, technological innovations are only valuable if part of coordinated initiatives. That coordination starts with communication about things that people need to accomplish together—their common goals. So while technological inventions might be a more obvious "tool" in the production process, their importance is overshadowed by effective communications that guide and energize the collective business population. It all starts there. And how well that communication is aligned with the overall organization goals may determine how effectively the goals are reached. So if the front-end communication is inadequate, then overall organization performance will be inadequate.

4.3.2 Purposes of Financial Reporting

- External reporting to satisfy regulatory requirements
- Guidance for internal performance improvement efforts

Few would argue with the need for financial business reporting. How else could you keep score of business success or failure? And besides, it's required by government business regulations (such as IRS and SEC). But many would argue about the value of financial reporting for business performance improvement efforts. Facile arguments would be that it's "too much nonvalue (waste) activity." More thoughtful arguments would point to the fact that financial measures tend to be too historical or after the fact—in other words, too late to be good measures for real-time business improvement work. An even more thoughtful view would point to the process management philosophies of the last 20 years that correctly describe how "upstream, causal measures" are needed to identify the things that need to be done to the front end and middle of a process to ensure predictable results out of the process. In other words, you have to manage the upstream process steps to achieve predictable downstream results.

4.3.3 If You Don't Measure It, You Can't Improve It

W. Edwards Deming, the late quality guru, led a dramatic Japanese industrial revolution after World War II, triggered U.S. Total Quality Management efforts in the 1980s, and spread the *statistical process control* (SPC) foundation for what Motorola evolved into the now-ubiquitous Six Sigma methods for process improvement and management. No doubt,

Deming and Taiichi Ohno (at Toyota) paved the way for several decades of continual improvement process advances in industries around the world.

Ohno pioneered the broad, cross-functional process improvement techniques (now called Lean Flow process methods), and Deming shined a bright light on the deep statistical process variation control tools. Between their broad and deep views we now have a comprehensive total view of the process performance fundamentals. That foundational view had been largely forgotten during the go-go years of the second half of the twentieth century when inflationary business conditions seduced us into a blissful ignorance of the business process fundamentals.

4.3.4   Metrics Fundamental to Process Improvement

Metrics are at the heart of all the continuous improvement methods and processes. There is ample evidence that the most dramatic improvement efforts start and follow through with good process metrics. And we are all familiar with sayings like, "If you don't measure it, you can't improve it." And, "People do what the boss measures."

Those are common-sense sayings, based on obvious reality. That is, by keeping score we give everyone a clear target that guides their efforts in the same direction. The clock adds efficiency by coordination of large-group efforts. And measurable goals add efficiency by preventing wasted effort in directions other than the ones indicated by the target metrics.

You cannot overestimate the power of metrics for organizational process performance.

4.3.5   Focusing on the "Vital Few"

Having the right metrics is critical. And having the wrong metrics can be worse than none at all. The wrong ones can lead people down counterproductive paths, wasting resources on efforts that may even run counter to the real goals. With no goals at all, at least everyone can exercise their best judgment about how to support the corporate mission, and not spend time in directions indicated by faulty metrics.

The wrong metrics can be a disaster, but too many metrics can be almost as bad. People can be confused if too many metrics are routinely reported, because taking action on many of them can have the same result as acting on the wrong metrics—activity without value.

So it's important to keep the scorecard simple. Pareto's law applies here, in that few of the many process indicators in any business are the most important keys to guiding performance management actions. Jim Collins' book, *Good to Great*, has several good examples, including the Walgreen's story.

A single performance metric, not even a handful, drives a lot of business performance improvement work at Walgreen's. And how they redefined that measure to alter the company's course illustrates how powerful a process measure can be in guiding business performance.

- *Old measure:* Profit per store
  - Focus was on the P&L and balance sheet.
  - Improvement thinking started at the operational level.
  - Operational tactics with immediate financial results were prominent.
  - Promotions were a primary tool to pump total revenues.
  - Controls focused on reducing or minimizing expenses.
- *New measure:* Revenue per customer visit
  - Focus is on customer behaviors at the points of contact.
  - Improvement thinking starts at the customer contact point, the reason for Walgreen's existence.
  - Operational tactics look to the future for repeat customer visits.
  - Store personnel collaborate on customer service issues.
  - Controls highlight service improvement opportunities.

You can "feel" the change in mind-set from the old to new measures. The old metrics were inward looking, so personnel focused their attention and energies on internal activities. Those were not bad moves when viewed individually. But they created an artificial barrier to thinking "outside the box" that would have helped them see more opportunities to serve the customers— and, in turn, help the customers find more things in the store to buy.

The new metrics are a constant reminder to everyone that their collective success depends on satisfying the customers who visit the store—every time. There is no fuzziness. No curtain obscuring the mission we are all committed to. So in our daily activities we all should find dozens of little ways to contribute to the mission.

A flywheel is the metaphor Collins uses to describe how an organization engages the energies of the workforce to accomplish the mission. Basically, if everyone is aware of the flywheel they can all make spontaneous little pushes on it, at will, whenever they have the opportunity to contribute something big or small to the flywheel's resident energy. That continuous, broad-based input to the mission is a key difference between industry leaders and the others.

4.3.6   Establishing Clear Baseline Metrics Provides Focus

You get what you measure.

Any road will do if you don't know where you're going.

People do what the boss measures.

These are all familiar sayings that describe common experiences with the impact, or lack thereof, of performance measures in business life. We are surprised over and over with how much change can be caused when a process measure is redefined.

- Shipping service mega improvement while decreasing finished goods inventories in just a few weeks.
- Manufacturing process changeover times reduced by 80 percent, just by measuring the interactions of the crew members involved.
- "Impossible" changes in workforce schedules once enough was measured to satisfy the interests of all the participants.

The list goes on forever, telling of business improvements that could not be imagined until the people involved began measuring the right things.

"If you don't measure it, you won't improve it." That's a paraphrase of a W. Edwards Deming quote. Perhaps one of his most important contributions was to clearly demonstrate that most, if not all, business performance improvement efforts begin with measurements of the current situation. In other words, you will make little improvement progress until you have defined your current situation (business process) in enough detail to measure it—end results, overall process metrics, and upstream predictive metrics.

The fundamentals of quality and productivity, as stated by most of the well-known gurus, always include measurement. The Cumberland experience is that it may be the most fundamental of the fundamentals. The most productive efforts of all kinds (new product development, production, service delivery, performance improvement, sports, government services…) always start with measurement. In other words, while many efforts start with a verbalized idea, the best ideas are those that include an articulation of the benefits in measurable terms to be derived that keeps the project headed in a productive direction.

4.3.7   Gunslinger Syndrome

Project teams often suffer from "gunslinger syndrome," especially when the project was triggered by operational problems with a sense of urgency about them. That's because corrective-action team members are often asked to undertake a difficult mission under time pressure, but not given adequate time or support to "do it right the first time." That leads to "Ready, Fire, Aim!" project behaviors that rush to the first possible solution so the team can accomplish the mission as soon as possible, satisfy the boss, and get back to their primary jobs. Everyone knows someone who works for a boss who is more interested in quick fixes than lasting results. "That's close enough."

4.3.8 Business Metrics in the Transition from Twentieth to Twenty-First Century

A few thoughts about the basic nature of business measurement may be useful here.

- "Unmeasurable" business issues
- The simplicity/complexity paradox
- It's in the details

In business a familiar mantra is "Just do it." No doubt, that action bias has been valuable. But that rush to completion has been accompanied by a simplistic view of business processes with a conclusion that many business processes are not measurable. Indeed, W. Edwards Deming even gave managers a pass by saying that "a large percentage of business issues are not measurable." A more complete view is that well-defined business processes are almost always measurable. Therefore, the challenge is to carefully define/design business processes so they can be measured and managed to produce predictable results.

The simplicity/complexity paradox is that better methods for viewing the complex process details are needed to achieve the simplicity promised by Lean and Six Sigma. Examples from the most successful Lean Sigma practitioners illustrate the importance of working the details to Lean Sigma sustainability. Is it "Take care of the big things and the little things take care of themselves?" Or is it the inverse? It's both! And that's why the Bridge Process is important—as a tool for making business metrics comprehensive enough to be a powerful lever for performance improvement efforts, yet organized enough to make routine use and maintenance relatively simple.

The HON Company's attention to process details in the 1970s avoided the myopic mistakes of their competitors that let the "MRP materials management" paradigm weigh them down with nonvalue overhead while the Lean folks (like HON) were focused on a much different paradigm— *moving materials* through more efficiently. That "forward thinking" view was actually the result of using "old-style process planning techniques" with on-going attention to the process details. SMED methods (single minute exchange of die) were new to companies discovering Lean in the 1990s, although Toyota had practiced it since the 1930s, and HON since the 1950s. Attention to detail was the key to those practices and operating efficiencies that kept their competitors wondering "how do they do it?"

It's in the details. We heard or read four references last week to the same new bestseller about the importance of little details in big changes (*The Tipping Point*; we will mention a couple of key points from it later). Four! In one week! Perhaps it's becoming obvious to more people that there is no way to accomplish big changes without working out the details. But the tools generally available for business process improvement are also generally inadequate for the detail work. Most often, project teams are left to their own devices to create spreadsheets of process data that are useful for the current project, but they're not maintainable as part of the central data files so they're soon out of date, out of sight, and out of mind. Lots of value lost.

4.3.9   Ready, Fire, Aim! = Strength Used to Excess = Weakness

A great American business strength is the action orientation that fostered many of the technology and business developments that made the United States the world's commercial leader for the entire twentieth century. However, when used to excess that strength becomes a serious weakness that looks like Ready, Fire, Aim! When unchecked and unbalanced, the cowboy culture has too short an attention span to be interested in details and resists "measurement" because it's a detailed process and might curtail favored cowboy behaviors. In the new global economy, attention to detail is becoming critical. "Just do it" is becoming a dangerous behavior in a world where the "its" are becoming smaller, more subtle, and more complex. Sorting out the important "its," eliminating the waste around them, and streamlining what's left is a detail-oriented process. Business people need tools to make that practical while not losing the action orientation that is still relevant today as global communication has accelerated the run rate worldwide.

4.3.10   Leadership's Role and Responsibility in Measure

"Walking the talk" is a highly praised management trait. Certainly, the opposite behavior is universally reviled as *pandering* from leaders who can't be trusted and, in return, engender no trust or loyalty from their employees.

So it's no surprise that a key leadership role is to demonstrate the use of intelligent business process metrics in maintaining high performance levels, and in using metrics to help identify new opportunities for improvement. The Financial Bridge Process provides a convenient structure and methods to facilitate that work.

4.3.11   Nonfinancial Metrics

Metrics are needed to quantify the impact of Lean and Six Sigma initiatives. They ensure the effectiveness of improvement activities. But on the shop floor and in an administrative environment, such metrics must be in the language of "things," not the language of "money."[*] On a shop floor they include days of inventory, first-pass yields, on time, complete. In a warehouse they might include pick-up time, complete, time spent looking for lost items, fill rates, and so forth. In an administrative environment (where such metrics are scarce) they might include on time, error rates, first-pass completion of task, wait time, rework, and so forth. These metrics can be translated to dollars, but cost reduction is only an interim target. The ultimate target is business growth. Just like the baseball industry, companies need to figure out leading, useful metrics that position their organization for growth.

At Allegheny General in Pittsburgh, the two intensive-care units had been averaging about 5.5 infections per 1000 patient days, mostly blood-stream infections from catheters inserted into patients. "That infection rate was a bit higher than the Pittsburgh average but a bit lower than the national average," says Dr. Shannon.

Over the previous 12 months, 37 patients, already some of the sickest people in the hospital, had 49 infections. Of those, 51 percent died. Dr. Shannon and the staff in the two units—doctors, residents, nurses—applied the Toyota root-cause analysis system, investigating each new infection immediately.[†]

Their main conclusion: A femoral intravenous line, inserted into an artery near the groin, had a particularly high rate of infection. So the team made an all-out effort to replace these lines with less-risky ones in the arm or near the collarbone. Dr. Shannon, who oversees the two units, gave the directive to keep femoral lines to an absolute minimum.

"I was one of those naysayers in the beginning," Connie Cibrone, the hospital's chief executive officer, says of the overall Toyota approach. "I wondered:

---

[*]Michel Baudin, "Cell Metrics;" *www.wefixfactories.com.*
[†]"To Fix Health Care, Hospitals Take Tips from Factory Floor: Adopting Toyota Techniques Can Cut Costs, Wait Times; Ferreting out an Infection, What Paul O'Neill's Been Up To," *The Wall Street Journal;* April 9, 2004.

What is he talking about?" she says of Dr. Shannon. But, "it really made sense."

As organizations wrestle with nonfinancial metrics there are six demons they need to watch:

1. Many *metrics are simply irrelevant* to the work being done. Information gets gathered, but no action is taken. Take a look at the performance metrics in your business and ask yourself, "When was the last time we took an action based on this number?" In many administrative and professional business processes the metrics don't even exist.

2. *Measures are used as a weapon.* Dr. W. Edwards Deming often said, "We need to drive fear out of the workplace." Many performance measurement systems do exactly the opposite. When management does act on a metric, they don't look at the business process. Instead they focus on someone, some other department, or outside factor to "blame" causing people to game the system and to point their fingers elsewhere when problems arise. *We cover this concept a number of times in this text.*

3. The *metrics selected are too general* or high level to provide information that someone can take timely action to address. An important result gets looked at, but it is impacted by so many variables it is difficult to know which one moved the dial. Is a 3 percent decrease in the rate of hospital patient infections due to improvements in the process or due to variability in the measurement system?

4. The metrics show a result, but *it comes too late to make a corrective action.* This is a problem with output-based metrics like on-time deliveries, total production, and total transactions processed. By the time a problem is discovered, it is too late to do anything about it. We are not saying output metrics are irrelevant, but they are not very useful for timely improvement.

5. The *wrong information is gathered*, and the resulting changes made to the process are, at best, neutral and likely do more harm than good. A classic example of this is "earned hours" in many manufacturing operations. In a desire to keep people busy, earned hours lead them to stay busy making something, rather than focusing on key customer needs. Companies fail to prove that improvements in nonfinancial metrics will in fact improve profitability. Linkages are not validated, they are assumed.

6. Finally, *metrics don't start with the customer* in mind or *key business strategies*. Another issue we come back to numerous times in this text. Despite the logic of making such connections, fewer than 30 percent of the companies surveyed by Ittner and Larker have developed causal

models, which show what areas are expected to improve as a result of commitments to particular courses of action, and then show how those improvements should affect long-term economic performance.[*]

These problems undermine the credibility of the entire business performance measurement process. An example of half-baked assumptions, from the Ittner and Larcker article, references a fast food chain. They assumed employee turnover caused cost to escalate. Subsequent analysis showed that profitability of restaurants with identical turnover varied dramatically. Further research revealed that turnover among supervisors was really the key, not turnover among lower-level workers. The company was not wrong in believing turnover was important; they just had not investigated far enough to understand what really mattered. This story is very similar to the baseball metrics example used earlier.

Actions need to be taken on the metrics without making people fearful of blame. Organizations also need to understand their performance drivers and have some backup data to support that belief. Otherwise, companies end up measuring too many things, with many of the metrics being irrelevant. Relevant metrics are those that people can use, those that address real business issues like the hospital infections example at the beginning of this section.

4.4   Company Examples

4.4.1   Wal-Mart

- *In-Stock:* Inventory turns and days on hand along with in-stock. They look at in-stock (available on the shelf for the customer) versus "customer perception of our in-stock." The idea being that Wal-Mart can be at 100 percent in-stock, but if customers don't think they are, they will go down the street to a competitor that they believe is in-stock. It only takes a brief period of out of stock before the perception kicks in, and a long time to get the confidence back. The linkage to sales is well defined and it is a great upstream indicator.
- *Customer perception:* They monitor numerous cuts of customer perception ranging from checkout experience to bathroom cleanliness to price perception. They have an extremely good database that tells them

---

[*]"Coming Up Short on Nonfinancial Performance," Measurement Christopher Ittner and David Larcker; *Harvard Business Review;* November, 2003.

how changes or trends in those areas impact sales. On a company wide level, those metrics are very stable, but the drill down to store level provides a goldmine of information. They can assess many aspects of their operations from these data.

- *Support services:* This is a process and internal business relationship metric. Think of it this way: the information technology group provides services to various business groups. Those business groups can describe (and quantify) the value of the IT services and impact on business objectives. This valuation can be based on project scoping and impact assessments (on the front end) or even impact assumptions—as long as the business group and IT agree. Those valuations are tied to certain service or project level delivery, and become the performance metrics for IT (or at least part of them). This arrangement drives IT to do a better job on project scoping/partnering/delivery, as well as creating a situation where the business group clearly defines success (which helps IT focus on the right things).

4.4.2   A Hospital

A member of one hospital's quality department noted that there were six "incident reports" (error reports) related to the wrong IV drip rate in the ICU. Now, this is pretty serious—if you're getting drugs through your IV and you're in ICU, you're likely pretty sick. Anyway, this person went up to the ICU, talked to the nurses, and made several discoveries: there were several different methods of calculating drip rates; the hospital had purchased some new IV monitors that were calibrated differently than the old ones, resulting in a different rate for a similar monitor setting; and there was a discrepancy in how the nurses reported from shift to shift. Obviously these are all about standardizing the work, which this person did, rallying agreement among the staff to standardize the machines. The result: No errors related to wrong IV drip rates in the next 3 months!

4.4.3   GE Business Unit

(First-hand report of a GE executive on key metrics… as you can see this feeds their version of a Bridge Report)

- We had a nine page report we looked at each month. We also had an event tracker deck that broke all projects into material, labor, and other variable costs (OVC) productivity, adding to total variable cost productivity.
- We also tracked deflation projects and added these to variable cost productivity to get total variable cost out. We called this executable cost

out. We also had a deck that measured accounting changes from prior year each month and how they impacted current year productivity.

- We also had a mix calculation that calculated mix impact on productivity each month. Now from the ledger we turned this year's costs into constant dollars before calculating VCP from the prior period the prior year. To do this we factored out price changes, FX changes, and labor (raises) and OVC inflation (fuel price increases, energy price increases, and so forth) from the costs this year so an apples to apples comparison to prior year was possible (we also tracked what these were against plan—price, FX, labor/OVC inflation). Then we calculated productivity on material, labor, OVC, and total. This was our true productivity; we calculated material deflation separately.

- True productivity was distinguished from material productivity: if we got cost out from a form, fit, or function change to a part, it was productivity; if it was from a supplier negotiation on the same component number and revision, it was material deflation.

- We then took the ledger productivity and subtracted the mix impact, the accounting plays (current and prior year), and what the teams claim they save off of their event tracker project deck, and what was left over hit a plug line that was called unidentified.

- All of this effectively excluded the effects of price, FX, inflation, mix, and accounting from the true ledger value and left hopefully close to true executable productivity.

- Now, we were required to have a very low unidentified. If it was much more than $50K we had to find ways to explain the gap. This may all sound complicated, and it was a tough metric, but highly automated, and forced us to be able to explain executable productivity and match it close to the ledger. GE Energy has similar requirements but not quite as stringent, and as such they often find reported savings do not show up in the ledger.

GE measures everything, holds people very accountable, and expects people to make their numbers.

4.5   Pulling It Together—Measure Phase in Bridge Process

Developing a Financial Bridge Model and Process in the DMAIC Measure phase.

At this point, you may be feeling somewhat disoriented. After the background review, you might be focusing on all the reasons business metrics are not as effective as hoped, or the apparent complexity of

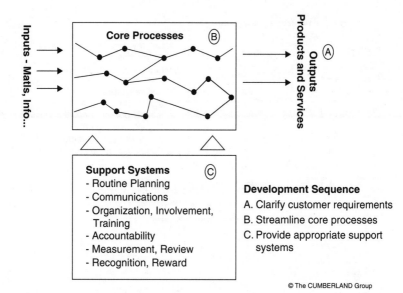

Exhibit 4.1   Business Process Model

business metrics that is one of the obstacles to effective business process measurement.

None of the concepts involved are particularly complicated (it's not rocket science), but the scope and interrelationships of the business metrics landscape are truly "complex" by virtue of multiple dimensions and all the overlaps. Let's add a perspective to your view that will help you get your bearings and keep you from getting lost in the trees while managing the forest.

First, reflect on the Business Process Model (Exhibit 4.1). Most of this book is focused on the Measurement Support System in the bottom block. However, it will be useful to keep in mind that these support systems are just that, and that they exist solely to help the business teams operate their processes as effectively as possible.

4.5.1   Bridge Structure and Development Steps

Exhibit 4.2 summarizes the Bridge structure and development steps discussed in the chapter. First, look at the three large arrows labeled Time, Metrics Types, and Causality. They indicate the main dimensions of information expressed in the Financial Bridge Model (Exhibit 4.3).

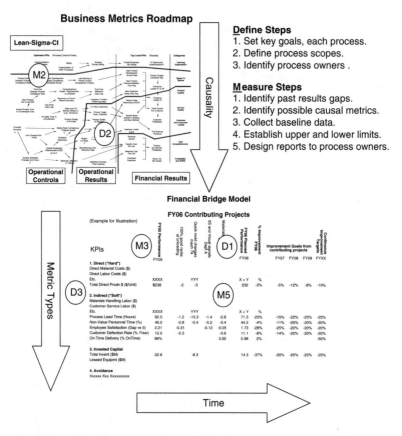

Exhibit 4.2   Building a Financial Bridge Model

- The Time dimension, discussed in the Bridge Model chapter, is focused on the big picture and how business improvements track into the financial statement. In this chapter we will take a more granular view to look at operational process metrics that become important in short time intervals, right up to real time.
- The Metrics Types dimension, also introduced in the Bridge Model chapter, outlines the main categories to be tracked. The submetrics will be discussed in more detail in Sec. 4.10.
- The Causality dimension addresses the cause-and-effect relationships that should be the foundation of a good business metrics set. It's a critical concept and will be described shortly.

Financial Bridge Model

(Example for Illustration)	FY05 Performance	FY06 Contributing Projects				FY06 Planned Performance	% Improvement FY06	Improvement Goals from Contributing Projects			Continuous Improvement Targets
	FY05	100% Good Racks at Unloading	Quick Mold Changes Mach 74	5S and Visual Signals Dept A	Materials Staged in Sequence	FY06	%	FY07	FY08	FY09	FYXX
1. Direct ("Hard")											
Direct Material Costs ($)											
Direct Labor Costs ($)											
Etc.	XXXX		YYY			X + Y	%				
Total Direct Prodn $ ($/Unit)	$238	−2	−3		−1	232	−3%	−5%	−12%	−8%	−10%
2. Indirect ("Soft")											
Materials Handling Labor ($)											
Customer Service Labor ($)											
Etc.	XXXX		YYY			X + Y	%				
Process Lead Time (Hours)	92.0	−1.2	−15.3	−1.4	−2.8	71.3	−23%	−15%	−25%	−25%	−25%
Nonvalue Personnel Time (%)	46.0	−0.8	−0.4	−0.2	−0.4	44.2	−4%	−11%	−25%	−20%	−20%
Employee Satisfaction (Gap vs 5)	2.21	−0.31		−0.12	−0.05	1.73	−28%	−25%	−20%	−20%	−20%
Customer Defection Rate (% /Year)	12.0	−0.3			−0.6	11.1	−8%	−14%	−20%	−20%	−50%
On-Time Delivery (% OnTime)	96%				0.02	0.98	2%				
3. Invested Capital											
Total Invent ($M)	22.6		−8.3			14.3	−37%	−20%	−25%	−25%	−25%
Leased Equipmt ($M)											
4. Avoidance											
Xxxxx Xxx Xxxxxxxxxx											

Exhibit 4.3 Financial Bridge Model

113

4.6   Measurement System Analysis

Measurement System Analysis is a critical part of any Six Sigma project, regardless of the environment (e.g., transactional and service). However, this type of analysis is often easier in a manufacturing environment since there are more techniques developed in this arena.

Depending on the type of data, the statistical analysis will be different. For a continuous measurement, there are a variety of statistical properties that can be determined: stability, bias, precision (which can be broken down into repeatability and reproducibility), linearity, and discrimination. For a discrete measurement, estimates of the error rates can be determined for within appraiser, each appraiser versus standard, between appraisers, and all appraisers versus standard. The properties related to both continuous and discrete measures are discussed in the following sections.

4.6.1   Continuous Measurements[*]

Stability is defined as the distribution of the measurement system remaining constant over time. Stability is often determined by measuring a standard or a golden unit on a periodic basis and plotting the results on a time-based chart, usually a control chart. Control charts are discussed in the Control phase. The purpose of this chart is to show that the variability and mean of the measurements remain the same over time. Assuming the standard or golden unit doesn't change, any changes in the variability or mean are due to the measurement system.

Bias is the difference between the observed average of the measurement data on a standard and the actual reference value. The purpose of doing a bias study is to determine if the measurement system is giving accurate values. To determine bias, a standard must be available that is traceable to the National Institute of Standards and Technology (NIST), or is an industry agreed-upon standard. To determine bias, a team would measure the standard several times (say 20 or 30) and compute the difference between the average of these readings and the reference value. This is the bias. The goal is to get this value close to zero.

Any measurements taken from a process will have variability. This variability can be broken into two main sources: process variability and measurement

---

[*]*Six Sigma Black Belt Handbook,* McCarty, Daniels, Bremer and Gupta; McGraw-Hill, 2004.

system variability. The goal is to have the variability due to the measurement system small in comparison to the process variability.

Precision is the measure of the measurement system variability, and is defined as the standard deviation due to the measurement system. A traditional way to determine precision is to take a sample of representative parts from the process and to have two or three people measure the parts two or three times. Usually this is conducted as a blind study; the people aren't aware that they are part of the measurement system analysis. Precision can be split into repeatability and reproducibility. *Repeatability* is the variability of the gauge itself. *Reproducibility* is the variability associated with using different operators under different conditions. Variability from part to part is due to the process, while repeatability and reproducibility are due to the measurement system. The goal is to have the repeatability and reproducibility be small.

To judge if the variability due to the measurement system is small enough, two metrics are commonly used. They are %R&R and % P/T. %R&R stands for percent repeatability and reproducibility. The formula is

$$\%R\&R = \frac{6\hat{\sigma}_{Measurement\_System}}{6\hat{\sigma}_{Total}} \times 100$$

where the numerator contains an estimate (the "^" indicates an estimate) of the variability solely due to the measurement system, and the denominator contains an estimate of the total variability. %P/T stands for percent precision to tolerance. The formula is:

$$\%P/T = \frac{6\hat{\sigma}_{Measurement\_System}}{USL - LSL} \times 100$$

where USL is the upper specification limit, and LSL is the lower specification limit. These give the allowable range of values for the process. For both metrics, usually the goal is to get these percentages to be under 10 percent.

Often a measurement system is used to measure parts that have a range of sizes. *Linearity* is the determination of the bias and precision over the expected operating range of the gauge; it helps to determine if these are acceptable for all part sizes. For instance, if a measurement system measures length, it may work well (small bias and precision) for parts that are 12 inches long. However, it may not work at all for parts that are smaller than one-half inch. If the business makes parts of both sizes, the measurement system may not be appropriate for both types of parts.

Discrimination is the capability of a measurement tool to detect and adequately indicate small changes in a measured characteristic. For example, measuring the width of a strand of hair with a tape measure that indicates to the nearest sixteenth of an inch would not be adequate. The discrimination of the tape measure is not small enough. If the measurement tool is not adequate to detect small changes, determining how to find and fix errors in the process will be difficult.

4.6.2   Discrete Measurements

For discrete measurements, a blind study may also be done. An expert would usually determine whether the product is good or bad. Then, a variety of good and bad units is given to two or three appraisers. The appraisers each then determine if they think the product is good or bad. They are asked to look at the same unit more than once, without knowing that they had evaluated the unit previously. This is called the *within appraiser error rate*. It can then be determined how well all the appraisers are able to get the same result on the same product—the *between appraiser error rate*. In addition, one can determine how well the appraisers agree with the expert, known as the *appraiser versus standard error rate*.

Software packages can help with the analysis of data from a measurement study for both continuous and discrete data.

If a team is unable to get repeated measures, as described above, the calculations of these statistical properties may be difficult. The team may not be able to conduct a formal measurement system study. However, they should still review the measurement system and consider ways in which the data produced may have error. They should consider using a cause and effect with people, machine, method, environment, and material as possible categories and measurement system variability and inaccuracy in the head of the diagram. The team would then brainstorm possible reasons for inaccuracy and variability in the data due to the measurement system. The team would choose the most likely reasons to address. In addition, teams that don't do a formal measurement system study should place even more emphasis on clear Operational Definitions, discussed in the next section.

Data collection can be difficult. To help, the team should use Operational Definitions and data collection plans (Exhibit 4.4). They may also need to create data collection forms.

Develop a Measurement Plan

- Determining current process performance usually requires the collection of data. When developing a measurement plan ensure that:
    - The data collected is meaningful.
    - The data collected is valid.
    - All relevant data is collected concurrently.

Questions to Answer

- What precise data will be collected?
    - Performance measurement?
    - Causes of process deficiencies?
- Do we analyze all relevant data or a sample?
    - What is the right sample size?
    - What is the right frequency?
    - What will be the sample selection method?
- What tools are necessary?
    - What formats will be used?
    - What logs will be kept?
    - Do we need a computer?

- What logistical issues are relevant?
    - Who will collect data?
    - Where are the data located?
    - When will it be collected?
    - What additional assistance is required?
- What do you want to do with the data?
    - Use daily, weekly, etc.
    - Identify trends in the process data.
    - Identify deficiencies in the process.
    - Demonstrate current process performance.
    - Identify variation in a process.
    - Identify a cause and effect relationship.

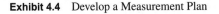

Exhibit 4.4   Develop a Measurement Plan

4.6.3   Operational Definition

An Operational Definition is a precise definition of the specific Y to be measured. These will be used to baseline the performance. The purpose of the definition is to provide a single agreed-upon meaning for each specific Y. This helps ensure that reliability and consistency are built in up front during the measurement process. Although the concept is simple, the task of creating a definition should not be underestimated.

A good Operational Definition will ensure that the first time the data are collected, they are collected correctly and the data will be useable.

Data Collection Plan

The data collection plan is an important deliverable from the team. It is a plan defining the precise data that will be collected, the amount of data that will be collected, a description of the logistical issues—who, where, when data will be collected, and what will be done with data collected. The purpose of the plan is to make sure that the data collected are meaningful and valid and that all relevant data are collected concurrently (the Xs and the Ys).

Steps for creating a data collection plan:

1. List the Y data. Each row contains a separate Y.
2. Enter the Operational Definition for each Y.
3. List the sources from which the team will need to get the data.
4. Enter the sample size. Consider the cost and practicality of sampling, how representative the sample is, and the variability of the population.
5. Determine logistical issues—who will collect data, when it will be collected, and how it will be collected.
6. List all the X data to be collected at the same time. Take this information from the cause-and-effect matrix or cause-and-effect diagram.
7. List what will be done with the data. Include any analysis to be done as well as any graphs to generate.

Data Collection Forms

Most teams need to do some level of manual data collection. Even in the most automated processes, some X data may not be available any other way. Changing an IT system to collect specific X data may not be a viable option.

For manual data collection, the team will have to develop a form to meet the data collection needs (Exhibit 4.5). The format should be straightforward

Sample Data Measurement Plan Form

Performance Measure	Operational Definition	Data Source and Location	Sample Size	Who Will Collect the Data	When Will the Data Be Collected	How Will the Data Be Collected	Other Data that Should Be Collected at the Same Time

How will the data be used?	How will the data be displayed?
Examples: ◆ Identification of Largest Contributors ◆ Identifying if Data is Normally Distributed ◆ Identifying Sigma Level and Variation ◆ Root Cause Analysis ◆ Correlation Analysis	Examples: ◆ Pareto Chart ◆ Histogram ◆ Control Chart ◆ Scatter Diagrams

MOTOROLA UNIVERSITY   *intelligence* **M** *everywhere*

Exhibit 4.5   Form for Data Gathering Measurement

and simple to minimize errors and the people gathering the information should be involved in its creation. If the team is collecting data about time, people in the process may be concerned how the data will be used. They may worry that their performance is being judged. It is important to address these concerns to avoid possible bias in the results.

Try using the form on a trial basis before full implementation and examine the data for unexpected results or missing data. Adjust the collection form as required. Another good idea is to have the team be as close to the data collection as possible to help with any problems.

4.7   Measure Substeps for Routine Bridge Process Use

Next, notice the Measure phase steps (upper right in Exhibit 4.2) for development of a Financial Bridge Model (FBM). They are easy to describe in context for FBM purposes, but they can be somewhat tricky to develop. In fact, that's probably one of the reasons business metrics systems in general are not consistently effective—the process of determining effective business metrics is just complex enough to be overrun often by our Ready, Fire, Aim! (RFA) cultural bias to "just do it," and worry about the details later. Maybe. If we survive the next wave of threats to our leaky boat…(Techniques are included in the Business Metrics Roadmap section for overcoming a RFA bias against measurement.)

The work involved in the Measure steps for Bridge Process development includes some things that are probably familiar in your business, and some that may be surprise "missing links."

1. Adjust or establish "upstream" causal process metrics; working backward from the process outputs or the key business performance goals. Organize new process metrics in Bridge categories. Establish routine measurement procedures.
   a. Convert VOC and VOB to critical voice of the process metrics (typically outputs).
   b. Identify the Big Y and Little X process metrics.
   c. Create or edit the Process Metrics Roadmap.
   d. Determine appropriate upper and lower limits for reporting.
   e. Create an Operational Definition of metrics and data to be collected.
2. Adjust the reporting procedures to communicate to process operators and owners; highlight the exceptions outside upper and lower control limits in "Discovery Sequence" for Analyze steps (next chapter).

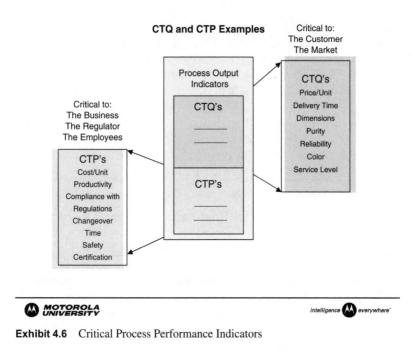

Exhibit 4.6   Critical Process Performance Indicators

3. Update the Process Diagnostics reference manual for use in the Analyze phase.

There is a lot going on in these three steps. The following sections will help you interpret them.

Exhibits 4.6 and 4.7 are from Six Sigma process management concepts. Exhibit 4.6 illustrates the typical metrics in *Critical to Quality* (CTQ) and *Critical to Process* (CTP) segments of a business process. Exhibit 4.7 illustrates the scope of metrics views that are needed to make complete sense of the performance metrics for a single business process. A key point is that all the pieces are needed. If any are missing, the process metrics will be incomplete, and probably ineffective. So all the stakeholders need to be involved in the development process.

4.7.1   The Big Ys

A strength of the Six Sigma methodology is its rational view of key business performance metrics. Business process owners and operators gain powerful insights from Six Sigma methods for correlating downstream business

Process Elements and Indicator Relationships

Effective improvement requires information from the entire supplier-customer, cause-and-effect relationship.

Start Boundary

Suppliers:	Inputs:

End Boundary

Outputs:	Customers:

Process

Input Indicators	Process Indicators	Output Indicators
Measures that evaluate the degree to which the inputs to a process, provided by suppliers, are consistent with what the process needs to efficiently and effectively convert into customer-satisfying outputs.	Measures that evaluate the effectiveness, efficiency, and quality of the transformation processes—the steps and activities used to convert inputs into customer-satisfying outputs.	Measures that evaluate dimensions of the output—may focus on the performance of the business as well as that associated with the delivery of services and products to customers.
Examples:	Examples:	Examples:
? # of customer inquiries	? Availability of service personnel	? # of calls/hour taken by each service rep
? Type of customer inquiries	? Time required to perform credit review	? 2nd year customer retention figures
? # of orders	? % of nonstandard approvals required	? Total # of meals delivered
? # of positions open	? # of qualified applicants	? % customer complaints
? Type of position open	? Total cost of service delivery	
? Accuracy of the credit analysis	? Total overtime hours	
? Timeliness of the contract submitted for review		

intelligence **M** *everywhere*

M MOTOROLA UNIVERSITY

Exhibit 4.7 Cause-and-Effect Process Indicators

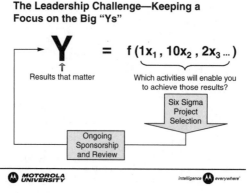

The Leadership Challenge—Keeping a
Focus on the Big "Ys"

$$Y = f(1x_1, 10x_2, 2x_3 \dots)$$

Results that matter

Which activities will enable you
to achieve those results?

Six Sigma
Project
Selection

Ongoing
Sponsorship
and Review

MOTOROLA
UNIVERSITY

intelligence everywhere

Exhibit 4.8   Big Ys

results goals (the Big Ys, Exhibit 4.8) with the upstream process control factors (the Little Xs). Once the metrics for financial results, market factors, product and service quality are defined, then you can identify which of them constitute the Big Ys that absolutely must be attained for strategic business advantage.

Better, faster, and cheaper are the umbrella headers for the balanced set of quality, time, and cost categories that should be reflected in the Big Ys for a core business process. Each of them can be subdivided into many possible component metrics. For example, *quality* may include metrics for product feature #4, service feature #12, customer relationship process #7, and employee satisfaction factor #6. *Time* may include on-time delivery, quickness of response to quote requests, hours per unit produced, and overall process lead time. *Cost* may include direct per unit costs, rework costs, warranty costs, and operating overhead costs. The point is that a balanced set of the few most important current metrics should constitute the Big Ys for any major business process. That provides focus for determining the upstream Little Xs that process operators will use to manage the process for predictable results.

4.7.2   The Causal X Factors

The last, but not least of the business process metrics are the upstream metrics that indicate status of the causal "X" factors that must be controlled to ensure predictable downstream results (product and service outputs that conform to customer requirements). In fact, the X factors may be the most important of the business process metrics because they are at the points in the process that must be controlled carefully to ensure predictable downstream results.

4.8   Business Metrics Roadmap—Extended Management Horizon

Measure Step 1 is about *causal metrics*. That needs some explanation to help you put it in context of the Bridge Process and business performance improvement based on process management concepts.

The roadmap in Exhibit 4.9 is an illustration of how business metrics are naturally linked to each other with an upstream/downstream "causality" view of process measures. In other words, it describes the linkages between the changes seen in the P&L and the upstream operating factors that caused them. The four "depth phases" of the roadmap form a complete view of how upstream activities contribute to downstream results that show up later in the P&L.

Consider the four views and a few "landmarks" in them:

- *Financial results:* After-the-fact view of profitability and return on net assets
- *Operational results:* Product and service quality, cost effectiveness
- *Operational controls:* Upstream process control points
- *Lean-Sigma-CI:* Business processes for accelerated performance improvement

Practical increases in the "business performance management *perspective*" are illustrated with percentages (for lack of a better term now) in the successive phases of Exhibit 4.9. In other words, management gains visibility and an important tool with a clear roadmap view of the upstream causal factors that can be managed for different downstream results. Over time, industry leaders adopt the broader view—including the far-upstream Lean-Sigma-CI process segments—giving them leverage that aligns the organization, and its results, for maximum competitive advantage.

The Bridge Process provides an understandable roadmap and methods for making that journey directly, with minimum rabbit-trails.

4.8.1   Driving in the "Rear-View Mirror"?

We are accustomed to first looking at the Financial Results view, because it's universally maintained to meet government regulations, presented

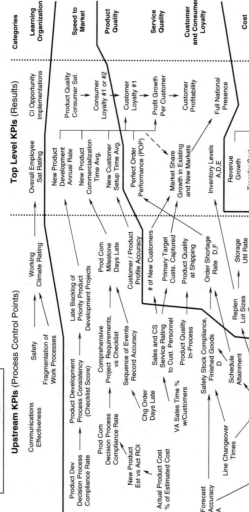

Exhibit 4.9 Business Metrics Roadmap

consistently according to standard rules (GAAP), and readily available as routine reports or queries from business information and ERP systems.

Next we look at the current Operational Results metrics to see how well we are meeting current customer demands for particular product and service features. Part of that view includes cost effectiveness, productivity, and profitability measures that summarize how well we are meeting key business performance goals.

But, the "rear-window" view in the financial, accounting, and operational summary records is inadequate for planning business performance improvements. That's especially true in our new global marketplace where internet-speed information is enabling once-isolated competitors to quickly fine-tune their operations for cost-effective solutions to rapidly changing market demands.

That accelerated change-speed means we all have to keep up, or perish. And a key to keeping up is to see our whole supply chain in more detailed views that are closer to real time—not just in the rear-view mirrors.

4.8.2   Roadmap and Clear View Ahead for Predictable Results

The future-oriented business metrics views are of the "upstream" Operational Controls metrics and the Lean-Sigma-CI metrics. Both views are quite different from the perspective traditionally exercised by many management teams even as the "information age" was entering its teenage growth spurt at the end of the twentieth century.

The Operational Controls view has been steadily gaining adopters with the process management practices from the Lean Manufacturing and Six Sigma camps. Both are effective tactics for finding and capturing improvement opportunities in business processes. The differences between Lean and Six Sigma are primarily in their focal points: Lean tends to emphasize "blitz-type" improvements of cross-functional operations, while Six Sigma places more emphasis on deep statistical analysis to identify cause-and-effect relationships that may not be immediately observable. So they both include process analysis methods to identify cause-and-effect relationships that indicate where management effort should be placed upstream for predictable results downstream. This causal factors view has been an important enhancement for process management methods aimed at reducing nonvalue operating costs and variations (defects, rework, scrap, waste, warranty claims, and so forth).

Finally, the Lean-Sigma-CI view also includes the organizational processes for accelerated *continuous improvement* (CI). The term *learning organization* has been applied because it paints an image of an entire workforce engaged in a business culture that is always looking for ways to improve and gain competitive advantage for growth. In other words, their culture is based on a foundation of "learning" as the first step toward all positive changes.

Unfortunately, the "learning organization" moniker too often gets bogged down in the learning methods to the point that there is more learning activity than actual improvement activity. That has been an all-too-often result of the many program-of-the-month initiatives that have come and gone in the last 40 years. All of them had good intentions, but missed the mark when trying to guide the practitioners toward real results.

In contrast, the Lean and Six Sigma processes have been easier to keep focused on the ultimate results goals, so they have been more sustainable to this point. And their sustainability is much enhanced when they are combined with the CI models that make continuous improvement a deliberate part of an organization's management process. To paraphrase an important quote from W. Edwards Deming, "Most business performance problems are process-caused, not people-caused." And, to extrapolate slightly, we can say that if the management process does not include specific segments to *cause* continuous improvement, then the workforce is less likely to do it as part of their business culture of "how we do things here."

Now if you look again at the whole roadmap you should see a natural transition from the lower right Financial Results to the upper left Lean-Sigma-CI metrics that indicate what an organization is doing now to ensure arrival ahead of the competition in 5 or 10 years. The Bridge Model is about making that transition and building a "bridge" that clearly links improvement efforts—sometimes far upstream—to financial results.

4.8.3   Metaphors for Bridge Model Concepts: "Onion peeling" and "car maintenance" in business process management

Beginning with the roadmap view we just described, you might already be forming a mental image of some of the steps to build your own Bridge Model. We will get to more about that shortly. First, let's use a couple of metaphors to help you with the mental imaging.

First, think of the layers in an onion. It's not hard to think of a company in layers that can be examined like the layers of an onion you're peeling.

The useful image is the "outside-in" view of stakeholders outside the company's day-to-day operations. Employees are on the inside with a less obstructed view. Customers, suppliers, stockholders, and often even top management are on the outside with a limited view of how the business really achieves its end outputs in the form of products, services, and financial results.

Now, consider that even the employees have a limited view since the cross-functional nature of processes in larger organizations makes it difficult for any one person to have a complete view of any current operating process. The views are all fragments of the whole. Therefore, Lean-Sigma-CI methods include cross-functional project team structures when the process at hand needs a comprehensive view to begin analysis work (see Project Teams chapter in *Black Belt Handbook**).

The useful idea here is that you can rarely see the key cause-and-effect relationships to be managed in a company from the outside. You have to spend some significant effort to "peel the onion" and eventually determine the few key control points deep inside. Having the patience for that more detailed view is sometimes difficult in action-oriented business cultures—but it is becoming crucial in the new global economy.

Now, try another view. Think about car maintenance. (Personal health maintenance would also work, particularly when the complexity of the human side of organizational performance is considered.) This is a simple analogy. If the fuel economy of our commuting vehicle has slipped lately, then we can check several indicators of "car health" to focus in on the possible causes of the problem for correction. Low tire pressure, low engine oil, and a malfunctioning fuel injection system are among the primary possibilities. Several others could be secondary causes. In any case, it's important to somehow observe the various indicators before we can make an accurate diagnosis for corrective action.

Business metrics serve that same purpose—to make causal factors observable for routine diagnostic work. And a key point is to be sure that the primary indicators are most visible. It takes some work to determine which are "primary," but it's necessary so that our diagnostic work down the road is always efficient and effective. If we hurriedly pull together a set of metrics for routine diagnostics, then we run the risk of missing the most important ones, overemphasizing minor/superficial ones, or worst of all, adopting the

---

Six Sigma Black Belt Handbook, McCarty, Daniels, Bremer, and Gupta; McGraw-Hill, 2004.

wrong metrics, causing counterproductive responses (á la the classic mindless "inventory turns" indicator). In any case, our business process management work down the road will be inadequate for good performance if we're not using the right diagnostic indicators.

You get the idea: It's about the details of true causal factors to be measured and managed.

4.8.4   Building Your Own Business Metrics Roadmap

Cause-and-effect clarity; one step at a time.

Considering the roadmap graphic in Exhibit 4.9, think of how you can develop your Business Metrics Roadmap in "depth phases" for each main road radiating out through production, distribution, logistics, customer service, sales, product development, and the like.

For example, if "quicker response to customer order changes" is a current improvement opportunity, then several "routes" in upstream business process segments should be examined for potential streamlining (inventory maintenance, order handling, demand forecasting...). And, that work will culminate with the identification of a few key upstream metrics that can be used to track improvement progress and continuous improvement in the future.

In summary, that upstream journey on the Business Metrics Roadmap looks like:

> *Phase I:* Extend the horizon of the roadmap from the Financial Results metrics in the lower right corner into the Operational Results metrics immediately left and above.
> *Phase II:* Extend into the Operational Controls sector next above and to left.
> *Phase III:* Extend to Lean-Sigma-CI at the top and left.

Each phase is actually a series of incremental linkage additions, maybe in parallel with improvement projects that are also working their way upstream in the business. The ultimate destination (Business Metrics Roadmap and Key Performance Indicators in the Bridge Model) is then a "business health" monitoring system for quick, accurate, routine diagnosis of business performance improvement opportunities. And the key to the model's effectiveness is in your careful analysis and identification of upstream causal factors for real power in everyday process management functions.

4.8.5   Not Too Distant Future—Get Ahead of the Pack

One last thought on business process metrics. On the horizon is a sea change in how management information systems are structured to support the work of business teams and individuals. The "Agent Rules" concept from complex adaptive systems theory (CAS, often incorrectly called "chaos" theory in the popular press) will be used to design future paradigms for process measurement as reported in MIS applications. The basic concept is that every "agent" in an organization (an operator, work cell team, manager, scheduler, machine, conveyor, and so forth) can act most effectively if guided by a unique set of rules that allow for "autonomous actions" within the intended boundaries of empowerment for that agent. The resulting systems of "autonomous agents" are far more robust than the brittle current systems driven by central-control paradigms.

The Financial Bridge and Business Metrics Roadmap recognize the CAS "Agent Rules" concept as the few key metrics are identified for use by each agent in a process or enterprise. That is a key contribution to the "people" side of continuous improvement business culture as the Bridge facilitates a clear view of the few *key performance indicators* (KPIs) one needs to perform one's role at peak levels. We will have more to say about the CAS impacts on CI processes in a later chapter. Having the few right metrics is "the springboard to improvement" in a CI process.

4.8.6   18-Month Rule

This was covered earlier in this book, but it bears repeating in part here.

One way to test the relevance of your metric system is to see how often it changes. If you have been using the same metrics for ever and a day, there is a high likelihood your metric system is not relevant to today's problems and business issues. Half of the metrics should focus on today's issues; from an overall organization perspective these are strategic issues. Over an 18-month period, as those issues become addressed and they cease to be a major problem, new metrics should replace them on the action screen.

4.9   Implementing a Bridge Model—Measure Phase

Project steps for developing metrics in the Financial Bridge Model.

The main Measure phase steps for developing a Bridge Process are:

1. Identify the current results gaps—that is, results that were expected from recent improvement projects but were not reflected in the current measurement system. In other words, what types of results have not been showing up as expected in the current performance reports? The other corporate performance improvement goals should also be front-and-center for a Bridge Process development, but the current project results gaps should get extra visibility as the model is first built.

2. Identify possible causal metrics needed for upstream process control that will yield dependable downstream results in line with the key process performance goals.

   Note: A YX matrix may be helpful for sorting the few high-correlation causal metrics from the many possibilities. Work "upstream" from a process output, as you might when "deconstructing" an output to re/design the process that creates it. In the upstream process steps, look for the "control points" where extra care is needed to ensure "in-spec" results downstream. Some control points will be obvious, based on easily observed cause-and-effect relationships. However, many are not obvious and will need deeper investigative methods such as Six Sigma statistical process analysis. Metrics in Bridge Categories. For each business process, align its key goals and causal metrics in the Financial Bridge Model according to the four categories. You might find it useful to do this step in parallel with the causal metrics, since the Bridge categories can be instructive in determining the relative importance of causal metrics candidates. Use the Pareto rule to help identify the few metrics that are most important to overall business performance. In any case, this is a critical step because the lack of appropriate upstream control metrics will allow process performance and output results to wander, sometimes disastrously. "You get what you measure."

3. Collect data and establish current performance baselines for initial process/es to be tracked in the Bridge Process.

4. Determine appropriate upper and lower control limits. For each metric added to the Bridge Model, establish upper and lower control limits that can be used for exceptions reporting to upper management of only those metrics that have moved outside the limits and may need some support from top management to overcome unexpected barriers to the process indicated. This is an example of a concept called *Hoshin Planning*, that includes "process control" methods to keep people focused on what's important now, and not on "in-spec" metrics that should not be distracting at that point in time.

5. Establish formats and procedures for reporting to process owners and operating teams.

Note: A summary outline of these steps is included in Chap. 14 along with the steps from the other DMAIC chapters.

A "Lean-Sigma-CI process owner" may be key to long-term sustainability of a Financial Bridge that realistically presents how improvement initiatives impact the key business goals. That is because recouping personnel time freed up by improvements in "indirect functions" ("soft" savings) may depend on having a corporate strategy and process for disposition of the now-available time. Otherwise, that fractional time may be retained in the remaining functional area so that the improvement will have no material impact on the overall financial results.

Alternately, a "Lean-Sigma-CI process owner" provides management of a process that's needed to "close the loop" on the individual projects that free up staff resources. That's done by providing proactive routes for them, including diversion to additional CI projects, beneficial outplacement if the firm isn't growing fast enough to absorb the excess resources, and often promotions as a result of success and visibility in important projects.

Also, the existence of a Lean-Sigma-CI process owner adds visibility to the performance metrics that indicate how resources are being freed from streamlined functions and put to better use in Lean-Sigma-CI functions. Without that visibility (and credibility and active management) it's likely that those resources will be poorly redeployed so short-term project benefits goals will be missed (disappointment), and long-term opportunities to accelerate the organization's CI rate will be squandered (blissful unawareness of threat to survival).

4.10 Tools for Doing It—Measure Phase

In most companies, the sheer range of possible business process metrics is one of the roadblocks standing in the way of developing (and maintaining) effective process measurement systems. To help you navigate that range and begin to build your own mental model of the process metrics landscape, the following sections provide brief overviews of process metrics that could come into play during Bridge Process development.

Note: Measure or Analyze? The tools for these two steps often overlap. So some of them may first appear in this chapter, but may come into play again later in the Analyze, Improve, or Control chapters.

4.10.1   Product and Service Quality—Practical Customer/Supplier Metrics

To make product or service changes measurable vis-à-vis sales volume changes.

The customers never let us forget about quality, do they? But how often does it feel like we're speaking two different languages? That's not unusual in our rapid-fire business world where clarity is often lost in the rush of the daily battles.

Some customer/supplier communication problems are caused by unclear or incomplete initial agreements on the specifics of their working relationship, or a lack of agreed metrics for on-going control. For example, we can be so focused on meeting specific product features and pricing that we overlook a key delivery-timing requirement. And the customer has worked with it so routinely that they treat it as "expected," so it's not even mentioned in the purchase order. Both parties are cruising for disappointment.

4.10.2   Three Levels of Customer/Supplier Requirements

Heading off that disappointment starts with basic voice of the customer (VOC) information, then uses a methodology that organizes the elements of a customer/supplier agreement on the requirements for their working relationship [for the detailed steps see Requirements Setting Guidelines in Chap. 3 (Define)]. The process includes several key questions that cause the customer and supplier to think more completely about the product and service relationship.

- *Specifications:* Ask the customer and supplier to list the several things that would be specifically written in an order to the supplier to describe the attributes of the product or service to be delivered.
- *Expectations:* After the two parties have exhausted the list of usual specifications, ask what other attributes they would expect that may not usually be written in the order. These are often quality attributes that have become traditionally "expected," and have become "out of sight and out of mind." But, if not delivered, they lead to major disappointments.
- *Future/delights:* (Optional) Ask the parties to think about an ideal future. What attributes would the product or service have in the ideal state? This is really research and development work (R&D), but just asking the question jogs people to think "outside the box" of everyday assumptions. They are often surprised to discover incremental changes

in products or services that provide significant new value with minimal investment of time or capital.

Note: The specifications, expectations, and delights conventions are just question labels for the discovery process. The information jogged by them usually fits in categories of product specifications, timing, and so forth.

Think about the future in terms of those three requirements questions. Where are the significant threats and opportunities? Expectations offer plenty of risk and threat to the customer/supplier relationship. Because they have become routinely expected, the parties are doing less monitoring of them so performance on them becomes more variable with more chance of unpleasant surprises at delivery time. So it pays to periodically redefine the expectations and move some of them into the written specification set by the supplier for routine product and service production. So they're not out of sight and out of mind.

Future/delights can lead the way to high-value product or service enhancements ahead of the competitor offerings. Some may not be practical or technically possible today, but awareness of them provides important guidance for R&D, business strategy, and tactical operations planning. Just knowing "where we *might* be going in the foreseeable future" can be a powerful driver of organizational performance since department heads and local work groups have frequent opportunities to make minor course adjustments in their operating plans that lend support to the long range vision. Just because it's not cast in stone doesn't mean it's not useful for planning the potential future.

Rigorously working those questions is usually enough to identify the full range of requirements that a customer and supplier must work to for complete satisfaction on both sides. That's also an example of the collaborative "people side" of business process performance that we mentioned earlier.

Once the full range of requirements is known, then metrics for them are usually necessary to make them easily maintainable. Exhibit 4.10 is a simple example of how the customer/supplier dialog can transition to measurable terms. Precision isn't necessary, as even approximate metrics provide scale and basis for eventual agreement from a common viewpoint that may not have existed before.

The *Requirements Setting Process* described in Chap. 3 structures the improvement process to produce agreements that participants support wholeheartedly. Those agreements become the performance basis by which business teams guide their routine operations and plan business process improvements.

Product or Service Description
(Function Output Description)

Product/Service	Interview reports for job applicants		
Customer	Countryside packaging department, Dave Martin		
Specifications		Tracking Metric (KPI)	Rating
Qualifications match job requirement		Match Points Ratio	3
Available to work date is accurate		Y/N Audit	4
Expectations		Tracking Metric (KPI)	Rating
Frequent updates on recruiting progress		Avg. Days/Update	4
Future/Delights		Tracking Metric (KPI)	Value
On-line or e-mail progress reports		Y/N Audit	$10K

Qty. per delivery	Frequency	How often actually needed	O. A. Rating
1 per applicant	14 per month	14 per month	3
Alternate available			Value
Outsourced interviewing by an independent personnel agency			H

Exhibit 4.10   Product or Service Rating Sheet

Clear customer requirements help them eliminate ineffective activities and continually improve the product and service features most important to the customers. Essentially, everyone is working toward measurable product and service targets which constitute "an offer the customers can't refuse."

4.10.3 Quality Function Deployment—World-Class, Precision Requirements

To measure changes in product or service features versus operating costs and sales revenue.

Conformance to Requirements is often cited as a fundamental definition of quality. Meeting the requirements—no more, no less—is key to both customer satisfaction and supplier business efficiency. And various gurus have presented their short lists of fundamentals of business process quality that usually include *prevention of defects* and *doing it right the first time* (DIRTFT) as process attributes necessary for high productivity. The obvious relationship involved is that DIRTFT and Prevention are focused on Conformance to Requirements. Therefore, having a more comprehensive and precise set of requirements for any product or service is a key to fine-tuning business processes for least-cost delivery of top-quality products and services.

There are examples all around us of leading companies that have worked very hard to get precise requirements from their customers so they can routinely hit the bulls-eye of "wants" and avoid delivering features with business processes that add no value in the eyes of the customers. Toyota and its Lexus division have been providing the global benchmarks for a broad range of product, service, and process examples for many years. You can also point to many other companies that are effectively emulating their methods, so quality standards and expectations have taken quantum leaps forward around the world.

Quality Function Deployment (QFD) is a methodology for developing precision requirements for products and services (Exhibit 4.11). It uses an interesting "House of Quality" structure for organizing the features of products and services relative to values expressed by the customers. And it links the product and service features to the producing processes so they can focus their improvement efforts on the value-adding functions, and continuously look for ways to eliminate nonvalue waste activities from the process.

You have probably already deduced from the Bridge Model and this chapter that measurement is a key differentiator between the leaders and the also-rans in the new global competition. The boldness and speed of "Ready, Fire, Aim!" methods often outweighed their inefficiency when the competition wasn't as focused on quality. That's history now, as the wastes in shotgun-style methods will sink a company quickly.

QFD-style methods will become the norm for industry leaders. No one really wants to drown in ever-deeper details for Conformance to Requirements. But it is becoming a competitive necessity to have a clear view of them; convenient forms of QFD can simplify the detail work so it's both effective and efficient. Looking at it from the "people side," you can see that the work involved in establishing more robust customer requirements can produce a "J-curve" dip in business cultures that are attacking them in earnest for the first time. But they can be a critical early step in adopting Lean-Sigma-CI processes

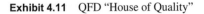

Exhibit 4.11 QFD "House of Quality"

Customer Requirements	Customer Importance	Short wait for live person on telephone	Competent, efficient order-taker	Internet ordering		Email or fax order confirmation	Route optim. program; saves drive time	Process for quick follow-up contacts w/customer	Check-list for 100% customer satisfaction	Competitor Comparisons (0–4)
Planning, Ordering, etc. — Quick, easy contact	3	2	2	2						OA (2) · J (3)
Flexible schedule options	2		1							O (1) · A (2) · J (3)
Freebie pitches	0									O (0) · A (1) · J (2)
Execution — Technician arrives on-time as scheduled	4					1	2	1		J (1) · OA (2)
Contact w/ customer if there is a problem meeting schedule	4					1		2	2	O (0) · A (2) · J (3)
Expert installation; professional materials, almost invisible	3		1	1		1			2	OA (2) · J (3)
No mess left behind	1								2	J (1) · OA (2)
Weighted Importance		6	11	9		11	8	12	16	
Relative Importance		0.4	0.7	0.6	0.0	0.7	0.5	0.8	1.0	

Product or Service:

Installation Service for Cable TV, Internet and/or Phone at Personal Residence

Correlations: −1, 1, 2

Characteristics of the Product/Service and Process*

Order Entry Functions | *Installation*

Competitor Comparisons:
O = Our Product/Service
A = ABC Company
J = JKL Company

CUMBERLAND

as the foundation for building world-class competitive capabilities. So a data organization tool like QFD can save a lot of development time, help minimize the depth of a "J-curve" dip, and ensure the availability of high-quality voice-of-customer information as front-end inputs to Six Sigma business process improvement projects.

4.10.4 Value-Stream Mapping

It's all about making the "value" visual, so it's easier to optimize the process around it.

The methods for Lean, Six Sigma, and continuous improvement (CI) have survived beyond many of the business fads that came before (see Exhibit 1.1 in the Overview chapter). That shouldn't be a surprise when we take a broad view of the business landscape and see that Lean, Six Sigma, and CI are fundamental to the goals faced by most companies competing in a new global marketplace that is clearly here to stay. That's refreshing, because it takes us back to operating fundamentals that had been given too little attention in the latter half of the twentieth century—but have again been proven to be essential to business success from now on.

Visual methods have played a prominent role in Lean processes that are clearly focused on the "value." Once the value was obvious it was possible to see the waste, eliminate it, and streamline what's left.

Value-Stream Mapping methods were a natural evolution of Lean development practices where visual methods work very well inside operating processes. And the visual methods of VSM make Lean development activities more effective and efficient. VSM makes communication of process improvement ideas easier, faster, and more complete.

4.10.5 Lead Time—The Common Thread

Some early Lean practitioners adopted a time-based view of the world that had a significant influence on the Value-Stream Mapping methods that eventually emerged. Interestingly, the now-common Value-Stream Mapping methods appear to have developed out of the involvement of several outsiders while observing inside Toyota; but like many other methods developed there, Toyota tends to make more of how people work together to use them than of the methods themselves. Given Toyota's obvious success, we should no longer be surprised at that.

By the early 1990s, our friends at Motorola had concluded that if they had focused on one single process metric during the previous 25 years, then they would probably have arrived at the same point without trying a new program every couple of years (e.g., SPC, JIT, and TQM) that eventually became the umbrella process now called Six Sigma. That metric was process span time, or lead time. Their conclusion came from the realization that a focus on lead time causes us to examine every element of a process, drive out the nonvalue waste, and streamline what's left. With that view we would then choose whatever tools were appropriate for the analysis or process design work at hand.

In our own work we have found that lead time is literally the common thread that ties all the process elements together. That has been especially evident when projects have required a Process Characteristics Chart (PCC; Exhibit 4.12) to display more data than can be shown on a Value-Stream Map.

Lead Time: The "Common Thread"

Process Characteristics

Process: *Airplane Factory*

Model Used On	Work Step or Item Description	ID	Value Add (X)	Quality (%)		Frequency		Time/Occur (Sec)		Setup Time (Sec)		Lead Time (Sec)		Capacity (U/Hr)		Avg Inventory (Pcs)		Space (SqFt)	
			Base/Oppty	Base	Oppty	Base U/Occur	Oppty U/Occur	Base	Oppty	Base	Oppty	Base	Oppty	Base	Oppty	Base	Oppty	Base	Oppty
11	1a Set-up to run model II	#1	X			1000	1000	36		36		0.0	0.0						
11	1b Get materials from stock	#1				10	100	17	17			1.7	0.2					0.1	2.1
11	1c Blue 16-pin blocks	B16														10	300	3.0	3.0
11	1d Assemble primary wing/airframe	#1	X			1	1	8	8			8.0	8.0						2.1
11	1e Get materials from stock	#1					500		20				0.04				750		
11	1f Blue 8-pin blocks	B08																3.1	7.2
11	1g Add nose section	#1	X					4				4.0							
11	1h Deliver to #2 and return	#1				5	1	25				5.0	1.0	244	272			1.5	0.0
11	S.T. #1											15	13						
11	WIP queue at #2											B16 20				18			
11	2a Set-up to run model II	#2				1000	1000	51	2	51	2	0.1	0.0					0.1	2.1
11	2b Get materials from stock	#2				10	125	20	20			2.0	0.2			25	750	3.0	3.0
11	2c Blue 8-pin blocks	B08	X																
11	2d Assemble nose & wing sections	#2				1	1	19	16			19.0	16.0					3.1	5.1
11	2e Deliver to #3 and return	#2				5	1	20	1			4.0	1.0	144	210				
11	S.T. #2											25	17			12	1		
11	2f WIP queue at #3											545	20					1.5	0.0

Base = Phase 1
Oppty = Phase 4 (Opportunity)

CT: Cycle Time
LT: Lead Time

CUMBERLAND

Exhibit 4.12 Process Characteristics Chart

Process Characteristics

Process: _Airplane Factory_

Model Used On	#	Step or Item Description	ID	Value Add X	Quality Base %	Quality Oppty %	Freq Base U/Occur	Freq Oppty U/Occur	Time/Occur Base Sec	Time/Occur Oppty Sec	Setup Base Sec	Setup Oppty Sec	Lead Base Sec	Lead Oppty Sec	Capacity Base U/Hr	Capacity Oppty U/Hr	Avg Inv Base Pcs	Avg Inv Oppty Pcs	Space Base SqFt	Space Oppty SqFt
11	3a	Set-up to run model 11	#3				1000	1000	46	7	46	7	0.0	0.0						
11	3b	Get materials from stock	#3				17	167	20	20			12	0.1						
11	3c	Blue 8-pin blocks	BOB														25	750	0.1	2.1
11	3d	Assemble large section of tail	#3	X			1	1	15	15			15.0	15.0					3.0	3.0
11	3e	Get materials from stock	#3					500		23				0.0						
11	3f	Blue 4-pin blocks	BO4															750		2.1
11	3g	Assemble cockpit	#3	X			1	1		4				4.0						
11	3h	Deliver to #4 and return	#3				5	1	15	1			30	1.0						
11		S.T. #3											9	20	187	178			3.1	5.1
11	3i	WIP queue at #4	#3										636	20			14	1	1.5	0.0
11	4a	Set-up to run model 11	#4				1000	1000	50	5	50	5	0.1	0.0						
11	4b	Get materials from stock	#4				17	333	23	23			14	0.1						
11	4c	Blue 4-pin blocks	BO4														50	1500	0.1	2.1
11	4d	Assm nose, fuslg, cbpt, tail, wing	#4	X			1	1	40	15			40.0	15.0					3.0	3.0
11	4e	Deliver to #5 and return	#4				5	1	20	1			40	1.0						
11		S.T. #4											45	16	79	224			3.1	5.1
11	4f	WIP queue at #5	#4										136	20			3	1	0.5	0.0

LC : Limiting Capacity

CUMBERLAND

Exhibit 4.12 (Continued)

139

Process Characteristics

Process: _Airplane Factory_

Model Used On #	ID	Step or Item Description	Value Add %X	Quality Base %	Quality Oppty %	Frequency Base #/Occur	Frequency Oppty #/Occur	Time/Occur Base Sec	Time/Occur Oppty Sec	Setup Time Base Sec	Setup Time Oppty Sec	Lead Time Base Sec	Lead Time Oppty Sec	Capacity Base U/Hr	Capacity Oppty U/Hr	Avg. Inventory Base Pcs	Avg. Inventory Oppty Pcs	Space Base SqFt	Space Oppty SqFt
11	5a	Set-up to run model 11	#5			1000	1000	23	0	23	0	0.0	0.0						
11	5b	Inspect finished units	#5		61%	100%	1	1	11	8			1.0	8.0					3.0	3.0
11	5c	Deliver to #6 and return	#5				5	1	25	1			5.0	1.0	225	400			3.0	3.0
		S.T. #5										16.0	9.0						
11	5d	WIP queue at #6										142	20			4	1	0.5	0.0
11	6a	Set-up to run model 11	#6																
11	6b	Tear down finished units	#6						NA	NA			NA	NA					3.0	3.0
11	6c	Return materials to stock	#6						NA	NA			NA	NA					3.0	3.0
		S.T. #6																	

CUMBERLAND

Exhibit 4.12 (_Continued_)

Improvement Goals and Progress

Process: _____ Airplane Factory

	Quality		Setup Time		Process Time		Capacity		Walking Dist		Transport Dist		Avg. Inventory		Space	
	Base	Oppty	Base	Oppty	Base	Oppty	Base	Oppty	Base	Oppty	Base	Oppty	Base	Oppty	Base	Oppty
U/M:	%	%	Sec.	Sec.	Sec.	Sec.	U/Hr.	U/Hr.	Ft./U.	Ft./U.	Ft./U.	Ft./U.	Pcs.	Pcs.	Sq.Ft.	Sq.Ft.
Totals (from sheet above)	61%	100%	51	7	120	76	48	178	0	0	18	4	161	4,805	24.0	28.5
Target	99.9%		15		70		180					4	3000		24	24
Status 6 / 15 / 97																
Status 9 / 30 / 97																
Status 12 / 31 / 97																

	Lead Time		Cycle Time		Takt Time		Productivity	
	Base	Oppty	Base	Oppty	Base	Oppty	Base	Oppty
U/M:	Sec.	Sec.	Sec.	Sec.	Sec.	Sec.	U/L.Hr.	U/L.Hr.
Overall Process	2,437	176	45	20	54	14	10	45
Target	150		18		14		40	
Status 6 / 15 / 97								
Status 9 / 30 / 97								
Status 12 / 31 / 97								

Base	Oppty	
5	4	= Crew Members

Base	Oppty	
7.5	7.5	= Net Avail. Prodn. Hrs. / Day

Base	Oppty	
500	2,000	= Planned Daily Output

Output Unit Description:
High-tech reconnaissance airplane

CUMBERLAND

Exhibit 4.12 (Continued)

141

The lead time common thread is always important in the spreadsheet PCC views since it is a bottom-line indicator of process development progress toward the Lean vision.

Let's continue with a basic description of lead time on the following example of a typical Value-Stream Map:

"Before" Map Example

A member company in the Chicago region of the Association for Manufacturing Excellence produced the map shown in Exhibit 4.13 as part of a kaizen project to make a key production process leaner, more efficient, and more responsive at serving customer demand changes quickly.

Notice that at a glance you can see several Lean opportunities.

- Lead time = 16 days; customer response time slower than desired
- Lots of "push-type" production controls and overhead expenses

Now look at the contrasting "After" map shown in Exhibit 4.14.

"After" Map Example

Notice that the visual clarity of the Value-Stream Map provides effective communication—at a glance—so you can easily see how the redesigned process has taken advantage of the Lean opportunities seen in the "Before" map.

- Lead time = 30 minutes; customer response time faster than expectations
- Use of "pull"-type production controls reduced WIP and overhead expenses

Notice the up-and-down stepped graphic at the bottom of the map. This is a key feature of Value-Stream Maps that differentiates them from other process map conventions. The stepped line is a graphic display of the lead time through the process, including both nonvalue time on the high-water steps, and value-adding time on the base-level steps. Think of that base level as the zero-base "value stream" of work that the customers are willing to pay money for. The rest of the time-in-process up to the high-water line is waste time caused by the current process configuration. That waste should be a prime target for elimination through process improvement efforts using Lean, Six Sigma, and other methodologies.

Now back to lead time: Notice that much of the overall lead time is in the nonvalue times on the high-water steps. That is usually because each unit

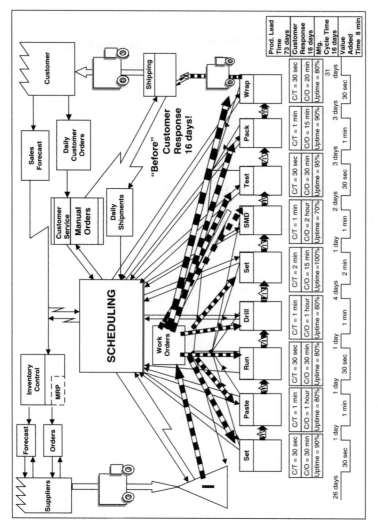

Exhibit 4.13 Value-Stream Map—"Before"

143

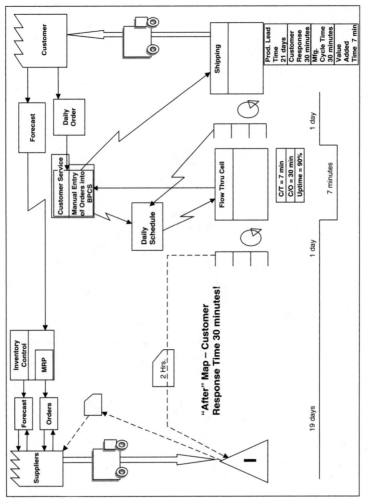

Exhibit 4.14 Value-Stream Map—"After"

spends a lot of time waiting its turn through the work-in-process (WIP) queues between the work centers. The lead time calculation for each queue = line cycle time × units in queue, where line cycle time is usually set by the slowest station that's acting as the bottleneck. So you can see that even small quantities of WIP in the queues represent a majority of the lead time through the line.

Now you can see why the Value-Stream Mapping technique has been such a powerful tool for making processes leaner. A big chunk of nonvalue lead time stands out like a sore thumb when displayed in the high-water line of a VSM. So a project team tasked with identifying new Lean opportunities can see them quickly and get right to work finding ways to eliminate the root causes behind such constrictions in a process.

And, by the way, you can also see why the Lean concept itself is so powerful in helping people find Lean opportunities in their everyday operations. The physical existence of WIP inventory sitting in a queue between workstations is a red flag. It's tangible evidence that the process is not lean and is wasting lead time, working capital, floor space, walking time around it, in-process damage, and other potential nonvalue costs.

Take a moment to think about the overhead implications.

Note: A host of process analysis questions usually come out during a VSM exercise. For example: What happens to queues downstream of the bottleneck? How much impact do line changeover times and production lot sizes have on WIP queues?

The focus in VSM is on the core value stream of work that converts materials, information, and energy into a product or service that the customer is willing to pay for.

But, VSM also makes it easier to see nonvalue overhead functions that can be eliminated along with the in-process waste. Make that a deliberate part of any VSM project. The Value-Stream Mapping technique is covered in more detail in Chap. 13.

4.10.6   YX Matrix

Sometimes picking the best upstream causal metrics from a Process Metrics Roadmap can be confusing because of the sheer range of possible metrics involved. It can be complex, although not necessarily complicated.

For many situations, the correlations between upstream and downstream indicators are relatively obvious once they're all viewed together. In that case, a simple tool like a YX matrix can be used to sort the possible metrics down to the few that may be critical.

Note: The different formats for the YX examples are not significant. Users customize them for each situation. Fields out of view to the right often contain additional information about tracking process design issues and implementation issues.

Exhibits 4.15 and 4.16 are typical of YX matrices for evaluating upstream metrics when the field has become larger. Notice the weight numbers under the overall business goals at the top and in the intersection cells to the upstream processes listed down the left hand side. They are not usually precise values. Rather, they are usually the nominal opinion of experienced process-group members. The concept here is to use their experienced process knowledge to estimate the correlation of various upstream process control metrics with the key downstream target results. The Pareto rule usually holds, so one or two metrics stand out within each process-segment metrics group (based on tabulated totals of their correlations to the weighted overall process goals). Those become prime candidates for routine process performance tracking. And a separate look at the high correlations under the most-weighted overall goals may identify a couple of other metrics that may be important as well.

A word about the "correlations" term here: Remember that this technique is not a rigorous statistical analysis. It's a shortcut for situations where the cause-and-effect relationships are not too subtle, but the number of relationships is enough to be confusing. The YX matrix is an easy way to organize the process metrics landscape, and focus on probable upstream control metrics options. When the relationships are fairly clear this can be a way to move ahead faster than expected and build project team enthusiasm.

4.10.7   Statistical Analysis of Process Metrics

PC-based statistical analysis software is a good tool for situations where the correlations between upstream and downstream metrics are less obvious. Six Sigma Black Belt practitioners are certified in the use of such software to quantify the extent to which specific upstream process factors are correlated with documented downstream results.

Since significant process performance data are needed, this analytical process usually takes much more time than the simple YX matrix method

Process Metrics
Ad Hoc Grants Process (Pilot test) --- Owner: Calvin / Jim M / John L ???

Key Process Indicators (= Downstream Results Ys)

Process Milestones and Control Metrics (= Upstream Xs)	Why Do We Care About This Metric?	Grant Quality (2)	Process Clarity (3)	Process Consistency (Grantees) (2)	Process Consistency (Staff) (4)	Waste Time (4)	Grant Efficiency (quality/cost) (2)	Negative Unintended Consequences (2)	Contribution Rating	Next-Stage Metrics (To be activated)
Current Weights =		2	3	2	4	4	2	2		
External / (Grantees)										
Prod & Service Quality, Grantee Satisfaction	Satisfaction of grantee: "My idea got a fair shake."	1							8	P
Batching (Owner = ???)										
Time from Receipt to Batching	Time is important.		1		1	1	1		13	P
Completeness % Nimble Proposals	Early-stage team input increases quality of proposal & avoids waste work downstream.		1		1	1	1		30	P
Number of Revisions in Following Steps			2			2	2		10	P
% Proposals Passed On In Error (vs. Strategy)	Eliminates a primary waste cause. Saves time spent on off-strategy proposals.	1	1	2	2	3	2		31	P
Applicant Notification (Owner = ???)										
Time from Batching to Applicant Notification	Time is important.		1		1	1	1		13	P
FP Team Vote (Owner = ???)										
Time from FP Request to Team Vote	Time is important.		1		1	1	1		13	P
Completeness % Full Proposals		1	2	1	2	2	2		30	P
Number of Revisions in Following Steps			1		1	1	2		10	P
% FPs not originally as BPs			2	1	2	2	2		28	P
% BP Grantees Asked for Extraneous Info										
GD Approval (Owner = ???)										
Time from Team Vote to GD Approval	Time is important.		1		1	1	1		13	P
PSM or / and Board Decision (Owner = ???)										
Time from GD Approval to PSM/Bd Approval	Time is important.		1		1	1	1		13	P
LOA Sent Out (Owner = ???)										
Time from Approval to LOA Out	Time is important. Possible unintended consequence: sloppy work due to heavy focus on time deadlines.		1		1	1	1	X	13	P
LOA Returned (Owner = ???)										
Time from LOA Out to LOA Return	Time is important.	(4)	1		1	1	1		13	P
% Done the First Time	Good indicator of LOA process effectiveness.		3	3	3				19	P
Check Issued (Owner = ???)										
Time from LOA Return to Check Out	Time is important.		1		1	1	1		13	P
Common Metrics, Most Milestones										
Average Time > Milestone Dates	Time is important.	(2)	1		4	4	2		37	N
Average % On-Time Milestones	Time is important.		3		3	2	1		39	N
Process Knowledge Scores by Staff	Answers questions about what is not contributing to team's work or strategic objectives.	2	3	2	3	2	1		27	N
Staff Satisfaction Ratings	Future use with enhanced workload balancing support system.					1	1		6	N
FTE Days per Grant	Future use with enhanced workload balancing support system.				4	4	4		24	F
Waste Hours per Grant (Excess of Std Hours)	Indicator for initial load balancing routine.			1	1	4	1		12	P
WIP Queue at each Milestone	Need to begin developing routine ways to level the workload spikes.			2	2	4	3		34	P
Grants per Week, History & Forecast	Need to begin developing routine ways to level the workload spikes.			3	3	4	3		34	P
Workload per Week, History & Forecast	Need to begin developing routine ways to level the workload spikes.			3	3	4	3		34	F

Exhibit 4.15 YX Matrix (Service Organization)

147

Processes and KPIs	Learning Organization	Speed to Market	Product Quality	Service Quality	Customer and Consumer Loyalty	Cost Competitive	Business Growth and Final Results	Contribution Rating
Current Weights:	4	4	2	2	3	3	2	
External Indicators								
Consumer Loyalty	1				1		1	9
Product Quality, Consumer Sat.	2		1		2		1	18
Customer Loyalty	1				1		1	9
Prod and Service Quality, Customer Sat.	2		1		2		1	18
Profit Growth Per Customer	2						1	10
Customer Profitability	2			1	1	1	1	18
Market Share Growth	2				1	1	1	16
Full National Presence							1	2
Revenue Growth							1	2
Product Commercialization								
Comprehensive Project Requirements	2	2			1	1	1	24
Change Order Timeliness	1	2						12
Sequence of Events Record Accuracy	2	2			1	1	1	24
Prod Com Milestones on Time	1	2	1	1	1	1	2	26
Prod Com Average Lead Time		1			1	1	1	12
New Customer Development								
Value-Added Sales Time w/ Customers		1		1	2			12
Sales and CS Rating from Cust Empls	2			2	2			18
Number of New Customers							2	4
Primary Target Customers Captured							2	4
Customer / Product Profile Accuracy	2	2		2	2	1	1	31
New Customer Set-up Time		2		2	1			15
Promotions % of Sales vs. Budget							2	4
Revenue vs. Budget by Div							2	4
Sales, Inventory, Opns Balancing (Mark Harris)								
Forecast Accuracy	1			2	1	1		14
Safety Stock Compliance, FG				2	1			7
Replenishment Lot Sizes						1	1	5
Storage Utilization Rate				1				2
Production Utilization Rate				1		2	1	10
Inventory Levels (dependent result)							1	2
SIO Balance	1			1		2	2	16
Order Fulfillment Process (Mark Harris)								
Order Fill Rate				2	1			7
Product Quality at Shipping	1		1		1			9
On-Time Deliveries				2	1			7
Perfect Order Performance (POP)	2			2	2			18

Exhibit 14.16   YX Matrix (Manufacturing)

above. Data may have to be collected over a period of time from a number of different process points; historical data records may have to be cleaned or formatted for loading into the PC program; and the statistical analyses may have to be run in several different ways to provide the interpretations required. However, such analyses are often the only way to get conclusive answers to questions about cause-and-effect relationships that are not easily observable.

4.10.8 Ask "Why?" Five Times

Cultural tendencies toward "detail-avoidance" were mentioned in the Background section in this chapter. One way to overcome that resistance and provide a balance for the "Ready, Fire, Aim!" bias in some cultures is to approach the development for each business process metric within a depth range that's no deeper than needed to identify the root cause factors that must be controlled for predictable results. Asking "Why?" five times is one of the techniques for searching one level deeper than needed, then backing up to the one that will be sufficient for routine control.

4.10.9 Metrics for Mixed-Model Manufacturing and Mass Customization

To measure nonlinear mixed-model production operations with respect to capacity, cost, customer response time, and overall productivity.

This will be discussed in the Analyze chapter (Chap. 5). But it deserves a couple of words here because some readers will wonder why the Logistics and Supply Chain Metrics section is included when the vision of "zero inventories" may actually be just around the corner with the advent of mass-customization technologies.

The answer is that the finished goods management issue is likely to be around for a long time yet, particularly if interest rates remain low for another decade so it's cheaper to carry some inventory than to invest early in changes for mass customization. So the next section addresses a couple of fundamental issues about shipping service that are not going away soon.

4.10.10 Logistics and Supply Chain Metrics—Tracking the Extended Process

To measure the contributors to shipping service levels versus costs, customer satisfaction, loyalty, and revenue.

Extended supply chains can have hundreds of localized upstream/downstream process metrics. Finding the few that matter can feel like searching for needles in a haystack. However, using the sorting tools described above can keep the task manageable.

Remember to avoid getting hung up on metrics that are not close enough to the root cause. Use the "Ask why?" technique to work back upstream. For example, an on-time shipping performance metric would point strongly at the stocking policies immediately upstream. But a little more probing would quickly identify the statistical analysis of historical demands, forecasted demand changes, and statistical analysis of supply variability a couple of steps further back. Those causal metrics may be key to the entire downstream chain:

On-time shipping performance

Customer loyalty

Market share growth

Higher margins

Higher profits and ROI

4.11   What Can Go Wrong

The Measure phase of DMAIC offers plenty of opportunities for failure in the DMAIC process itself, not just the subject process it's currently focused on. The typical pitfalls include

- Incomplete breadth, depth, and horizon
- Potential causes uncorrelated to effects
- Untimely
- Data collection not efficient

The reasons Measure might go wrong all have a common thread of "not working the details." In other words, if we are in a rush to just "get it done so we can check it off the list," then it's likely that we will have many "uncharted territories" (the missing details) in the roadmap where *unknowns will remain uncontrolled* so the end results will continue to be frustratingly unpredictable.

You might be tempted to blame a "Ready, Fire, Aim!" business culture bias for failure to work the Measure details, but a more fundamental reason may be just that—a lack of understanding about "the *fundamentals* of business process management and measurement." Conventional methods have used the tools at hand—financial statements, accounting records—because they're convenient and common to all businesses. But the upstream business process metrics have been an eclectic mix from a range of disciplines, not just accounting, so it's been difficult to provide a coherent "whole business" view that can serve as a foundation for planning business performance metrics. In fact, that's a reason for this book.

A few thoughts about how to avoid the pitfalls…

Incomplete Breadth, Depth, and Horizon

Asking "Why?" five times is important here. It's always amazing how effective that simple technique is at encouraging patience to find the true causal factors upstream of the downstream result to be improved.

Potential Causes Uncorrelated to Effects

Cause-and-effect "fishbone" diagrams are also effective because they expand the range of upstream channels with the categories assigned to the "bones"—materials, methods, equipment, personnel, time, and so forth.

Untimely

Too infrequent recordings can be a problem, especially when variations over time are meaningful in the subsequent analysis work. Ask what short term process cycles may be important later. Then set the recording schedule to capture data in appropriately short intervals.

Data Collection Not Efficient

Don't let process measurement become an off-line entity unto itself. Process metrics should be handled as part of the process they are measuring, so they are immediately available to the people involved for analysis and real-time process adjustments. That makes them both useful and efficient to collect.

4.12 Measure—Team Sponsor's Role and Responsibilities

Clear metrics are a key part of success. The phrase, "What gets measured is what gets done," was coined for a reason. For better or worse, measures provide focus. A key part of metrics is the goal. In the Measure phase of DMAIC, the team gathers hard data about the current actual performance of the target as-is process. Metrics that teams establish in Measure provide both a baseline and evidence that a problem/opportunity exists.

Based on new measurement data, the goal statement from Define is usually refined to become more specific. The right measures will make a significant difference. The team Sponsor should watch the metrics selected, be sure that the metrics measure significant process gaps, and assure that the metrics tie to strategic objectives. See Exhibit 4.17.

The team Sponsor should be tightly linked into all updates of performance improvement goals. It's often best to set some type of a stretch goal or BHAG. This acronym stands for *big, hairy, audacious goals*. It's pro-nounced "bee-hag." The concept was popularized in the 1995 business bestseller *Built to Last: Successful Habits of Visionary Companies* (Harper Business) by Jim Collins and Jerry Porras. For example, improve cycle times by 50 percent, decrease error rates or setup times by 90 percent, and increase customer face time (sales) by 70 percent, are all BHAGs.

4.12.1   Measure Phase Questions—Management Perspective

Goal Questions to Revisit (Answers May Change)

1. What are the key goals for this project?
2. What is the impact on the business? (What strategic objectives will be impacted on how?)

Questions about Metrics and Measurements

1. What Critical to Quality (CTQ) metrics have the team identified and how do they know the customer is impacted by them?
2. What Critical to Process (CTP) metrics are important to the business?
3. Which CTQ/CTP does this project focus on? Why?
4. How do you know that the data collected are representative of the process?
5. Is the team rigorously following the appropriate methodology?
6. Do they have adequate resources to complete the project?

Questions Relevant to Improvement Teams

1. What have they learned about the source of the variation from the initial data gathered? Is the process in control?
2. What is the current short-term process Sigma?
3. Did the team rescope the project as a result of the Measurement phase?
4. What are the next steps?

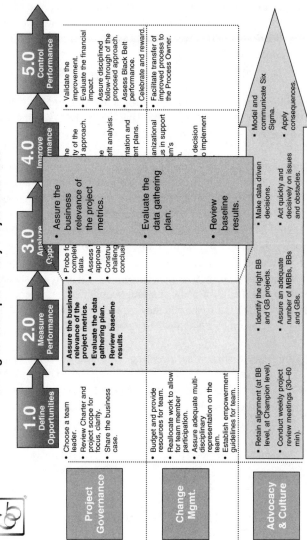

Six Sigma Champion—Key Project Activities

1.0 Define Opportunities	2.0 Measure Performance	3.0 Analyze Opportunity	4.0 Improve Performance	5.0 Control Performance

Project Governance

1.0 Define Opportunities:
- Choose a team leader.
- Review Charter and project scope for focus, clarity.
- Share the business case.

2.0 Measure Performance:
- Assure the business relevance of the project metrics.
- Evaluate the data gathering plan.
- Review baseline results.

3.0 Analyze Opportunity:
- Probe for complete data.
- Assess approach.
- Construct challenge conclusions.

4.0 Improve Performance:
- the ty of the d approach.
- efit analysis.
- ntation and ent plans.

5.0 Control Performance:
- Validate the improvement.
- Evaluate the financial impact.
- Assure disciplined follow-through of the proposed approach.
- Assess Black Belt performance.
- Celebrate and reward.
- Facilitate transfer of improved process to the Process Owner.

Change Mgmt.

- Budget and provide resources for team.
- Reallocate work to allow for team member participation.
- Assure adequate multi-disciplinary representation on the team.
- Establish empowerment guidelines for team.

- anizational us in support am's
- decision o implement

Advocacy & Culture

- Retain alignment (at BB level, at Champion level).
- Conduct weekly project review meetings (30–60 min).

- Identify the right BB and GB projects.
- Assure an adequate number of MBBs, BBs and GBs.

- Make data driven decisions.
- Act quickly and decisively on issues and obstacles.

- Model and communicate Six Sigma.
- Apply consequences.

Overlay box (2.0 Measure):
- Assure the business relevance of the project metrics.
- Evaluate the data gathering plan.
- Review baseline results.

intelligence **M** everywhere

M MOTOROLA UNIVERSITY

Exhibit 4.17 Sponsor's Responsibilities—2.0 Measure

4.13   Technical Business Unit Story—Measure Phase

The team then created a comparison chart that compared financial structure by quarter. The chart allows leadership to see at a macro level where the business is going and at what cost. Sales by customer and application—working with the customer team and with the SEC reports, the lead team created a fairly accurate picture of what products were sold to what customers to test specific chips (applications). This allowed them to see what products were really winning in the market and why.

Product Comparison: Each competitor was introducing a major new "system platform" product in FY06. They compared specifications, quality, and so forth for each of these new products to establish a competitive baseline.

Technical business unit (TBU) then launched four Six Sigma teams. One of the teams focused on faster and more effective rollout of new products to customers. During the Measurement phase, one of the senior engineers suggested using a Quality Function Deployment analysis to determine critical customer requirements. Beth Londonberry, a senior software engineer said, "Wait! We have gone down this path many times. We then become so enamored with the tool, that we lose site of what we are trying to accomplish. How about if we just go talk with a few customers?" The team she was working with discussed this for a while. Several people felt they needed the rigor of this analytical tool, but in the end they agreed they could still use this tool after talking with customers. So the team agreed to start there.

The team's findings were somewhat alarming. One new software testing product, launched previously by TBU, had four different computer chips. Due to differing understanding of customer requirements, only one of the chips had been tested at an early point in development. Quality issues later surfaced delaying the TBU customer's new product's introduction to market.

The TBU improvement team decided to ask customers two simple questions:

- *What software features do you need to test?*
- *How well do these features meet your needs?*

This team also looked at how TBU determined what new products to create. The company was using a classical market segmentation strategy and trying to develop appropriate products for each key segment. The problem here was this approach caused people to look at the markets in an objective, but very detached way. In fact, TBU only had 30 global customers they needed to serve. Six of those were critical customers and TBU was only selling to half of them. There was not very much emotion in TBU about the segments. It's a slight overstatement, but these were largely numbers on a spreadsheet, without much life or energy behind them.

4.14   Tollgate Questions

Measure is like Define in that it's a foundational step for later work in Analyze and Improve. If it's not done adequately, then the subsequent steps are likely to run into problems that require rework, causing delays and wasted time. At the completion of the Measure phase, the team members, team leader, Master Black Belt, and Champion should feel comfortable with the answers to all of the following questions and any others that might be specific to the organization.

To check for comprehensive Measure phase Bridge Process development:

1. For each major downstream process improvement goal, have we identified at least one well-correlated upstream metric that can be measured and tracked easily during routine operations?
2. Does the Measure segment of the process feed data to all possible users of it, so it's constantly in view for real-time analysis and opportunities identification? Has that communications flow been fully pilot tested?
3. Has the charter been updated? If so, how?
4. Has the scope changed?
5. What are the X data collected?
6. What are the Operational Definitions?
7. How much data was collected?
8. What was done to assure the reliability and validity of the measurement process?
9. Has the data collection provided consistent information throughout the data collection period?
10. If the data collection were repeated, would the team get similar results?
11. Are the data collected representative of the population?
12. Do the data collected provide the information needed?
13. What is the baseline value for the data?

5

Analyze—Identifying the Things That Are "Off Track"

A man who carries a cat by the tail learns
something he can learn in no other way.
                                    MARK TWAIN

5.1   Purpose

Chapter 4 (Measure) discussed methods to select for your company a set of business process performance metrics for effective support of your continuous improvement efforts. A prime objective was to identify process-control metrics with good cause-and-effect relationships to the bottom line, so resources for improvement action work can be aimed at high-value opportunities. Lastly, Chap. 4 described steps in building a routine for communicating the process metrics to people in positions to use them for business process improvements. So, the Measure phase ended with high-leverage process information in front of eyes that can use it.

This chapter (the "Analyze" in DMAIC) aims to make use of that process data. It addresses two systemic problems that get in the way of business process improvement efforts:

- Sorting and focusing on the few important issues now
- Quick selection and use of appropriate analytical tools

5.2   Introduction

Business people tend to be impatient as a consequence of conditioning in a work world that seems to get faster by the day. Many of them had expected that by now they would be making decisions with the sophisticated information technology (IT) tools they had been promised with the dawn of the "information age."

Instead, just to keep up with the competition, business teams find themselves still making decisions by the seat of their pants, and often repeating that old saying about "never enough time to do it right. But there's always time to do it over." Thankfully, the widening commitment to Six Sigma is providing relief with methods that are giving business teams the tools and support they need to *do it right the first time* (DIRTFT).

The Analyze phase of the Bridge Process is where the pay-off begins to appear for the new-found understanding of process management concepts, and patience to work the details with Six Sigma methods. Analysis is like placing the lever to start moving the mountain.

Caution: You may need a little extra patience to build your own mental image of how the Bridge Process can work for you. The text contains limited details about the subtopics so that the high-level Bridge Process view would not be obscured by too many "trees." You may have to go to other sources for additional information. However, there is no "rocket science" involved, so much of the missing detail can probably be filled in by business teams in your company as they discuss how to customize the Bridge Process for their own use.

5.3　Overview and Background

- Ready, Fire, Aim! (RFA)
- Fact-based decision-making
- Analysis paralysis

Looks like the makings of a conundrum, doesn't it? On one hand, we're pressed for time and need to make decisions and take actions in response to business conditions before we're really ready.

At the other extreme, we're sensing that seat-of-the-pants decision-making is less effective in the complex modern world, so we want to try more rigorous analytical methods. But we're afraid to get bogged down in excess detail, particularly if we have little experience with such methods and are afraid that a bungled application could be much worse than the RFA method.

In the middle, we hope for pragmatic methods that help us find enough information to make better decisions, but don't slow us down with methods that are more rigorous than needed, which could amount to overkill.

You can almost feel an inclination to hyperventilate. Too much information! Too little time to make sense of it! Have to keep moving! Hope we get through this current situation safely! Maybe we can take time to develop a better way to deal with this the next time around. Hopefully.

Remember the earlier reference to *Hope Is Not a Strategy*? As in Measure, it applies in Analyze and the other steps of DMAIC as they're used for business process improvement work. The pace and complexity of the new global economy might put us on the verge of panic, but we have to keep focused on our objective and find solutions to the business performance issues we're facing. If we don't, the competitors surely will.

5.3.1 Current Capabilities—Technical Processes

The jury is out—maybe gone and irrelevant—on whether heavy-duty information technology tools have had much impact on business performance improvement. Articles in the business press tend to indicate not much. Our observations while working with clients and other companies tend to support that view. Even though the buzz of Lean and Six Sigma continues at a high level, it's still surprising to find that relatively few companies are using process metrics for continuous improvement work, in spite of the information-handling power at their disposal in the local ERP system.

Meanwhile, there seems to be a shortage of analytical skills in the business staffs that might make use of the more sophisticated features in ERP systems. It's hard to tell which happened first—the arrival of "silver bullet" ERP tools that gave the impression of making staff expertise obsolete, or the deterioration of staff skills, causing management to look for automated replacements. Whether chicken or egg, the result has been the same: less and less resident capability for routine analysis and improvement of business processes.

For example, most ERP systems contain routines for analysis of demand variability by individual SKU (stock unit). But only a small percentage of companies are even aware of that capability, and that it can easily help them increase on-time shipping performance while simultaneously decreasing finished goods inventory levels. One client increased on-time ship rates from 86 to 99 percent, and decreased finished goods inventory by 23 percent in just three months. And they had to build a little off-line program to do it because the demand analysis routine they needed didn't exist in their older ERP version.

Even more disappointing, many companies stopped maintaining records of their standard product processing and times, even though that is a key database file in all ERP systems. So those companies are now finding that the data they need for analyzing their processes and applying Lean methods are no longer available. They have to be recaptured before they can begin the improvement project work.

Regardless of business process type—research and development, sales prospecting, order processing, insurance claim handling, manufacturing—most operating staffs complain of limited systemic capabilities to effectively analyze operating data on the fly. What's more surprising is when project teams charted for process improvement work find that it's not easy to extract data from the existing systems for their project, and it's at a pace much slower than real time.

5.3.2   Current Capabilities—People Processes = A Missing Link

Much has already been said about the lack of "process management" knowledge and management skills in the business population. However, Lean and Six Sigma initiatives are steadily gaining ground, so it appears that business staffs are slowly acquiring a skill set for continuous improvement in business processes.

One area is still a black hole in most business cultures. That is their capability for team-based, collaborative problem solving. As we have already said, many business cultures are conditioned to believe that creativity and a do-it-now action bias are keys to business success. But that's most often expressed in individual terms, alluding to individual leadership qualities. It's rarely expressed in team-based terms.

Our experience and observations are that this is a missing link in most business cultures. The most effective companies we have worked with have mastered team-based processes for continuous improvement in products, services, business processes, and working relationships. The team-based collaboration part is the most serious gap. For effective analysis (and all other DMAIC steps) collaboration must happen at all levels, from executive to shop floor. But in most companies, we have to bring those methods in from the outside because they don't exist inside. This issue is discussed in more detail in the Support Systems chapter; suffice to say that it's a serious weakness in most business cultures.

5.3.3   What Held Us Back

Earlier sections in this book offer explanations for why we're belatedly dealing with business metrics issues that should be as common as pencil and paper by now. Obviously, the rampant prosperity of western democracies during the latter twentieth century favored more of the same and distracted us from maintenance of fundamental practices for quality and productivity.

Powerful computer-based accounting tools (ERP, etc.) continuously promised that the perfect solution to every business operating problem was just around the corner. That myopic view has been all but eliminated since 2000 as optimism about major potential benefits from new ERP installations have mostly been replaced with disappointment, attempts to make good on hollow promises, and—in some high-profile cases—law suits over failures to deliver even basic functionality to replace the legacy systems supplanted.

The "information age" has been another paradox of sorts. Clearly, the worldwide quantum-leap upgrade in communications capability has been a key to the rapid new growth in countries that had formerly occupied second or third tier status. Communication has become the great equalizer. But it's been basic communications methods, usually with humans on both ends, that have had the most impact, giving populations and work forces access, like never before, to the global marketplace. It would be hard to judge whether e-mail or cell phones have been the most powerful new links. Perhaps it depends on the current state of the country involved. Some are getting the most value from e-mail, while others are benefiting most from cell phone communications that increase the pace of business in the less-automated economies.

All along, each new upgrade in ERP systems ended up looking like a shiny new accounting system to provide analyses of the same old financial data, with very limited ability to look upstream in business process data. Frequently, companies commissioned business process reengineering (BPR) projects to streamline their operating processes before installing a new ERP system. The theory was that automating ineffective processes was not a good idea. But that good theory was often subverted by less-capable execution that usually did lots of "process documentation," but fell short in the Analysis phase. Many ERP systems were laid over the old processes as time ran out on the implementation schedule. In the end, there was still little connection between the accounting, operations, and engineering processes. From a practical view, the analysis and management of upstream causal factors behind downstream results was still out of reach.

So how did things get this far out of whack? None of this is rocket science. It's all basic operating process management. It seems the root cause answer is that business was doing too well during the latter half of the twentieth century to worry about it.

5.3.4   Why Now

Ready, Fire, Aim! will no longer work in the hypercompetitive global marketplace. To survive, every company must master the skills necessary for fast, accurate analysis of complex business data. But, as Deming said during the go-go years after World War II, "You don't have to change. Survival is not mandatory."

5.3.5   The Road Ahead

The Lean and Six Sigma movements have been a strong breath of fresh air. They are the first business management programs in the last 50 years to focus attention on business process *fundamentals*. Many previous "acronym" programs either focused on a too-narrow issue (zero defects, just-in-time) or danced around the core business goals with too much programmatic activity that ultimately sank them for lack of enough immediate benefits (total quality management, business process reengineering).

But Lean and Six Sigma are focused on business process improvement fundamentals for near-term contribution to the key business goals. And Lean and Six Sigma bring tools that are useful for all levels in the business, and for short-term or long-term development work. The fundamentals used at Ford in the early 1900s and refined by Toyota since the 1930s are gaining new ground. There's no turning back.

Analytical skills and tools will be key to that renaissance.

5.4   Pulling It Together—Analyze Phase in Bridge Process

Understanding and Using a Financial Bridge Model in the Analyze Phase:

At this point, the Analyze stage of DMAIC, you might ask:

- *How can we use comprehensive Bridge metrics to easily analyze our current situation relative to our strategic business goals?*
- *How can that analysis work become a smooth, efficient part of our everyday business practices, so that our continuous improvement (CI) rate becomes a self-sustaining and accelerating part of our business culture?*

The answers in the following sections sound like the opposite of Ready, Fire, Aim! In other words, to use the Bridge Process effectively, we deliberately move "Aim" ahead of "Fire," so we always use a consistent "fire control" process to lock onto the correct improvement action targets before we pull the trigger.

Caution, repeated: Traditional business cultures are steeped in "action-oriented" and "just do it" dogma that gets in the way of methodical problem solving and improvement planning. If overuse of the action-bias strength has become an accidental weakness in your culture, then you may have to fight your own tendency to skip the instructions and go straight to the end point. If so, you might use a reminder about "balance" to keep your head in the details. That is, most people tend to seek more knowledge in areas they are already proficient in. But a key to high-performance business processes is the balanced use of the organizational Support Systems (shown in the lower box of Exhibit 5.2). You will begin to see the huge leverage and potential payoff from managing the measurement and review supports—if you hang in with the explanations of how DMAIC becomes a powerful business performance accelerator with the Bridge Process.

5.4.1 Bridge Structure

As in the other phases of Bridge, speed and ease are the by-words for how the Bridge steps are configured for the Analysis phase. They enable the user to "see" new opportunities fast enough to take advantage of them, on the fly if possible.

The routine steps in the Bridge Analysis phase are in the following section. Some are familiar methods from Six Sigma, Lean, process reengineering, TQM, and other business improvement processes from the last 40 years. Others may be less familiar since they are fundamental methods that didn't get marquee billing in the various improvement process reincarnations. You will see how they link together in the course of the Analyze Substeps section discussions.

Structurally, the Analyze phase of the Bridge Process is based on several design criteria:

- Communicate business process metrics to the eyeballs that can act on them.
- Present process metrics in context with logical analysis steps.
- Highlight relative values, sensitivities, and out-of-bounds metrics.
- Facilitate the search for causality; logical diagnostics menu and questions; statistical correlations (Ys and Xs) between actions taken and results measured.
- Identify the best opportunities.

You will see how these criteria come into play as you read through the Analyze Substeps discussions. Later, in the Tools for Doing It section of this chapter you will find the step-by-step description for how to build and install a Bridge in your business with the structural design described in Exhibit 5.1.

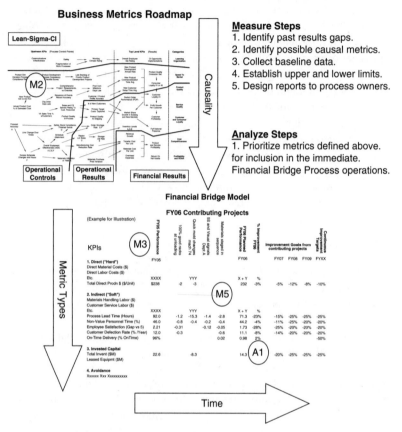

Exhibit 5.1   Financial Bridge Model Operations

5.5   Analyze Substeps in Routine Bridge Functions

The substeps in the Analyze phase of the Bridge Process are summarized next. You can create a customized version of them for use by everyone involved in using the Bridge Process day to day.

1. Review metrics status in "discovery sequence" to identify the most important issues for analysis at scheduled times. For example:

   a. Financial results in cost records, P&L statement, and balance sheet

   b. Market demand versus competitive capacities

   c. Product and service quality levels

   d. Process output performance levels; the Big Y's from a, b, and c above

   e. Upstream metrics that indicate status of the causal "X" factors

2. Analyze the "out-of-bounds" values for "root causes." Tools options:
   a. The process diagnostics manual (for the specific process)
   b. Visual/graphic analysis tools and checklists
      - Cause-and-effect diagrams
      - Force field analysis
      - Relationship matrices
      - Failure modes and effects analysis (FMEA)
      - Process analysis
      - Function analysis
      - Process waste checklist
      - Fundamentals of high-performance processes
   c. Statistical correlations analysis (PC software)
3. Identify the best opportunities (priorities) for operational improvements.
   - Pareto-type methods; focus on the "vital few"
4. Update the process diagnostics reference manual for improved use in Analyze.

Key concepts behind these Bridge steps are discussed in the following sections.

KISS (Keep it simple, stupid.) to organize the complexity for easier analysis:

- Collect and report current Bridge metrics to process owners and operators in a natural "discovery sequence" that's appropriate for your business process type. The Business Process Model and Business Metrics Roadmap in the following sections can be useful as you organize your business-specific metrics for a natural discovery process.
- Format reports to *highlight the exceptions,* i.e., the metrics that have wandered off track, outside the control ranges. The Exceptions Reporting section includes some discussion of relevant techniques.
- Schedule the review and diagnostic activities for appropriate frequency and timing. Upstream "X" metrics may be monitored more often (daily, hourly, or real time) to feed the control processes. Downstream "Y" metrics may be monitored less often (weekly, monthly, quarterly) for use in planning periodic operational improvements.

5.5.1   Discovery Sequence Metrics Review

Business operations are not complicated, but they can be complex. That's not a contradiction. The concepts involved in most business processes are relatively simple, once they are viewed in isolation. An apt description is that "It's not rocket science." Product and service descriptions, customer relationships, basic production steps, workload plans, schedules, accounting formats, and so forth are all simple building blocks that make up the enterprise.

But business operations do *become* complex because of the multiplicity of different pieces in each category of those building blocks—many customers and market segments, many different products and services, many distribution patterns, many production lines for the various products, and so forth. Multiplicity = complexity.

It's the complexity that can become overwhelming to the participants as they search for answers to everyday questions about how to maintain, improve, and grow a business. The complexity in front of them can become disorienting if they don't have ways to simplify the view for effective diagnostic analysis work.

Business Process Model

In Analyze, to take advantage of business process complexity, without drowning in it, we need a way to organize it for easy interpretation. The Business Process Model (Exhibit 5.2) is a useful construct for planning the reporting sequence for process performance metrics in the Bridge Model. It's an "outside-in" view that begins with the customer's view of the product and/or service and works backward into the business processes that produce them.

In the simplest view, business process improvement amounts to three steps:

A. Clarify customer requirements for the process outputs.
B. Streamline the core processes that add value to be sold to the customers.
C. Provide appropriate Support Systems to sustain the work team.

This model is a first checkpoint when one is confronted with a complex business problem and needs to sort the wheat from the chaff, so to speak. In initial analysis, the Support Systems tend to play the role of "chaff" because they are usually complex. They are necessary to support the core process as currently configured, but they add no value to the outputs from the core process. Their complex, ubiquitous nature tends to put them everywhere, in the line of sight to the core process, so they're often seen too early and too prominently in the analysis process.

For example, how often have you heard communications cited as a business process problem? It's possible that a process problem may be displaying symptoms that look like a communications problem. But it's too early to

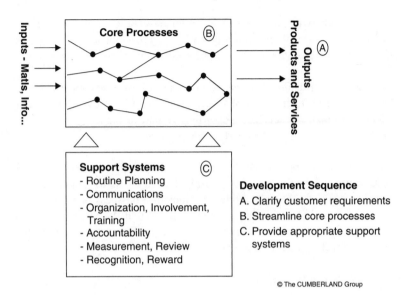

Exhibit 5.2   Business Process Model

look at the communications Support System if we have not first analyzed the core process for process-caused problems that need to be addressed before looking at the Support Systems. Thinking about the A-B-C Business Process Model development sequence will help you stay out of the Support Systems' "weeds" (C) until the core issues are taken care of.

The importance of that organized model was illustrated in an example cited in *The Tipping Point,*[*] about the learning process as discovered in the children's TV program *Sesame Street,* and research in more depth later for the Blue's Clues program. Prior to these programs, conventional academic wisdom about learning programs was that they had to be fast-paced and active with a lot of stuff happening to hold children's attention. But research with those programs proved just the opposite—that *complex* scenes and skits actually caused confusion and boredom. So both programs evolved to much simpler formats that allowed for earlier mental mastery by the audience so their incremental little personal "wins" kept them interested in doing more.

Adults can manage more complexity in problem-solving situations, but they still need organized ways to simplify the landscape of problems in front of them so that solving them one after another can be easier and continually

---

[*]M. Gladwell, *The Tipping Point,* Little, Brown & Co., March 2000.

satisfying. Otherwise, the complexity of business process problems can be confusing and boring to the point where it's easier to adopt a TCE (that's close enough) attitude than to take the extra steps to affect permanent solutions.

The ABC of the Business Process Model is a first-response mental construct that can be used to test bits of information to see if they're in the core process, products, or services—or if they're part of the Support Systems' "chaff" that should be pushed to the side until later.

Note: Chaff is an appropriate description of the Support Systems pieces in the Measure and Analysis phases of Bridge, when the focus for performance improvement is on the value-added portions of a business process. But, in the Improve and Control chapters you will see that the Support Systems become very important upstream causal factors for sustaining high performance levels in a redesigned business process.

Business Metrics Roadmap

The Business Metrics Roadmap (Exhibit 5.3) introduced in the Measure chapter is also a useful illustration of how cause-and-effect process metrics can organize the discovery process in Bridge reported process performance indicators. You can think of the roadmap as the next level of detail below the Business Process Model for viewing the range of metrics in your business that may be appropriate for routine review and analytical discovery.

Use the roadmap to help look upstream in the Little Xs for causes of downstream variances in the Big Ys. See Exhibit 5.3.

Exceptions Reporting

To ensure visibility of the few metrics that are currently important, format your Bridge reports so that any metric that is "out of bounds" is highlighted, so it's one of the first things seen by a reader. This will save time and effort in the routine diagnostic process so corrective action can be as timely as possible.

A basic concept behind statistical process control (SPC) methods is to organize data so that out-of-control conditions are easy to see quickly in "run" charts. With that timely (almost real-time) focus, process operators and managers can take action quickly to adjust the upstream controls as needed.

The increasing pace of everyday business has made that need even more important. With internet communications, few people feel that they have

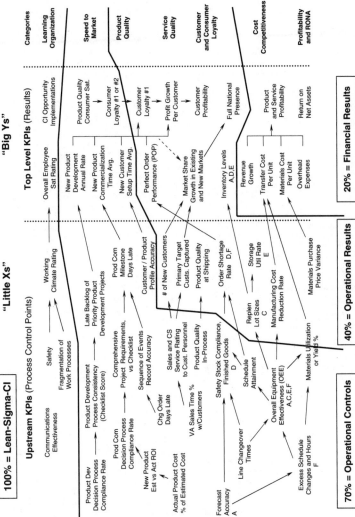

Exhibit 5.3 Business Metrics Roadmap

169

Financial Bridge Model

(Example for Illustration)	FY05 Performance	FY06 Contributing Projects				FY06 Planned Performance	% Improvement FY06	Improvement Goals from contributing projects			Continuous Improvement Targets
		100% good racks at unloading	Quick mold changes mach 74	5S and Visual signals Dept A	Materials staged in sequence						
	FY05					FY06	%	FY07	FY08	FY09	FYXX
1. Direct ("Hard")											
Direct Material Costs ($)	XXXX		YYY			X + Y	%				
Direct Labor Costs ($)											
etc.											
Total Direct Prodn $ ($/Unit)	$238	−2	−3		−1	232	−3%	−5%	−12%	−8%	−10%
2. Indirect ("Soft")											
Materials Handling Labor ($)	XXXX		YYY			X + Y	%				
Customer Service Labor ($)											
etc.											
Process Lead Time (Hours)	92.0	−1.2	−15.3	−1.4	−2.8	71.3	−23%	−15%	−25%	−25%	−25%
Nonvalue Personnel Time (%)	46.0	−0.8	−0.4	−0.2	−0.4	44.2	−4%	−11%	−25%	−20%	−20%
Employee Satisfaction (Gap vs 5)	2.21	−0.31		−0.12	−0.05	1.73	−28%	−25%	−20%	−20%	−20%
Customer Defection Rate (%/Year)	12.0	−0.3			−0.6	11.1	−8%	−14%	−20%	−20%	−50%
On-time Delivery (% OnTime)	96%				0.02	0.98	2%				
3. Invested Capital											
Total Invent ($M)	22.6		−8.3			14.3	−37%	−20%	−25%	−25%	−25%
Leased Equipmt ($M)											
4. Avoidance											
Xxxxx Xxx Xxxxxxxxxx											

Exhibit 5.4   Financial Bridge Model

time to review all the process data before taking action. They have only enough time to find the key factors, take action, and move on to the next issue that is already emerging.

Meanwhile, the proliferation of tools and techniques for business performance and quality improvement just seem to add to the complexity problem. That seems strange when considering that Lean, Six Sigma, TQM, and so forth, all include prescriptions for focusing attention (priority) on the few most important issues at any point in time. Yoji Akao described a process called Hoshin Kanri that pushed harder in the direction of exceptions reporting to keep people focused on the strategic improvement issues, but those techniques didn't get enough traction to spread far in the business community. Perhaps the Internet distractions of the 1990s (silver bullet expectations) kept it pushed to the side; perhaps it was also perceived as "another Japanese concept that won't work elsewhere."

But business metrics continue to be an underutilized and poorly applied element in all the improvement processes. Ready, Fire, Aim! attention spans may be partly to blame, but it seems that there is a more fundamental problem at work. The lack of a clear, simple business process metrics format is a huge gap in many CI Process efforts.

The Bridge is designed to fill that gap with a process that enables the users with easy-to-interpret business performance data that pave the way for decisive next steps for further improvement.

5.5.2   Analyzing Out-of-Bounds Values for Root Causes

Analyze the out-of-bounds values. Identify cause-and-effect relationships. For each, test for root causes—use the appropriate analysis tools and checklist questions (Secs. 5.7 and 5.8) to jog your thinking and extend your view of the process performance issue at hand.

5.5.3   The Important Few (versus the Trivial Many)

Pareto's rule (i.e., 20 percent of issues/items/incidents/etc. account for 80 percent of the problem/effort/cost/etc.) applies to business process management functions as well as to simpler examples of statistical distributions. So it follows that a small percentage of currently reported process performance data would represent the majority of important issues that should get immediate attention.

5.5.4   Update Process Diagnostics Handbook

Every process has a logical diagnostic routine based on how the upstream variations usually play out in downstream results. The "onion peeling" sequence often makes sense, because a question about a downstream variation can lead to successive questions about the upstream contributors.

Maintaining a diagnostic handbook for each process can be invaluable information for a process operating team and process owner as they routinely look for clues in the performance metrics that could lead them to corrective actions in current activities, or to opportunities for process improvements that need some significant development work. It's also a key training tool for new personnel as they join the operating team.

Details such as those in the Tools for Doing It section could be included. A key point would be that the diagnostic handbook is an important Support System piece that should be produced for ongoing use by the process operators and managers before any process improvement project is considered complete. Therefore, the learnings from Analyze should be put to use in Control as well as Improve.

To be most effective, a process diagnostics handbook should be the product of real-life experience. So editing while using it is the best way to keep it up-to-date and continuously improved. Include detailed steps in the routine Bridge Process for making approved changes in the handbook.

5.6   Implementing a Bridge Model—Analyze Phase

Project steps for developing and implementing a Bridge Process in your company:

The Analyze phase for implementing the Bridge Process amounts to one step:

1. From the results gaps identified in the first implementation step (Measure #1), identify the ones that should have shown the largest benefits in the financial statement (i.e., the priority results gaps).

This is a very important step because it defines where the Bridge Process *should* be used to fill in the measurement gaps in the current management processes. And, it enables your organization for better, faster, easier decision-making about business process improvements for strategic advantage.

Note: A summary outline of these steps is included in the Process Outlines chapter, along with the steps from the other DMAIC chapters.

5.7   Tools for Doing It—Analyze Phase

Process analysis work is somewhat like the flip side of process measurement. In Measure, you're confronted with a far-reaching landscape of possible metrics for business process performance assessment. A key question is: How can we organize all this so it's manageable? In Analyze, after you have lots of data in hand, you are confronted with that same question, plus: What tools should we use to simplify our diagnostic work and get conclusive answers quickly?

This section includes examples of the types of at-hand diagnostic routines that can enhance the performance improvement efforts of process operators and managers. Generally, they are discussed in an outside-in sequence, so diagnostics for customer, product, and service issues appear first and then tools for analyzing business process operations. Finally, there are thoughts about Support Systems diagnostics to determine if they may need modifications to sustain new or redesigned core business processes.

5.7.1   Product and Service Quality—What's Important, For Investment, Now

To measure specific customer satisfaction and loyalty versus sales volume and revenue changes:

Focus on the product and service features that make customers rather fight than switch.

Remember to periodically test the customer loyalty factors when adjusting the product and service metrics in the Bridge. They change faster than you might expect, so it's important to regularly check with the customers to be sure that the metrics in the Bridge are the ones that are currently most important to them.

In the not-too-distant past, customer satisfaction surveys often asked questions in only one dimension for each product or service feature—performance rating in the customer's opinion. To keep the forms simple, the survey was usually preceded by a "focus group" exercise to identify the important features that were worth asking about in the survey. So a small group of people set the agenda for the larger survey.

Since the 1980s, companies like the Customer Loyalty Institute and Bain & Company established standard methods for customer satisfaction research to include the importance rating for each product or service feature along with the performance rating. The real importance of the full range of features is thus measured in the eyes of a significant sample size group.

The data result of that two-dimensional view is a set of conclusive "voice of customer" measures for product and service features. In fact, these data are valid for hard decisions on where to invest time or capital to achieve increased customer satisfaction, loyalty, and market share.

Exhibit 5.5 is an interesting view of customer satisfaction data as used by the Customer Loyalty Institute since the 1980s. Notice the top and bottom halves of the grid formed by data from a customer survey. All the features rated as less important in the lower half are only interesting *attitudes* with limited business impact. In other words, customer behaviors (buying) are not likely to be changed by performance changes on the lower-half features. Therefore, you would have little to gain by spending resources to bolster performance on those features.

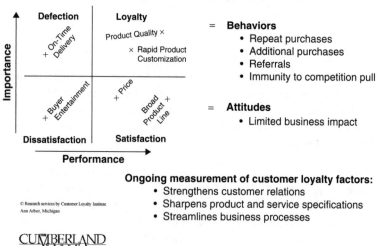

Exhibit 5.5   Customer Loyalty Factors

But consider the features that might appear in the upper half because they are rated as more important by customers. These features are important enough to cause shifts in real customer buying *behaviors* if the performance on those features is changed. If you are performing at subpar levels on some of them, then you might justify some resources to improve them and avoid customer "defections." However, if you are already performing at a high level on some of them, then they are already contributing to customer loyalty and business growth—and the returns from additional expenditures on them might be insufficient to justify more investment.

Customer Loyalty Factors Background

This is the measurement concept involved in customer loyalty factors. The following fills in some of the background that led to how it's currently used and how it should be included in the Bridge Model.

A Familiar Scenario

Businesses are working harder than ever to attract and keep loyal customers. It is the key to business success in increasingly competitive markets.

But the tactics businesses use and the results they get are often more random than orderly. Worst of all is the demoralizing frustration of failed efforts that stifles management attempts to improve customer loyalty. Some of their comments suggest a resignation to the assumption that customer loyalty is the result of luck or magic:

Why are we always competing only on price?
Our customer acquisition costs are too high. Margins are too low.
How can we achieve 'prime source' status with more of our customers?
How can we move from downsizing to growing?

The Ideal Vision

Customer-focused companies know what keeps their customers loyal. In return, their customers gladly pay higher prices, ignore sales pitches from the competitors, and provide noncompetitive bid situations. Both parties to a loyal customer-supplier partnership reap major benefits.

Solutions

Research has shown that customer surveys often measure only satisfaction *attitudes*. However, to be effective, they must measure the relative importance of product and service features which produce loyal buying *behaviors*. Those features, the customer loyalty factors, are the product and service attributes most important to customers. Businesses use those attributes as focal points toward which to align their operating processes for the most direct and efficient production and service methods.

Benefits

According to the Customer Loyalty Institute, customer loyalty is demonstrated by five profit-generating behaviors:

- Repeat purchases and long-term retention
- Increased volume of purchases
- Purchases across the product and service line
- Referrals
- Immunity to the pull of the competition

In addition, customer loyalty results in major internal productivity benefits. For example, experienced customers who are merely satisfied often return to the open marketplace and require significant new sales or marketing efforts to win succeeding purchases. Loyal customers, however, ignore the pull of weaker competitors and free the sales and marketing staffs to concentrate on acquiring new customers. Other productivity benefits result from concentrating organizational operations on loyalty factors, avoiding ineffective actions which customers don't value or appreciate.

Methodology

Precise service and product definitions help achieve win/win outcomes that not only meet customers' specific requirements, but also exceed their expectations and delight them with unique value-added features they begin to describe as necessities. Diagnostic assessments identify the requirements factors and their relative importance.

The four phases of the customer loyalty cycle described by the Customer Loyalty Institute are:

- Scan of the market place, customer base, and client organization
- Measurement and statistical analysis of loyalty and defection factors
- Review and presentation of findings
- Actions to take advantage of loyalty factors opportunities
  - Product or service enhancements
  - Critical business process improvements
  - Customer-supplier team development with facilitation
  - Support Systems infrastructure development

   Metrics in The Bridge Model should provide visibility for these opportunities.

Success Factors

Development of meaningful customer loyalty factors is a tricky business. One-dimensional surveys, measuring only customer satisfaction with product and service features, are often completely misleading. Even two-dimensional surveys, measuring both satisfaction and importance levels, can produce erroneous data if proper statistical analyses are not used. Either way, the dangers of imprecise measurement or methodology are wasteful allocations of resources to the wrong factors and, ultimately, disappointed customers. Meaningful use of customer loyalty factors comes from:

- Recognition of the difference between satisfied attitudes and buying behaviors
- A valid loyalty diagnostic model
- Ability to perform the statistical correlations necessary to correctly measure loyalty factors, defectors, satisfiers, and dissatisfiers.
- Understanding of the causal relationship between product and service factors and customer loyalty
- Ability to develop Support Systems for the customer-supplier relationship
- Frequent reappraisal of customer loyalty factors, before they become common market knowledge

For Bridge purposes, the customer loyalty factors often define the Big Y business process metrics that the entire organization is aiming at. Downstream from them are market share, sales volume, and profitability. Upstream from them are the business process metrics (little Xs) that must be managed to ensure dependable achievement of the Big Y goals.

5.7.2   Work Flow Linearity—A Major Cost Driver

The term *linearity* sounded surprisingly new about 20 years ago when the Lean process concepts began appearing in the business press. Perhaps that was because the issue it highlighted had been as poorly addressed as the more detailed process design aspects of Lean.

In any case, it's a fundamental process management indicator of how well the overall workload and processing capacities are balanced over time. The key point is that if the output demand rate is not smoothed (flattened, made linear), then the spiky workload it causes will have to be covered with a significantly higher capacity than the average workload would require. In other words, to handle the spikes without delays, more capacity in the form of production facilities and human resources will have to be maintained in place than actually needed on average. That extra capacity is waste cost, so if cost reduction is a key business goal, then an early place to look for waste cost is in an uncontrolled production demand curve (Exhibit 5.6).

Keep workload linearity in mind as you dig deeper into process analyses that uncover nonvalue (waste) resource time. Nonlinear workflows can be a prime cause from the macro level of process management.

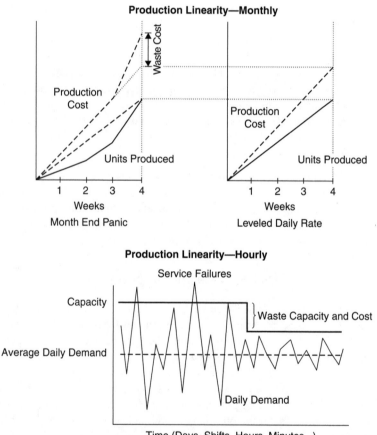

Exhibit 5.6   Cost Impacts of Production Variability

5.7.3   Process Synchronization and Workload Balancing

In Analyze, two other concepts come into play in the micro levels of process management. Workload balancing and process synchronization can have as much impact on operating team productivity as the macro issue of overall load linearity. That is especially true in business processes where the process team is doing many things in parallel, so the timing of their interactions is more difficult to coordinate than processes where everyone's work tends to flow in line from one to the next without crossovers from a process segment in one area to one in another area. Even if they are not physically far apart, the disconnected handoffs almost always create inefficient fits and halts in the process.

Exhibit 5.7 is a simple illustration of what is meant by station-to-station workload balancing. The objective is to distribute the process steps between the work stations so that the value-added time in each station is not much less than the cycle time set by the station with the most work time (the "limiting station"). The aggregate of waste times in unbalanced process workstations can be a large number that the Bridge Process tracks to the bottom line.

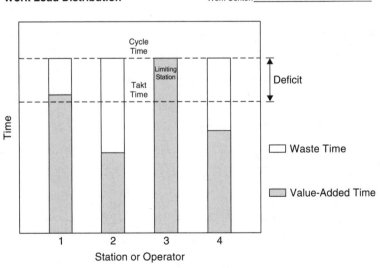

Exhibit 5.7   Workload Distribution

Exhibit 5.8 illustrates the process details you may have to manage in order to achieve Lean in processes with multiple subprocesses working in parallel. As mentioned in the Value-Stream Mapping comments of Measure, the process Lead Time can grow considerably if the subsegments are not synchronized and the WIP queues between them hold many units indexing forward at the process cycle time rate.

A sync chart (See Exhibit 5.9) can be a useful tool for analyzing workload balance between operating team members in parallel process segments. In the example, notice that there are several people identified in the columns. They are performing simultaneous functions within an overall process that has many adjacent and overlapping steps.

From a Bridge Process viewpoint, sometimes the value of team synchronization in such situations isn't obvious in either the shop-floor view or the downstream operating cost view. The sync chart makes all the start and stop points—the "sync points"—visible for process and team planning. In routine operations, that can make a performance comparison that looks like the difference between a hobbyist's backyard auto shop and an Indianapolis racing pit crew.

Synchronized Production

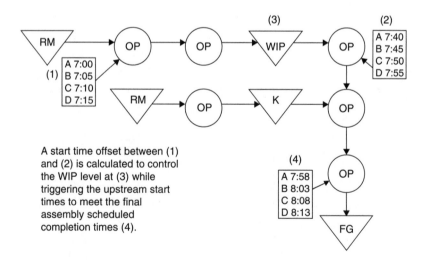

CUMBERLAND

Exhibit 5.8   Synchronized Operations

16-Oz. Meat Change-Over Sync Chart

Sync Points	A. Lead Operator	Times	B. Sanitation Operator	Times	C. Packer 1	Times	D. Packer 2	Times
	A1. Position tool cart, next packaging rolls, cleaning equipment	0:05:27						
	A2. Slack time	0:10:00						
	A3. Check line status, check CO prep items, turn line "Off"	0:01:35						
1	S.T. Prep Change-Over Sync Point	0:17:02 0:17:02						
			B1. Disassemble slicer, strip remaining meat	0:06:40	C1. Disassemble slicer, strip remaining meat	0:06:40	D1. Remove top and bottom film and put away	0:05:50
			B2. Strip remaining meat and add to rework	0:03:10	C2. Strip remaining meat and add to rework	0:03:10		0:05:50
2			S.T. Strip Line Sync Point	0:09:50 0:26:52		0:09:50		
			B3. Wash down and sanitize slicer	0:15:35	C3. Wash down and sanitize slicer	0:15:35		
			B4. Dry and reassemble slicer	0:12:10	C4. Dry and reassemble slicer	0:12:10		
3			S.T. Sanitize Sync Point	0:27:45 0:54:37		0:27:45		
	A4. Adjust slicer settings for next material	0:04:20	B5. Move cleaning equipment away	0:05:38	C5. Mount top and bottom film rolls and thread into place	0:08:10		
	A5. Move material tub into place and load meat into slicer	0:06:47			C6. Install date stamp	0:02:40		
	A6. Make trial cuts and adjustments	0:04:25			C7. Make adjustments to film packer	0:02:54		
4	S.T. Restart Steps Sync Point	0:15:32 1:10:09		0:05:38		0:13:44		

Line Running

Exhibit 5.9 Sync Chart

A key element of the sync chart format is the sync points labeled 1, 2, 3, 4 in Exhibit 5.9. During process planning, the operating team first balances their work to where everyone can hit the sync points without idle time or causing someone else to wait. Then, during routine operations, the team uses the sync points as visual cues that the process is going as planned. If a delay occurs at a sync point, it catches everyone's attention to look for a possible problem that might need immediate corrective action to get back on track. The sync points help with both pace and communications.

Note: Team synchronization methods can have interesting side effects when used to reduce line changeover times and production lot sizes. Sometimes that can allow a large enough increase in the number and frequency of changeovers that conflicts begin to occur in availability of changeover crewmembers. A large auto parts manufacturer recently discovered exactly that as availability of changeover crews became critical to more-frequent mold changes on their 4,000-ton injection molders. In that case, the departmental scheduling focus has to shift so that changeover resource schedules are as important as equipment operating schedules.

5.7.4   Process Characteristics Charts; Value-Stream Maps; Lead Time Analysis: Clear, organized "process data pictures" for fact-based decision-making

In Measure, you were introduced to Value-Stream Mapping and Process Characteristics Charting methods. They are commonly used for organizing the key process metrics used in project work for Lean redesign of operating processes. Their usefulness continues through the Analyze and Improve phases as well.

For Bridge purposes, the Process Characteristics Chart can be useful in validating how all the pieces of a redesigned process puzzle fit together, and how the aggregated savings track to the bottom line. The spreadsheet format of the PCC allows for easy coordination of related metrics as, for example, where in a particular process step (one row in the PCC) a reduction in changeover time leads to a production lot size reduction, average WIP inventory queue reduction, WIP floor space (and cost) reduction (See Exhibit 5.10). The relationships and changes are all easily related in the organized spreadsheet format.

That's the view when developing a revised process design or introducing a new product. But the PCC is equally valuable as a source of process improvement opportunities ideas since the PCC process data picture makes

Process Characteristics Chart
Clear "process data picture"

Process Characteristics

Process: _____

Model Used On	#	Work Step or Item Description	ID	Setup Time Base Sec.	Oppty Sec.	Process Time Base Sec.	Oppty Sec.	Capacity Base U/Hr.	Oppty U/Hr.	Transport Dist Base Ft./R.T.	Oppty Ft./R.T.	Avg. Inventory Base Pcs.	Oppty Pcs.	Supply Method Base	Oppty
22	3i	WIP queue at #4				938	37					14	1		
22	4a	Set-up to run model 22	#4	50	5										
22	4b	Get materials from stock	#4			1.4	0.1			20	10				
22	4c	Blue 4-pin blocks	B04									50	1500	K	K
22	4d	Asm nose, fuslg, ckpt, tail, whls	#4			40.0	15.0								
22	4e	Get materials from stock	#4			1.2	0.1			20	10				
22	4f	Yellow 4-pin blocks	Y04									50	1500	K	K
22	4g	Asm optional avionics package	#4			20.0	20.0								
22	4h	Deliver to #5 and return	#4			4.0	1.0			10	1				
		S. T. #4				67	36	54	100						
22	4i	WIP queue at #5				201	37					3	1		

Few example data fields shown.

CUMBERLAND

Exhibit 5.10 Process Characteristics Chart

183

it easier to see the bigger chunks of waste that need to be captured in the course of accomplishing the current business process improvement goals.

5.7.5 Miscellaneous Analytical Tools

There are a variety of simple tools for process analysis that can be useful in identifying upstream causal metrics. You can find instructions for them in the many problem-solving tools books on the market for business teams.

- Process waste checklist
- Fundamentals of high-performance processes checklist
- Priorities; the vital few; Pareto distributions
- Process analysis
- Function analysis
- Force field analysis
- Cause and effect diagrams
- Failure modes and effects analysis
- Relationship matrices

Notice that the tools and techniques in the previous sections tend to take a *broad, process-wide view*, then sort the possibilities to the few best ones for further analysis. That's in line with a rule of scientific methods that basically says that "the simplest solution is also the most probable solution," so initial analysis steps should be to take a broad view of the problem and possible causes, then sort down to the few best ones for more work.

In the next section, statistical analysis methods are described for when a *deep, process-detail view* is needed to identify cause-and-effect relationships that may not be apparent from direct observations.

5.7.6 Statistical Correlations Analysis

The Six Sigma process is built on a foundation of statistical analysis methods. Typically, as in the previous sections, Six Sigma begins with a broad, "outside-in" view to find the causes of business process performance problems in the most direct way practical.

However, the deeper view from statistical analysis methods often comes into play after asking a series of questions to determine if variation causes are still undefined:

- What is the statement of the statistical problem?
- What have you determined are the vital few Xs causing the variation in the output measure Y?

- How much of the problem have you explained with these Xs? How much unexplained variation exists?
- Are the vital few Xs statistically significant? Are the effects of practical significance?
- What statistical analysis have you used to verify the root causes?

If at that point deeper analysis is needed, then statistical methods are called into play.

5.8   Specialized Tools

The previous section reviewed the general purpose tools commonly used for business process analysis work in Lean-Sigma-CI projects. This section continues with several tools that may come into play as you make measurement for continuous improvement a more active feature of the business culture.

5.8.1   Analysis for Mixed-Model Manufacturing and Mass Customization

To analyze nonlinear mixed-model production operations with respect to capacity, cost, customer response time, and overall productivity

This is the next frontier in process analysis, planning, and management in the "mass-customization" age. Lean-Sigma manufacturing methods are recognized worldwide. And tools made popular by Lean practitioners (e.g., kaizen blitz, Value-Stream Mapping, kanban visual signals, etc.) have made initial Lean-Sigma efforts more understandable and team oriented.

But sustainability has been elusive, and Lean practitioners have commented that:

> We don't need more Lean education...We do need tools to make Lean sustainable.

They are frustrated and discouraged with current levels of success that are below their expectations. Asking "Why?" five or more times uncovers two key barriers to those expectations.

One emerged as we approached the twenty-first century with communications that promise "infinite variety" to consumers—and resulted in complex mixed-model production flows that overwhelm traditional manufacturing planning tools. The activities in mixed-model production are too variable (nonlinear) to be "seen" with conventional systems, so they offer little advantage over manual spreadsheet methods for process optimization, especially when factoring in the inherently high maintenance overhead of such systems.

The other has been here all along—but surprisingly unrecognized by Lean-Sigma proponents—in the form of clumsy process-data files. This problem has become painful as *leaner* staffs are faced with mind-numbing workloads of product-process changes to keep up with increasing "infinite variety" customer demands.

Manufacturers of complex, customer-configured products face a number of problems in their businesses. There have been some practical methods and processes adopted recently for efficient, mixed-model *mass-customization* operations.

They amount to data analysis and organization, using some new software tools to:

1. Organize complex manufacturing process data...to make Lean-Sigma-CI efforts practical, efficient, and sustainable.
2. Make complex process behaviors visible...to simplify process optimization efforts...including complex mixed-model manufacturing.

The first function makes use of methods like the Process Characteristics Chart mentioned earlier (in database format) to organize manufacturing process data for convenient use by people planning operations improvements, new product introductions, or routine product engineering changes (ECNs). The overall objective is to make those data-handling functions easy and powerful for Lean process development work. This is in contrast to many typical manufacturing process database functions that are mainly feeders for the ERP system so they are more like clumsy barriers to process improvement work.

The second function is a technical solution for optimization of the complex workflows caused by custom-configured, mixed-model production. This problem has been beyond the capability of conventional sequential equations software, so a platform using architecture from complex adaptive systems (CAS) theory was needed to realistically represent the complexity of mass customization for process analysis and routine operations planning. There is some work being done in this arena.

The bottom line here is that the Bridge Process Analyze work is more difficult for mixed-model production, but it can be done and specialized tools for it will be available in the foreseeable future.

5.8.2   Market Demand versus Competitive Capacities for Strategic Planning

Forecasting profitability based on competitive capacity versus market demand for Strategic planning metrics are discussed in another chapter because they are generally not part of the day-to-day operational and financial accounting that should be tracking the results from improvement efforts focused on internal operations. However, some linking of strategic and operational metrics is valuable in extending the view of the workforce as they search for improvement opportunities in the Bridge metrics, so a few words here will act as a placeholder for future reference.

A key factor that determines price levels in a particular market is the *utilization rate of existing capacity* to supply specific goods or services to a current demand level. Suppliers can usually charge higher prices as their aggregate industry capacity approaches full utilization because the greater uncertainty of supply in the near term causes customers to cave-in to price increases as insurance against future shortages.

Many companies "go with the flow," and build new capacity to chase new demand after it appears; so they're often disappointed later, after the market peaks, to be part of an "overcapacity" industry with cutthroat competition and low profit margins. The smart operators are looking into the future to anticipate market and competitive shifts to be exploited later. Building capacity late in a recession is an effective way to capture higher margins in the early stages of a recovery when capacity has been contracted by the loss of weaker players in the overcapacity environment of the recessionary tail-off stage.

Two metrics go into the utilization rate of existing capacity calculation:

* Market demand for specific product or service
* Supplier industry aggregate capacity that is unique to the specific product or service

For Bridge Model purposes, consider "capacity" in the broadest view. For example, the capacities of human resource pools with specialized core competencies can be more important than capital equipment system capacities. And that's becoming more so in the "knowledge age" of global competition where business agility is often a function of human resource capabilities. One saying is that "people-based business differentiators are often more difficult to copy than hard technologies" that can be reverses-engineered once they're available in the open market. So human resources can be the key capacity constraint in some industries, especially where specialized experience is involved. Even if hard industry data is not available, your business view will be richer for undertaking the exercise.

5.9   What Can Go Wrong

The Analyze phase offers plenty of opportunities for failure in the DMAIC process itself, not just the subject process it's currently focused on. The typical pitfalls include:

- *Wrong data:* Initial search for upstream causal metrics wasn't comprehensive enough to identify the key metrics for the roadmap.
- *Inaccurate data:* The routine data collection process is not disciplined to capture consistent, accurate data.
- *Skipped diagnostic steps:* Previous repetitive diagnostic results have led to assumptions and comfort with corrective actions that may have been valid only temporarily.
- Insufficient practice and Support Systems for disciplined follow-through, so people revert to Ready, Fire, Aim! behaviors when under pressure.

5.9.1   Why Silver Bullet Solutions Tend Not to Work

More often than not, untested faith in IT systems solutions for business process analysis has been a disappointment. Perhaps "Nothing ventured. Nothing gained," is a hint at a key reason why that is so. In other words, if we haven't first applied personal time to fully understanding the real process requirements in detail, then how can we know enough to apply an IT solution effectively? That must also be a source of disappointment for IT systems vendors as they try to coach users in the full range of functions in their systems. In any case, there is plenty of evidence that buying new software before establishing appropriate business process designs is like "putting the cart before the horse."

5.10   Analyze—Team Sponsor's Role and Responsibilities

The Analyze phase is about finding root causes of problems. The Sponsor does not want to do the analysis for the team. Analysis can be the most difficult DMAIC phase. It's the Sponsor's role to gently push or occasionally shove the team to dig deep into their process to find causes (See Exhibit 5.11). This encourages higher levels of team performance. Sponsor involvement is also key to keep the team on track and focused on the charter. The Sponsor is responsible for making certain a team does not jump to a solution in the Analysis phase. Evidence must be gathered to support the team's root cause hypothesis (what they believe to be true). Teams pressured for fast actions sometimes like to bypass this step and implement their first solution idea for a fix.

Six Sigma Champion—Key Project Activities

1.0 Define Opportunities	2.0 Measure Performance	3.0 Analyze Opportunity	4.0 Improve Performance	5.0 Control Performance

Project Governance
- Choose a team leader.
- Review Charter and project scope for focus, clarity.
- Share the business case.

- Assure the business relevance of the project metrics.
- Evaluate the data gathering plan.
- Review baseline results.

- Probe for the completeness of the data.
- Assess the analysis approach.
- Constructively challenge the team conclusions.

Change Mgmt.
- Budget and provide resources for team.
- Reallocate work to allow for team member participation.
- Assure adequate multi-disciplinary representation on the team.
- Establish empowerment guidelines for team.

Advocacy & Culture
- Retain alignment (at BB level, at Champion level).
- Conduct weekly project review meetings (30–60 min).

- Identify the right BB and GB projects.
- Assure an adequate number of MBBs, BBs and GBs.

- Make data driven decisions.
- Act quickly and decisively on issues and obstacles.

- Model and communicate Six Sigma.
- Apply consequences.

Overlaid box (Sponsor's Responsibilities—3.0 Analyze):
- Probe for the completeness of the data.
- Assess the analysis approach.
- Constructively challenge the team conclusions.

MOTOROLA UNIVERSITY

intelligence everywhere

Exhibit 5.11 Sponsor's Responsibilities—3.0 Analyze

189

Implementing premature, unanalyzed solutions is one of the primary reasons that so many performance improvement efforts have a poor record. A fix gets implemented, but it only takes care of a symptom, not the root cause, and within a short period of time the problem resurfaces. For example, one organization was looking to increase sales "face time" with customers. The team decided to take the administrative work the salesperson was doing and give it to a customer service assistant to handle. Not a bad idea on the surface, but unfortunately the process was rife with exceptions and redundancies. The salesperson was filling out over 15 different information reports. When a "pilot" implementation project ended up failing, the team went back and addressed "root cause" issues. They reduced 15 forms to eight; simplified data entry by only entering information once (common elements were automatically populated on other forms), and they gave the customer service assistant training in the new process. The resulting change was a 50 percent increase in face time and a 30 percent increase in revenues per salesperson.

5.10.1 Analyze Phase Questions—Management Perspective

Questions about Causes and Effects:

1. What is the statement of the problem in terms of cause and effect?
2. What are the vital few factors causing variation in the outputs?
3. What analysis exists to verify the root causes?
4. Are you being open minded and creative in your team thinking about causes?

Questions Mostly Relevant to Process Improvement Teams:

1. *How much of the problem is explained with the vital Xs? How much unexplained variation exists?*
2. Are the vital few Xs statistically significant? Are the effects of practical significance?
3. Are any of the current learnings transferable across the business? Is an action plan for spreading the best practice appropriate?
4. Do you have adequate resources to complete the project?
5. What are the next steps?

5.11   Technical Business Unit Story—Analyze Phase

Analysis of competitive customer and product information resulted in the development of three focused market penetration strategies, three focused installed based strategies, as well as a realigning of the new product roadmap to meet major competitive threats.

One of the teams met with four customers talking with a number of people in each organization. They learned that products took too long to roll out—no surprise. New products were too complicated. Many of the new product features went unused; customers were not even aware they existed—a big surprise and disappointment to the engineers on the team. When the team looked at the development process it was quite clear that new products were developed based on what engineers thought the market should use, not on what a specific customer needed, or more importantly, specific issues faced by that customer, where the technical business unit (TBU) could instead develop solutions for those issues.

Shouldn't they have done a process analysis of the functions to be included in the chips to identify the common and exceptional features? And use C&E fish bones to identify product features with the customers that are chip-related versus mother-board related, and so forth.

All along TBU improvement team members and the leadership team had felt the organization was "very" customer oriented. But during Analysis they gained a new *insight*. In the past TBUs engineers developed technical solutions that they strongly believed customers *should* do. The new approach stressed making their customers more successful by developing solutions to specific problems as stated by the customer. This was a major breakthrough in the way new products were developed at TBU. Part of this was mental. Previously engineers felt they knew better than customers. The engineers were incapable, at that point in time, of truly "listening" to what customers said. In the new model, they were seeking to learn, better understand, and solve something that a customer literally stated, "This would excite me." It was like the difference between night and day.

5.12   Tollgate Questions

At the completion of the Analysis phase, the team members, team leader, Master Black Belt, and Champion should feel comfortable with the answers to all of the following questions and any others that might be specific to the organization. To check for comprehensive Analyze phase Bridge Process development:

1. Does the process design present the operating process metrics in ways that are immediately useable by the operating teams and managers who are in position to take action for process improvements?
2. Is everyone involved prepared to perform analysis steps in a timely fashion?

- Diagnostic functions coordinated with rest of role's functions?
- Fully trained?
- Diagnostic handbook available?

3. Does the process include steps for continuously evaluating itself and making improvements in how it operates, when beneficial?
4. Have there been any revisions to the charter? Has the scope changed?
5. What was the approach to analyzing the data? Why were these tools chosen? What worked well/did not work well about these tools?
6. What are the root causes of the problems? How were these conclusions drawn?
7. How did the team analyze the data to identify the factors that account for variation in the process?
8. What is the opportunity represented by addressing this problem? What is the impact on customer satisfaction, retention, and loyalty?

6

Improve—Make It Happen, Effectively!

There are two kinds of people, those who do the work and those who take the credit. Try to be in the first group; there is less competition.
INDIRA GANDHI

The Improve phase is all about "execution." And since execution requires people to make it happen, Improve is also all about people. In DMAIC questions are asked, "What needs to be done?" and "Who needs to do it?" Data have been gathered in the measurement phase; the analysis phase identifies "root causes." The fact-based information is pulled together. And in the Improve phase these causes/facts are addressed. In this phase everything comes together from the first three steps. If the leadership team, project team, or functional department did a good job probing beneath the surface during the first three steps, this is likely to go well. Improve is not where you want to start figuring things out for the first time. People also need to step forward, take responsibility, and be held accountable for results. All too often great ideas get fumbled with poor or even nonexecution.

Deliverables for this phase include:

- Solutions to the targeted improvement opportunity
- Open dialog to consider alternate solutions for critical areas
- An action plan with implementation milestones
- Cost and financial benefits
- Accountabilities and timelines
- Communications plan
- Initial pilot plan, if appropriate

6.1   People and Processes

First a note on people. Significant improvement and sustained gains will not happen without good people. Many books have been written that discuss the importance of people. In his book, *Good to Great,* Jim Collins writes, "It all starts with good people on the bus." Good people can overcome many ills in an organization. Good people get things done! Collins also stresses the importance of having the right people in the right seats on the bus. In *Good to Great,* good people in the right seats was the single most important difference between companies that moved from a prolonged period of average performance to a 15-year cycle of "great" performance relative to their industry peers, and overall stock market performance in terms of shareholder value.

Dr. Deming stressed that, "85 to 95 percent of all productivity and performance problems result from an organization's processes and those processes are owned by management. Therefore, management is responsible for these issues; they are not the fault of the individual worker."

Over the years some consultants and some organizations working on improvement lost sight of the accountability aspect of Dr. Deming's statement. Some people interpret that statement to mean, "All people are equal in terms of ability, and desire to do work." In truth, 50 percent of all organizations are below average, and this is a pretty easy to prove mathematical fact. The same truth applies to individuals. Since "average" happens to be the middle, 50 percent of all people are above or below average for whatever criteria we want to apply (height, weight, desire, ability, and the like) At some point, if one could measure a single characteristic, one-half of all people in the world will be above the average and one-half will be below it.

6.1.1   Behavior Engineering Model

Create a matrix with two headers and six lines:

Performance happens when six characteristics are working together:	Which three cause your organization to not achieve its performance targets?
1. Information (directional and conformational)	•
2. Tools/resources (hand, mental, and access)	•
3. Incentives (monetary, removal of barriers)	•
4. Skills/knowledge	•
5. Capability	•
6. Motivation	•

When you ask managers to rate the characteristics shown on the matrix, they typically say that employees lack skills/knowledge, capability, and motivation. Employees typically rate the first three characteristics as lacking.

Try this exercise, it can get a good discussion going. There were several studies years ago that show that when performance fails, the failure can be attributed as follows:[*]

Management and organizational failure at providing:

- Information–38 percent
- Tools/resources–29 percent
- Incentives–8 to 75 percent

Employees lack of:

- Skills/knowledge–13 percent
- Capability–6 percent,
- Motivation–6 percent

6.1.2   People or Processes?

If you think about people you have worked with over the years, most likely some of them were outstanding performers. If you were ever part of a high-performing team, people on the team rose above personal limitations. Most likely there was true synergy on the team. Now imagine an organization full of people like that—an organization with trust, with high demands on performance, and most importantly, an organization that delivers what it promises. In all likelihood this type of organization will attract performers that are above average.

At the end of the day, organizations require "good people" if they aspire toward greatness, or even if they hope to be above average. Larry Bossidy and Ram Charan point out, "Some leaders drain energy from people and others create it. You can easily spot the doers by observing their work habits. They're the ones who energize people, are decisive on tough issues, get things done through others, and follow through as second nature."[†]

Now think about the other end of the spectrum. Imagine the increased difficulties an organization experiences when leaders drain energy, or when employees in an enterprise build their power by tearing other people down. An organization with a low level of trust, with poor execution, and where it

---

[*]Valarie Washington, *Knowledge Broker—using Gilbert's Engineering Behavior Model.*
[†]*Execution—The Discipline of Getting Things Done,* Larry Bossidy and Ram Charan; pp. 120–121; Crown Business, 2002.

is hard to get up and go to work the next day is probably not a candidate for "greatness." People may actually work against one another in this type of an environment. Above-average performers are less likely to remain in this environment, so who does that leave? Some departments of some organizations are stuffed with low-performing leaders and low-performing doers. They tend to attract one another. If you find yourself in that type of an environment, with no real opportunity to change it, go find a new bus. Life is too short to be dragged down to the lowest common denominator.

This is not saying "find 'perfect people' "—other than our spouses, we're not sure if perfect people exist. But obviously, an organization needs to attract high-level talent if it hopes to prosper in the global marketplace.

So which is most important, people or processes? Which one needs to be addressed first? The answer is probably, "yes," and, "it depends." Processes are most likely a good starting point. It is also easier to do something about processes than it is to make a mass people switch. If processes generate large numbers of problems that not only cause good people to leave, but also issues at that level would also cause customers to defect. So most likely, processes get addressed first. And if you think about it, "good people" are a result of good processes. If an organization has a preponderance of less-than-great people, management is responsible. Because management owns the hiring process, the performance evaluation process, the promotion process, the developing process, and the firing process—all people-related processes. Furthermore, the manner in which people are held accountable is a business process. We will come back to this "people topic" in the accountabilities section of this chapter.

6.2   Selecting a Solution

All solutions are not equal. Some are better than others. And always, *always*, there is more than one "good" way to get it done. Leadership and project teams face some common dangers here: selecting the solution they had before any measurement or analysis work was started; selecting the first solution someone develops; or adopting partial solutions that may cause more problems than good. Carlos Ghosn is famous for "starting with a clean slate"—the ability to wipe away preconceived notions and instead to focus on the facts and the reality of the current and anticipated future situation. When people can let go of their biases and preconceived ideas, many more intriguing possibilities spring into existence.

Again, *The Six Sigma Black Belt Handbook* covers tools and approaches for selecting solutions. It describes how Kaizen teams, Lean teams, and Six

Sigma teams select solutions. So this text will focus more on solution effectiveness (i.e., improving the quality of the selected solution).

Telecoms equipment giant, Lucent Technologies, ousted its chief executive, Richard McGinn, in an attempt to improve their financial performance.[*] The giant telecommunications company had just reported a $1 billion loss in the first quarter of 2000. Part of their problem was due to internal controls and some accounting irregularities (never a good thing), while another part of their problem was attributable to poorly thought-out "solutions" that they were then unable to execute.

Lucent was spun off from AT&T during the 1990s. It was a combination of the old Bell Labs and Western Electric operations. The Bell Labs research center was a fantastic place—it had a long pedigree of patents, breakthrough technology inventions, and bright people. But the company also had the AT&T culture. Not exactly a fast-paced, fleet-footed organization.

McGinn failed to hold underperforming executives accountable, even when people underneath were pleading for him to act. Lucent was late to market with router hardware that competed with Cisco and Juniper Networks. And they were slow to develop new optical equipment. When much of the market outside of AT&T was looking to buy, sales of old products were dropping. New products were not coming to market on a timely basis, yet McGinn failed to aggressively reduce costs. They actually increased spending, poured millions of dollars into new facilities in the Chicago suburbs, and acquired a number of businesses that Lucent could not integrate. While the telecommunications market was hit hard by the downturn in 2000, Lucent was hit far harder than the rest and appeared to come within a few days of filing for bankruptcy. The former CEO, Henry Schacht, was brought back out of retirement and he instituted a series of rigorous cost controls; but significant damage had been done to the brand and 5 years later the organization is only now beginning to recover.

The Lucent story is featured because, while a little extreme in its dire consequences, it is a typical corporate story. In this instance, the CEO and some other members of the leadership team did not want to hear what they did not want to hear. So in the end, most folks (those who survived or those who hung around) told the CEO what he wanted to hear, not what was reality. Most of the time it does not end so horrendously, but that is because most of the time people end up performing in an average way. That is what "average"

---

[*]Jo Ticehurst, vnunet.com 23 Oct 2000; http://www.vnunet.com/news/1112878.

is—clustered around the middle. Most organizations are not great, nor are they disasters; they continue to exist and get along, pushed mostly by momentum from the previous year. In a global economy this may get harder and harder to do over time, but average will always be with us. It is just that tomorrow's average will be a little bit better than today's average.

6.2.1   Average Organizations

Three things are missing in an "average" organization regarding solutions:

1. Commitments are made at a very high level, with little or no understanding of the underlying details. Numbers are provided, but there is no roadmap on how those numbers will be realized, or even justification for why the presented number is appropriate.
2. Assumptions, especially those believed by the senior staff, go unchallenged. People do not say what is really on their minds, and as a result the project or leadership team does not think as deeply about their opportunities as they might.
3. There is little accountability until the financial results are disastrous. Somehow there is always some outside factor to blame: the economy, the government, "those people," and so forth.

So while this book is about the numbers, once again you can't start there. The numbers are simply symbols on pieces of paper. Just saying something does not make it happen. If the numbers are going to be met, several things have to happen first, one of which is simply creating space for open, honest communications.

6.3   Open Dialog

Open dialog is discussed in this phase. But it really applies to every step of the DMAIC model and to leadership. Anything said in the *Improve phase* about "open dialog" certainly applies equally to the other classifications.

Some organizations create more space for people and some shrink a person's space. Consider a simple situation: A leadership or project team has done its homework, the baselines are known, evidence has been gathered about the opportunities, and analyses has been conducted to identify root causes of problems or to hone business opportunities. The people working on the project have opinions; now it's time to share their ideas and get input.

In today's world, ideas typically get shared through presentations. There is nothing magic about doing a presentation, nor for that matter, is there anything magic about getting input from others. Magic comes from open dialog, where at the end of the day, we know more than when the day started.

If "input" is simply a group of people sitting and listening quietly to a PowerPoint presentation, a valuable learning opportunity has been lost. If ideas do not get challenged, or if the executive team simply rolls over and accepts them without pushing on the edges to see if even more opportunities exist, then an opportunity to possibly turn an average idea into a great one has been missed!

Also, if a presentation has been made and folks who are not on the team use this as an opportunity to shoot it down, stomp it, and totally crush the sucker, that would not be a good formula for creating more space. It's moving in the opposite direction. Linus Pauling said, "The best way to have a good idea is to have a lot of ideas." That is the purpose of early discussions, before decisions get made.

If the presentation is a real learning opportunity, and people are expected to ask challenging questions, and team members are expected to get more specific with their thinking, then this can be a very powerful exercise. Nissan followed a similar process—the cross-functional teams were encouraged to go deeper, to push further, and to maximize the results of their efforts. This is also a very normal way to act within General Electric. Consider two short stories from other industries.

6.3.1 A Story of Two Teams Focused on Innovation

Team One was working on pulling cost out of the production process. They had been meeting for several weeks, had mapped the production processes at three different facilities in detail, and had identified 75 key improvement opportunities. At the project launch meeting, the team's Sponsor (Bob G., VP of Global Operations) said, "I expect this team to come up with a number of creative new innovations." The team was expected to reduce cost by 5 percent on a very low margin, somewhat commodity product; this was a big time "stretch goal" for this product line. The team felt they could reach that goal with the changes they wanted to make.

Bob G. came in to listen to the team's presentation. After they were finished and had walked Bob through one of the plants, they came back to the meeting room to hear what he had to say. There was a quiet pause, then Bob said, "You call that creative innovation? We have talked about all of these ideas before." Somehow the room got colder, and the quietness was uneasy. Finally, Mary stood and said, "Bob, this time we are going to do them!" Bob seemed a little taken aback; then he smiled and asked to discuss the ideas in more detail. Subsequent conversation was energized, and Bob then shared several important additional ideas for the team to consider.

Team Two was working on the new product development and rollout process. They would periodically get together when they had some time available. The president of the Milwaukee area business unit kept asking why they had to work on this—that the new product coming out of engineering should take care of past problems. It was a sure hit! After 6 months and several stops and starts, the team invited a few folks to hear their presentation. The VPs of marketing and engineering had planned to attend, but at the last minute had other issues needing their attention. The team gave their presentation. People said, "Great idea," and then everybody went back to work. The "hot new product" was rolled out in the fall, and pretty much followed the same scenario as previous hot new products. It was a little late to market. Somehow their number two competitor once again scooped them, and had a product to the market 3 months earlier, which customers seemed to be snapping up. Their "hot new product" was doing OK, but was not meeting targets or expectations.

Team One's organization has been written about and is nationally recognized as a team-based organization. At the same time they heve a pretty "blunt" speaking culture. During the ideas dialog that eventually followed Bob's statement, someone on the team looked at Bob and said, "Hey 'B', do you think you might ask that question about innovation in a little bit different way, if you had it to do over again?" Bob, not usually shy, turned a little red in the face, and said, "Possibly." Then he smiled and the group returned to talking about the changes they wanted to make. Bob asked several penetrating questions:

- What is the likelihood of a quality problem happening in the production process as a result of the changes they wanted to make? And what precautions were they considering?
- How were they going to gain buy-in and support from the workforce for the 24/7 changes they wanted to make for scheduling? And if the workforce was not convinced this was a good idea, what was their alternate plan?

Other questions were asked as well, but these questions stimulated an interesting dialog with team members and they developed two additional options to explore from a scheduling perspective. At the end of the day, everyone agreed they were a little taken aback by Bob's opening remark, and they congratulated Mary for standing up to him, but they all felt an even higher sense of energy and commitment for the changes they wanted to make.

Team Two was pretty much doing things the same old way. The Business Unit President was an ex-GE employee, but did not seem to be a practitioner of GE standard practices. There were many discussions, but more importantly, no substantive actions were taken to improve the process. The new product development team had committed to certain goals and numeric targets, but there was no deep discussion regarding how those targets would be realized, or how the company could do a better job of hitting the customer's requirements, and so forth. They certainly had discussions on those two topics. But no deep thinking, no challenging of the team or the functional departments took place to change their thinking or change their actions to do anything differently from past actions and activities. In theory, accountabilities existed, but at the end of the day, no one was held accountable.

Questions the leadership team might have asked Team Two include:

- "Why are our products late to market?" *A Team Response, then,* "Why does that happen?" *A Team Response, then,* the leadership team probes deeper to gain an understanding for all, and to drive toward finding key actionable items.
- "What customer group does this new product target?" "Who makes the buying decision for the customers?" "How many of those people have you spoken to?" "Why would they buy this product?"
- "What competitor(s) are likely to go after this same target market?" "What is their track record in the past?" "Why would the target market buy from us versus this competitor?"

Some of these questions should have been asked before the team's final presentation. The idea is to create a healthy debate that will improve the concept, bring a dose of business reality, and increase the likelihood for higher levels of success. Too often this deep questioning and challenging of assumptions does not take place. The resulting financial returns are then below expectations and short of what they could be.

Leadership needs to first clearly agree on the priorities. Ideally, they set some direction (with a strong customer focus), and then they really need to step back and listen. That is a hard thing to do when you are paid to have the answers. But the most solid improvement happens when the changes are embraced by broad numbers of people in the organization, really more inspired by the top than driven by the top, and the top listens to what people in the organization are saying needs to happen. Then leadership needs to help people see reality. A healthy challenging debate can help greatness to emerge! As long as this is done in a positive fashion, focused on the facts, and does not degenerate into a set of personal attacks, much can be learned by all parties with an open dialog. Dialog with the executive group paves the way for their buy-in, as well as giving team members additional ideas on how to implement the change.

6.4   Alternate Solutions

When one of the authors of this book was a younger man he had an opportunity to lead a project team evaluating a company-owned corporate research center. Beatrice Foods (a Fortune 30 Company at the time) had a research center that would develop new products for a diversified set of independent businesses that Beatrice owned. Beatrice had over 440 separate businesses spread around the globe, including companies like Samsonite, Tropicana, Culligan, Meadow Gold, Dannon, and so forth. Most of the products developed by the research center were not picked up by any of the 440 profit centers. They would typically come up with an idea and then look for someone to adopt it (meaning, provide more funding to further develop a concept).

Some of the senior managers wanted to fire the research center's director; others wanted to shut down the entire center. A small cross-functional team looked at the work being done and talked to customers (internal businesses) that did or could use the R&D center. This was done in the days before "benchmarking" was a hot word, but R&D centers at a few other companies were checked. The team's recommendation was to give the corporate R&D center to the two divisions (i.e., a group of profit centers) that used it the most. When the recommendation was made to the executive committee, they asked what other ideas the team had. They asked what sort of return might the company realize if the R&D unit served just two divisions. And, to make a long story short, they really did not like the ideas of not making any personnel changes and having just two divisions serviced.

Now, our young author's first reaction to this conundrum was: "this leadership team is resistant to change," and he tried to sell the idea—harder. Picture a sword coming up from the middle of the floor where our young colt could impale himself and bleed on the floor. He believed that if the executive team saw enough blood and realized the degree of his emotional commitment to the team's recommendations, they would go along with this idea. The reality was no one really cared how much the young man bled. Fortunately for our young author, a couple of people on the executive committee did like him and called a halt to this painful process, inviting the young man for a chat after the meeting was ended.

6.4.1   Rule of 3

At that point the "Rule of 3" was explained. It's not clear what is so magic about the number 3, but when project or leadership teams come up with three ways to do something (such as solve a problem, or capture an opportunity) somehow the third way seems to rise above the other two. The *Rule of 3* tends to result in a breakthrough solution on the third pass, provided the first two solutions are real alternatives that the organization could adopt. Not just one idea we really want to do, and two other throwaway ideas.

The first solution tends to address the primary problem that the organization is experiencing. If the team comes up with a second workable solution, it tends to be an extension or slight modification of the first idea. If they have the mettle to push forward and develop a third workable solution, that idea tends to be more of a breakthrough—a different way of working.

A project team working on a controversial project should never, ever, have just one major recommendation, for several reasons. First, you will have a choice other than simply falling on your sword if the first idea does not fly. But more importantly, team members realize that there is more than one way to accomplish an objective that automatically makes team members more receptive to questioning by the key stakeholders in the process. This is actually another way to create more space inside an organization.

The team regrouped and looked at the problem again. A second solution was developed but it was really a slight variation of the first idea. The roles and responsibilities of the R&D executive director were looked at and the team realized that none of the profit centers really stepped up early in the game to provide any direction to R&D personnel. It was a pretty passive relationship from the profit center perspective (e.g., wait and see what these guys come up with and if it interests me, I may commit funds to it.) So the third solution tried to address these issues. The final recommendation approved by the executive committee allowed R&D personnel to spend 15 percent of their time working on whatever technologies or ideas interested them (staying within budget guidelines). Eighty-five percent of all R&D work needed to be funded at the start by a profit center. Several new communication channels were provided to stimulate this. The R&D Center was also to focus on just the food side of Beatrice's businesses, not the manufacturing operations. The food divisions accounted for about 70 percent of Beatrice's overall revenue dollars.

The end result of this activity was 40 percent of all R&D projects now made it as far as a market test. Millions of dollars of new revenues resulted from the project and staff turnover at the research and development facility decreased by more than 25 percent.

One other short example: A process improvement team was working on an Enterprise Resource Planning (ERP) integration project. One of the problems was how to get equipment operating information to people in the field (customers, maintenance, and modification shops). The team's first solution was to publish a paper or digital manual. The second solution was a toll-free hotline that anyone could call, 24 hours a day, 7 days a week. The third solution was using a Web-based application that was menu and keyword driven. The team was able to make direct links to OEMs for relevant parts and direct connections to engineers inside the customer's organization. All three solutions could have worked. The third solution provided the most differentiation, and customers valued this service.[*]

A great example of the "Rule of 3" is the Nissan Revival Plan. They had launched nine major cross-functional teams. But the work done by those teams largely fit under three key goals shown in Exhibit 6.1.

It is not all that difficult to gather key things an organization needs to do under two to three drivers. The beauty of doing this is communication becomes so much simpler and people can so easily sense the alignment. The amazing thing is that all companies don't do this all the time. The way most senior leadership teams talk about their overarching goals is more like a laundry list: "there are 20 key things we need to do." The 20 may be true, but people can't absorb it that way and stay focused. Sometimes the goals can be synthesized down to one key goal, as the "Global Tech" example used elsewhere illustrates: *Cash Flow as the only key goal.* The 11 companies listed in Jim Collins' book, *Good to Great* identified one key metric as their primary driver.

Note: Following the 18-month rule, Nissan modified the goals as soon as they were obtained. They kept their key goals and overarching drivers relevant to their business and alive in the sense that the organization was not working toward the same old goals year after year. They focused on issues relevant to customers, business growth, and, in their case, survival. In doing so, they provided fair returns to their shareholders and they were profitable, but those were not the driving goals.

---

[*]*The Six Sigma Black Belt Handbook*, McCarty, Bremer, Daniels, and Gupta; p. 193.

Nissan Revival Plan (NRP)

Key Goal Themes	Return to Profitability in One Year		People Development	Revenue Growth
Big Ys Reduce Operating Cost by $1 trillion; purchasing, manufacturing and SG&A	Reduce purchasing cost 20% (60% of overall costs)	Reduce net debt 50%	Transparency (openness) in all communications	Create 'Exciting' New Products; introduce 4 new models
Little ys Operating Profitability (target 4.5%)	Centralize global purchasing	Sell off non-core assets	Cross Functional Teams to deploy NRP	Faster rollout of new models from Japan to US
Metrics Reduce # of Manufacturing Platforms from 24 to 12	Give more buys to cooperating suppliers	30% inventory reduction target	Create a system of accountability for goal execution	Share research with Renault
Reduce Headcount (excess capacity) by 21,000 employees	Cut # Suppliers by 50%	Debt level from 1.4 trillion yen to 700 million	Performance-oriented compensation	New product sales as % of total sales

Source: mostly the Nissan Press Release, October 18, 1999.
Originally a 3-year plan; accomplished in 24 months

Exhibit 6.1 Nissan Revival Plan—Key Goal and Big Ys

6.5   Action Plans (60- to 90-day Timeframe)

In some ways this is Project Management 101. And in other ways there is an opportunity for a major breakthrough here. Most projects take too long. Rapid project implementation can result in meaningful financial results and be very energizing.

In general, it is better to implement quickly than to drag something out over a long period of time. Most projects can be implemented in a 60- to 90-day timeframe, six months at the longest. Including software projects! When a big (three year or longer) project gets implemented with no interim (useable) deliverables, requirements are likely to change (they are also harder to identify), the key players involved in the process are likely to change, the people on the team are likely to get bored, and the world is likely to pass you by—well, maybe that last one is a slight exaggeration.

Most people take too long to get improvement projects completed. Think about it. Typically 70 to 80 percent of what people do before an improvement project is implemented, they are likely to continue doing after the implementation. Invoices get processed, pharmaceutical drugs get delivered to patients, new products make their way to market, and so forth. The power of improvement comes from identifying the right change levers. The team's action plan should guide them away from excessive "as-is" process analysis and instead help them to focus on execution, once clear baselines have been established and root cause analysis is completed in the targeted leverage areas.

Carlos Ghosn at Nissan said, "95 percent of time should be spent on execution and 5 percent on planning." Now that may seem a little high, but he is trying to make a point. In *Execution—The Discipline of Getting Things Done,* Larry Bossidy and Ram Charan don't share a percentage, but they stress the need to avoid inch-thick planning books and instead to spend less time talking (about the same idea, over and over again) and more time executing (doing). Some planning is certainly needed, but it is far easier for many people to talk about what they are going to do than to do it. There is no real value added until the doing gets done!

Teams working on improvement projects typically do not need all of the power of Microsoft Project or other similar software. Complex software projects would be an exception to the above rule; they may need a software project management tool. Action plans can be kept for many projects simply using Post-it notes on a wall, or an Excel spreadsheet.

6.6   Cost and Financial Benefits

Project teams often select metrics that are either too high-level or too general, so it is difficult to know if their actions really had an impact. When gains are reported, many organizations don't adjust the base. Were revenues supposed to be accelerated? If yes, were revenue targets adjusted? Or was cost (budget) reduced? This is often not the case, and thus the project reporting becomes a feel-good system; this is one of the reasons gains don't make their way to the financials.

6.6.1   Project Team Reporting

A project team is going to have a more granular level of savings reporting than the senior level leadership. Savings begin with the team's charter. If the charter is a general statement with no specific way to measure results, then the overall savings the leadership team is trying to achieve will be lost.

The Project Savings Report shown in Exhibit 6.2 is used by several global businesses. Reported savings are distinguished by "hard" and "soft" classifications. They are also classified into fairly common categories. There is nothing sacred about the various categories shown. This report is typically filled out by a Black Belt or team leader working on a project and reviewed with the team's project Sponsor. This actual report may not get prepared until near the end of a project when the improvement team is preparing to wrap up its work. In the interim leading up to the end of the project, the team should have been taking test measurements and experimenting with changes. Typically, the results of those activities are covered in a simple weekly project report to the team's Sponsor (Exhibit 6.3).

6.6.2   Leadership Team Reporting

Launch leadership-level projects with appropriate goals that relate in a measurable way to the organization's key business objectives. On a quarterly or monthly basis the results of improvement activities should be reported to the leadership team. Effective financial measurement serves as an indicator of how well the improvement process works and also contributes to shared learning. The importance of "integrity" cannot be overstated. It is better to foster the building of "quality" results, rather than quantity (i.e., How large can the number be?). Twenty percent of projects underway in an organization will most likely yield 80 percent of the benefits. So those 20 percent are the ones to track most closely and get very specific with improvement targets and metrics.

Projected Savings Calculation Sheet

All dollars in (000s)

Project Name: _____   Project #: ___

Black Belt: _____   **Date**

Process Owner: _____

Monthly Increased Revenue Savings

Show Calculation

Quarterly Revenue:
- Hard Dollar
- Soft Dollar

Annualized:
- Hard Dollar
- Soft Dollar

Monthly Direct Labor Savings

Show Calculation

Quarterly:
- Hard Dollar
- Soft Dollar

Annualized:
- Hard Dollar
- Soft Dollar

Monthly Direct Material Savings

Show Calculation

Supplier Info:
- Name:
- Address:
- Contact:
- Phone:

Material Cost and Usage:
- New Mat'l Cost:
- Old Mat'l Cost:
- New Qrtly Usage:
- Old Qrtly Usage:

Material Cost Savings:

Monthly:
- Hard Dollar:

Annualized:
- Hard Dollar:

Monthly Overhead/Outsourcing Savings

Show Calculation

Note: Overhead includes: receiving, material handling, setup, maintain tooling, engineering...

Quarterly:
- Hard Dollar
- Soft Dollar

Annualized:
- Hard Dollar
- Soft Dollar

Other Expense Savings

Note: May include R&D, marketing, Admin. Exp.

Show Calculation

Quarterly:
- Hard Dollar
- Soft Dollar

Annualized:
- Hard Dollar
- Soft Dollar

Reduction in Invested Capital

Show Calculation

Net Capital Reduction

Quarterly:
- Hard Dollar:

Annualized:
- Hard Dollar:

Investment Cost (if not netted above)

Show Calculation

Quarterly:
- Hard Dollar:

Annualized:
- Hard Dollar:

Total Savings

Total Projected Savings
- Hard
- Soft

Exhibit 6.2   Project Team Reporting Form

C: Corporate, G: Group, B: Business Unit, D: Division

Weekly Report Template

Black Belt		Division		Champion	
Project				Master BB	

Achievements This Week	• X
Key Findings	• X
Issues and Obstacles	• X
Next Steps	• X
Champion's Comments	• X

MOTOROLA UNIVERSITY

Exhibit 6.3   Weekly Progress Report

6.6.3   Savings classifications

Reported business performance improvement savings should be classified into four savings categories with a fifth classification for avoidance dollars.

"Hard" Savings Related to Revenue Growth

Hard savings are directly traceable to the bottom line. They provide measurable, incremental benefits to the current base business. Improvements could be from margin growth or increased volumes from specific sources—existing customers, existing products or new products, and new customers. Projects should indicate which groups are targeted and how much revenue is expected. Examples include:

- Higher volume
  - New customers
  - New products
  - New product category
  - Over quota for a focused program
- Accelerated customer acceptance time (time value of money):
  - New product development (faster cycle times)
  - More sales person or engineer time with customers versus administrative or fix-it work
- Discount reduction

- More throughput out the door (lean manufacturing...)
- New customer acquisition (due to improvement projects)
- Additional sales to existing customers of existing or new products (due to improvement projects)
- Changing net price (negotiated term with indirect sales)

Revenue savings may take longer than cost savings projects to see the benefits. Earnings contributions from new revenues are typically gross profit margins, less any direct overhead expenses associated with the product or service; or, in the case of accelerated sales, the savings would be the time value of money.

Hard Dollar Cost Savings

Net hard cost savings demonstrate a clear and direct impact (traceable) in the financial results. Hard cost savings come from a net reduction in resources used (materials, people, outside contractors, transportation cost, and so forth) or an increase in outputs that results in more revenue. Savings can also revolve around a specific customer or customer group. Time is not usually a "hard" business cost savings (see soft savings). Examples of hard savings include:

- Net direct labor/direct material savings.
- Reductions in the cost of poor quality (CoPQ) improvements; these often yield direct savings from scrap reduction, reduced defects, or warranty costs.
- Elimination or reduction of net overhead and indirect costs: operations, production, transaction, storage, outsourcing, subcontractors, energy, and so forth.
- Productivity can also yield measurable direct savings improvements, where the same resources are generating more output. However, if productivity improvements do not decrease resources or increase throughput, then it is probably not a direct "business" cost savings. Productivity improvements upstream of a bottleneck operation or process step will usually not yield measurable bottom line improvement.
- Other period costs, possibly including the elimination of unprofitable customers or products. For example:

Reported Savings	Measure	Factors
Revenue	Revenue – (variable mfg costs + variable field selling costs)	All before tax
Cost	New cost – previous cost of activity	Cost of sales, operating costs all before tax impact

Soft Dollar Savings

Soft savings come from projects that are not directly traceable to the bottom line, but that over time should yield a business benefit, if the freed time or resources are managed in a prudent way. Soft savings will become 'hard savings' only if something else happens. That is why they are important to track separately. It is a leadership team's responsibility to turn soft dollars into hard dollars. Soft dollar savings come from:

Faster Cycle Times

Projects that yield a time or capacity savings. Unless these savings are directly traceable to a reduction in resources used or increased revenues, they are an indirect or soft cost savings. For example, setup time reduction. If one can't say for certain the freed-up time is being used to produce product going out the door, it is a soft savings. This savings could be turned into hard savings if, for example, "Reduce cycle time with the 'X' automotive products in order to increase sales with these customers by XX percent" was the original goal, and metrics tracked to see if it happened.

Freed-up Engineering or Sales time (Resources)

Projects that reduce the amount of engineering or sales person time might be tracked. One way to do this is to determine the cost per engineering or sales hour and show this as a soft dollar savings. One would expect to see increased revenues in the following quarters as a result of freeing up these resources. If a direct linkage can be made between the freed time and increased revenue, this could be a "hard" savings.

Freed-up Indirect Time (Resources)

Projects that reduce the amount of indirect time or overhead resources, (e.g., less material handling, less time spent bill processing, and less time expediting orders). A straightforward calculation: cost of the indirect time multiplied by hours saved, but it is typically not traceable to the bottom line.

Projects that improve cycle time or help to get work done faster need to be looked at beyond just the simple project. For example, reducing changeover time yields a process improvement savings. It does not necessarily yield a business or bottom line savings. The bottom line only benefits if that time gets used to make more products that go out the door to customers. If the time gets used to make additional inventory, then no savings are realized; actually the company incurs additional cost.

Reductions in Invested Capital Savings

Reductions in invested capital include improvements (typically reductions in net assets) to invested capital that are measurable and incremental in absolute dollars. These savings come from:

- Reductions specific to a project (i.e., specific part number, specific region)
- Sustainable asset "dollar" reductions, working capital improvements could be counted as savings.

Invested capital savings are counted one time in the year that they are realized.

Invested capital	Change in invested capital × groups'annual cost of capital (COC)	Adjust according to length of savings (e.g., % of year − 18% COC for 2 quarters would be 9%)

Cost Avoidance

These savings are tough to quantify. For example, if a series of improvements help to avoid a major capital expenditure, an avoidance savings may be realized. But because the cost is never actually incurred, there is no change in the P&L. The argument is, "the P&L would have been worse if…." That is very difficult to prove. These savings also result in very emotional arguments, more so than any of the other categories due to the different perspectives people have regarding avoidance issues.

Generally it is best not to include avoidance savings in reported totals. If a disagreement arises as to whether or not something is an avoidance or a hard cost savings, it is really the call of the appropriate manager responsible for the P&L of that unit to decide. If avoidance savings are recognized as "hard" we would expect to see a measurable impact at some point in the P&L. If this category is abused from a savings perspective we could "save our way into bankruptcy," so use common sense when reporting this type of savings.

This is not to say that important avoidance benefits are not obtainable or that they are not important. Benefits could include avoiding:

- Safety problems
- Losing a customer (customer retention)
- Environmental disasters
- Business disasters (e.g., information system disaster recovery programs)
- Governmental compliance problems

In some instances "avoidance savings" indirect benefits can be traced to the financials. For example, risk mitigation (clean rooms, earthquake mitigation, and so forth) might actually translate to a hard savings due to lower premiums, higher employee retention, ex-ergo efforts, or lower worker's compensation counts.

6.6.4 Savings Reporting

Exhibit 6.4 shows a simplified version of the above information. In this organization they reported all hard and soft savings, but did not report other classifications. Invested capital savings would have been nested into one of the above two classifications.

Exhibit 6.5 shows another simple report. This one was for a smaller company and it contains a longer list of projects.

And finally Exhibit 6.6 shows a report from a global technology business. The executive leadership team originally monitored about 80 projects as the organization was rolling out a new Six Sigma initiative. They planned to reduce that number to less than 20 projects once the start-up period was finished. The executive group was also going to focus mostly on the effectiveness of using Six Sigma, rather than actual projects, after the start-up period.

Significant time and expenses are invested in improvement activities. Organizations that simply toss numbers on a report, and do not take the time to probe into deeper understanding of what is happening will never obtain profound levels of knowledge.

6.7 People and Accountabilities

If you were going to make just one change in your organization after reading *Six Sigma Financial Reporting and Tracking*, this section may give you the most mileage. Many organizations do not manage reported savings in a proactive manner. Numbers get reported, and someone or some team may have accountability for hitting certain numbers, but the concept does not get carried to its logical conclusion. Reported savings do not get clearly linked to business results. Business results are not the same as project results.

Throughout this book the idea of using improvement resources to focus on business results has been stressed. An organization, a business unit, or a department is only going to focus improvement resources on a few selected issues. Successful accomplishment of the targeted improvement should do one of two things:

Six Sigma Financial Benefits Calculation Worksheet

Project Name: **Saving in Over Rejection in Test**
Black Belt: **Mike**
Project Type: **Reducing retest time**
Division: **ISD**
Financial Benefit Type: Hard and Soft Savings
Process Owner: GIO Team (usually this will be a name)
Date of Calculation: 25-Feb-05

Project #: **ABCD**
Project Start Date: **Q1 FY05**
Savings Start Date: **Q3 FY05**
Completion Date: **Q2 FY06**
Savings reporting not to exceed 12 month period
All dollars ($000)
FY

Reporting shown for actuals as though the 12 month implementation were completed

Six Sigma Savings Calculation (show savings by quarter)	Hard or Soft Savings (H or S) by Quarter	Projected Savings (000)			Actual Savings (after implementation)				
		Projected Savings (list by quarter, show TY, NY)	Annualized 12 Month Projected Net Savings	Projected Pilot Project Net Savings	Actual Pilot Project Net Savings	By Quarter	Cumulative Fiscal Y-T-D	2nd Fiscal Y-T-D (when overlaps to second year)	Total 12 Month Actual Savings
Improvement in margins due to fewer rejects of good product									
3rdQ	Hard Savings	88		25	29	85			
4thQ	Hard Savings	88				90	175		
1stQ	Hard Savings	88				89			
2ndQ	Hard Savings	88	350			100		189	364
Savings in Manhours (operators and Testers productive time is saved)									
3rdQ	Soft Savings	42		10	14	35			
4thQ	Soft Savings	42				45	80		
1stQ	Soft Savings	42				38			
2ndQ	Soft Savings	42	168			56		94	174
Total Projected Savings		518	518	35	43	538	255	283	538

Calculation working notes:

Exhibit 6.4   Leadership Savings Report

Six Sigma Savings Summary Report

Date: _____

Project Name	Hard/Soft Savings	Projected Benefit This Y-T-D (000's)	Actual Savings This Y-T-D (000s)	Projected Annual Savings (000s)	Process Owner	Black Belt	DMAIC Status
Division Name #1	H or S						
Restructure Outsource IT	H	$75	$82	$150	Chuck Jones	Mary Smith	Improve
New Wire Source Cost reduction	H	$25	$50	$100	Marty Hoover	Jason Short GB	D&M
Cost reduction Siemens	H	$25	$30	$70	Marty Hoover	Doug Nummerdog'	Measure
CBG Races from Rings	H	$50	$60	$290	Pat Smith	Jon Rennie	Analyze
Scrap reduction	H	$86	$90	$130	Pat Smith	Ian Rudling	Analyze
Cosmetic IMP	H	$27	$15	$54	Pat Smith	Jon Rennie	Improve
Optimax	H	$20	$25	$180	Kat Malone	Sid Von Feldt	Define
CoPQ Reduction	H	$135	$175	$135	Mark Whisler	Jim Hungate	Improve
MAS (two slip rings) Applied CR	H	$110	$140	$225	Glenn Dorsey	Jim Hungate	Measure
CAD-CAM CAI	H	$15	$20	$50	Frank Pinckney	Joan Hollin	Define
Design for Customer	H	$10	$45	$50	Frank Pinckney	Joan Hollin	Define
Total Hard Savings Division #1		$578	$732	$1,434			

Exhibit 6.5 Small Company Project Savings Report

Vital X Project	Big Y	Sub Y	Estimated $ Savings	Actual $ Value	Champion	BB	DMAIC Phase	Target End Date
Project 1	New Product Dev.	Innovation	$xxx	$xxx	Howard J	Lynn	Measure	xx/xx/xx
Project 2	Quality Leap	Operating Cost	$xxx	$xxx	Martin Y	Kate	Define	xx/xx/xx
Project 3	Customer Acquisition	Revenue	$xxx	$xxx	Mary L	Andy	Control	xx/xx/xx
Project 4	Cost Target	Operating Cost	$xxx	$xxx	Margret	Lynne	Analyze	xx/xx/xx
Total			$CCCC	$CCCC				

Exhibit 6.6 Global Technology Company Six Sigma Savings—Senior Leadership Report

1. Help the unit reach its current year performance targets.
2. Raise the bar for next year's performance improvement targets.

As was stressed at the very beginning of this chapter, and hopefully throughout the book, people are critical to making any of these changes happen. People ultimately determine just how far an organization goes on the path toward greatness.

Accountabilities exist at several levels. If the organization and leadership set goals that are too high, financial results are less likely to occur. If the organization does not allow a healthy dialog and does not give people space to say when a problem exists, it is less likely to have substantive financial results. People are generally willing to be held accountable, but the *way* they are held accountable makes a tremendous difference.

The culture at Nissan prior to Carlos Ghosn was also short on account-abilities. There was always someone outside that could be blamed when the company did poorly. Departments blamed regions, sales blamed production, the United States blamed Japan, Tokyo blamed Europe. This is a common dilemma in many large businesses.

Accountabilities do not need to be a painful process, nor is forced ranking of employees required. GE and Allied Signal do forced ranking, but it is not as biased or as brutal as it sounds. First though, let's look at a more genteel example of accountability. Sometimes people just need to know someone is looking at related information to realize that something is important.

6.7.1 Health Care Foundation Story

A New Jersey Healthcare Foundation did not hold people as accountable as the senior leadership team thought they might. This foundation gave grants to health care personnel and researchers working on health care related projects or studies. When a team looked at how long it took to process a grant request, a number of improvement opportunities were identified.

One of the changes involved setting target dates for completing analysis of a funding request within certain timelines. It turned out that grant requests sat for an inordinate amount of time on the desk of senior officers needing to sign off on the ultimate dollar amount awarded to grantees. Applications were also held up at the front end of the process, where a fairly straight-forward decision was made regarding whether or not grant applications met the foundation's funding guidelines. Once people realized these delays existed and a spotlight was shone on them, the delays went away.

Another goal of the foundation's Six Sigma quality improvement team was to improve "teamness" in the enterprise—"the way people work together and support one another." The foundation was organized into a series of programmatic-related teams. At any given point one team's workload might be significantly higher than the other teams. So the Six Sigma team developed a workload report that took into account the different grants in process. When one program team's workload exceeded 12 grants in motion, a team with a lesser workload was expected to step in and assist with the reviewing of grant requests. The leadership team used this report to break down the boundaries or walls between teams. Over time, associates indicated they welcomed the change. It gave them an opportunity to work with more people inside the foundation and to learn more about the different types of initiatives the foundation funded.

6.7.2   GE

In 1994 Jeff Immelt was the vice president and general manager of GE Plastics–Americas, and his division was caught in a classic profit squeeze—the crunch that comes when the cost of raw materials rises and a company is locked into fixed-price contracts with customers. Instead of making his 20 percent profit growth goal, he delivered earnings growth of just 7 percent, missing his earnings number by $50 million. At the annual leadership meeting in Boca Raton, Florida, he hoped to avoid the "tough" talk with Jack Welch. Jack caught up with Jeff and ended his comments by saying, "I love you, and I know you can do better. But I'm going to have to take you out if you can't get it fixed."

In a Fast Company interview Jeff Immelt went on to say,

> I believed in myself. There was only one person at that time who thought I had a future at GE, and it was me. It's like you see people at a meeting looking at you and covering their eyes quickly. They're thinking, "Dead man walking." I recognized that I had made a few mistakes in the whole thing, and I recognized that the only person who could get us out of it was me.... I was able to play through it, fix it, and it gave me a lot more confidence to face other things.[*]

Immelt clearly points out how accountability starts with you. What could/should you have done differently? Begin there before jumping to the "blame game." Once we accept accountability for our own actions, it

---

[*]"Interview with Jeff Immelt," John Byrne, Fast Company; July, 2005.

becomes much easier to work with the other players involved in the situation. You become more open minded, and less likely to drive fear into the situation.

Ram Charan, a longtime consultant with GE and Allied Signal, has a great example of deeper thinking. He is talking with a CEO of a consumer products company who plans to promote someone to a chief marketing position. The company has been losing market share, and the leadership team felt they had weak marketing leadership. At first the CEO talked about what a great person their inside candidate was. "She's great, she's fantastic!" When Ram asked why she was fantastic, the CEO could not respond. Ram pressed the CEO to explain the three (there is that rule again) nonnegotiable criteria for the job. After a few minutes the CEO said, "Be extremely good in selecting the right mix of promotion, advertising, and merchandising; have a proven sense of what advertising is effective and how best to place this in TV, radio, and print; have the ability to execute the marketing program in the right timing and sequence so that it is coordinated with the launch of new products; and (the CEO added a fourth element) be able to select the right people to rebuild the marketing department."[*]

With the deeper thought process the CEO realized the inside candidate was not likely to succeed in the new position. The ability to ask probing questions and determine the 'key' criteria is critical to greatness and positive financial results. This sets the stage for accountability. The demands of the position are defined at the start. If the CEO makes this hiring decision, he or she should have done enough homework to know the critical criteria.

6.7.3 Accountability out the Window!

Beatrice Foods or, as it was known during the last 2 years of its corporate existence, Beatrice Companies was listed on Dun's best managed companies list. It had over 10 years of record earnings and revenues. For the most part, over the years, it was a well-managed business. But in a 2-year period it was pretty much destroyed by its senior leadership team. It happened on two fronts.

First, no one was held accountable for results. Somehow the company lost its focus. The CEO surrounded himself by "yes" people. So meaningful dialog

---

[*]*Execution—The Discipline of Getting Things Done,* Larry Bossidy and Ram Charan; p. 114; Crown Business, 2002.

did not take place; as a matter of fact it was highly discouraged. One's career was shortened quickly if one said something the CEO did not want to hear. As a result, people did not talk about any of the key issues facing the business, and many talented senior leaders (high performers) left the organization. That left the senior leadership team with politicians (in the worst sense of the word) and people that might not have been high performers.

Secondly, Beatrice made a very misguided acquisition. Beatrice was traditionally an operating company. It had over 400 profit centers (independent businesses all over the globe) ranging from company brands like Samsonite, Culligan, Tropicana, LaChoy, Meadow Gold, Stiffel, Callard & Bowser. In the early 1980s the CEO of Beatrice and the CEO of Esmark (another, smaller conglomerate) got into a catfight over who should acquire whom. Esmark had great brand names like Avis, Playtex, and Hunt-Wesson. But instead of focusing on operations, Esmark's leadership was extremely astute in taking advantage of tax strategies. Just prior to the Esmark acquisition, Beatrice had reorganized into 14 operating divisions, which could have switched Beatrice from an eclectic group of profit centers to (at least) 12 very strong operating companies. The Esmark acquisition threw this strategy out the window. Beatrice's leadership never did come up with a sound strategy for structuring and managing the new combined entity. Beatrice's leadership may have won the acquisition battle, but it certainly lost the war.

Beatrice's board of directors and its senior leadership lost sight of why the company existed. In a misguided attempt to improve shareholder value (at least in theory), the leadership team totally undermined the organization's key strengths. After the CEO was ousted, the remaining senior leaders quickly proved incapable in turning the business around. Customer service levels declined on a number of fronts after the Esmark acquisition, and the shareholders were rewarded with a declining stock price, while Beatrice's peers were appreciating. Accountabilities were subordinated to egos. This was an extremely unfortunate turn for many employees at both Beatrice and Esmark, because many jobs were lost during the subsequent break up of two once well-managed organizations.

The questions that the board of directors should have asked the CEO and the leadership team prior to the Esmark acquisition were really quite simple:

- How do you plan to gain synergies and improved margins from this acquisition? Response was: "By combining the distribution organizations of the businesses, headcount reductions, synergies from cross selling, and so forth."

- Who will run these combined entities? Response was: "Our talented group of executives who have years of experience in running similar businesses."

Probing questions might have included:

- Who is the first line buyer (customer) for the products sold by the combined entities? *It turns out they were different people.*
- What will the combined entity do differently than the two separate businesses in terms of selling products/services? *It turns out that Esmark had a direct sales force, and Beatrice's products, for the most part, were sold through distributors. Beatrice did not actually know who the first line buyers were for most of its product lines. Asking this question may have opened the door for a few more questions.*
- What are the key qualifications for the leadership teams in the newly combined entities (Beatrice's 14 operating divisions and Esmark's four super profit centers were being combined into three new mega divisions inside Beatrice)? *Response might have been: Experience with new product rollouts, experience with customer management, customer acquisition, successful global new product introduction, experience with managing more than 1000 people, and so forth. Answer: For the leaders promoted to these positions—not much direct experience—but of course they are all good people and quick studies (which they were). But the plan to do this, all at the same time, for every megabusiness was a pipe dream; it was total nonsense. However, no one asked these questions at a board level.*

This reads like a recipe for disaster from the get-go, which it turned out to be. While this story seems extreme it happens more often than one would like to believe. Look at all of the once great businesses that no longer exist. Sometimes a company survives these disasters, but it is never pretty. Motorola lost its leadership in cell phone manufacturing due to the power held by one senior executive who wanted to maintain the profits from analog phones. That one person prevented Motorola from switching to digital technologies, opening a door for Nokia to jump to a leadership position. While it is easy to know the right decision in hindsight, organizations that promote an "open" nonjudgmental dialog increase the likelihood that they will at least have an opportunity to make an informed choice.

At Motorola, the senior corporate team might have asked the following questions, because they were well aware of the turmoil:

- How fast was the conversion from analog to digital in other industries once the technology was available?

- What are the risks to Motorola if customers decide to switch? Are there any global competitors that might supply the new technology? *Think Nokia, Erickson, maybe Samsung.*
- Electronic manufacturing leadership has been lost to Asia in many industries. If Motorola does not lead the way to digital, what opportunities exist for Asian competitors to exploit the opportunity? *The initial onslaught turned out to come from Europe, but the company should have been looking to what could happen if they were not ready with the new technology. Other models existed to show how rapidly a leading position could evaporate.*

While all of these questions, and many more, were asked at lower management levels, no mechanism existed at the time to bring these issues to the attention of senior leadership. And senior leadership (of a technology business) was not asking the hard penetrating questions about market realities that should have been asked.

6.7.4   Importance of Conflict!

In Jim Collins' *Fortune Magazine* interview, he was asked about the importance of conflict and also about getting information to flow freely inside an enterprise. He responded,

> I really want to underscore something. This is not about consensus. (Conflict!) That's the key. What we found in companies that make good decisions is the debate is real. When Colman Mockler at Gillette is trying to decide whether to go with cheaper, disposable plastic razors, or more expensive ones, he asks marvelous questions. He's Socratic. He pushes people to defend their points of view. He lets the debate rage. And this is, by the way, not an isolated case. We found this process in all the companies we studied, when they made a leap to greatness. The debate is real. It is real, violent debate in search of understanding.[*]

> It's conflict and debate leading to an executive decision. No major decision we've studied was ever taken at a point of unanimous agreement. There was always some disagreement in the air.

> Our research shows that before a major decision, you would see significant debate. But after the decision, people would unify behind that decision to make it successful. Again, and I can't stress this too much, it all begins with having the right people—those

---

[*]"Collins on Tough Call," Jerry Useem, *Fortune Magazine*; June 27, 2005.

who can debate in search of the best answers but who can then set aside their disagreements and work together for the success of the enterprise.

Conflict does not mean trashing one another. You gain more influence on others when you analyze a situation and strive to see the other individual's point of view. One can be calm, and not be a doormat. One can be calm and still have high energy and enthusiasm. Sri Daya Mata, from the Self Realization Institute said, "When people become angry, they talk at each other at the same time, each one determined to have his say...The most important point is not to impress people with my opinions, but to get to the truth of the situation. So first let the other individual have his say. I already know what I am thinking; I want to understand what she is thinking and why she thinks that way."*

Earlier in this book we shared an expression that we have found to be a truth over the years:

Reasonable people

Equally well-informed

Seldom disagree

Reasonable People: Most people have a similar set of core desires. They want to do interesting, meaningful work, they wish to serve customers well, and they don't like waste. We each have a responsibility to be open-minded if we wish to maximize our learning.

Equally Informed: We all have our own perspectives on situations. Part of the challenge is walking in the other persons' shoes, to learn their view of the world. Certainly some people are better at doing this than others. The point to remember is what actions will help different people to become more equally well-informed. Focus on making those links. Once the first two conditions get met, people can usually find some common ground on which to build an agreement.

While the conflict dialogs can have high energy and emotion, they can still include active listening, avoid trashing people, focus on the facts (not the person), and search for the best alternative solutions. Remember at all times that there is more than one way to hit the target. Make certain several doable choices surface in your discussions.

---

*"Our Relationship with God Influences Our Relationship with Others," Sri Daya Mata; *Self-Realization*; Summer, 2003.

6.8   Communications

Communications should of course occur throughout the course of a project. Teams and leaders should not wait until the last minute, or until they are ready to begin implementation and say, "Oh my! We'd better communicate." For convenience we will talk about it here, but keep in mind this is a critical requirement throughout the life of a project. The same is true for a major corporate change initiative. There is a tendency for some people to say, "Wait! Let's not begin communicating until we know what we want to do." This is an interesting theory, but unfortunately once people know something big is underway, they begin to make up their own theories. These stories usually focus on the negative and consist of a series of "half-truths" that are usually far worse than actual reality. The effectiveness of communication has a direct bearing on financial results. Before we cover some of the financial aspects of communication, let's briefly consider what people experience when an organization undergoes major change.

A lot of research has been done in this arena. Creating value requires meaningful organizational change. Harvard University Professor John Kotter has done considerable research in this area. He said there were eight reasons why many change initiatives fail:[*]

- Allowing too much complexity
- Failing to build a sustainable coalition
- Understanding the need for a clear vision
- Permitting roadblocks against the vision
- Not planning and getting short-term wins
- Declaring victory too soon
- Not anchoring changes in the corporate culture

These failures would also decrease the likelihood of significant financial improvement. In order to prevent these mistakes from occurring, Professor Kotter created an eight-step change model (Exhibit 6.7):[†]

Professor Kotter felt it was critical to apply the eight phases of change in that exact sequence. These steps pretty much outline a project management approach to change. Notably, Kotter's model does not start with a vision. That comes after the organization's leaders have established a strong sense of urgency for change, and built a coalition to support it. Skipping the first stages, warns Kotter, will ultimately lead to failure. And although cultural

---

[*]*A Force for Change: How Leadership Differs from Management;* John Cotter, 1993.
[†]Ibid.

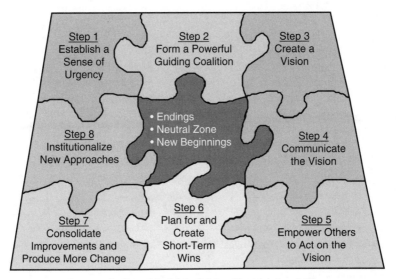

Exhibit 6.7   Communications Model for Major Organizational Change

change is critical to long-lasting change, Kotter puts it at the end, rather than the start of the process. He states, "Culture only changes after you have successfully altered people's actions and new behaviors produce some group benefit for a period of time." You might note that the eight steps are fairly similar and link to the DMAIC model:

- Define
  - ○ Create a business case.
  - ○ Define the opportunity (sense of urgency).
  - ○ Focus on high leverage targets.
- Measure
  - ○ Gather evidence to substantiate opportunity.
  - ○ Establish a performance baseline.
- Analyze
  - ○ Determine root causes.
  - ○ Define leverage areas (lower level of detail than define).
- Improve
  - ○ Pilot changes, learn from results and use them to build support.
  - ○ Create an implementation plan.
  - ○ Communicate with effected parties.
- Control
  - ○ Leadership governance to sustain the gains.

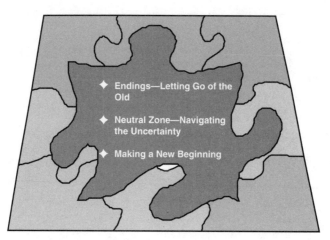

Exhibit 6.8 Managing Transitions: The People Side of Change

• Key metrics to measure performance.
• Hold people accountable for commitments.

The Kotter "change model" in Exhibit 6.7 surrounds a center core. The center puzzle piece shown in Exhibit 6.8 is the William Bridges component. It focuses on the people side of change.*

Leaders' failure to manage transitions also causes change initiatives to fall short of expectations. By the time a leadership group has made a decision regarding major organizational change, they have worked through Bridges' three stages: endings, neutral zone, and new beginnings. Leaders forget, or perhaps overlook, that other people in the organization are at different phases of change. Leadership needs to decide at the beginning of a major change initiative how many people they wish to bring along to the new frontier. If they don't care, then they don't need to spend too much time managing transitions. But if they hope to bring along the bulk of their employees, managing transitions is critical to pulling off the change quickly and to obtaining the highest level of financial results.

Transition leadership recognizes that people undergo three separate processes, and all of them are upsetting. The leadership team has already gone through this before they ever start talking to other employees about

---

Managing Transitions: Making the Most of Change, William Bridges; Harper & Collins, 1993.

the changes needed. They are ready to move on, that is one of the reasons it is so difficult to communicate. After the leadership team has worked through these transitions they are standing in a different place than the rest of the organization. Transition phases include:

- *Endings—saying goodbye to the old:* "People have to let go of the way that things—and even worse, the way that they themselves— used to be," the authors note. You can't steal second base with your foot on first base; you have to leave where you are. Many people have spent their life standing on first base. "It isn't just a personal preference you are asking them to give up. You are asking them to let go of the way of engaging or accomplishing tasks that made them successful in the past. You are asking them to let go of what feels to them like their whole world of experience, their sense of identity, even 'reality' itself."
- *Shifting into neutral:* Even after people let go of their old ways, they find themselves unable to start anew. They are now in the neutral zone, and that in-between state is so full of uncertainty and confusion that simply coping with it takes up all their energy. Since this zone is uncomfortable, people try to get out of it—some trying to backpedal and retreat. "This time in the neutral zone is not wasted, for that is where the creativity and energy of transition are found and the real transition takes place. It's like Moses in the Wilderness: it was there, not in the Promised Land, that his people were transformed from slaves to a strong and free people." The change can continue forward on something close to its own schedule while the transition is being attended to, but if the transition is not dealt with the change may collapse.[*]
- *Moving forward:* Some people fail to get through the transition because they don't let go of the old ways and make an ending. Others fail because they get frightened or confused in the neutral zone and don't stay in it long enough to let it do its work on them. Some, however, get through the first two phases but freeze when they face the next phase, the new beginning, because it requires that they begin to behave in a new way. "That can be disconcerting—it puts one's sense of competence and value at risk. Especially in organizations that have a history of punishing mistakes, people hang back during the final phase of transition, waiting to see how others are going to handle the new beginning."

---

[*]*On Leading Change: Insights from the Drucker Foundation's Journal,* edited by Frances Hesselbein; Jossey-Bass Books, 2002, referencing Bridges' and Mitchell's change management research.

Senior executives and project teams need to understand the transition. When the leadership team hits the road with their 100 PowerPoint slides to talk about how great the change is going to be, how well do people listen? Typically (during major change) they listen for the negative. So right at the outset, people impacted by a major process change do not hear the message. They only hear what negatively impacts them. So perhaps they are absorbing 25 percent of the overall presentation at most. All negative! The proponents of change are so close to the proposed "new way of doing things" that they may forget it took them some time to come to terms with the proposed changes. They need to understand why people might not embrace the changes; rather than viewing followers as ignorant, rigid, or hostile. They need to see that it is the transitions, not necessarily the changes themselves, that hold people back.

While this may sound like change management, communications are also about actually achieving financial results. If the organization communicates in a poor, ineffective manner, the financial results are less likely to be realized or sustained.

6.9   Improve—Team Sponsor's Role and Responsibilities

A surprising number of teams falter when they get to this phase. This is a critical point in the process. The Sponsor needs to make certain the team transitions from analysis to "doing it" (Exhibit 6.9). Too often teams stall, saying "We need more information," or any one of a dozen other perceived crises that can delay getting something implemented. This is the whole purpose of having a team do the analytical work. Motorola is big on the use of pilot projects to test concepts and fine-tune before a full rollout. The learning from a pilot is valuable, and adjustments can be made accordingly. The trade-off is that the implementation process takes more time. There is no one right way to do this.

Try to fix the problem, not fix the blame! At this point communication with the rest of the organization is critical. The team and the Sponsor should have been communicating all along to gain buy-in and support for their ideas to be implemented sponsor questions:

1. What alternative solutions did the team consider for solving the problem?
2. How was the current solution selected?
3. What are the expected benefits from the selected solution? What are costs?

Six Sigma Sponsor—Key Project Activities

	1.0 Define Opportunities	2.0	3.0 Analyze Opportunity	4.0 Improve Performance	5.0 Control Performance

5.0 Control Performance
- Validate the improvement.
- Evaluate the financial impact.
- Assure disciplined follow-through of the proposed approach.
- Assess Black Belt performance.
- Celebrate and reward.
- Facilitate transfer of improved process to the Process Owner.

4.0 Improve Performance
- Assess the practicality of the proposed approach.
- Revisit the cost/benefit analysis.
- Oversee implementation and deployment plans.
- Build organizational consensus in support of the team's approach.
- Influence decision makers to implement changes.

3.0 Analyze Opportunity
- ...e for the ...pleteness of the ...
- ...ss the analysis ...oach.
- ...structively ...nge the team ...lusions.

Project Governance
- Choose a team leader.
- Review Charter and project scope for focus, clarity.
- Share the business case.

Change Mgmt.
- Budget and provide resources for team.
- Reallocate work to allow for team member participation.
- Assure adequate multi disciplinary representation on the team.
- Establish empowerment guidelines for team.

Advocacy & Culture
- Retain alignment (at BB level, at Sponsor level).
- Conduct weekly project review meetings (30–60 min).

(Center enlarged panel — 4.0 Improve Performance)
- Assess the practicality of the proposed approach.
- Revisit the cost/benefit analysis.
- Oversee implementation and deployment plans.
- Build organizational consensus in support of the team's approach.
- Influence decision makers to implement changes.

(Arrow callout)
- Make data driven decisions.
- Act quickly and decisively on issues and obstacles.
- Model and communicate Six Sigma.
- Apply consequences.

Exhibit 6.9 Six Sigma Sponsor Responsibilities—4.0 Improve Performance

4. How will the solution get communicated to the organization?
5. Will the team make use of pilot project teams or do they have a complete fix?
6. Do they have adequate resources to complete the project?
7. What are the next steps?

6.10   Improve Close

We talk a lot about the voice of the customer and the importance of listening to the customer. It's true and we believe that. But it's also true that organizations are driven by an internal drive. Most people start with the outside world and try to figure out, "How do we adapt to it?" Greatness doesn't happen that way. It starts with an internal drive.[*]

Jeff Immelt said customers do not pick GE's strategies. Daya Mata said to search for the truth of the situation. So organizations need to understand: What are our real core values and our real aspirations? What do we really stand for? What do we really want to get done? This internal imprint drives all key actions. Everybody harps about, "It's all about responding to the outside world." But the great companies are internally driven, and externally aware. Think of Johnson & Johnson and their credo, which sums up the responsibilities we have to the four important groups we serve:

- *Our customers:* We have a responsibility to provide high-quality products they can trust, offered at a fair price.
- *Our employees:* We have a responsibility to treat them with respect and dignity, pay them fairly, and help them develop and thrive personally and professionally.
- *Our communities:* We have a responsibility to be good corporate citizens, support good works, encourage better health, and protect the environment.
- *Our stockholders:* We have a responsibility to provide a fair return on their investment.

The deliberate ordering of these groups—customers first, stockholders last—proclaims a bold business philosophy. If we meet our first three responsibilities, the fourth will take care of itself.

Johnson & Johnson is very customer aware, but this awareness comes from deeply seated internal beliefs and values.

---

[*]"Collins on Tough Calls," Jerry Useem; *Fortune Magazine*; June 27, 2005.

So the first question is: What is really driving us internally? The second question is: What is the truth about the outside world? and in particular: What is the truth about how it operates and how it is changing? The third question is: When you intersect your internal drive with external reality, what is the truth about what you can distinctively contribute potentially better than anyone else in the world?[*]

These questions and the organization's key business strategies drive, and should drive, improvement activities.

6.11 Technical Business Unit—Case Study

There were some major culture issues the TBU leadership team needed to address. This was not the first time TBU had rolled out an improvement initiative. Credibility was established when the leadership team shut down a new project. This was not typical leadership behavior. The new product was shut down when the TBU leadership learned, after talking to customers, that the product currently under development would only have about a 6-month life. The new product development team had just focused on an immediate problem needing to get solved right now, not giving any consideration to what solutions were most likely needed over the next 3 years by that customer. The action was like a tidal wave hitting the engineering product development group. They realized that some new behaviors and more conversations with customers were critical requirements for future development.

One of the new strategies was to ensure transition of the installed-based to the new system platform product. TBU initiated another Six Sigma project to define what was required to transition their installed base rapidly to the new product. The activities were handed off to the functions except for one item which was focused specifically on the issue of upgraded customer software for the new system platform. TBU is in midproject for this effort. The financial bottom line for installed-based transition is in excess of $100M. Leadership felt that the first Six Sigma project contributed to $50M of that amount. A second follow-up project is planned to accelerate those dollars by one quarter.

TBU also looked at the three key customers missing from their critical customer list, and decided to target two of the companies. Within a 6-month

---

[*]Ibid.

period significant sales (in excess of several million dollars) were made to both organizations. Leadership at the two new critical customers commented that TBU had a refreshing approach to the market and really seemed to grasp their problems.

TBU also had one product in the marketplace that was performing significantly below expectations. Rather than incurring significant expense to totally reengineer a product with a short life, they decided to make it "good enough" for the time being, and to set up for future success. Customers were pleased with the changes made and increased orders by 25 percent over a 4-month period.

6.12 Tollgate Questions

As the team progresses through the Improve phase, the leadership team should meet with the Sponsor/Champion and Master Black Belt to review everything that has been accomplished. The team can use these questions to make certain they have covered all the important items. At the completion of the Improve phase, the team members, team leader, Master Black Belt, and Champion should feel comfortable with the answers to all of the following questions and any others that might be specific to the organization.

1. How did the team generate ideas? How was the list of ideas narrowed down to the best few? What methods were used to encourage creative thinking?
2. What criteria were used to evaluate the potential solutions? How does the preferred solution address the root cause of the problem?
3. What alternative solutions did the team consider for solving the problem?
4. Were at least three workable solutions considered for high risk or sensitive issues? Why didn't you go further with this idea?
5. Where can these improvements be duplicated?
6. When should the organization come back to further improve this again?
7. How did the team develop the revised process design? What are the critical elements of the design?
8. Did the team conduct a cost/benefit analysis? What assumptions were made? Did a financial subject matter expert validate the cost/benefit analysis?
9. How was the compelling need for change explained? How will the team communicate this explanation to stakeholders? How is this reflected in the communication plan for implementation?

10. How will the team answer the stakeholders' "What's in it for me" question? What can be done to mobilize their support? How is this reflected in the communication plan for implementation?
11. What training is required to ensure the people affected will be able to support the new process design with minimal frustration and maximum preparedness?
12. What were the lessons learned from the pilot?
13. What mechanisms are in place to measure actual benefits?
14. Has leadership or the project team tested their ideas with the people impacted by proposed changes?
15. To what extent are communications being done in an open (full disclosure) and honest fashion?
16. To what extent is effective listening taking place by all sides?
17. What mechanisms are in place to sustain the gains?
18. What mechanisms are in place to make adjustments on learnings from pilot implementation actions?
19. How will the solution get communicated to the rest of the organization?
20. Do they have adequate resources to complete the project?
21. What are the next steps?

7

Control—Sustain the Gains

*Those who are too smart to engage in
politics are punished by being governed by
those who are dumber.*

PLATO

7.1 Overview

In the Control phase the organization is trying to sustain the gains from past improvement activities and to build momentum for ongoing improvement. In this phase leadership and participants in the improvement process are trying to understand, "How did we do?" And one might add, "Where do we go next?"

At this point an organization would actually like to leverage the results from its improvement activities. Plans need to exist for replicating and standardizing solutions to other relevant parts of the organization. This is a key part of shared learning, and to minimize nonvalue-added attempts to reinvent solutions already known inside the business. Somehow this last action is not done frequently enough in U.S. and European organizations. Asian operations seem to do a better job of replicating best practices. Deliverables in this phase include:

- Pilot evaluation plan
- Implementation and execution
- Implementation rollout plan
- Clarified roles and responsibilities (accountabilities)
- Process and performance control metrics
- Financial assessment
- Leadership governance

Another issue for this phase is trust and transparency. The word "control" implies we're in charge, like somehow one can just make it happen. *Control* in fact is another paradox. When Carlos Ghosn came in to Nissan as the COO, he could have taken control and began dictating orders. In fact, that was what most people expected him to do. Instead he created nine cross-functional teams, spent much time listening, and with minimal personnel changes had the employee teams develop solutions to major business challenges. More on this later.

7.2   Pilots and Pilot Evaluation Plan

Like everything else in this book, a "pilot evaluation plan" can operate at multiple levels. From one perspective the "pilot" might be the organization's overall approach to improvement or implementation of key new strategies. At another level pilot project teams will have typically handed off their improvement activities to the line managers and people responsible for the processes being worked.

Certainly in the case of project teams, early preparation for this handoff goes a long way toward predetermining the extent of success or failure. Whether it's company-wide or one strategic process, leadership needs to make certain implemented improvements are relevant to business needs and to continue to provide active support for sustaining gains and moving forward.

The steps for project or process "Solution and Implementation Planning" are outlined in *The Six Sigma Black Belt Handbook* (Chapter 16), so except for the measurement components they will not be reiterated here.

Assuming the concept is proven in the Improve phase now the idea is to standardize and replicate the process. There is a tendency or desire to believe that if people see it, they will believe it, or if it is good for you, you will do it. Unfortunately, seeing and believing are not always easy to do. People still eat too much, smoke when they know it is lethal, and consume too much alcohol. So if these activities with visible, damaging, long term results are difficult to control, imagine how much more difficult intangibles like change programs are.

You might ask, "Why do a pilot?" It's not always necessary. It is appropriate to do a pilot when:

- Scope of the design is complex or large.
- Cost is high or implementation resources for a full scale rollout are not available.
- Unintended consequences or unexpected outcomes could be significant.

- Credibility for the design/concept needs to be established.
- It is difficult to reverse the solution.
- Substantial training and changes to job design are required.
- You're just not sure, and the risks are high.

Sometimes the above situations exist, but the organization goes ahead with an overall rollout anyway. That is what happened at Nissan. Carlos Ghosn felt they did not have time for a pilot, survival was at stake, and large scale change was necessary to accomplish this. Lou Gerstner did the same with the revival he led at IBM.

Pilot evaluation criteria should:

- Be done ahead of time to avoid being compromised by the solutions
- Measure the effectiveness of the implementation
  - Degree proposed solution is adopted
  - Degree of acceptance by key stakeholders
- Measure the effectiveness against the targets (sometimes this is difficult for a partial roll out)
  - Results against goals
  - Results from key metrics
- Determine if the selected metrics provide the desired feedback on the process
- Determine if cost-benefit targets and expectations are likely to be met
- Determine if the solution addresses identified "root cause" problems

Good pilot planning takes into account the various challenges and barriers to success and addresses them ahead of time. For example, open communications throughout the DMAIC process with affected parties go a long way toward planting seeds for change.

Even a small change in a business process can affect many other processes. During a pilot, leadership teams should check ripple effects from changes. Do the changes adversely impact suppliers to the process? Are the outputs from the changed process(es) still in alignment with what the recipients or customers of the process need? Unintended consequences in this area can quickly wipe out any gains. (See Exhibit 7.1.)

Somehow people think, "They'll know it when they see it" and they don't put together a clear set of metrics. Two categories of success criteria established for a pilot are:

1. *Effectiveness of implementation:* The degree to which the organization understands and adopts the solution(s).

Summarizing Pilot Conclusions

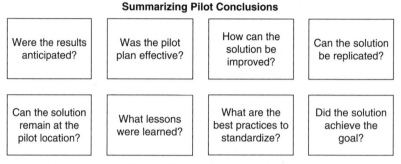

Were the results anticipated?	Was the pilot plan effective?	How can the solution be improved?	Can the solution be replicated?
Can the solution remain at the pilot location?	What lessons were learned?	What are the best practices to standardize?	Did the solution achieve the goal?

Exhibit 7.1   Measure and Verify Pilot Results Process Map

2. *Impact on the target*: The degree to which a solution helps move overall process performance toward its improvement goals and targets.

Pilot success criteria should be established for both these categories. One without the other will lead to either the failure of a good solution from bad planning, or the good execution of a bad solution. Good pilot planning takes into account the various challenges and barriers to success and addresses them before the failure occurs.

A pilot should test not only the solution, but also the proposed measures and measurement techniques. The measures will serve to assure that gains are being maintained and identify areas for further improvement. The pilot will test:

1. The effectiveness of the measurement techniques to provide the desired feedback
2. The ease of capturing the metrics
3. The time and cost associated with performing measurements

Ideally, measures will already be in use. However, don't limit your metrics to that. A balance must be established between the effectiveness, the ease of use, and the time and cost associated with obtaining the metrics. The correlation of the measure to the goal is the most important consideration. Without a strong correlation the measure is meaningless.

The number of measures should be limited to three to five. Anything beyond five measures, the management of the results becomes difficult. Therefore, the selected metrics must provide the insight necessary to determine if customers or other key stakeholders are ultimately going to be satisfied.

Everything takes longer than you think, so pilots should be planned accordingly. Do not underestimate communication needs. Set the metrics before the pilot is started.

The experiences and feedback gathered throughout the pilot and initial rollouts can support implementation on a larger scale if the organization plans for this to happen. As part of a pilot and solution evaluation, a project team should capture information and feedback regarding:

- The effectiveness of the original process design and impact on performance
- The effectiveness of the implementation plan

This feedback helps in making decisions regarding future deployments, as well as improvement to the solution(s).

7.3   Implementation and Execution

Somewhere between the pilot and actually doing it, things often seem to get lost along the way. In the Overview chapter, there is a description of how often leadership teams are disappointed in the actual results of their company-wide improvement initiatives versus the leadership team's expectations. Implementation is typically a primary source of this frustration. The leadership team may set a direction, but for whatever reason it does not work the way they thought it would. Think about it though, 50 percent of the population will be below average and 50 percent above at any given point in time. The average may be manipulated a little bit by working with modes or weighted averages. But most things, most improvement initiatives, and most products and services will be right around the middle. If it is too far below average, it goes away, so the bulk of the population is "average."

Larry Bossidy, CEO of Allied Signal, describes "execution" as the proof at the end of the day regarding how well we are doing. Plans are great, but execution is what counts! Carlos Ghosn at Nissan fostered the same idea, "95 percent (of time) on execution and delivery" and "5 percent on planning."[*] He says, "Too much time within a company gets spent planning and not enough doing." When the leadership is not clear in its directives and if it does not insist the job get done now, that is when organizations get into trouble and people act with uncertainty.

---

[*]*Turnaround*, David McGee, Harper Collins, 2003 p. 103.

Staying focused on implementation is a fundamental difference between success and mediocrity. First, leaders should give employees the opportunity to change by discussing and listening at all levels of an organization. The voice of the customer and any other key stakeholder needs consideration. Then, leadership needs to set a clear direction for the organization and do it. Too much time spent listening and planning erodes effective implementation. When actions drag out, people lose heart and their spirits wane. Even the requirements may change if it takes too long to do. As the Nike commercial states, "Just Do It!"

The telltale sign for too much time listening and planning: You start hearing the same messages over and over again or plans get put together over and over again—continual refinements versus clear new directions or new ideas. And the temptation to do this is great; it is far easier to talk than to act. While Ghosn did not do a pilot at Nissan, he did an incredible amount of listening to employees and involving employees in developing solutions to the challenges outlined in the Nissan Revival Plan. The success of these actions was pretty much proven when the organization met all of its goals, almost 1 year ahead of time.

7.3.1   A Sense of Balance

Obviously, the planning versus acting needs some sense of balance. Just acting without thinking or acting without data produces many false starts and mediocre results. Depending on the cultural tendencies of any individual company they may swing to one or the other side of that fulcrum. For meaningful change to happen the weaknesses need attention.

Balance is needed in several other ways as well. The key goals at Allied Signal in 1999 were: "Driving growth by providing products and services of enhanced value to customers; increasing employee skills and opportunities by a commitment to learning; and applying Six Sigma tools to drive productivity and generate cash flow."

If the leadership team operates only at a surface level, it is very likely that people inside the organization will not interpret these goals in the same manner as the leadership team. The leadership team will also most likely have a very shallow understanding of key issues in these categories faced by the organization. This fits with a theme we stress consistently throughout this book: One needs to probe without judgment, beneath the surface, to begin developing profound knowledge.

Let's take just one goal example (increasing employee skills and opportunities by a commitment to learning) and begin to probe some of the issues in more depth. Subgoals below the corporate scorecard might include cross-training, high performance, work/life balance. Staying with the last one: If employees always choose home life over work life, it is little different than the organization *always* choosing shareholders over the other key constituencies. From an employee perspective, sometimes the organization needs to preempt family life, especially if you are an executive responsible for hundreds or thousands of employees. But not all the time, and hopefully the decision is left to the employee to make the right choice in a given situation. The employee, of course, then bears responsibility for the decision.*

Leadership has a responsibility to understand what is below the surface. Then, they will do a better job of communicating their expectations. If they only communicate from a top-level goal perspective, then real life issues and real life trade-offs (and there are trade-offs for every decision that gets made) don't receive much consideration or thought. At a top level only, communication becomes a "yes you did," or "no you didn't," on/off type mantra. When employees realize leadership is disconnected from the real world, their credibility erodes and much of what the leadership team is trying to accomplish is undermined.

7.4   Implementation Rollout Plan

Effective solutions, whether at a leadership, a team, or a project level have built-in steps and controls for reducing risk. During the Analyze phase a risk assessment should have been done. Depending on the degree of risk, it may be a formal or an informal assessment. Carlos Ghosn assesses risk by talking to people with a stake in the problem. That may include folks on the shop floor, customers, suppliers, functional departments, and so forth. Obviously, the results of any risk assessment should be taken into account in implementation.

A large scale rollout may touch multiple locations, large numbers of people, a myriad of processes, and have major timing considerations. On a smaller scale, perhaps a project team simply needs to leave implementation tools behind to help the people responsible for the process to do

---

*"Allied Signal Case Study," Sharon Lobel ©2000; The Wharton Work/Life Integration Project; www.bc.edu/bc_org/avp/wfnetwork/loppr/alliedsignal.pdf.

the implementation. Chapter 16 of *The Six Sigma Black Belt Handbook* provides a Solution Implementation outline, so this book will touch mostly on the measurement related aspects, plus a few other action steps not touched on in the other book.

Teams fill out a financial benefits calculation worksheet or some other type of cost benefit summary. An example of a form is shown in Exhibit 7.2.

This worksheet should guide the measurement control aspects throughout the implementation cycle. In the case of an overall organizational change, surprisingly, leadership does not typically prepare this type of analysis. But they do lay out goals and expectations for major change initiatives, so those become the guiding measurement factors in the Control phase.

7.4.1   Error Mode Effects Analysis Form

This form can be used to anticipate and prepare teams to address key implementation risk (Exhibit 7.3). Used correctly, this form helps teams build in the necessary controls to prevent interference with project objectives. *Error mode effects analyses* (EMEAs) require a team to make qualitative assumptions about the likelihood and potential impact of errors on a solution. Once each of the criteria is discussed and a given value is assigned, the degree of effect is totaled for each error. Occurrence prevention should match the degree of effect. This form is very similar to a failure mode effects analysis (FMEA) form, which is used in the Analyze or Improve phases.

This form is used mostly by project teams, although it works equally well with leadership teams working on broad scale improvements. While it is shown in the Control phase, it could be used in the Define, Analyze, or Improve phases as well.

Steps to complete the EMEA include:

1. Describe the objective or area of focus for the EMEA. Try to be as specific as possible. Different risks or objectives may require the completion of more than one EMEA for the same process.
2. Identify and list each of the major process steps (activities and decisions) currently under review.
3. Determine potential errors that may occur for each of the process steps—staying focused on the EMEA objective. Answer the question: What could go wrong with this process step?

Project Name: _____
Black Belt: _____
Project Type: _____
Division: _____
Financial Benefit Type: _____
Process Owner: _____
Date of Calculation: _____

Project #: _____
Project Start Date: _____
Savings Start Date: _____
Completion Date: _____

Savings reporting not to exceed 12 month period
All dollars ($000)
FY _____

Six Sigma Savings Calculation (show savings by quarter)	Hard or Soft Savings (H or S) by Quarter	Projected Savings (000)			Actual Pilot Project Net Savings	Actual Savings (after implementation)			
		Projected Savings (list by quarter, show TY, NY)	Annualized 12 Month Projected Net Savings	Projected Pilot Project Net Savings		By Quarter	Cumulative Fiscal Y-T-D	2nd Fiscal Y-T-D (when overlaps to second year)	Total 12 Month Actual Savings
Total Reported Hard Dollar Savings		0	0	0	0	0	0	0	0
Potential Soft Savings									
	Soft Savings								
	Soft Savings								
	Soft Savings								
	Soft Savings								
Total Soft Savings		0	0	0	0	0	0	0	0

Calculation working notes:

Exhibit 7.2 Six Sigma Financial Benefits Calculation Worksheet

243

Description:

Step #	Process Step	Error	Cause	Effect	Degree of Effect				Occurrence Prevention (Countermeasure)
					Frequency	Severity	Detection	Total Points	

Exhibit 7.3   Error Mode Effects Analysis Form

4. For each error identified in Step 3, identify the likely root causes using appropriate analytical tools.
5. Briefly describe the consequences of each of the errors. What adverse impact may the error have on the solution or process?
6. Calculate and total the degree of effect for each of the errors identified (assign a point total to each category (high might equal 5 or 3 points, low equal 1 point).
   a. What is the likelihood that the error will occur? High, medium, low, none (nothing magic about this scale; others could be used).
   b. How severe or damaging would the error be? Critical, high, medium, low, none.
   c. How easy is the error to detect? Difficult, somewhat difficult, medium. somewhat difficult, easy.
   d. Total the points in each row for a priority rating.
7. Determine a way to prevent the high-priority errors or have a counter-measure plan of action.
   a. Describe the action that can be taken or designed into the solution.
   b. Determine what can be done to prevent the error from arising.
   c. If the error does occur, what steps should be taken to address it to eliminate or minimize any consequences?

Error Modes and Effects Analysis

Description: _Team to develop strategic new product for trade-
show xx/mm/yy_____

Step #	Process Step	Error	Cause	Effect	Frequency	Severity	Detection	Total Points	Occurrence Prevention (Countermeasure)
							Degree of Effect		
3.1`	NPD Requirements	Keep changing	Definition or commitment to require-ments set	Cost, delays, frustration, less likely to succeed	2	5	5	12	Leadership needs to layout core requirements at project outset, that will not change.
									Rapid prototyping for customer feedback

Exhibit 7.4   EMEA New Product Development Example (One Step of Process)

Uses of this form for a project are probably obvious. So let's consider two unrelated examples from a leadership level shown in Exhibits 7.4 and 7.5.

There is nothing magic about the two examples. In the steps, ideally just one idea per block is shown. The examples have several ideas in the Effects column. It might be better to separate them into different line items, so that each factor can be separately weighted.

7.4.2   Implementation Rollout

After the pilot concept is tested, the solutions or actions need to be spread to other parts of the organization. Hopefully cross-functional teams were utilized in developing the initial solutions and approaches. Those teams

Error Modes and Effects Analysis

Description: _Roll-out of company wide six sigma
initiative_____

Step #	Process Step	Error	Cause	Effect	Frequency	Severity	Detection	Total Points	Occurrence Prevention (Countermeasure)
							Degree of Effect		
4.2	Measurement of results	Savings do not show up in P&L	Poor definition of "hard" vs. other savings	Loss of support for initiative, less credibility, etc.	4	5	2	11	Define hard savings
									Institute hard savings reporting mechanism

Exhibit 7.5   EMEA Six Sigma Rollout Example (One Step of Process)

provide resources for improvement acceleration throughout an enterprise, improvement acceptance, and improvement ownership.

Nissan

At Nissan, Carlos Ghosn launched nine cross-functional teams to look at all aspects of the enterprise. Over the course of three months those teams assessed more than 2000 improvement ideas. They ultimately presented ideas dealing with new model launch, reduction in the number of suppliers, a realignment of Keiretsu relationships, cost reductions, capacity reductions, and so forth. The final recommendations accepted by the executive committee became the foundation for the Nissan Revival Plan (NRP).[*]

Implementation began immediately and also had significant time pressures. Success depends on early results. Nissan shuttered five plants (an unprecedented action in Japan), agreements were made with suppliers and those who reduced costs were rewarded with more business. A host of other changes were also made.

The fact is, leadership acted. They did not continue to study. In this instance employees did not need training on a new methodology. They needed to execute the plan. And that is what happened. Over the course of 2 years Nissan:

- Returned to profitability
- Achieved an operating profit in excess of 7.9 percent
- Reduced debt
- Rolled out several new products.

Implementation was done through a steady stream of communications, a clear direction that did not change, accountability enforced throughout the enterprise, the breaking down of barriers between functions, departments, and regions, and building on a steady stream of successes. Ghosn frequently uses the word "commitment." Once you commit you are expected to deliver. If a problem arises, people are expected to bring it forth immediately, otherwise the commitment is expected to be on track. The executive committee reviewed critical commitments every month and worked immediately to find solutions if promises were not met.[†] In Six Sigma language, these critical commitments are the "Big Ys" that are targets for an enterprise.

---

[*]*Turnaround*, David McGee; HarperCollins, 2003.
[†]Ibid.

United Airlines and General Motors

Compare the very quick turnaround at Nissan to the recurring pain that takes place at United Airlines and General Motors. The main differences are:

- The degree of focus on the key commitments
- Other goals were subordinate to the big ticket items
- The executive group agreed on the priorities
- The executive group followed through on its commitments

The other major difference is that Nissan had a reasonably well thought-out plan, created after listening to the "voice of the customer" and the "voice of the business." The customers' voice was pretty clear from the lack of purchases of products and declining market share. The plan was not dreamed up in a white-walled conference room by an out-of-touch group of executives.

At United Airlines and GM, each year senior leadership complains about the unions, pensions, and unfair competition (*Wall Street Journal*; June 16, 2005; "GM Warns UAW about Cutting Health Benefits"). What competition is fair? The goal is to win in an ethical manner. People look for advantages against competitor weaknesses; that is a key fundamental of business in a free market. United and GM complain about energy costs, and presumably they complain about the weather. Leadership cannot keep going back to the employee group, year after year, and ask for a new round of sacrifices. United has been through four or five CEOs. The last one with a vision was Richard Ferris. It's not clear if it was a good vision or a poor one, but at least the guy had a picture. And this is not to say that pension costs are not a problem for United and GM. They are! But the leadership teams seem to lack a clear picture on how to change their fundamental competitive position. And their financial performance proves it.

While United and GM complain, companies like Nissan, Toyota, Hyundai, Southwest Airlines, and Virgin Atlantic, who also face tremendous competitive pressures, continue to do fine. Compare the Nissan Revival Plan to United Airlines' launch of TED, the new low-cost carrier designed to compete with the likes of Southwest Airlines.

United spent considerable marketing dollars to launch the new brand, but it is largely nonexistent from a customer perspective. They paid to get a number of aircraft painted in a new color. They also presumably paid some PR firm to come up with the new company name and logo. Then how was this low-cost airline launched? If you go to the United web site, *www.ual.com* to make a reservation, you can see a "TED" name, but when you book your flight you have no idea which brand you are flying. TED flights do not show on the Web as a cheaper alternative. If you go into the United terminal at O'Hare or Denver airports, TED planes are randomly sprinkled throughout the United gates. There is no differentiation! TED is not a different airline. The only presumable difference between TED and United is the pilots and flight attendants are paid less.

This is hardly a noticeable or meaningful difference from a customer perspective. Not to pick on United, but so many companies that reorganize and launch major new change initiatives do it in a similar fashion with average results at best. From a governance perspective in many organizations, people just go about it in the average way.

Can you imagine United's leadership team receiving a message from employees saying, "I think we need to launch a low-cost airline and pay employees less money"? Or if they had bothered to ask the question, if they sincerely went out and listened to the "voice of key stakeholders" in the business, might they have heard something else? What might the market reaction be if United simplified pricing, treated customers like adults rather than price schemers, or had flexible ticketing policies such that if customers needed to change a flight, they could take their chances on an empty seat or pay for a guaranteed ticket change? These ideas may be no better than the name change, but at least they touch customers. United Airlines suffers from poor execution and poor planning, a combination that is often fatal.

A major problem for United and GM today is employees have lost confidence in the leadership. A blame culture exists: it's always somebody else's fault. Hopefully, these companies will regain their footing. Both have many bright, hard-working people inside their organization. At one time they were both great institutions, and they can certainly become so again at some point in the future. But to make that happen they will need to quit continually doing things in the same old way while hoping for different results.

Nissan reduced headcount by more than 21,000 employees, many of whom were in Japan, an unheard-of practice. Yet the leadership team was very transparent with their reasoning, employees understood there was too much production capacity and that a cost was associated with that. There was no sabotage and employees largely cooperated until the doors closed. They were treated fairly with severance packages, but that does not lessen the pain. Nissan's leadership set out to keep these employees as potential customers and ambassadors for the future, even though people were losing their jobs. Most people understood this sacrifice was necessary to save the greatest number of jobs over time. Transparency, focus, and execution— three things missing from the ongoing turmoil at GM and United today, and yesterday at U.S. Steel, Eastern Airlines, Xerox, Continental Bank, Polaroid, and Zenith.

Nissan's plan—and any successful revival plan—touches customers. At the end of the day the organization offers products or services that excite customers. Just like good people, great products and services cover many other ills. Lou Gerstner came in to shake up IBM, but it was the people inside IBM that made the changes happen. Proctor and Gamble, another old-line company, has reinvented itself over the last several years, albeit in a little more quiet manner.

7.5   Standardization and Replication

Replication is taking a solution and applying it to the same type or a similar process. *Standardization* is taking the lessons/solution learned and applying them to processes or organizational entities that are different from the original. Standardization and replication reduce variation (see Exhibit 7.6.). These two factors are a key foundation element of the Toyota Production System's standard work.

Replication and standardization are also key outcomes of any enterprise looking to operate as a "learning organization." Too often organizations end up with islands of improvement. Active steps need to be taken to institutionalize new processes and procedures. A map for replication and standardization across the enterprise is shown in Exhibit 7.7.

| | Replication | | | Standardization |
Solution Focus	Pilot	Site	Company-Wide	Similar Process
Solution to reduce cycle time where rented equipment is inspected, serviced, and turned around for new rental	Selected one type of equipment, at one rental location, in 3 different districts	All types of equipment at one rental location in the same 3 districts	All equipment at all locations, in all regions and districts	Adopt a bar code tracking system from original solution is printed as an element of the customer rental agreement and invoice to reduce cycle time

Exhibit 7.6   Example: Solution Standardization

Replication and Standardization Plan

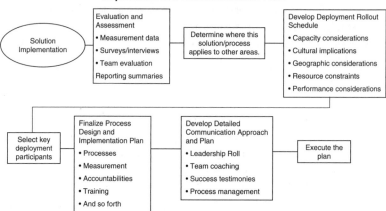

Exhibit 7.7   Replication and Standardization Map

Standardization and replication can be a tough challenge when it bumps up against an organization's cultural norms. Managers stationed at Pitney Bowes customer sites took great pride in their ability to act entrepreneurially and to customize Pitney's services. In their new competitive environment they needed to change. Pitney was losing customers to remote locations in India and elsewhere around the globe that could provide desktop publishing services at a fraction of the cost. So what Pitney needed in their new world was a set of standardized highly cost-effective offerings that provided different degrees of handholding to customers where they provided on-site services. They provide mailroom and back-office services to scores of banks and law firms in New York city. Rather than PB managers sending work backlog to another company down the street, Pitney now has high-speed capacity to support all of its NYC business. They are currently in the process of selecting which of their services will be core offerings in the new competitive environment.[*]

7.6   Clarified Roles and Responsibilities

This is an easy thing to overlook. Perhaps there is a built-in assumption that once the solution is obvious, people will take responsibility for what

---

[*]"Back Where We Belong," Michael Critelli; *Harvard Business Review*; May, 2005.

needs to happen. Unfortunately in today's world, people are already pretty overburdened, and they do not have much extra time on their schedules.

The roles and responsibilities beyond the leadership or project team are not always well thought through. A project team can use a Roles and Responsibilities Matrix for the actual process (Exhibits 7.8 and 7.9). A detailed description of how to use this tool is provided in *The Six Sigma Black Belt Handbook.*

This is easier to do for a process, although it is one of the more difficult steps for a process team. Sometimes people get upset when their responsibilities are modified. In the case of a leadership team looking to make major change happen, roles and responsibilities also need to be addressed.

The ideal Sponsor of a project team owns at least 70 percent of what an improvement team is working on. Otherwise a team is reporting to a sales person (idea sales) and that can make it difficult to move to implementation. In the case of broad scale organizational change you also need a Sponsor or Champion with "clout." Otherwise, not much change is likely to take place. See Exhibit 7.10.

Roles/Decision Clarification Guidelines

R - Responsible — ultimately accountability for completion of the activity. *Only one per activity.*

A - Approval — makes the decision.

C - Consult — involved, contributes but not responsible for the activity, is not the decision maker.

I - Inform — needs information or update from the activity.

↓ Roles Activity →								

MOTOROLA UNIVERSITY   intelligence everywhere

Exhibit 7.8   Roles and Responsibilities Matrix Form

Example: Cross Functional Role and Responsibilities Matrix

Subprocess: Work Planning

Need Identified → Define Work Tasks → Identify Human Resources → Identify Materials → Identify Service Requirements → Review and Approval

Process Roles / Steps	Define Work Tasks	Identify Human Resources	Identify Materials	Identify Service Requirements	Review and Approval
System Owner (System Engineer)	• Check backlog • Review systems • Compare across system for common cause • Review best practices • Set priorities for planner • Combine work requests across functional equipment groups				
Planning Function	• Develop list of tasks to be performed by: • Conducting walkdown • Refer to vendor manuals • Research work history • Refer to Procedures and standardization • Check for other deficient tags	• Match skill level and FTE by discipline to job (how many, how long, skill set type) • Refer to personal qualifications database	• Specify materials	• Identify service provider • Identify requirements	
Operations	• Prioritize emergency and expedite requests • Review and manage routine work	• Validate planning input		• Validate planning input • Initiate search for new provider or validate request	• Review and approve
Maintenance	• Provide input as requested (lead times and delivery dates)	• Review and validate planning input			• Review and approve or recommend, rewrite requirements on an exception basis
Engineering Production Design	• Provide input or evaluation as requested by planner		• Maintain bill of materials and quality levels		• Review and approve

MOTOROLA UNIVERSITY — intelligence everywhere

Exhibit 7.9 Roles and Responsibilities Matrix Example

Digital Six Sigma Governance Plan			
Campaign Target What? By When?	Dashboard Metrics:		
Sponsor(s):	Campaign Manager(s):		
	What?	Who?	When?
Review Process			
Communication Process			
Coaching Support			
Training Plan			
Recognition			

Exhibit 7.10   Six Sigma Governance Plan

7.7   Process and Performance Control Metrics

These key metrics should mostly be known from the work done in the Analyze and Improve phases. But let's just consider here how they play out. Several examples have been used throughout this book regarding Carlos

Ghosn's turnaround at Nissan. They had very specific performance metrics in the Nissan Revival Plan. Big Ys at Nissan included one trillion yen cost reduction, 50 percent reduction in manufacturing capacity, cut number of parts and suppliers in half, launch over 22 new models (automobiles) during the next 3 years, return to profitability and operating margins over 4.5 percent. The metrics in this instance are quite clear. A reduction in the number of suppliers, the reduction of the number of manufacturing platforms, and the reduction in manufacturing capacity were all related to the cost reduction goal. One could argue the Big Y here is the cost target and the others are Little y goals or supporting vital xs, to use Six Sigma language for a moment. The fact is the metrics and metrics targets were very clear.

Nissan is a global manufacturing giant. How do these same concepts apply on a smaller scale?

7.7.1   The Old Town School of Folk Music

The Old Town School of Folk Music (OTSFM) is a small not-for-profit Chicago institution. In the early 1980s the OTSFM was going out of business. It had approximately $200,000 in revenues and was losing $40,000 per year. Not exactly an enviable position. What happened here to turn this institution around? It is a similar story to Nissan. A new executive director, Jim Hirsch, was named at the beginning of the turnaround. Jim and one member of the board reviewed all of the financial numbers and decided what they could control, and where cuts were necessary. Just like the closing of plants was painful for Nissan, so was the laying off of guitar instructors who were already struggling to make a living as artists. The little that the OTSFM paid them was still a meaningful amount in their lives, but an expense the school had to reduce in order to survive.

Each creditor—and there were many—to whom the school owed money, was met. A plan was offered to pay them if they could extend a little more credit to the school. The school also needed to look at its programs and concert offerings to the public. Just like Nissan's cars were boring, the school's programs were pretty much geared to a middle class, white-faced public. If the school wanted to survive over the long term, just like Nissan, it needed to offer exciting products (concerts, lessons, and so forth) and draw in a broader, more diversified customer base.

Growth takes time to build; cost reductions can happen (no matter how painful) immediately. The school faced several tough choices. The school owned two buildings. It was a painful choice, but the school needed to sell one of its buildings so that bills could be paid and agreements kept. The layoffs were even more painful, but amazingly half of the staff that was laid off agreed to work for free during the transition. Once costs were under control, the school expanded its concert offerings and guitar instruction lessons. A whole new program was put together to teach music to little children (under 5 years). Jim put together a Latin music festival that was the first such offering in Chicago by a non-Latino institution.

A number of other changes were also made, but cost reductions came first. And the metrics for the school, while simpler than Nissan, were very much the same—reduce excess teaching capacity, free up cash, pull down all nonvital cost, make and keep agreements, and fulfill all commitments made.

Fifteen years later the school has had a renaissance. Its revenues are in excess of $7 million, it has renovated its old building and purchased a new one, its programs are full, and there is a very healthy involvement of volunteers, customers, and staff at the school. It impacts more people's lives today than at any time in its history.

The key thing about metrics is they need to be few in number, and the organization's leadership needs to believe they are important enough to take action if they begin to move out of alignment. If an organization has too many metrics, or if leadership and associates do not believe in the credibility of the metric system, then it becomes a useless exercise that simply sucks life out of the institution.

7.8   Financial Assessment

Cost reduction is not the only goal in life. As a matter of fact, if an organization only focuses on reducing cost, it will never be a great company or a great organization. Greatness comes from doing things that people care about. Carlos Ghosn said, "There's no problem in a car company that good products can't solve." This is true of most organizations. It is perhaps a slight overstatement because distribution of the product, market awareness (that you have it), and a few other fundamentals also hold true. While the world may not beat a path to your door, all other things being equal, the organization with great products will do much better than the rest.

The very beginning of this book talked about the scenario, "I had a million dollars in savings, but my P&L did not change." The Financial Bridge Model offers one approach to better manage turning savings into dollars. This Financial Report does not need to be complex. A quarterly savings report from a global electronics manufacturer is shown in Exhibit 7.11.

Date: _____

| Project Name | Group | BU | Division | Actual Hard$ Savings (000's) *No more than 12 months savings to be shown* | | | | | | | | | | | Projected Annual S$ Savings (000s) | Projected B/S Improvement Y-T-D (000's) | Actual B/S Improvement Y-T-D (000's) | Process Owner | Black Belt |
				Q1	Q2	Q3	Q4	FY One Total	Q1	Q2	Q3	Q4	FY Two Total	Total 12 Month Savings					
Project 1																			
Project 2																			
.																			
.																			
.																			
.																			
.																			
.																			
.																			
.																			
Project n																			
Corporate Total																			

Exhibit 7.11 Six Sigma Savings Report Form

To simplify this example, the current quarterly reporting number columns were pulled out. The organization has several hundred projects underway. The senior executive staff focuses on less than 15 global projects.

7.9   Leadership Governance and Sustaining the Gains

Organizations still fall short in one primary area: budgets are rarely adjusted to reflect the gains from improvement projects. This has been a classic problem in every major improvement initiative over the last 20 years. In TQM initiatives, people were actively discouraged from adjusting the budgets for fear that would lessen enthusiasm for improvement. Today if a project is supposed to increase revenues by 20 percent, then the related budget needs to be bumped up an additional percentage beyond the original expectation, unless the project being worked is a specific commitment (initiative) in the current year's plan, and implementation is being done to hit specific current year commitments.

We discuss leadership governance further in a separate chapter, but because it is a key part of control, it will be covered here also. The whole idea of the Financial Bridge Model is to understand what is happening with earnings on a year-to-year basis. Earnings are the most visible number seen by shareholders, bankers, and senior executives. While shareholders are not the only key stakeholder, they are a pretty influential group, especially for large publicly held enterprises. If an organization is going to have true, meaningful improvement, leadership must be actively involved and balance the interest of all key stakeholders.

The senior executive level, at the very top of the organization, should be focused on three to four key business goals at the most *where change is needed.* Anything more than that and there is not much focus. The executive group will look at more than three numbers for sure. But for the most part, if something was done well last year, it is most likely to be done well this year. Momentum makes many things happen. And unless some of the control dials begin to show fluctuation, the actions an organization does well do not need the same level of attention as the actions an organization hopes to change.

Leaders execute their focus on a very few priorities that everyone can grasp. Why just a few? First, anybody who thinks through the logic of a business will see that focusing on three or four priorities will produce the best results from the resources at hand. Second, people in contemporary organizations need a small number of clear priorities to execute as well. When decision making is decentralized, as in a matrixed organization, people at many levels have to make endless trade-offs. There's competition for resources and ambiguity over decision rights and working relationships. Without carefully thought out and clear priorities, people can get bogged down in warfare over who gets what, and why. A leader who says, "I've got ten priorities," doesn't know, himself, what the most important things are.[*]

A senior leadership team at a business unit level ideally looks at 10 or fewer projects at any given time. If the list is any longer than that the group probably loses focus. This means the senior leadership is intimately familiar with up to 10 projects, some of which may not be in a particular executive's line of responsibility. The key projects should not just be a number on a page or a name on a list, which the leadership team knows little about. They've got to understand in depth the key milestones, have debated the assumptions behind the numbers, and improved the quality of those projects as a result of their discussion. At GE and Allied Signal this is called a *healthy debate*. You cannot set realistic or challenging goals until the assumptions have been debated.

For example, if one of the organization's key priorities is to roll out a new product, the discussion does not end when the project teams says, "We will increase sales by 20 percent as a result of this new product." For the leadership team to have more in-depth understanding they need to ask questions like:

- Which customers are targeted for these new products? *Then probe.*
- Why would they buy from us? *Then probe.*
- Who makes the buying decision? *Then probe further or start a new line of questioning.*
- Will the new product cannibalize existing products?
- How/when/where will materials be sourced? And so forth.

Probing down, challenging assumptions (not trashing people), increasing the learning for everyone involved in the discussion, and the leadership team offering ideas, are the factors that teams should consider.

During implementation of the Nissan Revival Plan, senior executives looked at critical commitments on a monthly basis. People were held accountable for coming forward early if a problem arose and otherwise were expected to

---

[*]Bossidy and Charan; *Execution—The Discipline of Getting Things Done;* p. 69.

deliver the results. But leadership did not just look at numbers. The assumptions made by project teams were challenged and they were encouraged to run as far with the improvement as they could. This open dialog is key for any enterprise to gain an in-depth understanding of what is important and what is real.

If people desire a longer list, the critical (top 10) projects should be segregated from the rest of the pack. Additional ones could be there for informational purposes, but they should belong to the realm of subordinates and outside the scope of the leadership team. Consider it an opportunity for the leadership team to trust their subordinates.

The report shown in Exhibit 7.12 includes key summary information: project name, key goals impacted (Big Y), estimated and realized savings, Champion and Black Belts on the project, and how far along the project is in the DMAIC problem/opportunity cycle. This particular form was used for Six Sigma project-related reporting, but it could apply to any improvement methodology.

The management levels below senior executives should also be looking at a list of 10 or fewer projects. Obviously, if your boss is looking at a project, it most likely makes your list. Once you have covered the projects of concern to people higher in the organization related to your responsibilities and controllable resources, additional projects can be added. All functions and departments will not be working on every one of the leadership team's projects. So there should be slots available to add a few more.

Nissan had nine cross-functional teams. Each of those teams spun off subteams. But the nine core teams were responsible and accountable for reporting at the executive level. Ten or less, ideally five or less, is a manageable number.

Managing projects this way clarifies priorities. Everyone clearly knows which projects are most important and which projects should preempt lower (less strategic) projects if there is a conflicting demand over use of resources.

"What gets monitored is what gets done." This popular phrase has many variations. While it may not be true 100 percent of the time, it is still a key part of maintaining any gains. Numerous studies have shown that up to 70 percent of improvement gains are lost in the next three to 6 months. Is this due to resistance to change or some other evil force? Not likely. Think about

Vital X Project	Big Y	Sub Y	Estimated $ Savings	Actual $ Value	Champion	BB	DMAIC Phase	Target End Date
Project 1	New Product Dev.	Innovation	$xxx	$xxx	Howard J	Lynn	Measure	xx/xx/xx
Project 2	Quality Leap	Operating Cost	$xxx	$xxx	Martin Y	Kate	Define	xx/xx/xx
Project 3	Customer Acquisition	Revenue	$xxx	$xxx	Mary L	Andy	Control	xx/xx/xx
Project 4	Cost Target	Operating Cost	$xxx	$xxx	Margret	Lynne	Analyze	xx/xx/xx
Total			$CCCC	$CCCC				

Exhibit 7.12 Six Sigma Governance Report Form

what happens on a day-to-day basis. People are under time pressures. When it comes to getting work done, which way is simplest and which way is fastest? Probably not the new way! So what tends to happen is exceptions get made. Just this one time, let's do it the old way—just this one more time. Over time the gains just drift slowly away; it's hard to even notice while it is happening.

So the metrics, for better or worse, become a key part of sustaining any gains and leadership governance. They provide a reference point. The more visual the metrics, the easier they are to maintain, and the more credibility in the number, the more likely they will foster the desired new behaviors and results. For most operational (manufacturing and distribution) processes appropriate metrics probably already exist. For most administrative or professional processes, they probably do not exist. Earlier in the book we describe how leading metrics are better than lagging metrics. Sometimes output metrics are the only ones available. If that is the case, fine, but if a leading indicator can be identified, it will result in earlier action.

A health care foundation that funds health-related research projects uses time as its key metric. The institution always looked to turn around proposal ideas in a 6-week period, but they just had the one overall date. At the end of the period they either met the date, or they missed it. It turned out they were missing it about 45 percent of the time. So in addition to making a few process changes, they added a few more date gates, which provided a leading indicator for the overall process. The process began with a review of the idea, a go forward to explore this proposed project or to reject it; that date kicked off a timeline. The next date was to get a full proposal from the research institution and complete all internal reviews, where again a "go/no go" decision was made. For accepted proposals, the funds needed to be released to the research institution; this was the final date.

This information provided the leadership team with data they could use for more profound knowledge and action. One result was leadership learned that workload spikes would take place periodically, overburdening some of the funding program staffs. This led to a backup plan where program staffs that did not have heavy loads stepped in and assisted another group with heavy volumes. A number of benefits accrued to the organization as a result of these activities: less overtime, improved customer satisfaction (due to timeliness), improved proposal reviews, and so forth.

Financial managers who simply run a company by the numbers may hold things together for a while, but when they leave, the house of cards usually crumbles. Remember just a few: ITT and Harold Geneen, International Harvester and Archie McCardell, or Robert McNamara and Vietnam, and his reign at the World Bank; all were numbers judges and each of those organizations had major problems after the "by the numbers" executive left. And if unethical behaviors were added to the list for number manipulation or downright fraud, the list of problematic organizations would be much longer.

With a year remaining in the Nissan Revival Plan, Carlos Ghosn refers to the sequel as *Nissan 180*, which sets future growth targets from which the *180* figure is derived: One million more units sold globally in 2005 than in 2001, an 8 percent operating profit margin, and zero debt.[*] "The key facts and figures point to one reality," Mr. Ghosn says. "Nissan is in bad shape."[†] It just goes to show that you never get there. New challenges always lie waiting in the future.

7.9.1   Control or Let it Go?

In Lou Gerstner Jr.'s successful turnaround of IBM in the 1990s, he learned the surprising importance of emotional persuasion. This type of story must be simple, easy to identify with, emotionally meaningful, and suggest positive rather than negative consequences. When Gerstner took over as CEO, he was fixated on what had worked for him throughout his career: coolheaded analysis and strategy. He thought he could revive the company through maneuvers such as selling assets and cutting costs. He quickly found that those tools weren't nearly enough. He needed to transform the entrenched corporate culture, which had become hidebound and overly bureaucratic. That meant changing the attitudes and behaviors of hundreds of thousands of employees. In his memoir Gerstner writes that he realized he needed to make a powerful emotional appeal to them to "shake them out of their depressed stupor, remind them of who they were—you're IBM, Damn it!" Rather than sitting in a corner office negotiating deals and analyzing spreadsheets, he needed to convey passion through thousands of hours of personal appearances. Gerstner, who is often brittle and imperious in private, nonetheless responded admirably to the challenge. He proved to be an engaging and emotional public speaker when he took his campaign to his huge workforce.

---

[*]*Ward's Auto World*, Feb 1, 2002.
[†]"Nissan 'in Bad Shape,' But Now Has the Plan;" Bill Visnic and Mack Chrysler; *Ward's Auto World,* Dec 1, 1999.

7.9.2   Reframing the Case for Change

We discussed this concept earlier in the book with the example of a poor school district in Misiones, Argentina. Here is an additional perspective on the power of reframing the problem. Approximately 600,000 people in the United States have heart bypass surgery every year; 1.3 million heart patients have angioplasties—all with a cost in excess of $30 billion. The procedures temporarily relieve chest pains but rarely prevent heart attacks or prolong lives. Half the time, the bypass grafts clog up again in a few years, the angioplasties in a few months. Many people could avoid this problem by switching to healthier life styles, but few do. Dr. Dean Ornish realized the importance of going beyond the facts. "Providing health information is important, but not always sufficient," he says. "We also need to bring in the psychological, emotional, and spiritual dimensions that are so often ignored." He established a holistic program that focused on diet, and patients attended twice-weekly sessions led by a psychologist. They also took instruction in yoga and aerobic exercise. The program only lasted for 3 years, but a study found that 77 percent of the patients stuck with the lifestyle changes and safely avoided future surgery. Mutual of Omaha, the insurer for patients in this study, saved over $30,000 per patient compared to traditional treatments.[*]

Nothing is magic about the specifics of Dr. Ornish's work: the idea is to move beyond the problem staring you in the face and look for more holistic alternative approaches. At Nissan, they changed the performance measurement system, provided more focus on a new business direction, increased accountability, and communicated, communicated, communicated. Employees at Nissan were feeling beaten, depressed, and inferior to Toyota and even Hyundai, and the company faced bankruptcy. Once leadership created a new direction, they shared progress with employees, stayed positive on the opportunities, and shared successes along the way. And, far from a Pollyanna view of the world, they demanded new performance. The leadership team also said, "If they could not deliver the goals and objectives laid out in that first two-year plan, they should be fired." These big decisions and the thousands of smaller decisions made in alignment with the "Big Y's" so clearly expressed by the leadership team caused a major transformation of this enterprise. Today Nissan enjoys a profit margin at the top of its industry.

---

[*]"Change or Die," Alan Deutschman, *Fast Company*; May, 2005.

7.10   Control—Team Sponsor's Role and Responsibilities

The "easy" part of the project is completed. It's after the team disbands that the wheels can fall off the cart. Organizations that do not plan on how to control the gains ahead of time risk losing the gains shortly after the improvement team is disbanded. From project day one, the Sponsor and the team should be giving consideration to how the gain (the improvements) gets sustained over time (see Exhibit 7.13.)

A number of studies have been published over the last 10 years indicating rates of failure ranging from 30 to 70 percent. Is this simply due to resistance to change? Probably not! Think about how hard it is to learn something new to a high skill level. If you've ever played tennis and did not initially learn to watch the ball all the way into the racquet, you know how hard it is to change that behavior. You know you should do it, and if your opponent hits a soft shot you probably can, but if the ball comes whistling back across the net, it is all too easy to revert to your old ways. The same is true with organizations. People are usually willing to try the new way. But what happens during the first crunch period or crisis? We move to automatic, or someone says, "I know we are supposed to follow this new procedure, but if we just make this one exception and do it the old way, I can get it out much faster." One exception follows another and we simply drift back to our old ways, then "Poof!"—the gain is gone.

The Sponsor needs to plan ahead of time, and to work with the team during the course of their project to identify ways to sustain the changes. Simply posting the results and developing a few measures to maintain the gains over time can go a long way toward sustaining the gains. It is also necessary to keep a spotlight on the changes, until the new behaviors are burned in. New habits are hard to learn. Dr. W. Edwards Deming once said, "It takes 25 repetitions to burn in a new habit." If something is only done once a month or once a week, this can take a long time.

To change behaviors, one literally needs to forge new neural pathways in the brain and, once they're initially formed, they need reinforcement over and over. New scanning methods show that this deep section of the brain lights up when we develop and express sequential motor acts, and also in response to rewards. With the new ability for researchers to see the brain's electrical activity while learning is in progress, they can actually see patterns of activity change permanently after learning takes place. Learning a habit is different from other kinds of learning; often we are not aware of developing a habit, and we develop it slowly over time. "The process doesn't seem to go in reverse, or else we

Six Sigma Sponsor—Key Project Activities

1.0 Define Opportunities
- Choose a team leader.
- Review Charter and project scope for focus, clarity.
- Share the business case.
- Budget and provide resources for team.
- Reallocate work to allow for team member participation.
- Assure adequate multi-disciplinary representation on the team.
- Establish empowerment guidelines for team.

2.0 Measure Performance
- Assure the relevance of the project metrics.
- Evaluate the gathering p...
- Review bas... results.
- Identif... and C...
- Assure... numb... and C...

3.0
- Validate the improvement.
- Evaluate the financial impact.
- Assure disciplined follow-through of the proposed approach.
- Assess Black Belt performance.
- Celebrate and reward.
- Facilitate transfer of improved process to the Process Owner.
- Develop Pilot Plan and Pilot Solution
- Verify Sigma Improvement Resulted from Solution
- Identify If Additional Projects are Necessary to Achieve the Goal
- Integrate
- Identify and Integrate Lessons Learned from Project

4.0 Measure Performance
- ...ss the ...cality of the ...sed approach.
- ...sit the ...benefit ...sis.
- ...see ...mentation and ...yment plans.
- ...nsus in support ... teams
- ...organizational
- ...nce decision
- ...rs to implement
- ...ges.

5.0 Control Performance
- Validate the improvement.
- Evaluate the financial impact.
- Assure disciplined follow-through of the proposed approach.
- Assess Black Belt performance.
- Celebrate and reward.
- Facilitate transfer of improved process to the Process Owner.

Project Governance

Change Mgmt.

Advocacy & Culture
- Retain alignment (at BB level, at Sponsor level).
- Conduct weekly project review meetings (30–60 min).
- ...nven
- Model and communicate Six Sigma.
- ...and ... issues ...s.
- Apply consequences.

Exhibit 7.13 Six Sigma Sponsor Responsibilities—5.0 Control Performance

265

don't have access to the means to reverse it," Professor Graybiel said,[*] "Unlike an association between an object and a word ('Oh, so that's a blue jay!'), learning a habit is very slow. It takes many repetitions, often reinforced with positive feedback, before an action or series of actions become a habit." Strong positive or negative motivators help develop or break habits. Positive feedback works better than negative. "The brain has an absolutely fabulous system for getting reward signals," said Professor Graybiel. The system is so sensitive that researchers have seen nerve cells fire in response to a single word, evoking a craving long after an old habit has been kicked.[†]

The degree to which communications have been maintained throughout the project can go a long way toward preparing people in the organization for change. A periodic walk through by a senior manager to check on "Did the change stick?" is valuable and communicates the importance of the project. Clear lines of accountability will also help to sustain changes once the spotlight of the team event has passed.

7.10.1   Control Phase Questions—Management Perspective

1. Did the team conduct a pilot of the new process? What was learned and changed as a result of the pilot?
2. What is the new process result (Sigma)? Has the project achieved its goals? Has the team demonstrated the new results with data?
3. Is the learning transferable across the business? What is the action plan for spreading the best practice? What lessons did the team learn?
4. What are the variables being monitored to assure that process performance improvement continues?
5. What training has been conducted to assure the new process runs as expected? How are new habits or behaviors being learned?
6. What are the financial results of the project? How have they been calculated and documented? What changes is the customer seeing?
7. Are there any spin-off projects from this one?

7.11   Case Study

The senior leadership team knew they had some problems to address. Part of their challenge was that TBU had a long history of success. In many ways

---

[*]http://web.mit.edu/newsoffice/tt/1999/sep22/habit.html.
[†]"TechTalk," MIT News Office, Deborah Halber, 9/22/99, http://web.mit.edu/newsoffice/tt/1999/sep22/habit.html.

letting go of the past was their most difficult challenge. The steps they took killing a new product also helped in the Control phase. It established credibility that leadership would act, rather than just talk.

The leadership team also took this opportunity to really incorporate Six Sigma into their business practices rather that just thinking about Six Sigma as an improvement project tool. At a TBU planning retreat, Ted, VP of Operations, stated, "We really should not be doing anything at our level with Six Sigma; that is not something we would have needed to do anyway to improve our business."

This comment opened up a whole new paradigm for the management team. Rather than talking about "What do we need to improve?" the conversation shifted to "What do we need to do with our business?" They had recently started up a new manufacturing operation in China. The initial production was exported from China, but they also had many opportunities to sell in China. They decided to launch a new team, using Six Sigma's DMAIC methodology to plan their course of action. They took a similar approach to environmental compliance with new European regulations.

These actions further reinforced the new behaviors they were looking to adopt as a leadership team. In the past, they tended to go from, "what is the problem," to, "what is a solution," and then run with it. Now they did a much better job of defining the problem, seeing that evidence was gathered to support it, and using the Analysis phase to foster development of several workable solutions instead of running with the first workable solution that someone came up with in the past.

TBU also instituted a two-tier Balanced Score Card. The core score card tracked business fundamentals—orders, revenue, inventory, inventory days, and so forth. They are tracked on a monthly basis with corrective action taken immediately. They also had a Business Priorities Score Card (same quadrants) that identified and tracked specific initiatives necessary to deliver the business basics. They track this score card on a quarterly basis—also employing corrective actions to resolve issues. All Six Sigma projects were initiated from the Business Priorities Score Card.

7.12   Control Phase—Tollgate Questions

As the team progresses through the Control phase, the leadership team should meet with the Sponsor/Champion and Master Black Belt to review everything that has been accomplished. The team can use these questions to make certain they have covered all the important items. At the completion of the Improve phase, the team members, team leader, Master Black Belt, and Champion should feel comfortable with the answers to all of the following questions and any others that might be specific to the organization.

1. How has the scorecard been integrated into the management review process?
2. What is the leadership team doing to guide, monitor, and support the performance improvement process?
3. How is the leadership team keeping in touch with the organization's top three improvement priorities?
4. How are improvement projects being transferred from project team responsibilities to line management responsibilities?
5. Did the team conduct a pilot of the new process? What was learned and changed as a result of the pilot?
6. Describe the implementation plan. How will the plan be monitored to ensure its success? Who is accountable?
7. What are the potential problems with the plan? What are the contingency plans?
8. What controls are in place to assure that the problem does not reoccur?
9. Who is the process owner? How will the responsibility for continued review be transferred from the improvement team to the process owner? How frequent are the reviews?
10. What is being measured? What evidence does the team have that would indicate the process is "in control"? What are the variables being monitored to assure that process performance improvement continues?
11. How well and consistently is the process performing? Is a response plan in place for when the process experiences "out-of-control" occurrences?
12. How has the process been standardized? Have the process changes been documented?
13. How has the training plan been revised from the Improve phase? How has training been conducted to assure understanding of the process changes? How effective was this training? What continuing issues need to be addressed in the area of training?
14. What is the communication plan for implementation? How will the team use communications to manage this change, minimize resistance, and mobilize stakeholders?
15. Based on the implementation and communications with key stakeholders, what are the barriers to successful change? What actions are planned to overcome these barriers?

16. Was the solution tested on a small scale? How representative was the test? How are the learnings from the pilot integrated into the implementation plan?
17. What gains or benefits have been realized from the implementation?
18. What are the financial results of the project? How have they been calculated and documented? What changes are the customer seeing?
19. How can the improvements be replicated elsewhere in the organization? What is the action plan for spreading best practice?
20. What did the team learn from the project? What are the best methods to share the learnings of the team?

Chapter

8

Assessment Instruments

If everyone is thinking alike, then somebody isn't thinking.

GEORGE S. PATTON

There are a number of national assessment instruments available to organizations:

- Malcolm Baldrige National Quality Program (which was the first of these instruments)
- Software capability evaluation (CMM/SEI)—from Carnegie Mellon University
- People capability model (also at SEI)
- Shingo Prize for Excellence in Manufacturing
- Others: Deming award criteria—Japan's national quality award, Industry Week's Best Plants award, and so forth

Some people love these criteria and have spent countless hours preparing award applications. Other people feel, given the complexity of applying for these various awards and certifications, that they are not worth the effort. Motorola, for disclosure purposes, was a two-time Baldrige Award winner. So perhaps there is a bias in our thinking that you, the reader, need to take into account.

Here is a summary of the above award/certification programs for your information. Personally, we find the criteria very valuable, but one needs to be careful not to get too crazy with applying for awards. Some organizations merely focus on getting the award. They lose sight of the "real" changes these criteria intend to cause in a business.

8.1 Malcolm Baldrige Quality Award

This was the first U.S. version of a national quality award. Japan's Deming Prize was in place many years before. President Reagan signed the Malcolm

Baldrige National Quality Award Improvement Act on April 20, 1987. The award criteria have changed a lot since its original incarnation:

Original Criteria	2005
Leadership	Leadership
Information and analysis	Strategic planning
Strategic quality planning	Customer and market focus
Human resource	Measurement, analysis, and knowledge management
Management of quality process	Human resource focus
	Process management
	Business results

Not even knowing the detailed descriptions of each classification, it is pretty easy to tell there was a shift toward business results and objective data. Quite a few states in the United States, provinces in Canada, and other countries around the world have used these criteria to create their own versions of awards for excellence. Versions have also been created for health care, education, and government excellence.

The criteria were intended to accomplish three things:

1. Improve organizational performance improvement practices
2. Facilitate communication and sharing of best practices
3. Serve as a working tool for understanding and managing performance and for guiding organizational planning and opportunities for learning

Robert Austin in *Measuring and Managing Performance in Organizations* puts all of these award descriptions in a chapter titled "The Measurement Disease." So he does not see a lot of value added from using these instruments. Personally we feel there is much merit in understanding the criteria, and using them as a guide for improving the "improvement process." If an organization applies for these awards, especially at a state level, they can have a free team of outsiders come in and assess the organization's application against the criteria. This can definitely point out improvement opportunities. Applicants for the national award are less likely to receive a site visit.

We describe the Baldrige Award criteria in detail in the Baldrige National Quality Program section. The information was taken directly from the 2005 award instruction booklet, available from www.baldrige.org.

We condensed it somewhat, mostly dropping Notes sections and paragraph reference numbers. If you are working on amending your Six Sigma financial reporting and tracking systems or simply looking to improve your improvement processes, we suggest you read it.

8.2   Capability Maturity Model Integration

Carnegie Mellon's Software Engineering Institute sponsors these assessment criteria. The Capability Maturity Model Integration (CMMI) for software is a model used by many organizations to identify best practices. Originally known as the SEI/CMM software maturity model, it is used to help increase the maturity (efficiency and effectiveness) of software development processes. There are multiple CMMI models available. Consequently, people need to decide which CMMI model best fits their organization's process improvement needs. The models have been shown to facilitate process improvement, increasing product and service quality as organizations apply it to achieve their business objectives. Today, the CMMI is intended to facilitate process improvement by providing the latest best practices for product and service development and maintenance.

In CMMI models with a staged representation, there are five maturity levels, each a layer in the foundation for ongoing process improvement, designated by the numbers 1 to 5:

1. Initial
2. Managed
3. Defined
4. Quantitatively managed
5. Optimizing

8.2.1   Maturity Level Details[*]

Maturity levels consist of a predefined set of process areas. The maturity levels are measured by the achievement of the specific and generic goals that apply to each predefined set of process areas. The following sections describe the characteristics of each maturity level in detail.

---

[*]*Capability Maturity Model Integration*; Carnegie Mellon University, System Engineering Institute, Copyright 2002.

There are five levels of the CMM. According to the SEI, "Predictability, effectiveness, and control of an organization's software processes are believed to improve as the organization moves up these five levels. While not rigorous, the empirical evidence to date supports this belief."

Initial

- At maturity level 1, processes are usually ad hoc and chaotic. The organization usually does not provide a stable environment. Success in these organizations depends on the competence and heroics of the people in the organization and not on the use of proven processes. In spite of this ad hoc, chaotic environment, maturity level 1 organizations often produce products and services that work; however, they frequently exceed the budget and schedule of their projects.
- Maturity level 1 organizations are characterized by a tendency to overcommit, abandon processes in the time of crisis, and not be able to repeat their past successes.

Repeatable

- At maturity level 2, software development successes are repeatable. The organization may use some basic project management to track cost and schedule.
- Process discipline helps ensure that existing practices are retained during times of stress. When these practices are in place, projects are performed and managed according to their documented plans.
- Project status and the delivery of services are visible to management at defined points (for example, at major milestones and at the completion of major tasks).

Defined

- At maturity level 3, processes are well characterized and understood, and are described in standards, procedures, tools, and methods.
- The organization's set of standard processes, which is the basis for level 3, is established and improved over time. These standard processes are used to establish consistency across the organization. Projects establish their defined processes by tailoring the organization's set of standard processes according to tailoring guidelines.
- The organization's management establishes process objectives based on the organization's set of standard processes and ensures that these objectives are appropriately addressed.
- A critical distinction between level 2 and level 3 is the scope of standards, process descriptions, and procedures. At level 2, the

standards, process descriptions, and procedures may be quite different in each specific instance of the process (for example, on a particular project). At level 3, the standards, process descriptions, and procedures for a project are tailored from the organization's set of standard processes to suit a particular project or organizational unit.

Managed

- Using precise measurements, management can effectively control the software development effort. In particular, management can identify ways to adjust and adapt the process to particular projects without measurable losses of quality or deviations from specifications.
- Subprocesses are selected that significantly contribute to overall process performance. These selected subprocesses are controlled using statistical and other quantitative techniques.
- A critical distinction between maturity level 3 and maturity level 4 is the predictability of process performance. At maturity level 4, the performance of processes is controlled using statistical and other quantitative techniques, and is quantitatively predictable. At maturity level 3, processes are only qualitatively predictable.

Optimizing

- Maturity level 5 focuses on continually improving process performance through both incremental and innovative technological improvements. Quantitative process-improvement objectives for the organization are established, continually revised to reflect changing business objectives, and used as criteria in managing process improvement. The effects of deployed process improvements are measured and evaluated against the quantitative process-improvement objectives. Both the defined processes and the organization's set of standard processes are targets of measurable improvement activities.
- Process improvements to address common causes of process variation and measurably improve the organization's processes are identified, evaluated, and deployed.
- Optimizing processes in an agile and innovative way depends on the participation of an empowered workforce aligned with the business values and objectives of the organization. The organization's ability to rapidly respond to changes and opportunities is enhanced by finding ways to accelerate and share learning.
- A critical distinction between maturity level 4 and maturity level 5 is the type of process variation addressed. At maturity level 4, processes

are concerned with addressing special causes of process variation and providing statistical predictability of the results. Though processes may produce predictable results, the results may be insufficient to achieve the established objectives. At maturity level 5, processes are concerned with addressing common causes of process variation and changing the process (that is, shifting the mean of the process performance) to improve process performance (while maintaining statistical predictability) to achieve the established quantitative process-improvement objectives.

Some of Motorola's business units have used these criteria and found them to be very valuable. The following performance targets and scores are from Motorola's Global Software Group.[*]

Metric	Goal	Actual
Cost of poor quality	8%	6.4%
Cost of quality	35%	42%
Cycle time reduction (X factor)	1.6x	1.62x
Customer satisfaction	8.5	8.8

Again the criteria are powerful. For an organization with many software developers and complex systems this assessment instrument offers a powerful set of assessment and organizing criteria. But it is not simple, and takes a fair amount of resources to implement.

8.3   People Capability Maturity Model[†]

The People Capability Maturity Model (People CMM) is a framework that helps organizations successfully address their critical people issues. Based on the best current practices in fields such as human resources, knowledge management, and organizational development, the People CMM guides organizations in improving their processes for managing and developing their workforces. The People CMM helps organizations characterize the

---

[*]http://www.sei.cmu.edu/cmmi/results/state_39.html
[†]http://www.sei.cmu.edu/cmm-p/version2/

maturity of their workforce practices, establish a program of continuous workforce development, set priorities for improvement actions, integrate workforce development with process improvement, and establish a culture of excellence. Since its release in 1995, thousands of copies of the People CMM have been distributed, and it is used worldwide by organizations, small and large.

The People CMM consists of five maturity levels that establish successive foundations for continuously improving individual competencies, developing effective teams, motivating improved performance, and shaping the workforce the organization needs to accomplish its future business plans. Each maturity level is a well-defined evolutionary plateau that institutionalizes new capabilities for developing the organization's workforce. By following the maturity framework, an organization can avoid introducing workforce practices that its employees are unprepared to implement effectively.

Given the commonality of sponsorship this assessment instrument parallels the CMMI model described earlier.

8.4   Shingo Prize for Excellence in Manufacturing*

The prize was established in 1988 to promote awareness of Lean manufacturing concepts and recognize companies in the United States, Canada, and Mexico that achieve world-class manufacturing status. The Shingo Prize philosophy is that world-class business performance may be achieved through focused improvements in core manufacturing and business processes.

The Shingo Prize for excellence in manufacturing is named for Japanese industrial engineer Shigeo Shingo who distinguished himself as one of the world's leading experts in improving manufacturing processes. Dr. Shingo has been described as an "engineering genius" who helped create and write about many aspects of the revolutionary manufacturing practices which comprise the renowned Toyota Production System.

The mission of the Shingo Prize is to:

- Facilitate increased awareness of excellent-to-world class manufacturing practices and techniques that maintain and enhance a company's competitive position in the global marketplace

---

*http://www.shingoprize.org/AboutUs/

- Foster an understanding and sharing of successful core manufacturing and business improvement methodologies
- Encourage research in all aspects of manufacturing by both academic and business practitioners

This prize started out focusing on manufacturing, with a heavy emphasis on setup time reduction. It has expanded to include a research prize to promote research and writing regarding new knowledge and understanding of manufacturing processes.

Its assessment classifications include:

- Leadership culture and infrastructure
- Manufacturing strategies and system integration
- Nonmanufacturing support functions
- Quality, cost, and delivery
- Business results
- Summary of achievements

So it is similar to the Baldrige criteria, but focuses more on manufacturing.

8.5   Baldrige National Quality Program: Criteria for Performance Excellence[*]

Senior Leadership

Describe how senior leaders guide and sustain your organization. Describe how senior leaders communicate with employees and encourage high performance.

Vision and Values

- How do senior leaders set organizational vision and values? How do senior leaders communicate, deploy your organization's vision and values through your leadership *system to* all employees, key suppliers and partners, and customers, as appropriate? How do their personal actions reflect a commitment to the organization's values?
- How do senior leaders create, promote an environment that fosters and requires legal and ethical behavior?
- How do senior leaders create a sustainable organization? How do senior leaders create an environment for empowerment performance

---

[*]Source: Baldrige National Quality Program; 2005 Award Criteria; http://www.baldrige.org/

improvement, accomplishment of strategic objectives, innovation, and organizational agility? How do they create an environment for organizational and employee learning? How do they personally participate in succession planning and the development of future organizational leaders?

Communication and Organizational Performance

- How do senior leaders communicate with, empower, and motivate all employees throughout the organization? How do senior leaders ensure, encourage frank, two-way communication on these topics throughout the organization? How do senior leaders take an active role in employee reward and recognition to reinforce high performance and a customer and business focus?
- How do senior leaders create a focus on action to accomplish the organization's objectives, improve performance, and attain your vision? How do senior leaders include a focus on creating and balancing value for customers and other stakeholders in their organizational performance expectations?

Note

- A sustainable organization is capable of addressing current business needs and possesses the agility and strategic management to prepare successfully for its future business and market environment. In this context, the concept of innovation includes both technological and organizational innovation to succeed in the future.
- A focus on action considers both the people and the hard assets of the organization. It includes ongoing improvements in productivity that may be achieved through eliminating waste or reducing cycle time, and it might use techniques such as Six Sigma and Lean Production. It also includes the actions to accomplish the organization's strategic objectives.

Governance and Social Responsibilities

Describe your organization's governance system. Describe how your organization addresses its responsibilities to the public, ensures ethical behavior, and practices good citizenship.

Organizational Governance

- How does your organization address the following key factors in your governance system:
  - Accountability for management's actions

- ○ Fiscal accountability
- ○ Transparency in operations and selection and disclosure policies for governance board members, as appropriate
- ○ Independence in internal and external audits
- ○ Protection of stakeholder and stockholder interests, as appropriate
- How do you evaluate the performance of your senior leaders, including the chief executive? How do you evaluate the performance of members of the governance board, as appropriate? How do senior leaders and the governance board use these performance reviews to improve both their personal leadership effectiveness and that of your board and leadership system as appropriate?

Legal and Ethical Behavior

- How do you address any adverse impacts on society of your products, services, and operations? How do you anticipate public concerns with current and future products, services, and operations? How do you prepare for these concerns in a proactive manner, including using resource-sustaining processes, as appropriate? What are your key compliance processes, measures, and goals for achieving and surpassing regulatory and legal requirements, as appropriate? What are your key processes, measures, or indicators for addressing risks associated with your products, services, and operations?
- How does your organization promote and ensure ethical behavior in all your interactions? What are your key processes, measures, and goals for enabling and monitoring ethical behavior in your governance structure, throughout your organization, and in interactions with customers and partners? How do you monitor and respond to breaches of ethical behavior?

Support of Key Communities

- How does your organization actively support and strengthen your key communities? How do you identify key communities and determine areas of emphasis for organizational involvement and support? What are your key communities? How do your senior leaders and your employees contribute to improving these communities?

Strategy Development

Describe how your organization establishes its strategy and strategic objectives including how you address your strategic challenges.

Strategy Development Process

- How does your organization conduct its strategic planning? What are the key process steps? Who are the key participants? How does your process identify potential blind spots? What are your short- and longer-term planning time horizons? How are these time horizons set? How does your strategic planning process address these time horizons?
- How do you ensure that strategic planning addresses the key factors listed next? How do you collect and analyze relevant data and information pertaining to these factors as part of your strategic planning *process:*
  - Your organization's strengths, weaknesses, opportunities, and threats
  - Early indications of major shifts in technology, markets, competition, or the regulatory environment
  - Long-term organizational sustainability and business continuity in emergencies
  - Your ability to execute the strategic plan

Strategic Objectives

- What are your key strategic objectives and your timetable for accomplishing them?
- What are your most important goals for these strategic objectives?
- How do your strategic objectives address the challenges identified in response to in your organizational profile? How do you ensure that your strategic objectives balance short- and longer-term challenges and opportunities? How do you ensure that your strategic objectives balance the needs of all key stakeholders?

Note

- *Strategy development* refers to your organization's approach (formal or informal) to preparing for the future. Strategy development might utilize various types of forecasts, projections, options, scenarios, or other approaches to envisioning the future for purposes of decision making and resource allocation.
- Strategy should be interpreted broadly. Strategy might be built around or lead to any or all of the following: new products, services, and markets; revenue growth via various approaches, including acquisitions; new partnerships and alliances; and new employee relationships.

Strategy Deployment

Describe how your organization converts its strategic objectives into action plans. Summarize your organization's action plans and related key measures or indicators. Project your organization's future performance on key measures or indicators.

Action Plan Development and Deployment

- How do you develop and deploy action plans to achieve your key strategic objectives? How do you allocate resources to ensure accomplishment of your action plans? How do you ensure that the key changes resulting from your action plans can be sustained?
- How do you establish and deploy modified action plans if circumstances require a shift in plans and rapid execution of new plans?
- What are your key short- and longer-term action plans? What are the key changes, if any, in your products and services and your customers and markets, and how you will operate?
- What are your key human resource plans that derive from your short- and longer-term strategic objectives and action plans?
- What are your key performance measures or indicators for tracking progress on your action plans? How do you ensure that your overall action plan measurement system reinforces organizational alignment? How do you ensure that the measurement system covers all key deployment areas and stakeholders?

Performance Projection

- For the key performance measures or indicators identified, what are your performance projections for both your short- and longer-term planning time horizons? How does your projected performance compare with competitors' projected performance? How does it compare with key benchmarks, goals, and past performance, as appropriate? If there are current or projected gaps in performance against your competitors, how will you address them?

Customer and Market Knowledge

Describe how your organization determines requirements, expectations, and preferences of customers and markets to ensure the continuing relevance of your products and services and to develop new opportunities.

Customer and Market Knowledge

- How do you identify customers, customer groups, and market segments? How do you determine which customers, customer groups, and market segments to pursue for current and future products and services? How do you include customers of competitors and other potential customers and markets in this determination?

- How do you listen and learn to determine key customer requirements and changing expectations (including product and service features) and their relative importance to customers' purchasing decisions? How do your determination methods vary for different customers or customer groups? How do you use relevant information and feedback from current and former customers, including marketing and sales information, customer loyalty and retention data, win/loss analysis, and complaint data for purposes of product and service planning, marketing, process improvements, and other business development? How do you use this information and feedback to become more customer focused and to better satisfy customer needs?
- How do you keep your listening and learning methods current with business needs and directions, including changes in your marketplace?

Note

- *Product and service features* refers to all the important characteristics of products and services and to their performance throughout their full life cycle and the full "consumption chain." This includes all customers' purchase experiences and other interactions with your organization that influence purchase decisions. The focus should be on features that affect customer preference and repeat business—for example, those features that differentiate your products and services from competing offerings.
- Listening and learning might include gathering and integrating surveys, focus group findings, Web-based data, and other data and information that bear on customer' purchasing decisions. Keeping your listening and learning methods current with business needs and directions also might include use of newer technology, such as Web-based data gathering.

Customer Relationships and Satisfaction

Describe how your organization builds relationships to acquire, satisfy, and retain customers, to increase customer loyalty, and to develop new opportunities. Describe also how your organization determines customer satisfaction.

Customer Relationship Building

- How do you build relationships to acquire customers, to meet and exceed their expectations, to increase loyalty and repeat business, and to gain positive referrals?
- How do your key access mechanisms enable customers to seek information, conduct business, and make complaints? What are your

key access mechanisms? How do you determine key customer contact requirements for each mode of customer access? How do you ensure that these contact requirements are deployed to all people and processes involved in the customer response chain?

- How do you manage customer complaints? How do you ensure that complaints are resolved effectively and promptly? How do you minimize customer dissatisfaction and loss of repeat business? How are complaints aggregated and analyzed for use in improvement throughout your organization and by your partners?
- How do you keep your approaches to building relationships and providing customer access current with business needs and directions?

Customer Satisfaction Determination

- How do you determine customer satisfaction and dissatisfaction? How do these determination methods differ among customer groups? How do you ensure that your measurements capture actionable information for use in exceeding your customers' expectations, securing their future business, and gaining positive referrals? How do you use customer satisfaction and dissatisfaction information for improvement?
- How do you follow up with customers on products, services, and transaction quality to receive prompt and actionable feedback?
- How do you obtain and use information on your customers' satisfaction relative to their satisfaction with your competitors and/or industry benchmarks?
- How do you keep your approaches to determining satisfaction current with business needs and directions?

Note

- Determining customer satisfaction and dissatisfaction might include use of any or all of the following: surveys, formal and informal feedback, customer account histories, complaints, win/loss analysis, and transaction completion rates.
- Actionable customer satisfaction measurements provide useful information about specific product and service features, delivery, relationships, and transactions that bear on the customers' future actions—repeat business and positive referral.

Measurement, Analysis, and Review of Organizational Performance

Describe how your organization measures, analyzes, aligns, reviews, and improves its performance at all levels and in all parts of your organization.

Performance Measurement

- How do you select, collect, align, and integrate data and information for tracking daily operations and for tracking overall organizational performance, including progress relative to strategic objectives and action plans? What are your key organizational performance measures? How do you use these data and information to support organizational decision making and innovation?
- How do you select and ensure the effective use of key comparative data and information and information to support operational and strategic decision making and innovation?
- How do you keep your performance measurement system current with business needs and directions? How do you ensure that your performance measurement system is sensitive to rapid, unexpected organizational, or external changes?

Performance Analysis and Review

- How do you review organizational performance and capabilities? How do your senior leaders participate in these reviews? What analysis do you perform to support these reviews and to ensure that conclusions are valid? How do you use these reviews to assess organizational success, competitive performance, and progress relative to strategic objectives and action plans? How do you use these reviews to assess your organization's ability to rapidly respond to changing organizational needs and challenges in your operating environment?
- How do you translate organizational performance review findings into priorities for continuous and breakthrough improvement and into opportunities for innovation? How are these priorities and opportunities deployed to work group and functional-level operations throughout your organization to enable effective support for their decision making? When appropriate, how are the priorities and opportunities deployed to your suppliers and partners to ensure organizational alignment?

Information and Knowledge Management

Describe how your organization ensures the quality and availability of needed data and information for employees, suppliers, partners, and customers. Describe how your organization builds and manages its knowledge assets.

Data and Information Availability

- How do you make needed data and information available?
- How do you make them accessible to employees, suppliers and partners, and customers, as appropriate?

- How do you ensure that hardware and software are reliable, secure, and user friendly?
- How do you ensure the continued availability of data and information, including the availability of hardware and software systems, in the event of an emergency?
- How do you keep your data and information availability mechanisms, including your software and hardware systems, current with business needs and directions and with technological changes in your operating environment?

Organizational Knowledge Management

- How do you manage organizational knowledge to accomplish the following:
  ○ Collection and transfer of employee knowledge
  ○ Transfer of relevant knowledge from and to customers, suppliers, and partners.
  ○ Rapid identification, sharing, and implementation of best practices

Data, Information, and Knowledge Quality

- How do you ensure the following properties of your data, information, and organizational knowledge:
  ○ Accuracy
  ○ Integrity and reliability
  ○ Timeliness
  ○ Security and confidentiality

Work Systems

Describe how your organization's work and jobs enable employees and the organization to achieve high performance. Describe how compensation, career progression, and related workforce practices enable employees and the organization to achieve high performance.

Organization and Management of Work

- How do you organize and manage work and jobs, including skills, to promote cooperation, initiative, empowerment, innovation, and your organizational culture? How do you organize and manage work and jobs, including skills, to achieve the agility to keep current with business needs and to achieve your action plans?
- How do your work systems capitalize on the diverse ideas, cultures, and thinking of your employees and the communities with which you interact (your employee hiring and your customer communities)?

- How do you achieve effective communication and skill sharing across work units, jobs, and locations?

Employee Performance Management System

- How does your employee performance management system, including feedback to employees, support high-performance work and contribute to the achievement of your action plans? How does your employee performance management system support a customer and business focus? How do your compensation, recognition, and related reward and incentive practices reinforce high-performance work and a customer and business focus?

Hiring and Career Progression

- How do you identify characteristics and skills needed by potential employees?
- How do you recruit, hire, and retain new employees?
- How do you ensure that the employees represent the diverse ideas, cultures, and thinking of your employee hiring community?
- How do you accomplish effective succession planning for leadership and management positions? How do you manage effective career progression for all employees throughout the organization?

Employee Learning and Motivation

Describe how your organization's employee education, training, and career development support the achievement of your overall objectives and contribute to high performance. Describe how your organization's education, training, and career development build employee knowledge, skills, and capabilities.

Employee Education, Training, and Development

- How do employee education and training contribute to the achievement of your action plans? How does your employee education, training, and development address your key needs associated with organizational performance measurement, performance improvement, and technological change? How does your education and training approach balance short- and longer-term organizational objectives with employee needs for development, ongoing learning, and career progression?
- How does employee education, training, and development address your key organizational needs associated with new employee orientation, diversity, ethical business practices, and management and leadership development? How does employee education, training, and development

address your key organizational needs associated with employee, workplace, and environmental safety?

- How do you seek and use input from employees and their supervisors and managers on education, training, and development needs? How do you incorporate your organizational learning and knowledge assets into your education and training?
- How do you deliver education and training? How do you seek and use input from employees and their supervisors and managers in determining your delivery approaches? How do you use both formal and informal delivery approaches, including mentoring and other approaches, as appropriate?
- How do you reinforce the use of new knowledge and skills on the job and retain this knowledge for long-term organizational use? How do you systematically transfer knowledge from departing or retiring employees?
- How do you evaluate the effectiveness of education and training, taking into account individual and organizational performance?

Motivation and Career Development

- How do you motivate employees to develop and utilize their full potential? How does your organization use formal and informal mechanisms to help employees attain job- and career-related development and learning objectives? How do managers and supervisors help employees attain job- and career-related development and learning objectives?

Employee Well-Being and Satisfaction

Describe how your organization maintains a work environment and an employee support climate that contribute to the well-being, satisfaction, and motivation of all employees.

Work Environment

- How do you ensure and improve workplace health, safety, security, and ergonomics in a proactive manner? How do employees take part in these improvement efforts?
- What are your performance measures or improvement targets for each of these key workplace factors? What are the significant differences in these workplace factors and performance measures or targets if different employee groups and work units have different work environments?
- How do you ensure workplace preparedness for disasters or emergencies?

Employee Support and Satisfaction

- How do you determine the key factors that affect employee well-being, satisfaction, and motivation? How are these factors segmented for a diverse workforce and for different categories and types of employees?
- How do you support your employees via services, benefits, and policies? How are these tailored to the needs of a diverse workforce and different categories and types of employees?
- What formal and informal assessment methods and measures do you use to determine employee well-being, satisfaction, and motivation? How do these methods and measures differ across a diverse workforce and different categories and types of employees?
- How do you use other indicators, such as employee retention, absenteeism, grievances, safety, and productivity, to assess and improve employee well-being, satisfaction, and motivation?
- How do you relate assessment findings to key business results to identify priorities for improving the work environment and employee support climate?

Note

- Specific factors that might affect your employees' well-being, satisfaction, and motivation include effective employee problem or grievance resolution; safety factors; employees' views of management; employee training, development, and career opportunities; employee preparation for changes in technology or the work organization; the work environment and other work conditions; management's empowerment of employees; information sharing by management; workload; cooperation and teamwork; recognition; services and benefits; communications; job security; compensation; and equal opportunity.
- Approaches for employee support might include providing counseling, career development and employability services; recreational or cultural activities; nonwork-related education; day care, job rotation or sharing; special leave for family responsibilities or community service; home safety training; flexible work hours and location, outplacement, and retirement benefits (including extended health care).
- Measures or indicators of well-being, satisfaction, and motivation might include data on safety and absenteeism; the overall turnover rate; the turnover rate for customer contact employees; employees' charitable contributions; grievances, strikes, other job actions; insurance costs; workers' compensation claims; and results of surveys. Survey indicators of satisfaction might include employee knowledge of job roles, employee knowledge of organizational

direction, and employee perception of empowerment and information sharing.

Value Creation Processes

Describe how your organization identifies and manages its key processes for creating customer value and achieving business success and growth.

Value Creation Processes

- How does your organization determine its key value creation processes? What are your organization's key product, service, and business processes for creating or adding value? How do these processes contribute to profitability and business success?
- How do you determine key value creation process requirements, incorporating input from customers, suppliers, and partners as appropriate? What are the key requirements for these processes?
- How do you design these processes to meet all the key requirements? How do you incorporate new technology, organizational knowledge, and the potential need for agility into the design of these processes? How do you incorporate cycle time, productivity, cost control, and other efficiency and effectiveness factors into the design of these processes? How do you implement these processes to ensure they meet design requirements?
- What are your key performance measures or indicators used for the control and improvement of your value creation processes?
- How does your day-to-day operation of these processes ensure meeting key process requirements? How are in-process measures used in managing these processes? How is customer, supplier, and partner input used in managing these processes, as appropriate?
- How do you minimize overall costs associated with inspections, tests, and process or performance audits, as appropriate? How do you prevent defects and rework, and minimize warranty costs, as appropriate?
- How do you improve your value creation processes to achieve better performance, to reduce variability, to improve products and services, and to keep the processes current with business needs and directions? How are improvements and lessons learned shared with other organizational units and processes to drive organizational learning and innovation?

Note

- Your key value creation processes are those most important to "running your business" and maintaining or achieving a sustainable competitive advantage. They are the processes that involve the majority of your organization's employees and produce customer, stockholder, and other key stakeholder value. They include the processes through which your organization adds greatest value to its products and services. They also include the business processes most critical to adding value to the business itself, resulting in success and growth.

- Key value creation processes differ greatly among organizations, depending on many factors. These factors include the nature of your products and services; how they are produced and delivered; technology requirements; customer and supplier relationships and involvement; outsourcing; importance of research and development; role of technology acquisition, information and knowledge management; supply chain management; mergers and acquisitions; global expansion; and sales and marketing.
- To achieve better process performance and reduce variability, you might implement approaches such as a Lean Enterprise system, Six Sigma methodology, use of ISO 9000:2000 standards, or other process improvement tools.

Support Processes and Operational Planning

Describe how your organization manages its key processes that support your value creation processes. Describe your processes for financial management and continuity of operations in an emergency.

Support Processes

- How does your organization determine its key support processes? What are your key processes for supporting your value creation processes?
- How do you determine key support process requirements, incorporating input from internal and external customers, and suppliers and partners, as appropriate? What are the key requirements for these processes?
- How do you design these processes to meet all the key requirements? How do you incorporate new technology, organizational knowledge, and the potential need for agility into the design of these processes? How do you incorporate cycle time, productivity, cost control, and other efficiency and effectiveness factors into the design of these processes? How do you implement these processes to ensure they meet design requirements?
- What are your key performance measures or indicators used for the control and improvement of your support process? How does your day-to-day operation of key support process ensure meeting key performance requirements? How are in-process measures used in managing these processes? How is customer, supplier, and partner input used in managing these processes, as appropriate?

- How do you minimize overall costs associated with inspections, tests, and process or performance audits, as appropriate? How do you prevent defects and rework?
- How do you improve your support processes to achieve better performance, to reduce variability, and to keep them current with business needs and directions? How are improvements and lessons learned shared with other organizational units and processes to drive organizational learning and innovation?

Operational Planning

- How does your organization ensure adequate financial resources are available to support your operations? How do you determine the resources needed to meet current financial obligations? How do you ensure adequate resources are available to support major new business investments? How do you assess the financial risks associated with your current business operations and major new business investments?
- How do you ensure continuity of operations in the event of an emergency?

Product and Service Outcomes

Summarize your organization's key product and service performance results. Segment your results by product and service types and groups, customer groups, and market segments, as appropriate.

Product and Service Results

- What are your current levels and trends in key measures or indicators of product and service performance that are important to your customers? How do these results compare with your competitors' performance?

Customer-Focused Results

Summarize your organization's key customer-focused results, including customer satisfaction and customer-perceived value. Segment your results by product and service types and groups, customer groups, and market segments, as appropriate.

Customer-Focused Results

- What are your current levels and trends in key measures or indicators of customer satisfaction and dissatisfaction? How do these compare with competitors' levels of customer satisfaction?
- What are your current levels and trends in key measures or indicators of customer-perceived value—including customer loyalty and retention,

positive referral, and other aspects of building relationships with customers, as appropriate?

Financial and Market Results

Summarize your organization's key financial and marketplace performance results by customer or market segments, as appropriate.

Financial and Market Results

- What are your current levels and trends in key measures or indicators of financial performance, including aggregate measures of financial return and economic value as appropriate?
- What are your current levels and trends in key measures or indicators of marketplace performance, including market share or position, business growth, and new markets entered, as appropriate?

Human Resource Results

Summarize your organization's key human resource results, including work system performance, employee learning, development, well-being, and satisfaction. Segment your results to address the diversity of your workforce and the different types and categories of employees, as appropriate.

Human Resource Results

- What are your current levels and trends in key measures or indicators of work system performance and effectiveness?
- What are your current levels and trends in key measures of employee learning and development?
- What are your current levels and trends in key measures or indicators of employee well-being, satisfaction, and dissatisfaction?

Organizational Effectiveness Results

Summarize your organization's key operational performance results that contribute to the improvement of organizational effectiveness. Segment your results by product and service types and groups, and by market segments, as appropriate.

Organizational Effectiveness Results

- What are your current levels and trends in key measures or indicators of the operational performance of your key value creation processes?

- Include productivity, cycle time, supplier and partner performance, and other appropriate measures of effectiveness and efficiency.
- What are your current levels and trends in key measures or indicators of the operational performance of your other key processes? Include productivity, cycle time, supplier and partner performance, and other appropriate measures of effectiveness and efficiency.

Leadership and Social Responsibility Results

Summarize your organization's key governance senior leadership, and social responsibility results, including evidence of ethical behavior, fiscal accountability, legal compliance, and organizational citizenship.

Leadership and Social Responsibility Results

- What are your results for key measures or indicators of accomplishment of your organizational strategy and action plans?
- What are your results for key measures or indicators of ethical behavior and of stakeholder trust in the senior leaders and governance of your organization? What are your results for key measures or indicators of breaches of ethical behaviors?
- What are your key current findings and trends in key measures or indicators of fiscal accountability, both internal and external, as appropriate?
- What are your results for key measures or indicators of regulatory and legal compliance?
- What are your results for key measures or indicators of organizational citizenship in support of your key communities?

9

The Role of Leadership and Governance in Driving Financial Impact

When men and women think, the first step to progress is taken.

ELIZABETH C. STANTON

9.1 Overview

Any discussion of continuous improvement systems—particularly when the subject is breakthrough improvement as measured by financial impact—is typically based on a set of assumptions: the notion that a leadership team is leading the way, pointing teams to appropriate targets, and then monitoring improvement efforts to make sure that projects stay on track to achieve desired financial returns.

In practice, unfortunately, case after case of failed efforts illustrates that despite all the talk about the role of leaders, it is often the lack of cohesive, continuous leadership that is a key driver of failed attempts at continuous improvement. This is especially true when the reason for failure is the inability to achieve a desired financial impact.

Most leaders understand intuitively that their organization's Six Sigma business improvement efforts will have a higher likelihood of sustainable success if they remain active in the process. Yet, few appear to have a concrete model for putting that understanding into practice.

A review of successes at organizations like General Electric, Allied Signal, Honeywell, Caterpillar, Bank of America, and Motorola demonstrates that breakthrough improvements, and the financial gains associated with them, occur when senior leadership moves *beyond* thinking about Six Sigma as simply a tool set for driving continuous process improvement. Successful leadership teams view Six Sigma as an integrated set of management practices supported by a specific set of their leadership behaviors.

Such leaders share common themes in their practice of Six Sigma:

- A Six Sigma macro model for driving organizational change
- A continuous management process for monitoring and driving execution
- An established set of expected leadership behaviors

In this chapter we will review these themes and illustrate how to put them into practice through case examples.

9.2   The Six Sigma Macro Model at Apex

Ron Brown is the general manager of a fully integrated business unit named Apex Electronics (name changed to protect confidentiality). Apex Electronics develops, produces, and markets products and services used in high-tech electronics applications. Ron recently replaced a general manager who had managed the business for 10 years, and he found himself facing a number of challenges.

9.2.1   From a Decade of Growth to Diminishing Cash Flows

With a solid reputation as technology wizards, Apex and its employees built their success on a formula of one new technology breakthrough after another. As a result, the company sustained a 20 percent growth rate for the past 10 years.

But after a decade of growth, Apex customers lost their appetite for investment in speculative technologies. Instead, they demanded more performance at a lower price and more responsive service on currently installed products and systems. New competitors found ways to copy Apex products and deliver them at a lower price. As customer order rates dramatically declined, inventories quickly increased, with the result that Apex is finding it difficult to reduce product costs or attract new customers for its higher margin products. Cash flow is suffering, and Apex cannot fund new product development opportunities as it had in the past. Needless to say, Ron is not sleeping well.

9.2.2   Dilemma: When Six Sigma Does Not Create Measurable Financial Gain

The leadership team at Apex has deployed Six Sigma improvement teams to drive specific process improvements for the past 2 years. While each member could point to specific projects that had shown some solid process improvements, it didn't seem that those improvements were creating measurable financial gain. Margins continued to decline, and the organization was dangerously close to negative cash flows.

Reflecting on Six Sigma project level wins as well as disappointments, Ron was convinced that this was not the time to drop Six Sigma and try a different approach to improvement. He believed that there was a way to build on the experiences, positive and negative, of the past 2 years and develop a more comprehensive, bottom-line oriented approach to Six Sigma business improvement.

9.2.3 Asking a Key Question

Ron pulled his leadership team together for a working session focused on a key question: How can we achieve more consistent weekly results *as well as* more sustainable improved performance?

Starting with this question, members of the leadership team discussed their performance over the past 2 years. They agreed that Six Sigma had been a useful approach to solving some critical problems. Inventories were more manageable. Product launches were going more smoothly. Numerous processes were operating more efficiently and more productively. At the same time, the team was perplexed by the fact that overall organizational performance, as measured by profitability and shareholder value, had not seemed to have improved in spite of these efforts. To help solve this conundrum, the team developed a list of what was working and not working in the quest for rapid and sustainable business improvement. See Exhibit 9.1.

WORKING	NOT WORKING
▪ Improved yields/reduced scrap in production	▪ Other functions not fully on board
▪ Certified Black Belts and Green Belts access the organization	▪ No documented return on investment for the dollars spent on training
▪ Project level savings in excess of $5,000,000	▪ Savings don't seem to show in bottom line
▪ Problem-solving tools helping teams get to root causes	▪ Leaders are not supporting breakthrough investments
▪ Many enthusiastic supporters	▪ Employees wonder if the commitment to change will last

Exhibit 9.1   Six Sigma at Apex—What's Working and Not Working

After reviewing the list, Ron told the team that he had observed many of the same things. It seemed to him that they had achieved reasonably good adoption of Six Sigma tools for support in discrete problem solving situations. On just about every problem, Ron was seeing much deeper levels of analysis and much better identification of root causes before solutions were being implemented or investments were being made. In addition, during the past 2 years, 20 Black Belts and 50 Green Belts had been certified with projects that demonstrated an average savings or incremental revenue gain of $200,000 per project. Still, Ron said, overall organizational performance remained flat or was declining in certain key areas.

9.2.4   A Common Phenomenon

What Ron was observing is a common phenomenon in the adoption levels of Six Sigma (see Exhibit 9.2.) Many organizations use Six Sigma tools to help solve discrete problems using discrete tools like the seven basic quality tools, Failure Mode Effect Analysis, and sources of variation studies. As organizations mature in their adoption of Six Sigma, they become effective in deploying Six Sigma teams on high-impact projects using an integrated methodology to yield improvement in a focused area. But few organizations realize the full impact of the Six Sigma methodology until they realize the power of Six Sigma to drive organizational transformation.

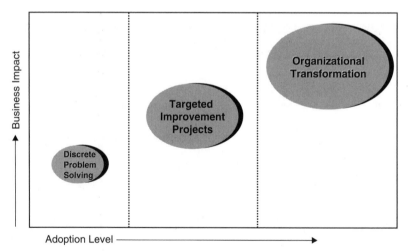

Exhibit 9.2   Six Sigma Adoption Levels of Implementation

9.3   The Holistic Six Sigma Model

The path to organizational transformation and more sustainable improvement for Apex could be in the adoption of a more holistic Six Sigma model that can be adapted to drive all three levels of business improvement. An example of a more holistic model can be found in use at Jones Lang LaSalle, a global leader in real estate services and money management. The company, with approximately 19,300 employees worldwide, serves clients' real estate needs in more than 100 markets in over 35 countries on five continents.

Jones Lang LaSalle's full range of services includes agency leasing; property management; project and development services; valuations; capital markets; buying and selling properties; corporate finance; hotel advisory, space acquisition and disposition (tenant representation); facilities management (corporate property services); strategic consulting; and outsourcing. The company provides money management on a global basis for both public and private assets through LaSalle Investment Management. Jones Lang LaSalle has grown to become the leading supplier of global real estate services to corporate clients by building its business model around superior client relationship management and consistently high quality, worldwide service delivery.

9.4   Jones Lang LaSalle's Client-Driven Six Sigma Continuous Improvement Model

During the past 3 years, which have been marked by rapid growth for the company, the firm's senior leadership came to realize that to sustain growth and deliver on the dual promise of strategic partnering and superior service to their clients, they would need a robust model for driving breakthrough improvements across their business. In response, they developed and adopted what they call the *Client-Driven Six Sigma model.*

9.4.1   Leveraging Lessons Learned from Clients

The model was developed by the firm's Strategic Consulting team based on learnings gained from a number of the company's clients who practiced Six Sigma. A close partnership with Motorola helped the team understand the importance of leading projects with a clear understanding of the voice of the customer (VOC), and converting the VOC into hard requirements. Motorola also provided an excellent example of the role that strong governance, led

Six Sigma at Jones Lang LaSalle is an integrated process improvement system that drives breakthrough performance for our clients.

Five Focus Areas of Client-Driven Six Sigma:

1. Voice of the Customer
2. Performance Metrics
3. Lean Process Design
4. DMAIC Process Improvement
5. Governance

Exhibit 9.3   Client-Driven Six Sigma at Jones Lang LaSalle

by a committed senior leadership team, plays in the overall success of a Six Sigma implementation.

Another global client, Whirlpool, helped the firm understand the important role that process-based performance metrics play in guiding focused Six Sigma execution. At Xerox and Solectron, the firm learned the value of integrating lean process design and lean thinking into their Six Sigma approach. Finally, through collaborative projects at Bank of America and Eli Lilly, the firm discovered the value of utilizing the Define-Measure-Analyze-Improve-Control (DMAIC) framework for structured problem-solving and focused project management. The resulting experiences and learning generated a model that represents best practices from many of the best known Six Sigma practitioners and a model that is compatible with Jones Lang LaSalle's valued clients (Exhibit 9.3).

9.4.2   Client-Driven Six Sigma Model

The Client-Driven Six Sigma model is useful because it integrates the higher impact Six Sigma tools in a framework that can be utilized across all three levels of business improvement from a micro problem-solving level to leadership-driven organizational transformation.

1. *Voice of the customer:* All improvement efforts begin—and are constantly monitored for alignment—with customer requirements. Tools and methods are in place to continuously listen to customers and take definitive action based on that voice. See Exhibit 9.4.

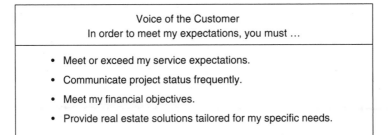

Exhibit 9.4   Voice of the Customer Example

2. *Performance metrics:* Operationally driven performance metrics establish a baseline, as well as stretch goals, by which leaders judge the quality of execution. These operational metrics provide linkage between customer requirements and continuous improvement to critical processes. Tools such as the Six Sigma dashboard, and Jones Lang LaSalle's single client view reporting process ensure that the performance metrics are up to date and being acted upon (see Exhibit 9.5).

3. *Lean process design:* Driven by a clear understanding of customer requirements and desired performance metrics, teams focus on streamlining service delivery processes with an eye on eliminating waste, improving service quality, and reducing process variation. See Exhibit 9.6.

4. *DMAIC process improvement teams:* Once processes are streamlined and predictable, real performance breakthroughs can occur as Six Sigma DMAIC teams are deployed on specific projects within each process. Key attributes of these Six Sigma projects include customer-collaborative, team-based problem solving; consistent use of the model; trained resources working in projects; project selection and prioritization process, and metrics monitoring to drive project execution.

5. *Governance and leadership:* At the heart of successful implementation of Customer-Driven Six Sigma is an active leadership team that applies a rigorous monitoring and review process. This ensures that the model is consistently applied and that real customer impact is occurring. A disciplined governance and review process is established with each client to ensure that Client-Driven Six Sigma is generating high-impact improvement. Jones Lang LaSalle has developed a particularly interesting model for governance driven by the company's need to partner closely with key clients to drive success for both parties. This governance model, called the *Collaborative Management*

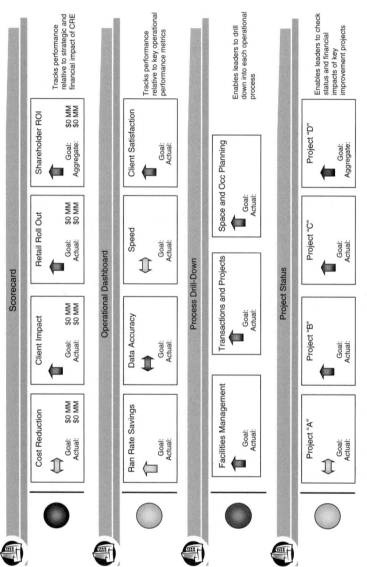

Scorecard

Cost Reduction
Goal: $0 MM
Actual: $0 MM

Client Impact
Goal: $0 MM
Actual: $0 MM

Retail Roll Out
Goal: $0 MM
Actual: $0 MM

Shareholder ROI
Goal: $0 MM
Aggregate: $0 MM

Tracks performance relative to strategic and financial impact of CRE

Operational Dashboard

Ran Rate Savings
Goal:
Actual:

Data Accuracy
Goal:
Actual:

Speed
Goal:
Actual:

Client Satisfaction
Goal:
Actual:

Tracks performance relative to key operational performance metrics

Process Drill-Down

Facilities Management
Goal:
Actual:

Transactions and Projects
Goal:
Actual:

Space and Occ Planning
Goal:
Actual:

Enables leaders to drill down into each operational process

Project Status

Project "A"
Goal:
Actual:

Project "B"
Goal:
Actual:

Project "C"
Goal:
Actual:

Project "D"
Goal:
Aggregate:

Enables leaders to check status and financial impacts of key improvement projects

Exhibit 9.5 Jones Lang LaSalle's Single Client View Reporting Process

302

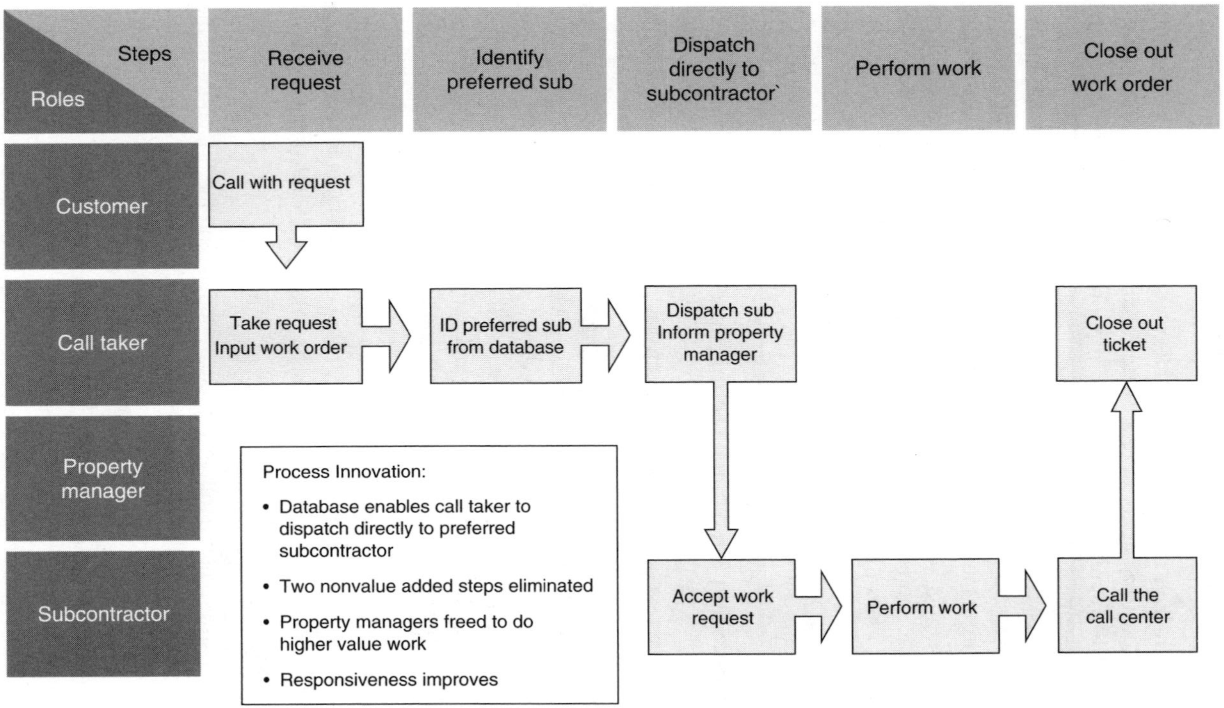

Exhibit 9.6 Call Center Process Innovation Enables Call Takers to Dispatch Work Orders Directly to Subcontractors

The diagram shows a process flow with the following columns across the top (Steps): Receive request, Identify preferred sub, Dispatch directly to subcontractor, Perform work, Close out work order.

Roles (rows): Customer, Call taker, Property manager, Subcontractor.

Process flow:
- Customer: Call with request
- Call taker: Take request / Input work order → ID preferred sub from database → Dispatch sub / Inform property manager
- Subcontractor: Accept work request → Perform work → Call the call center
- Property manager: Close out ticket

Process Innovation:
- Database enables call taker to dispatch directly to preferred subcontractor
- Two nonvalue added steps eliminated
- Property managers freed to do higher value work
- Responsiveness improves

Model, enables Jones Lang LaSalle and its clients to jointly plan and manage Six Sigma project to execute as well as monitor core process activity. (The model is explored later in this chapter.)

As luck would have it, Jones Lang LaSalle was a partner to Apex, providing the company with a variety of real estate services. Jones Lang LaSalle was providing full facilities management support at all Apex facilities and project management support of a new office expansion. The firm had also represented Apex in a number of real estate lease transactions. Through a series of conversations, Ron had learned from Peter Roberts, CEO of Jones Lang LaSalle, Americas, how the Client-Driven Six Sigma model had helped Jones Lang LaSalle move from "project-at-a-time" execution of Six Sigma to the holistic, organizational/client transformation currently underway at Jones Lang LaSalle.

Ron was convinced that the model could work for Apex.

9.5   Integrating Six Sigma Techniques

Apex had been gathering voice of the customer input for 2 years and had already adopted a Balanced Scorecard approach to manage their business through performance metrics. Their teams were very familiar with Lean process design techniques like Value-Stream Mapping, and they had demonstrated success with any number of DMAIC project teams. They had just never put it all together in an integrated, organization-wide change campaign. And Ron doubted that they had really committed to driving this level of transformation as a collaborative leadership team.

So Ron brought together his leadership team for a second Six Sigma strategy discussion. He shared the Client-Driven Six Sigma model with the team and emphasized the importance of its five components operating as an integrating system.

The team realized that, intuitively, they all understood the principles of the model. Customer requirements should drive the metrics that guide the business and those metrics should absolutely determine which processes were critical to the success of the business. Critical investments and resource decisions should be made in ways that enabled the core processes to deliver maximum value to customers.

At the same time, however, the team admitted that, in practice, that was not the way they ran this business. Each leadership team member operated its specific area of responsibility as if it were a stand-alone business. Accountabilities and rewards were established primarily against financial objectives. There had always been an unstated pact between team members: "You stay out of my business and I'll stay out of yours. If we all perform well within our function, the business will prosper."

9.5.1   Aligning Apex with the Client-Driven Six Sigma Model

At this point, Ron asked the team to describe ways that they could more closely align Apex to the Client-Driven Six Sigma model.

Mary, the vice president responsible for sales and marketing, had good data that showed a clear set of customer priorities. Henry, the chief technology officer, had already been in discussions with Fred, the vice president of supply chain operations (procurement, production, and order fulfillment), about how they could work more closely together to get products to market more rapidly. Jack, the chief financial officer, could see that, while financial metrics represented the "bottom line" and that financial discipline was critical, financial metrics were actually after-the-fact measurements. He had always been frustrated by the team's inability to predict changes in financial outcomes in time to make operational adjustments. Jack believed that operational metrics, aligned to customer requirements and linked closely to the key operating processes, would allow the team to run the business with a more "hands-on" proactive approach rather than an end of the month, looking back perspective. With all that in mind, the team developed a Client-Driven Six Sigma framework for Apex (see Exhibit 9.7.)

It was clear to the team that Apex could be run in a more integrated fashion. The obvious challenge was putting the framework into day-to-day practice.

9.5.2   From Functionally Focused to Customer Driven

Ron had learned that moving from a functionally focused business to a customer-driven integrated business required a leadership shift: from functional experts operating as an efficient staff to process owners operating as a collaborative leadership team. In the client-driven, integrated business model, the functional experts would become process owners, accountable for process performance, while the team would take shared ownership of the performance of the entire business. The leadership team collectively would own the performance metrics and assume shared ownership for collaboration and integration between and across the business processes.

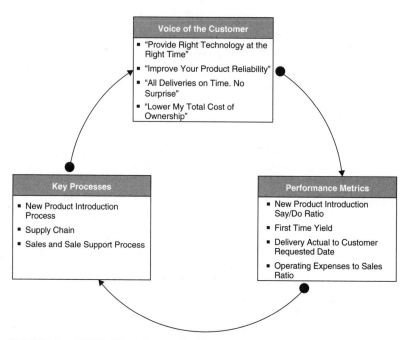

Exhibit 9.7   APEX: Client-Driven Six Sigma Framework

To illustrate, Ron drew a diagram to further illuminate the integration of the business processes and the end-to-end connection between customer expectations and the business performance dashboard (see Exhibit 9.8.)

The team agreed that the diagram made sense and said they could start to understand the integrated business. Ron observed that the two keys to putting Client-Driven Six Sigma into practice would be:

- Leaders moving from functional experts to process owners
- Leaders sharing ownership of the business and collaborating to achieve shared performance metrics

To illustrate the point, Ron drew a matrix assigning process ownership and the shared performance metrics (see Exhibit 9.9.)

What's the Connection?

The team was energized by this opportunity to run Apex as an integrated business unit. At this point, however, Fred, the supply chain leader (who had

Voice of the customer

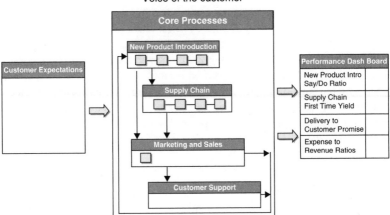

Exhibit 9.8   APEX Integrated Process Model

previously demonstrated the most success with Six Sigma projects), asked a question: What does all of this have to do with Six Sigma?

A History Lesson

Ron reminded the team where they had started. Six Sigma is an integrated set of business practices focused on driving breakthrough business performance.

Process	Process Owner	Critical Customer Requirement	Shared Performance Metrics
New product development and launch	Henry	Right technology ahead of competition	NPI say/do ratio
Supply chain	Fred	Reliable products out of the box	Yield
Marketing and sales	Mary	On time, every time	End-to-end delivery cycle time
Customer support (including all back room functions)	Julie	Delivered value	Revenue to expense ratios

Exhibit 9.9   APEX Integrated Process Ownership Matrix

During the past 2 years the team had experienced project-level success in lowering inventories, reducing product costs, improving internal processes.

But despite those successes, financial results remained flat. Ron explained that by operating Apex as an integrated business system and collaborating as a leadership team to achieve shared performance goals, the team would be in a better position to identify and lead Six Sigma improvement projects that honestly transformed the business. These projects could more closely link to the highest priority customer needs and could focus on the intersections and hand-offs between the processes and across the processes.

In the past, focused improvement projects may have pushed the problem into another process area or attacked a minor part of the problem. Financial gains in one project were dissipated in another part of the overall process.

9.5.3   Focusing on High Leverage Points of Improvement

The new Client-Driven Six Sigma framework for Apex would enable the leadership team to see opportunities more holistically and then focus cross-functional teams on high-leverage points of improvement. Able to see the entire business system, and no longer concerned with stepping into each other's turf, the team could sponsor and lead Six Sigma projects that could truly search out and eliminate the root causes of their toughest business performance problems. Driving solutions to true systemic root cause would be the key to translating Six Sigma improvement to sustainable financial impact.

The team had come a long way in expanding their view of how to achieve breakthrough business performance. The Client-Driven Six Sigma framework provided an enlightened view of Apex as an integrated business system and helped the team understand the importance of process ownership combined with collaboration across the team.

9.5.4   The Critical Perspective of Suppliers and Customers

But Ron also knew that, to achieve true breakthrough performance, the team needed an additional perspective. When he looked closely at each of the critical processes, it was clear that some key roles in each of them were not represented on the leadership team. The missing players were key suppliers and certain critical customers. Ron knew that to make Apex processes most effective and deliver the greatest amount of value, suppliers and customers would have to be part of the analysis and part of every solution. Ron wanted his leadership team to view the critical processes beyond the Apex boundaries: from suppliers at one end to customers at the other (see Exhibit 9.10.)

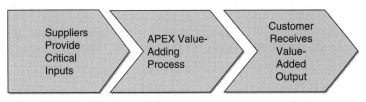

Exhibit 9.10 The APEX Value Chain

Ron realized that the total value chain concept represents another idea that is intuitively obvious but has significant implications for how his leadership team would operate moving forward. The broad implication was that the team was going to have to find mechanisms for bringing customers and suppliers into the Apex leadership and decision-making process. This would go beyond traditional notions of supplier councils and customer advocacy boards. Customers and suppliers would have to participate directly in the Six Sigma improvement projects. But beyond that, Ron knew that certain suppliers and key customers would have to become part of the leadership and governance of the Apex integrated business process model.

9.5.5 The Need for Discipline and a Collaborative Leadership Environment

At the same time that the leadership would be challenged with the need to collaborate much more closely with customers and suppliers, they would also be challenged with the need to be more disciplined and rigorous as a management team while, at the same time, be much more collaborative in their analysis and decision making.

Breakthrough performance requires a team that is willing and able to lead in a very "hands-on" and collaborative way. Superior execution occurs when a team has full operational awareness and is able to drive activity across the entire business.

In this collaborative leadership environment, work flows seamlessly across the value chain. Expectations established at one end of the value chain are delivered upon, according to the requirements. New products are brought to market on time and at the forecast volume and profit levels (the say/do ratio). Everyone delivers on the promises they make to each other and to their customers. Improvement projects are resourced properly and completed as forecast, delivering the financial impacts that were expected. In this environment, sustainable, breakthrough business performance becomes a reality.

Ron set out to find a leadership and governance process that would become the fifth component of the Apex Client-Driven Six Sigma model and enable the leaders to execute in the manner that he was envisioning.

9.6   The Collaborative Management Model

As members of the team at Jones Lang LaSalle were putting its Client-Driven Six Sigma model into practice, they realized—as our friend, Ron Brown, had realized—that getting the most out of an integrated Six Sigma framework and effectively driving performance through a set of integrated processes required a new model of leadership and governance.

This is especially true for Jones Lang LaSalle, because of the unique relationships the company enjoys with top corporate clients. Many of the real estate services that Jones Lang LaSalle provides to corporate clients (such as Bank of America, Motorola, Procter & Gamble, Xerox, and Microsoft) are performed at client sites and involve direct interactions with the client employees and client work processes. Such services include providing engineering and maintenance support to client facilities, managing the physical movement of offices and whole businesses, and helping the client reduce office and real estate space, and associated costs.

Strategically, the company advises clients on overall real estate portfolio strategy. These services include advice on lease-versus-buy decisions, finding optimal labor markets, and optimizing a corporation's in-house workplace services organization. All of these services require tight integration and close coordination with clients. This tight integration is critical if Jones Lang LaSalle is to deliver the kind of continuous cost reductions and service improvements that their clients have come to expect. For a strategic alliance to be sustainable over the long term at Jones Lang LaSalle, both parties must win, as illustrated in Exhibit 9.11.

9.6.1   Developing a Set of Leadership and Management Practices

Given this challenge, the Strategic Consulting team at Jones Lang LaSalle developed the Collaborative Management Model. The model comprises a set of leadership and management practices to guide client teams and their client partners in new ways of managing and governing business alliances. The model suggests that breakthrough performance occurs when all members of the leadership team have an equal seat at the "leadership table." All members also need to have a common view and shared ownership of both the business outcomes and the operational performance

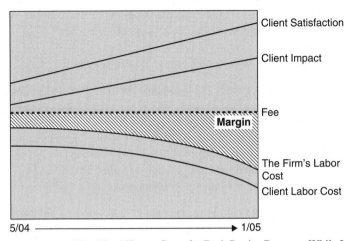

Exhibit 9.11   In a Win-Win Alliance Costs for Both Parties Decrease While Impact and Satisfaction Increase

required to achieve them. The Collaborative Management Model can be visualized as a control room equipped with a large round table and live screens which deliver various views of activity status and performance metrics (Exhibit 9.12). The model puts into operation a collaborative,

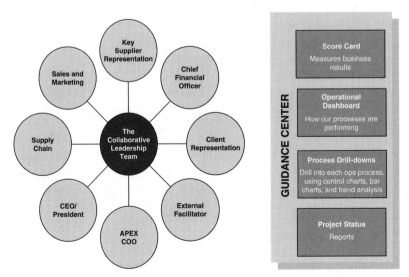

Exhibit 9.12   Collaborative Management Model

team-based approach to strategy and planning, solution development, and shared decision making across the leadership team.

9.6.2   Working in a "Guidance Center" Environment

Within this Guidance Center environment, the leadership team meets at weekly, monthly, and quarterly intervals. Unlike traditional management meetings, where functional managers provide function updates and senior managers issue the next set of orders, the Collaborative Management Model establishes an environment and an agenda focused on driving shared learning, innovative solutions, and breakthrough improvements. This outcome is made possible through the major elements of the model:

- A forward-looking continuous management process enabled through an established schedule of weekly, monthly, and quarterly leadership team meetings
- An established agenda focused on creating shared learning and innovative solutions
- A team commitment to a specific set of leadership behaviors
- A skilled, external facilitator/coach capable of keeping the team focused on learning and innovation while practicing appropriate leadership behaviors
- A set of dashboards that deliver real-time performance data that enable fact-based decision making to drive timely execution of decisions and solutions.

The Forward-Looking, Collaborative Management Process

The Collaborative Management Model is brought to life through a continuous cycle of monthly leadership dialogue sessions that follow an agenda designed to drive the leadership team toward creative strategy and solution discussions. The output of the session is an agreed-upon set of strategies and actions that guide day-to-day resource allocation and management of execution activities.

Functional leaders have full responsibility for management and execution between leadership sessions. The leadership team is informed regarding progress through weekly updates in the Guidance Center. At the same time, other leaders have responsibility for managing client relationships.

9.6.3   An Ongoing Team Dialogue

The Collaborative Management Process is an ongoing team dialogue organized to enable continuous review of the external factors that should impact business direction and then converting these external factors into strategy and purposeful action. This objective is achieved through a series of workshops that establish an annual, quarterly, monthly, and weekly cadence to the leadership process of listen, plan, execute, review, and adjust.

On an annual and quarterly basis, the Collaborative Management Team focuses on listening to the customer voice, prioritizing investment in key initiatives, and making adjustments to the strategy. On a monthly basis, the team focuses on driving operational priorities through careful review of performance metrics, process drill downs, and key Six Sigma projects. On a weekly basis, the team is alerted to major variations in performance metrics or in the status of critical projects. Meetings are held only when they will resolve a key performance alert. A system of workshops and infrastructure drives this cadence.

9.7   Annual Planning and Strategy Development Workshop

The annual planning and strategy development workshop is focused on reviewing and understanding the organization's strategies. Through dialogue, with the support of an external facilitator, the team develops a shared understanding of the strategic inputs and the implications to the business strategy. Once the strategic implications are understood, a series of facilitated activities drive the Collaborative Management Team to establish shared objectives (3-year horizon), key initiatives (this year's actions that support the objectives), performance metrics that indicate progress toward the objectives, and a set of Six Sigma improvement projects that focus on major cost reduction opportunities and breakthrough process improvement opportunities. Together, the objectives, key initiatives, performance metrics, and Six Sigma projects become the Collaborative Management Team's strategic plan for the year. The plan is summarized in a one-page document (see Exhibit 9.13), which becomes the foundation for execution and review for the year.

9.7.1   Collaborative Management Team Strategic Planning Dialogue Agenda

- Create shared understanding of business strategies
- Conduct SWOT and performance driver analysis
- Agree on mission objectives and initiatives
- Establish performance metrics
- Launch Six Sigma improvement teams
- Finalize strategic plan

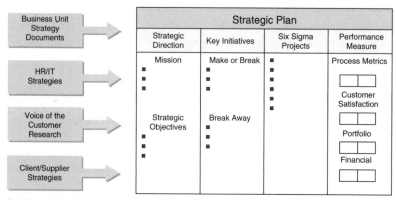

Exhibit 9.13   Strategic Planning Dialogue

9.7.2   Monthly Dialogue Session

The monthly dialogue session is the primary vehicle for driving joint accountability for performance, integrated planning, shared understanding of client needs and collaborative, innovative solutions. It is in these sessions that the linkage to key clients and resulting solutions is clearly established. Supported by structure and a facilitator/coach, client representatives present updates of client strategies and focus the team on emerging needs.

With these client needs as a backdrop, the team then reviews the performance status provided by the control center. The focus of this operational review is to develop a shared understanding of the sources of variation from operational plans. Where variation is apparent, process owners will be on hand to walk through a process drill-down. Similarly, Six Sigma projects are reviewed for positive and negative variation to schedule, and financial impact. Team leaders are on hand to review specific projects where CMT input is critical.

Once the operational reviews are completed, the team moves to dialogue focused on adjustments to the strategy and dialogue regarding emerging business unit needs, and innovative solutions to those needs. At a minimum, 50 percent of the focus of a monthly dialogue session is devoted to strategy and solutions. Each session focuses on developing shared understanding and enabling open and honest dialogue that drives innovative solutions and rapid execution.

Successful sessions result in leaders feeling confident that they can focus their month on client relationships and strategy, while the functional leaders focus on execution. These goals are achieved through a structured process and an establish set of shared behavioral expectations, supported by a skilled facilitator coach familiar with both the strategy and the process.

9.7.3 Weekly Reviews and Alerts Dialogue

Critical to maintaining focus and driving execution is the timely resolution of unplanned variation in key performance metrics. In anticipation of occasional variations, a weekly check-in call is on the calendar of all Collaborative Management Team members. Participation on the call is determined by the nature of the issues to be discussed. The call is facilitated by the COO, with support from the facilitator coach as required.

9.8   Collaborative Management Process Summary

When all the elements of the Collaborative Management Process are knit together, a leadership team emerges that is focused on fulfilling customer needs with innovative solutions, driving execution, and trusting one another to contribute appropriately. See Exhibits 9.14 and 9.15.

9.8.1   Commitment to a specific set of Leadership Behaviors

The Collaborative Management Model is dependent on a team of leaders committed to the shared success of the business and willing to engage in a set of leadership behaviors that foster open inquiry and continuous improvement while insisting on focused execution. The leadership team is assessed, first by one another and then by other stakeholders, on their ability to demonstrate the leadership behaviors and work with an executive coach to improve their use of the behaviors as a team and as individuals (See Exhibit 9.16.)

Leaders who adopt the collaborative model typically demonstrate common key beliefs and behaviors.

Behavior #1: Passion for Delivering Customer Value

Critical to both the Client-Driven Six Sigma framework and the Collaborative Management Process is the realization that effective leadership is grounded in and driven by an obsession for doing what is right for the customer. Effective leaders are constantly aware of their customers' needs and evolving requirements. Every decision they make and every action they take are weighed against its impact on customers. To deliver maximum value to customers, they search passionately for ways to improve effectiveness and eliminate waste within their organization.

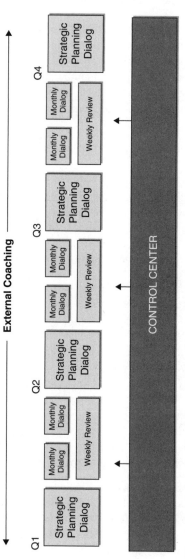

Exhibit 9.14 A Steady Leadership Cadence Drives Superior Execution

Process / Roles	Listen →	Plan →	Execute →	Review →
Integrated Strategy, Development, and Deployment	Review of Various Stakeholder Business Strategies	Share Strategy with Stakeholders	Provide Feedback and Changes from Business Units and Others Back to CMT	Adjust CRE Strategy and Begin Cycle Over
Operations Management	Establish Priorities and Performance Metrics	Allocate Resources Drive Daily Execution	Provide Updates and Performance Data Status to CMT	Adjust Operations
Six Sigma Improvement Projects	Identify Improvement Targets, Charter, and Launch Teams	Drive Teams through Six Sigma Project Milestones DMAIC	Provide Updates and Performance Data to CMT	Adjust and Launch Additional Projects
Solution Development and Deployment	Identify and Prioritize Emerging Client Requirements	Create Solutions and Develop New Resources Plans	Communicate and Negotiate Solutions with Business Units	Adjust and Track Solution Deployment through CMT

Exhibit 9.15 The Collaborative Management Team Process

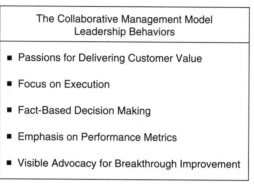

The Collaborative Management Model Leadership Behaviors
■ Passions for Delivering Customer Value ■ Focus on Execution ■ Fact-Based Decision Making ■ Emphasis on Performance Metrics ■ Visible Advocacy for Breakthrough Improvement

Exhibit 9.16   Leadership Behaviors

Behavior #2: Focus on Execution

Proper application of the Client-Driven Six Sigma framework and the Collaborative Management Process requires leaders to develop a laser-sharp focus on the vital actions that will most effectively produce the specific results they are trying to achieve. Strong leaders avoid trivial activities that keep average managers distracted and maintain a persistent course of purposeful progress toward end goals.

Behavior #3: Fact-Based Decision Making

Leaders are able to commit deeply to a given course of action because the decision to take that action is based on facts and data rather than gut feel. In the Client-Driven Six Sigma framework, leaders know when to demand analysis and how to use that analysis to drive better decisions. They also know when enough analysis is sufficient for the decision, respecting the fine line between "rigor" and "rigor mortis."

Behavior #4: Emphasis on Performance Metrics

For the Collaborative Management Process to work effectively, leaders need to know how to use a small but critical set of performance metrics to sustain focused activity. They also need to know the effect of this activity on a week-to-week basis. An operational dashboard is used to display trend data supporting these metrics. Daily use of the dashboard guides the leader's decisions.

Behavior #5: Visible Advocacy for Breakthrough Improvements

Confident in their ability to execute, supported by better decision making and guided by performance metrics that matter, the collaborative leadership team sets goals that require breakthrough improvement. They are able to sponsor and support the kind of activities that generate breakthrough improvements.

To encourage strong leadership behavior and make it possible for leadership teams to manifest these behaviors on a regular basis, effective leadership teams understand their governance responsibilities, and associated behaviors, in the context of the Client-Driven Six Sigma framework, and a continuous management process. These leadership teams develop a weekly, monthly, quarterly cadence in which they set priorities, review operational metrics, and make necessary decisions to drive effective execution.

9.8.2   The Need for Real-Time Performance Data

The Collaborative Management Model is informed through a set of dashboards (collectively referred to as the Guidance Center; Exhibit 9.17) that deliver real-time performance data that enable fact-based decision making to drive timely execution of decisions and solutions.

9.9   The Guidance Center

While the foundation of the Collaborative Management Team process is the strategic plan, the "nervous system" is the Guidance Center. This is an integrated set of management information displays that provide real-time or near–real-time updates and alarms related to critical performance objectives. There are four displays:

- The scorecard, which tracks performance relative to strategic and financial impact
- The operational dashboard, which tracks performance relative to key operational performance metrics
- Process drill downs, which enable leaders to click down into each operational process
- Six Sigma project updates, which enable leaders to check status and financial impacts of key improvement projects.

The Guidance Center enables members of the leadership team to spend less time collecting and interpreting data and more time communicating with clients and driving strategy.

GUIDANCE CENTER

Score Card

Measures business results

Operational Dashboard

How our processes are performing

Process Drill-downs

Drill into each ops process, using control charts, bar charts, and trend analysis

Project Status

Reports

Exhibit 9.17 Guidance Center

9.9.1   The Role of the Facilitator/Coach

The role of the external coach/facilitator should not be underestimated in the Collaborative Management Model. Leadership teams attempting to practice this model are learning a new set of processes, interactions, and personal behaviors.

While driving superior execution, the team is operating in a collaborative, learning-focused dialogue.

Old behaviors and deep functional knowledge in certain areas often drive leaders to want to jump to what they see as a foregone conclusion informed by previous experience. Or they may be inclined to "trump" another team member's opinion because of either deeper expertise or higher organizational status. The result is a missed opportunity to develop a holistic system view and a potentially innovative solution.

Only a skilled external facilitator can manage the structured agenda while coaching team members on appropriate behaviors. There will be times when the team will feel that all of the effort involved in attempting to collaborate is wasteful. The external facilitator/coach can push the team through these low spots.

9.9.2   Moving from Model to Practical Application

When all the elements of the Collaborative Management Model are put into practice, leadership teams can reach new levels of sustained breakthrough performance, both operationally and financially. And when the model is extended to include suppliers and customers in the governance and decision-making processes, players win across the value chain.

It should be recognized that the Collaborative Management Model is "aspirational" in nature. The team that developed it at Jones Lang LaSalle recognizes that complete implementation of the model, especially a model that drives deep collaboration between supplier partners and clients, requires mature relationships and deep trust across all parties.

The Key to Breakthrough Performance

Technical hurdles to delivering fully automated, real-time performance metrics must be overcome. And the tyranny of the urgent tends to derail the best laid plans for proactive, forward-looking leadership dialogue.

But as Jones Lang LaSalle introduces both the Client-Driven Six Sigma model and the Collaborative Management Model to them, more and more clients are recognizing that true breakthrough performance improvement and the associated financial gains can only come when a rigorous approach to problem-solving and innovative solutions is combined with leaders who can facilitate collaborative governance and decision making across the value chain.

As a result, elements of the Collaborative Management Model are in play across a number of key clients. Partnerships are being formed to drive collaborative Six Sigma projects. A number of business alliances are being governed through a common view of shared performance metrics. Governance boards are in place at a number of alliances where leadership is shared by the client and Jones Lang LaSalle. These developments point clearly to a future in which Client-Driven Six Sigma, enabled by the Collaborative Management Model, will become the preferred management model for enlightened clients in need of best-in-class service delivery from the professional service providers.

9.10   Conclusion

Informed by his new learning, Ron Brown was now prepared to introduce the Apex leadership team to the Collaborative Management Model. It was time to launch a Client-Driven Six Sigma framework using the Collaborative Management Model to drive more flawless execution across all of their business processes. Various team members agreed to take responsibility for key elements of the launch process. An action plan was developed, which is shown in Exhibit 9.18.

With commitments from his leadership team in place, Ron felt confident that he and his team were on track to deliver breakthrough performance for Apex. He was resolute in his intention to drive rigorous execution of the Apex Client-Driven Six Sigma framework through the Collaborative Management Process. He knew that his ultimate objective, superior financial performance, was now achievable.

The premise of this chapter is that a Six Sigma approach to achieving breakthrough financial results is most effective when an informed, committed leadership team is driving the effort, and is continuously monitoring, guiding, and leading the way. To be effective in that role, most leadership teams need to rethink their approach to continuous improvement. Sustainable improvement

Action	Owner	Timing
Update and validate voice of the customer input.	Mary	June
Establish and validate performance metrics.	Jack	Q3
Launch and complete IT project to create collection mechanisms, data base linkages, and live display capabilities for the Apex Guidance Center.	Liz	Q3
Launch four cross-functional teams to streamline and then integrate the four core processes.	Various process owners	Q3
Select key suppliers and customers to participate in Collaborative Management Team.	Ron	June
Administer baseline leadership skills assessment for all members of the Collaborative Management Team.	Barbara	Q3
Commit to the calendar of quarterly, monthly, weekly leadership sessions.	All team members	June
"Go Live" with the Annual Strategy Workshop.	All team members	August1

Exhibit 9.18   APEX Six Sigma Implementation Action Plan

is only possible when leaders understand that continuous improvement must be part of an overall organizational transformation. That transformation must include key shifts in management thinking (Exhibit 9.19).

The Client-Driven Six Sigma model enabled by the Collaborative Management Process provides the operational framework for making these organizational shifts. Once this framework is put into practice, organizations

FROM	TO
Internally focused business decisions	Voice of the customer driven decisions
Primary focus on financial results	Daily focus on performance metrics
Functionally focused organizations	Process-based organization
Management as a functionally focused staff	Collaborative leadership team
Quarterly "after the fact" review of functional results	Continuous "hands on" leadership and rapid decision making

Exhibit 9.19   Fundamental Shifts in Management Approach

realize maximum financial gains from their Six Sigma improvement efforts, *if* they keep the following principles in mind:

- Six Sigma is most effective when practiced in a holistic framework like Client-Driven Six Sigma.
- Six Sigma is most effective when practiced in the context of an integrated business process environment.
- Six Sigma is most effective when practiced across the value chain in collaboration with both suppliers and customers.

Finally, sustainable financial results will be greatest when an operationally aware leadership team follows the steady cadence of a Collaborative Management Process and remains committed to staying with the process for the long term.

10

Shareholder Value and Business Profitability

They that can give up essential liberty to obtain a little temporary safety deserve neither liberty nor safety.
BENJAMIN FRANKLIN

This chapter covers a broad front ranging from shareholder value to different profitability views to quality costs. A lot of organizations are trying to simplify their reporting while making certain they comply with Sarbanes-Oxley (U.S. businesses). They are trying to find useful nonfinancial metrics, which is always a challenge. And they are trying to identify metrics that steer them toward greater profitability. *A quick note:* Sarbanes-Oxley was a perfect example of a potential strategic Six Sigma project using the DMAIC model, but very few organizations implemented SOX following that thought process.

We discussed nonfinancial metrics in the Measurement chapter. They are hard to get right, because unlike the financials they don't usually have an overall reconciliation, so you're never sure if the number is exactly right. People have a reasonable idea of good nonfinancial reporting numbers they would like to see. But they leap to conclusions about the validity of these metrics without testing them, they fail to validate the number, and usually don't probe deeply enough to get the number they really need. In the Measurement chapter, we site an example regarding employee turnover in total versus employee turnover of cooks and supervisors at a national restaurant chain—the latter numbers had a much higher correlation to profitability. But the parent company was measuring the former. If the nonfinancial metrics provide misleading information, the actions taken as a result may do more harm than good.

The same problems happen with profitability reporting. On the surface this seems simple. Find the unprofitable and kill it! Unfortunately once again, it's not quite so simple. Rarely is a product unprofitable with all customers who buy it, and rarely is a single customer unprofitable for everything they buy. So once again probing and understanding the differences between profitable and unprofitable transactions and using that knowledge for action will serve an organization far better results. This is not to say that some customers and products are not dogs (no offense intended) and shouldn't be dropped. It's simply not as simple as it first seems. *(Say that sentence fast three times.)*

10.1   Shareholder Value

This is another subject where much has been written, so we will only touch on it lightly here. An examination of share prices shows that expectations of future performance are the main driver of shareholder returns: In almost all industries and almost all stock exchanges, cash flow expectations beyond the next three years account for 70 to 90 percent of a share's market value. These longer-term expectations in turn reflect judgments on growth and long-term profitability—a lesson relearned after the dot-com bust.[*]

Long-term expectations vary from one industry to another. Cash flows in the global semiconductor industry, for example, must grow by more than 10 percent a year during the next 10 years to justify current market valuations. In retailing and consumer packaged goods, the required growth rate ranges from 3 to 6 percent; in electric utilities, it is around 2 percent.

Future expectations also clearly drive the stock price of individual companies, thus explaining the often widely differing P/Es or market-to-book ratios of companies with similar reported earnings. In the pharmaceutical sector, for example, the market ascribes great value to a healthy drug pipeline, despite the fact that it will not affect earnings in the short term.

Shareholder value can be calculated as follows:

Shareholder value = NPV or all future cash flows
+ nonoperating assets − future claims (debts)

---

[*] *"Building the Healthy Corporation,"* Richard Dobbs, Keith Leslie, and Lenny T. Mendonca; *McKinsey Quarterly,* #3, 2005.

Nonoperating assets include

- Marketable securities (such as stocks and bonds)
- Excess cash
- Excessively funded (pension plans, real estate, or other assets)

Future claims include

- Interest-bearing debt
- Capital lease obligations
- Underfunded pension plans
- Contingent liabilities (if any)

Economic value added (EVA) calculates the true economic performance of a corporation. Unlike *return on net assets* (RONA), EVA takes into account an organization's debt and real cost of capital. This is another macro shareholder type metric. EVA is calculated by taking

Operating profit − income taxes − (a charge for debt + capital employed)

Both of these are good macro measures. The problem with them for operating decisions is they are like net cash flow: they are the net result of everything the organization does. So from that perspective they are good numbers to know. But they are long-term metrics. They will not help with day-to-day operating decisions. When organizations make short-term decisions simply to move these numbers, except in the case of a real crisis, leadership may be shortsighted for the long term. That short-term-sightedness deprives those metrics of their long-term value.

10.1.1   Misguided Shareholder Value

In the Define chapter we pointed out the danger of listening to just one stakeholder voice. If shareholders always dominate the other key stakeholders, an organization can't possibly be in balance. At some point, the organization will get so far out of alignment with the voice of the customer, the voice of the employee, the voice of the regulator, or whoever else is a key player, that ugliness will happen.

From a U.S. perspective, a dangerous obsession with shareholder value and a myopic focus on bottom line profitability has driven many multinational organizations to the point that one must question what value will be generated by the remaining core over the next 20 years. Even General Electric, which we have repeatedly praised elsewhere in this book, has so undermined its R&D capabilities that one wonders if they will be the superstar tomorrow that they are today. Consider just a few old line U.S.

industries and where the value-added work gets done today: Zenith (actually name any TV manufacturer)—the brand exists, but the company is gone; name any personal computer manufacturer—the brand exists, but the manufacturing portion of the U.S. company is gone; the U.S. machine tool industry is largely gone. These products are now made in Asia. Similar patterns are now cropping up in the outsourcing of R&D, information system development, and basic research. Some of this is simply the result of global capacity and capability. Some of it also appears attributable to CEOs who do not truly understand the "value" their organization creates. If all of this outsourcing is so good, why has Toyota done so little of it?

Here is another "repeating pattern—a depressing one": A "troubled" Fortune 500 company recruits a superstar CEO. The new CEO, pockets bulging with a host of lavish pay "incentives," announces a bold new plan to turn the company around. That bold plan amounts to spending billions of dollars to buy out some other company and create a synergy that, shareholders are assured, will cut costs and gain market share. The newly merged company does cut costs by firing a few thousand employees. But rarely does it actually create new "value."

Carly Fiorina's half-dozen years at HP followed a similar script. Fiorina, in her six years at Hewlett-Packard, did a good bit more than cut merger deals and destroy jobs. She was at the helm while a corporate culture that actually seemed to have redeeming social value has been destroyed, or at least severely harmed. It's not fair to blame all of HP's woes on Fiorina, but when you have a high profile CEO leading the chase, it's hard to point fingers elsewhere. At least there were no major ethics issues with Fiorina at HP.

"Chainsaw Al" Dunlap at Sunbeam was a bigger disaster on many fronts, and ethics was a major factor. Sunbeam was left in shambles after infamous CEO Al Dunlap's cost-cutting and acquisition spree sent the company into bankruptcy. Enron's Ken Lay and WorldCom's Bernie Ebbers are simply today's versions of the infamous superstar with stupendous lapses of ethics, along with fiscal irresponsibility. They all committed major accounting irregularities and were so out of line with voice of the customer and voices of the business that these are easy disasters to see. In your typical "average" organization, ethics aside, the same misguided thinking takes place on a smaller scale, when shareholders always dominate other constituencies. Boats float because they are balanced. When they get out of balance, they sink. The same happens with business organizations.

Cutting costs helps survivability, but it does not create new value. Value comes from growth-oriented strategies that ultimately generate cash.

Lou Gerstner, another high-profile CEO, managed to lead the charge at IBM in a very positive way. J&J has bounced back from setbacks in the marketplace, and CISCO has had a best-practice process for integrating new acquisitions. So these things can be done in the right way.

10.2   Strategic Business Planning Metrics

10.2.1   Market Demand versus Competitive Capacities

This needs some explanation. The key factor that determines price levels in a particular market is the *utilization rate of existing capacity* to supply specific goods or services to a current demand level. Suppliers can usually charge higher prices as their aggregate industry capacity approaches full utilization because the greater uncertainty of supply in the near term causes customers to cave in to price increases as insurance against future shortages.

You see this at the macroeconomic level during recovery from a recession as the U.S. Commerce Department reports industrial utilization increases into the 80 percent range. That usually causes a bump up in the *producer price index* (PPI) as suppliers can "name their price" for products from their now-less-available production capacity. Then the Federal Reserve Bank often interprets the PPI uptick as "potentially inflationary," so their near-term economic analysis announcements and changes in the federal funds interest rate are tilted toward "tightening" policies to keep the economy from growing faster than new capacity can come on line.

Similar dynamics occur in commerce within individual market segments and small or specialized niches. Many companies "go with the flow," and build new capacity to chase new demand *after* it appears; they're often disappointed to be part of an "overcapacity" industry with cutthroat competition and low profit margins. The smart operators are looking into the future to anticipate market and competitive shifts to be exploited later. Building capacity late in a recession is an effective way to capture higher margins in the early stages of a recovery when capacity has been contracted by the loss of weaker players in the overcapacity environment of the recessionary tail-off stage.

Two metrics go into the utilization rate of existing capacity calculation:

- Market demand for specific product or service
- Supplier industry aggregate capacity that is unique to the specific product or service

For Bridge Model purposes, supplier industry capacity is the more important of the two, because it's generally less available than market demand statistics that the customers are openly communicating to the suppliers in an effort to find the least-cost sources. But supplier capacity is a different story. Most are reluctant to share capacity information as a general principle, so that what their customers and competitors don't know can work to their own advantage. Thus, getting competitive capacity data is rarely as simple as checking the Commerce Department or Bureau of Labor Statistics data. But it doesn't have to be as hard as it sounds.

Start with a survey of your field sales people. Chances are they have had conversations with the customers that allude to the competitors' capacities. A little organized, but subtle, additional questioning may be enough to build a reasonable picture of competitive capacities, particularly if the questions are couched in terms of how to ensure long-term, low-cost support for the customers' future needs.

Consider "capacity" in the broadest view. The capacities of human resource pools with specialized core competencies can be more important than capital equipment system capacities. And that's becoming more true in the "knowledge age" of global competition where business agility is often a function of human resource capabilities. One thought is that people-based business differentiators are often more difficult to copy than hard technologies that can be reverse engineered once they're available in the open market. So human resources can be the key capacity constraint in some industries, especially where specialized experience is involved.

10.3   The One-Page Strategic Growth Model

10.3.1   How Exciting! It's "Annual Planning" Time...Not!!

Many organizations spend considerable time putting together the annual plan. Once completed, they breathe a sigh of relief and relegate the planning documents to the shelf, to await next year's planning revival meeting. Most organizations also use some type of key performance measurements. But most likely, other than the sales department, very few of the metrics focus on business growth. Then management wonders why people working inside the walls have so little customer focus!

Imagine Thousands of Spontaneous Employee Actions...

...In Concert, and Aligned With Your Strategic Goals

Jim Collins, in *Good to Great*, describes a flywheel metaphor for thousands of autonomous employee pushes on the strategic flywheel of the business.[*] That kind of unanimous movement has to start with a clearly understood, compelling business strategy. To be effective—guiding the whole organization in a productive direction—your strategic planning efforts should include the following capabilities:

- Does your team have a clear vision of your best opportunities? Or is your organization somewhat out of alignment, because people perceive key opportunities differently?
- Has your company timed your capacity investments for optimum ROI so you are putting capital to work just-in-time (not too early or not too late)? Or have you made investments only to find later that the timing of them was wrong? Or you under- or overinvested in the wrong things?
- Do you "own" your customer relationships, so achievement of the strategic plan is supported by dependable execution? Or do your customers and suppliers own you?
- Have you taken the guesswork out of strategic planning with fact-based decision making based on clear cause-and-effect market dynamics? (Yes, the laws of supply and demand play a role in practical strategy.) Or do you have a planning shelf document?

10.3.2 Making the Transition to a One-Page Model

Let's look at a simple but effective way to create a one-page Strategic Growth Model with meaningful information to help drive, or at least guide, business growth. The strategic planning process usually begins with a series of questions about the business situation.

- Which market niches offer the best potential returns for your core competencies and invested assets?
- Should you invest money (plant, equipment, human resources, or other) in our business today?
- What impact will it have on the marketplace where you play?
- What is the best timing for specific strategic investments?

Note: The last question can be crucial, but often goes unanswered as the planning team has usually spent a lot of energy researching current and historical market data, so they're uncomfortable forecasting future market shifts without a dependable "crystal ball." That's typical of internal management groups that spend most of their time analyzing "hard data" from operations.

---

[*]*Good to Great*, Jim Collins; HarperCollins, 2001.

Occasionally, an entrepreneurial spirit in the group may say something like, "Wait a minute. I've heard rumors that competitors DEF and XYZ are gearing up to serve this niche too. If all that capacity hits at the same time, and early in the market demand ramp-up, we could be selling the product at a loss for quite a while unless somebody drops out." Others might take that as negative, not supporting the team's plan, even though it's a legitimate concern about the future market dynamics. It's about the timing of the investment, not about the basic market opportunity. Unfortunately, most such discussions go unresolved because there is no convenient tool at hand to sort the issues in the future view.

The Strategic Growth Model (SGM) addresses the planning problem described earlier. It creates a one-page, time-based view of the key relationships between the following:

- Total niche market demand for your products or services
- "Net" competitive capacity available from your industry
- Your own company's capacity

The one-page SGM shows the factors driving niche market profitability and guides individual company decisions about when to increase or decrease participation in a market niche.

There are a variety of ways to approach this. The approach described in the following sections outlines a method several organizations have used to increase profitability, grow their business, and guide business investments. It also fits with our views on the importance of meaningful "key performance indicators" and "continual improvement of business performance."

10.3.3   Market, Competitors, and Us—The Causal Relationships

The Strategic Growth Model summarizes the time-variable key factors in a niche strategy (Exhibit 10.1). You can create your own version of this. Since it uses current operations data in a conventional financial spreadsheet format as a starting point, the niche extensions and roll-ups can be obvious and easy to interpret during planning discussions.

10.3.4   Industry Perspective

At an overall *industry level,* your SGM needs to include factors like GNP, expected growth, estimated production capacity, overall estimated market

1. Build Niche Strategy Data Models (see Notes sheet)

2. Roll Up to Segments and Business Total

3. Evaluate Segments and Business Totals vis-à-vis Biz Goals

4. Adjust Guidelines for Segments and Niches

5. Repeat Until Balanced and ROIC is Optimized

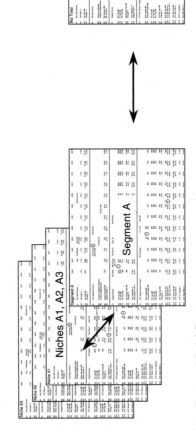

Exhibit 10.1   Strategy Model Structure

demand, human resources capacity, and so forth. You might come up with one or two other capacity factors, but keep it simple.

Example 1: Determining Your Net Capacity

In the case of human resources, think back to a few years ago, when software developers were at a premium. The industry demand exceeded the available supply, so if your growth plans needed that type of talent, you might not have been able to grow as fast as you hoped. Surprisingly, in many industries fixed asset production capacity is not a key factor. Often, based on equipment (such as molders and headers), there appears to be more supply than demand, so your competitors may expect that to put downward pressure on pricing. But their HR capacity to serve a specific niche may actually be the controlling capacity. So the companies that correctly support that relationship with adequate levels of quality HR capacity will reap the best margins and market share growth—in spite of what appears to be an unfavorable demand versus supply relationship based on the simple fixed asset capacities. That's the type of strategic relationship to be clarified in the SGM.

Example 2: Strategic Timing

In the following chart a niche market appears to be growing at a healthy rate, but still within the available capacities, so additional hard assets don't appear to be justified through FY2. But the competitor who sees that HR capacity is at 86 percent in FY3 might decide to invest in more HR capacity for FY3 when higher margins are likely.

	FY2	FY3
GNP growth (for reference)	3.0%	3.5%
Niche market total demand (sales $) (a)	$75M	$95M
Niche-specific supply capacity:		
General fixed asset cap. (equipment)	$200M	$200M
Proprietary/IP asset cap. (process, patents)	$120M	$120M
Human res. cap. (niche-specific expertise)	$110M	$110M
Net niche-specific supply capacity(b)*	$110M	$110M
Capacity utilization (a ÷ b)	68%	86%

*Net niche-specific supply capacity = the lowest capacity of fixed assets, proprietary, and HR. (The capacity constraint.)

Two points are important in this example:

- The demand versus supply relationship (capacity utilization) drives niche market profitability.
- Capacity comes in different forms, so you have to know which is the current constraint before making additional investments. Just like on a production line, additional investment in the unconstrained areas would be wasted.

The formula truly does show people as an asset: when you consider skills, capabilities, and availability.

Example 3: Company = Sum of the Niches

You need to develop this model for each industry (marketplace) niche that your company serves. For example, an automotive supplier might serve Detroit's Big 3, Japanese U.S. Operations, and perhaps another industry outside of automobiles. So there could be three data models, one for each market niche. The three views can be added together to get an overall segment or company view as shown in the chart in "Example 2: Strategic Timing".

10.3.5 Entrepreneur's View

People do not always know what the "real" market or competitor numbers are. Government, industry, and company databases are not usually detailed to the level you need for specific market niches. But you need to start somewhere. So at the very least, use estimates from your sales people to obtain an "entrepreneur's view" of the market factors that result in either high- or low-profit markets. Over time, you will find better information to replace the estimates—as long as you keep them in view so day-to-day interactions continue to look for the facts. However, even estimates help answer key strategy questions like: Do the Strategic Plan numbers that people talk about make any sense from a holistic perspective? And: will the niche market and competitive dynamics expected in FY3 provide margins to justify a capital investment now?

10.3.6 Company Perspective

Once you develop an SGM for your target market niches, you can begin to work on your company in total. The same information on capacity needs to be captured for your overall business. If you are looking at fixed assets, proprietary assets, and human resources, the overall capacity would be based on the portions of those capacities allocated to the individual niches.

Example 4: Financial Impact

After the above steps you can begin to compare performance between years. It would be unrealistic to assume that a company could increase prices or that revenues would rise significantly if an overall industry capacity has actually increased by 10 percent while total niche demand has increased by 10 percent or less. Unless the company has a dynamite plan of action or some grand new technology, it is likely to experience a flat to declining share for this industry niche.

The play-off between the industry and company figures can be used to estimate profit changes and return on invested capital (ROIC) for the company. As the company looks at the overall industry activity over time it can evaluate a wide range of issues:

- If overcapacity will hold down returns.
- When a shakeout is likely.
- When investment is most appropriate.
- When you should aggressively pursue market share, and so forth.

10.3.7   Getting Started Summary

You can build your own Strategic Growth Model by taking several key steps:

1. Identify the main capacity components in businesses serving your target market niches.
2. Research your competition to determine their capacities in the main capacity components. Remember that this will probably be very crude information the first year.
3. Research the total demand in each target niche.
4. Build a spreadsheet to display the market demand versus net industry capacity in future years. This is where the "entrepreneur's view" comes into play.
5. Add your own company's capacities to the spreadsheet model.
6. Identify the customer loyalty factors your company must deliver to dominate your chosen niches. This could be the most important part of the process since it provides the goals your people need to meet to execute the strategy successfully.
7. Add an industry margin % line to the model, with your interpretation of the margin to be expected in each future year based on the supply/demand ratio in place at that time.
8. Integrate the data used for strategy and operations so they present a clear roadmap and diagnostic base for use by everyone in the company, regardless of their role.

9. Replace the annual strategic planning "event" with an ongoing strategic planning "process" that's seamlessly woven into the day-to-day management routine.

Note: Step 7 is key to the investment timing questions in a strategic plan. Your team may not be able to fill the model with concrete data in the first year, but it will help them maintain that holistic entrepreneur's view of the marketplace and will provide a roadmap for on-going data collection work that can become a part of routine business activities throughout the year. So next year the numbers will be closer to reality, and need less guesswork to fill the gaps.

10.3.8   Do it!

The Strategic Growth Model concept is relatively simple although it can sound complicated since we rarely use supply and demand information in a holistic view of a business on a daily basis. The supply/demand view is out of context with our routine business operating views. Use the SGM to step back from the "trees" in your day-to-day view, and take a look at the "forest" of each niche you're operating in. Identify the forces that will drive the supply/demand market dynamics in the years ahead. Those are the factors you need to build into your Strategic Growth Model.

10.4   Customer Profitability

Most organizations calculate some form of customer, product, and services profitability. Unfortunately, the logic used in these calculations may be misguided, and the conclusions drawn from the information may sometimes do more harm than good.

Beatrice Foods owned a confectionery and snack division in Australia. They were using a simple activity-based cost system for determining customer profitability. In the interest of confidentiality and simplicity, let's consider just one of their logic streams. One of the cost assumptions dealt with deliveries. On the surface, the logic used by management in determining cost drivers made total sense. Management believed the large hypermarkets were their most profitable customers. They would buy several full truckloads of product per week. When the cost per shipment to the customer was considered, the large retail stores looked considerably better than medium-sized stores that required longer truck runs (distances) and more frequent runs for replacement of smaller quantities (replenishment). Unfortunately, when one dug beneath the surface, it revealed a picture that was not quite so rosy, nor quite in line with management's beliefs.

Full truckloads were sent to the large markets, but they would often wait for hours to be unloaded. If the trucks missed a delivery window at check in, the order would be refused and a redelivery expense and penalty charge for lateness were incurred. Medium-sized retail outlets on the other hand tended to pay a higher margin for products and they received fewer promotional dollars. The number of invoices required to hit $1,000,000 U.S. sales with a medium-sized retailer exceeded the number of invoices sent to the large retail stores to hit the same revenue dollars. But on further analysis there was virtually no problem with shipping counts or invoice adjustments with the mid-market; while it was an ongoing confrontation with the large retailers.

Now there are many ways the problems with the large retailers could be addressed. A project team could reduce the problem with late deliveries. Once some of the root causes of invoicing problems were identified, presumably the extent of these problems could also be decreased. But if leadership stayed at a high level of analysis and simply made management decisions based on the profitability reports, the changes they made to the business would not have the P&L impact they expected. In fact, this company was in the process of strategically distancing itself from the mid-market retailers, which were its most profitable business. As has been stressed throughout this book people need to be more in touch with reality, to probe and discover the "real" issues, beneath the surface.

10.4.1   Profitability Mental Models

One of the problems with profitability reporting is the mental model people develop (i.e., the way people think, talk, and act) inside a business. Sometimes these models become hard coded and make it difficult for people to see beneath the surface. People look at the numbers and they believe the numbers are real. But in fact, numbers are based on a set of assumptions. They represent one version of reality. If leadership teams or people inside an organization become too rigid in their thinking, they risk missing marketplace opportunities and they increase chances of suboptimizing processes rather than making the world a better place.

The easy solution is simply to say, "Let's drop this product, service, or customer group." The more meaningful action might be to say, "Let's understand why one group of products, services, or customers appears to be unprofitable, and what is different about these groups from profitable products, services, and customers?"

So once again the number is not what is important! The understanding of what the number represents is much more meaningful. If an analysis is done of revenues, typically 80 percent of revenues come from 20 to 30 percent of total customers. Another typical number is 5 percent of revenues come from 50 to 60 percent of total customers. Now on the surface, one can conclude: Simply drop the bottom half of the customer base, redeploy or get rid of the excess resources, and the organization will become more profitable. In the very short term, this belief is probably true, but if one digs deeper another story may emerge.

10.4.2   Misguided Profitability Thinking

A global bank did a study of its account base. It determined that 77 percent of revenues due to money deposited with the institution came from 20 percent of its customer base. And that 3 percent of revenue came from a whopping 40 percent of its customers. The leadership team immediately ordered all of those "small deposit accounts" canceled. Within 30 days a number of the bank's large deposit account holders were taking their business elsewhere. When bank employees interviewed some of these customers they learned the accounts were closed because the bank had canceled small balance accounts that belonged to their children. Once leadership had this realization, they dug further into the numbers. They learned they were also canceling the accounts belonging to young families in their 20s. They were really killing off future "large" deposit holders. If the bank had asked two simple questions when they were reviewing the data, they might have avoided these problems:

- What connections to larger accounts exist with these small deposit holders?
- What are the common attributes of these small deposit holders?

A large global manufacturing company did a product profitability study. They determined that 70 percent of revenues came from 22 percent of their product line. Eight percent of revenues came from 50 percent of their products. They decided to kill off the 30 percent of their product line that was contributing less than 2 percent of revenues. Shortly thereafter, a number of their largest and most profitable customers threatened to take their business elsewhere, if they could no longer procure these items from this company. This organization also dug more deeply into their data. They gained several new insights. This happens when people turn data into knowledge.

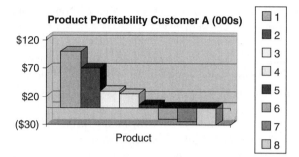

Exhibit 10.2   Graph of Product Profitability Purchases by One Customer

Several of their customers that purchased high-margin large machinery were also ordering small tooling, which was one of the negative-margin products. Customers purchase a variety of products, some of which have higher margins than others from a product profitability perspective. A graph might look similar to Exhibit 10.2, with machinery on the left hand side and tooling on the far right.

When they spoke to Customer A they learned that the tooling was used at various sites for field support of the machinery. The customer kept a supply of the tooling at the local sites, so that different maintenance teams would have the tools they needed when they were sent into the field as part of the customer's preventative maintenance program. Once the company saw what this customer was doing, it opened their eyes to opportunities with other customers where they might provide the preventive maintenance services.

10.4.3   Traditional Profitability Analysis Uses Averages

In Six Sigma, "variation" is evil. Improvement teams seek to reduce variation. In understanding customer, product, or supply chain profitability, "averaging" is evil. Averages mask complexity. People like to use averages, because they represent the presumed "norm." But in reality 50 percent of a population, work, activity, and so forth is above average and 50 percent is below. In terms of an "actual" transaction there may never be one that is actually "average." When averages are used to determine the profitability of customers, services, and products, actions can be taken that are 180° wrong.

10.5   Supply Chain Profitability

Most people don't seem to talk about supply chain profitability the same way they do customers and products or services. But this is really just a variation of the same concept. The other problem going into supply chain profitability is many organizations do a poor job of managing these relationships inside their walls, between functional departments that need to cooperate. So imagine the additional difficulties added when a business goes beyond its walls trying to foster this cooperation and synergy for the key players.

The idea missed here most often is the one of total or hidden costs. This includes new costs for managing the supply chain as well as any additional cost that may be directly related to the outsourced products. Sometimes when organizations elect to outsource a product they simply look at their labor costs plus material costs versus the supplier's labor costs and selling price for the product they are procuring. Organizations need to give consideration to the hidden costs: travel, loss of communications, legal, loss of intellectual property, response time, shipping/transportation, inventory levels, customer responsiveness (risks), reliability, and so forth. Opportunity cost may also be a factor. If two engineers are sent monthly to China, does that mean other work is not being done, or that other work needs outsourcing as a result of fewer available resources?

10.6   Cost of Quality

Cost of quality is another useful metric. It can be measured in terms of dollars and cents. But these numbers pale when compared to an organization's reputation. Like the VISA credit card commercial states: "some things are priceless." Just consider the actions taken by Johnson & Johnson when they had a product tampering problem in the 1980s versus the actions taken by Firestone with the tire problems in the 1990s, where precious time was wasted trying to place blame. The sad thing about Firestone is that in the 1970s they made a company film called *23/28*. The story of the film was about quality and productivity. *23/28 represents the percentage of time per week an average person spends working.* In the movie there was one line that proved prophetic, "If Firestone has problems, companies like Bridgestone will take its market share." After a series of tire debacles over the years, Bridgestone actually acquired Firestone Tire and Rubber Company. A reputation for quality is priceless; slipups can cost you the entire enterprise.

J&J dealt with its problems so quickly and so honorably that it established a new standard for dealing with product problems and improved its image in the marketplace, taking it to new heights.

The cost of poor quality is ultimately measured by lost customer bids, lost market share, and declining margins. Classifications might include prevention, appraisal, internal failures, and external failures:

- *Prevention costs:* Planned costs incurred to ensure that errors are not made at any stage during the delivery process of that product or service to a customer. For example, quality management, preventative maintenance, factory training, and supply chain process improvement.
- *Appraisal costs:* Costs of verifying, checking, or evaluating a product or service during the delivery process to ensure conformance to quality standards and to detect any failures inserted into the product or service before formal release of the product. For example, transaction inspection, factory inspection, material inspection, engineering maintenance of line costs, and technical operations.
- *Internal Failure costs:* Costs resulting from nonconformance to quality standards, and effort associated with overcoming the impact of failures *found before* the product or service is formally released. For example, scrap, excess and obsolete inventory, and rework.
- *External Failure costs:* Costs resulting from nonconformance to quality standards and effort associated with overcoming the impact of failures *found subsequent to* formal release of the product or service. For example, warranty costs, and call service centers.

Do not build a separate or new accounting system to track this information. This was a major problem organizations experienced in the 1980s, when they tried to adopt Phil Crosby's "Cost of Quality."[*] To track, measure, and reduce the cost of poor quality, a quality tracking system must be implemented. But it is simply a report that kicks out of the regular accounting system. In order to implement this type of tracking system an organization needs:

- Organizational agreement and understanding on what will be included in the cost of poor quality measurement
- Reliable systems to track the criteria being measured
- Leadership goals cascaded through personal commitments, and reviewed at operational and performance reviews
- A system to track the Green Belt/Black Belt quality improvement plans must be established by the organization and reviewed at the operations reviews

Quality costs get minimized by optimizing the trade-off between prevention and appraisal activities. Marginal cost with respect to defect prevention of

---

[*]*Quality is Free,* Philip B. Crosby; McGraw-Hill; 1979.

the combined prevention and appraisal costs is equal to the marginal cost of the combined internal and external failure costs. Cost of quality, or cost of poor quality report examples are shown in Exhibits 10.3 and 10.4.

Sometimes taking such information and turning it into a more visual report reveals patterns that are not always visible when looking at numbers (see Exhibit 10.5.)

In this instance, leadership noticed patterns that were recurring. When they probed further, they learned that certain actions were being taken at the end of each quarter. The rush to get products out the door for customer delivery was resulting in quality problems. Once the problem was visible, the fix was relatively simple.

10.7   Shareholder Value and Profitability Summary

Managing an organization against a broad range of time frames is difficult, to say the least, epecially during turbulent times! To maintain appropriate balance, organizations need:

1. A clear, meaningful strategy: Something people can get excited about, commit to, and work on. Some strategies may focus on the near term, but others need a three- to five-year window.
2. A robust set of metrics: While half the metrics may be permanent, things the business always needs to keep an eye on, the other half should be changing. Probably one-third of that second group should change annually as the organization goes after key opportunities. Once those opportunities are met, related metrics should drop to the background. Make certain numbers get probed to create new knowledge. Never make a decision based solely on a blind number!
3. Maintain focus on the voice of the customer and then blend in other key stakeholder voices so there is a sense of balance and reality over time.
4. Open and honest communications: Elsewhere we described a model for internal communications. From a strategic perspective, external financial analysts also need an understanding of the organization's plans. The organization should not only communicate results, but should also let these folks know its long-term intentions.
5. Leadership and Governance: These actions are discussed extensively in the Control chapter and in the Leadership and Governance chapter.

Oligopoly Corp.
Balanced Scorecard

	Responsibility	Measurer		GREEN	YELLOW	RED
CUSTOMER/MARKET						
Conversion Cost Performance to Budget	Plant Manager	Plant Controller		At/Above Budget	Within 2.5% Trend down	>2.5% below Budget
Delivery (Product) On-time delivery to Customer required ship date	Plant Manager	Logistics		97% or better	95%–96%	<95%
Customer Satisfaction Improvement in Survey "Yes" responses	Plant Manager	Quality Director		5% Survey Improvement	3% Survey Improvement	<3% Improvement
Escaping Defects PPM Field returns - 6 mos prior	Plant Manager	Plant Quality		110 or lower	110–120	>120
CONC Reduction Performance to Budget	Plant Manager	Plant Controller		Within 5% of budget	Within 10% of budget	>10% above Budget
Software Process Improvement Measured against SEI criteria	Plant Manager	S/W Director		70% SEI goals satisfied	60%–70 % SEI goals	under 60%
Cost Reduction-gap closure Performance against cost reduction plan	Plant Manager	Mfg. Director		At Plan	5%–10% below	>10% below
New Product Launch Status Achievement of customer launch timing	Plant Manager	Plant NPL		On schedule		Will miss

Exhibit 10.3   Quality Scorecard

$000	Oct-01	Nov-01	CURRENT MONTH Dec-01	% OF TOTAL C.O.Q.	YTD Dec-01	% OF TOTAL C.O.Q.	YTD Dec-00	% VARIANCE FROM LAST YEAR
FAILURE								
COST OF NON-CONFORMANCE:								
WARRANTY	280	326	627	15%	3,510	11%	4,158	-16%
PREMIUM FREIGHT	47	31	70	2%	508	2%	208	144%
SCRAP	582	585	767	18%	7,467	23%	7,267	3%
REPAIR and REWORK	13	(8)	(30)	-1%	249	1%	874	-71%
EXCESS & OBSOLETE	5	(40)	183	4%	1,426	4%	2,299	-38%
SHRINKAGE	203	134	438	11%	1,846	6%	1,513	22%
SLOW MOVING Finished Goods	0	0	56	1%	254	1%	331	-23%
OTHER CONC	232	287	636	15%	3,237	10%	1,873	73%
TOTAL CONC	1,361	1,315	2,748	66%	18,498	56%	18,524	0%
MFG DEPARTMENT COSTS	139	149	182	4%	1,750	5%	1,762	-1%
BUSINESS QUALITY	67	52	76	2%	751	2%	793	-5%
TOTAL FAILURE	1,568	1,515	3,006	72%	20,998	64%	21,080	0%
APPRAISAL								
MFG DEPARTMENT COSTS	119	209	271	7%	2,949	9%	2,223	33%
TOTAL APPRAISAL	119	209	271	7%	2,949	9%	2,223	33%
PREVENTION								
MFG DEPARTMENT COSTS	581	563	759	18%	7,261	22%	6,353	14%
BUSINESS QUALITY	131	146	122	3%	1,625	5%	1,583	3%
TOTAL PREVENTION	712	710	882	21%	8,886	27%	7,936	12%
TOTAL COST OF POOR QUALITY	2,399	2,433	4,159	100%	32,833	100%	31,239	5%

Exhibit 10.4 Cost of Poor Quality Monthly Report

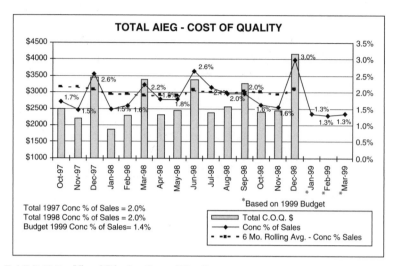

Exhibit 10.5   Visual Display Cost of Quality

The need would seem obvious. Carlos Ghosn at Nissan is probably the most extensive example we have covered in this text.

a. Start with an open mind, don't prejudge or feel that you are the one leader who has all the answers.

b. Set a clear direction.

c. Hold people accountable for their commitments.

d. Use metrics to track progress and maintain objectivity.

e. Focus on the facts, don't trash people.

f. Be relentless in demanding execution, not perfection; get something done, learn, and grow from there.

g. Take responsibility for your action, avoid placing blame.

11

Support Systems—People Side of Bridge Process

For every problem, there is one solution
which is simple, neat and wrong.
H.L. MENCKEN

11.1   Purpose

This chapter describes how the organizational Support Systems are used to sustain critical business processes, including the Bridge Process. This topic actually started in the Control chapter when we discussed what should be done to ensure dependable Bridge functions going forward. However, the Support Systems topic needs a separate explanation to fully understand its role within a business, and how the Bridge Process forms a solid foundation for the Measurement Support System.

11.2   Introduction

"Practice makes perfect." We are all familiar with this saying. It's a part of growing up and realizing that few things worth mastering come without repeated effort to perform them well. And we know family, friends, and business associates who have put in extra practice to excel at something they are passionate about. This is common sense.

But how do you apply that to a complex business organization? What does practice look like? What should people be practicing to reach for *better*, let alone *perfection*? And how can you provide guidance that helps everyone continuously evaluate what is needed to stretch for the next level?

The organizational Support Systems are very much about facilitation of "practice." They are the things that keep us focused on what's important that should be practiced. And they remind us when we're veering off course and need to refocus. One of the Support Systems is Measurement and Review. It amounts to keeping track of where we are now versus where we want to be in the foreseeable future.

Most organizations have trouble maintaining effective metrics for Support Systems purposes. The reasons are varied, but a common problem is that the measurement functions can become overly complicated if there is not a logical game plan to keep them focused on the few key metrics. So there is a tendency to put off developing definitive solutions to them because we have urgent customer and production issues to deal with first.

To counteract that tendency, this chapter offers a rationale for making Support Systems metrics a management priority, and explains how the Bridge Process can be used to put efficiency and effectiveness in Measurement Support System development work.

Measurement is like a high hurdle in the development of most Support System structures. Once it's cleared, the others present less of a stretch to reach the finish line dependably. Think of the Bridge Process as a technical edge for clearing the measurement hurdle.

Another subtle aspect of why Support Systems are often underdeveloped might be in the "practice makes perfect" saying. Subconsciously we all doubt that perfection is ever possible. It's an unrealistic goal. In fact, it feels like a destination that doesn't really exist. So why bother to reach for it? And why bother to put effort in developing Support Systems for an unrealistic goal? Besides, won't "just do it" get us there quicker?

That last line is our frontiersman persona talking. Brute force and awkwardness that gets the job done, but is probably too inefficient to be successful in the competition of the modern global economy. So we may need a way to counter our tendency to slight important systemic solutions in favor of "Ready, Fire, Aim!" behaviors.

One countermeasure might be to set a more realistic expectation about why and how we use Support Systems to guide our organized behaviors. Perhaps that could be a replacement of the unrealistic "perfection" with a more practical "possible." In other words, shift our focus from the *end point* to the *journey*, so we can use Support Systems to guide our daily practice of key business processes, and thereby improve our ability to reach difficult goals.

"Practice makes possible." That's an objective we can all be confident of achieving.

11.3   Overview and Background

"Why do we bother to do a strategic plan? We rarely follow through on it."

"Another spate of errors on customer orders! Why can't we do it right all the time?"

"We worked hard last year to fix the xxxxxx process. Why has it drifted off again?"

Those are typical of frustrations voiced by business people every day. You could probably come up with 10 more from your own company with just a few seconds reflection.

The point is that *things too rarely happen the way they were planned.* Or would it be more correct to say as "hoped?" That might sound like a cynical jab at business leadership, but it's really a recognition of a gap in how management processes are structured and practiced almost everywhere. To explain, let's go back to the Business Processes Model we introduced earlier.

By now you are familiar with the three development steps noted in the model (Exhibit 11.1). Steps A and B have been the focus of hundreds of publications dealing with customer satisfaction, customer loyalty, service quality, product quality, and operating process performance. Indeed, the Lean and Six Sigma processes have been welcome refinements of many previous business performance improvement methods focused on quality and productivity. You probably recognize their acronyms immediately: BPR (business process reengineering), TQM (total quality management), SPC (statistical process control, the lead-in to Six Sigma), JIT (just-in-time), TBM (time-based management), ABC (activity-based costing), zero defects, and a host of others.

All of the "acronym programs" have been valuable in improving business performance. But they have all been weak in one area that is critical to their long-term sustainability. Not surprisingly, Lean and Six Sigma are already beginning to suffer from the same weakness, as the early adopters are beginning to say things that sound like the Peggy Lee song, "Is that all there is…?" Some of them are saying, "Don't give us more education, training, or

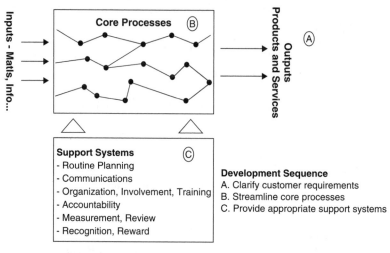

Inputs - Matls, Info...

Core Processes (B)

Outputs
Products and Services (A)

Support Systems   (C)
- Routine Planning
- Communications
- Organization, Involvement, Training
- Accountability
- Measurement, Review
- Recognition, Reward

Development Sequence
A. Clarify customer requirements
B. Streamline core processes
C. Provide appropriate support systems

CUMBERLAND
THE
GROUP

© The CUMBERLAND Group

Exhibit 11.1   Business Process Model

methods geared for quick fix, surface-level adoption of Lean-Sigma. We have that mastered. Rather, we need help with our fundamental infrastructure for making Lean-Sigma *sustainable.*"

Sustainable is an interesting word. At face value, it could mean to maintain the current level of proficiency for their Lean-Sigma programs. But that's probably not what these early adopters mean by it. More likely, they're disappointed with the rate of improvement they're realizing from Lean-Sigma to date, and they're trying to understand what they need to do to achieve a permanent acceleration of the Lean-Sigma adoption rate for company-wide culture of *continuous improvement* (CI). So, in this case sustainability probably means *significant continuous improvement.*

It may be an ominous sign for the Lean-Sigma movements that adopters are voicing "sustainability" concerns. Are they approaching the end of a fad life cycle? Or it may be that the adopters view these "acronym processes" as fundamentally important to their future business success, and they are sincerely frustrated with their ability to take full advantage of the power offered by Lean-Sigma methods. Our view is the latter.

So how do we explain the sustainability frustration? Look at step C in the Business Processes Model (Exhibit 11.1). That step is focused on the

Support Systems modifications that may be necessary to sustain a change in a core business process. A business process improvement project is not complete until the Support Systems have been adjusted to align with the core process changes. Unfortunately, the acronym processes give only cursory attention to Support Systems issues, so the operating teams often run into sustainability problems soon after implementation. The business process reengineering movement of the 1990s was especially vulnerable because it spawned many large-scale projects that were doomed from the outset because they did not address the Support Systems for sustainability. One Baldrige Award winning company went into bankruptcy soon after, partly owing to inadequate Support Systems for their reengineered core processes.

11.3.1   Support Systems Process Management

Process management is the now-familiar term that describes the shift in management philosophy that's taken place over the last 25 years. The 1981 NBC White Paper documentary, "If Japan Can, Why Can't We?" constituted a wake-up call to businesses around the world, not just in America. But Americans had been especially effective at *managing for results* in our "cowboy" culture where "Ready, Fire, Aim!" methods had been successful in an environment where lots of targets were profitable. So, with that tradition ingrained, the change in focus to *process management* has not been without lapses and pitfalls.

We have written whole books on the processes involved in maintaining or changing a business culture. That's been the core of our consulting practice for about 20 years. Over the years we have seen many fad-like techniques repackaged as the latest new management tool; these grab attention for a few years until enough companies have tried it and start looking for the next "new thing." But through all the fads the objectives have never changed—to improve business process for better, faster, cheaper performance. And the ways to do that are influenced by each situation and are drawn from the broad body of management techniques that have been part of the public domain for at least the last 100 years, probably much longer for some of the fundamentals. In any case, most business process improvements include both technical and human process elements. Our experience is that the latter is the more important.

The technical issues are rarely the main obstacles to business improvement. They are usually well known, available, and clear-cut in how they can or should be deployed.

But the human issues are often more difficult, less clear, and much more variable in how to deal with them. However, it's also been our experience that a lesser-known truism of business is correct. That is, people-based business differentiators are more sustainable than technical business differentiators that are usually easier to copy.

Think about that for a minute. Think of your own business experiences—inside your company, with another company, or with a retailer. How many of the memorable experiences (good or bad) were the result of human interactions? How many were the result of new or unique technologies? In modern times technologies are pervasive. They are copied quickly, so it is a rare surprise to find only one company with the "best" technology.

The people-based differentiators are a different story. As we have become more aware of business competition through communication, rate of personal transactions, and availability, we have also become more aware of quality differences. We are not surprised when "TCE" attitudes play out as poor service quality because we see it every day. But we *are* surprised when we run across business quality that is significantly above the average.

Disney, Toyota, Ritz-Carlton are names that immediately come to mind when thinking of companies that set the standards for their industries. They and others like them have a demonstrated history of high-quality product and service that's recognized by everyone who comes in contact with them.

But how much of that high-quality performance is technology driven? Not much, as close inspection usually finds that their use of technology is not much different than their competitors. In fact, it's the people differences that have put these companies at the head of the pack—and keeps them there for decades.

In developing a business culture of "people-based differentiators," a prime leadership responsibility is to develop and maintain a set of organizational Support Systems that "cause" the behaviors needed. Metrics are one of the Support Systems. We would argue that they are the most important Support System, the one that can cause the most harm or good, depending on how carefully it's handled.

11.3.2 A "Tipping Point" Analogy

A recent best seller provides some insight about why Support Systems are important to changing and sustaining cultural practices. Malcolm Gladwell, in *The Tipping Point* describes how some cultural changes suddenly spread very widely and very quickly. He calls that sudden spread the "tipping point." And he calls the factors behind the tipping point the *three rules of epidemics*:

1. *The law of the few: connectors, mavens, salesmen.* The law of the few is that there are a few key personalities in any local culture that influence everyone else. If they adopt something new, then many others will quickly follow.
2. *The stickiness factor: Sesame Street, Blue's Clues, educational virus.* The stickiness factor is that for a new cultural practice to be adopted quickly it must be interesting enough to "stick" once exposed to it. Like a good advertising name, slogan, or jingle that you can't seem to get out of your head, but simple enough for immediate personal mastery for quick ownership.
3. *The power of context.* The power of context is that when something new just seems "right" and fits comfortably in the local culture, it is viewed as a natural evolution that's adopted almost automatically with no questions asked. Richly detailed, relevant environmental features contribute to human acceptance and "belief" in them. In other words, it becomes obvious that "everyone is going in the X direction, so I should expect to go that way too." Context provides powerful expectations about the community and the individual's role in it. "If you build it, they will come."

All three rules offer examples of how Support Systems work in a culture of people in a community or business.

As one of the examples to explain the power of context, Gladwell pointed to the dramatic drop in the New York City crime rate during the 1990s. Several issues were uncovered as causal factors, including one that initially sounded somewhat indirect but was actually a primary cause. That was the city's program to clean up the neighborhoods that amounted to a dramatic decrease in the number of "broken windows" evident to people on the streets. That set of changes influenced a spontaneous behavior change in the community. The obvious environment changes caused a corresponding change in attitudes from an expectation of hopeless, inevitable decline to an expectation of optimistic, continuous improvement. The context of the neighborhood now indicated a new direction, so it was natural that the community should go in the same direction.

New context → new expectations → new behaviors

11.3.3 Bringing a Dying Plant Back To Life

Now let's look at the law of context in a business situation. Over a long and successful career, Jim Nolan held the senior manufacturing executive's position at divisions of several major U. S. corporations. Turnarounds were a de facto specialty, probably because his bosses could see that he was good at it. And some of his first actions at each newly assigned plant were to reestablish order and discipline in the work environment. That might have seemed odd to some onlookers because the business problems that brought him there were usually described in "bottom line" terms like slipping sales due to quality problems, or inadequate profit margins due to low productivity.

But Nolan saw businesses from a holistic view, so while bottom line improvement was the ultimate goal, he was looking at all the pieces of the puzzle, not just the results missing in the financial statement. That included operating fundamentals that had slipped in recent years as the previous management teams were often preoccupied with quick-fix solutions to what they thought were simply "misalignments in the strategic plan." In one case, after just a few weeks in a new assignment Nolan informed the CEO that the entire plant would have to be idled for several days while the operating management team "gets its act together." You can imagine the angst that caused. In another case, soon after taking command of a grimy old fabrication plant, Nolan got advice from an architect and interior designer on what shade of creamy white to paint the interior of the plant as part of a major clean-up campaign.

The white plant case is a good example of the subtle power of Gladwell's law of context. The clean-up campaign was just one piece of an overall renovation from customer relationship functions through product design upgrades, improved production processes, equipment, tooling, materials management practices, shop floor work instructions, and all the support functions—right down to the addition of "critical dimension" indicators on the production part drawings—so everyone was always aware of what's most important for successful downstream operations and delivery to the customers.

But the white walls were more than just a coat of paint. They were a visual signal that "things are different now." Holdovers from the previous management team said the changes wouldn't work because "these people don't care enough to maintain it. That's why we painted the walls black before; so they wouldn't show their foot and hand prints when they lean on the walls." But they were wrong. People avoided touching the white walls because they knew they might leave a mark. And it took only a few minutes a week to clean the few spots off the walls that happened accidentally. That one visual facilities "context" change caused a significant behavior change in the entire workforce.

It would be a mistake to give too much credit to the plant paint job. All the other "foundational" improvements played a role in the overall change. But the paint was a powerful communication element of the organizational Support Systems that enabled the workforce for dramatic improvements in quality and productivity. It all worked together in obvious new "context." And people just automatically go with the flow when it all feels right.

11.3.4   Accidental Success?

As a postscript to the paint story, 15 years later the engineering member of Nolan's management team reflected on the success of that turnaround and other major manufacturing changes he had been involved in elsewhere. It had always seemed to him that the key to those successes was in "working the details" of the subject production process. In other words, careful engineering would ensure that the system would be as efficient and effective as envisioned by the sponsors.

But in the years since he had become familiar with the broader range of management concepts that included the acronym programs mentioned a few pages back. They all focused on the core processes to be improved for better overall business performance. And they helped people understand how to strip the waste steps out of processes while finding simple ways to streamline the value-adding steps that were left. In many cases that meant elimination of off-line "indirect" functions that may have been added from time to time as "band-aids and bailing-wire" fixes for temporary problems.

However, when you look at the most successful applications of the acronym programs, it's obvious that they have also been careful to manage the Support Systems necessary for solid workforce adoption of the new processes. The engineering manager really began to see that, as the total quality management program of the late 1980s began to explain the true nature and importance of Support Systems in business culture for continuous improvement of business operations. And then the business process reengineering program of the '90s took several steps backward as management looked at it as a "silver bullet" for instant business improvements. Perfect for the short attention span of the TV generation, but sadly lacking in Support Systems attention, so long-term results were often very disappointing—not sustainable.

So at that point the former engineering manager "got it." In retrospect, those highly successful projects in the past were the result of both thorough engineering *and* "accidental" attention to Support Systems that were necessary for workforce adoption of the new production processes. "Accidental" isn't an accurate characterization, because the things that were done had seemed appropriate at the time based on informal prior experiences with business team situations. But that informality, lacking defined structure and methods, made them feel less than deliberately planned. In any case, the conclusion was obvious: organizational Support Systems are key to the effectiveness of business groups adopting new operating practices and developing a sustainable culture of continuous improvements thereafter.

11.3.5   Jack Welch Got It

Much has been made of the General Electric story during Jack Welch's tenure as CEO. His focus on meeting customer requirements, emphasizing the value-adding steps in business processes, and developing strategies to be #1 or #2 in any industry are well known. And by now, considering the number of books on the market, nearly everyone in a management role in the United States must be aware of how GE adopted Motorola's Six Sigma methods to organize their efforts for continuous improvement in business operations.

In those GE Six Sigma accounts there is usually at least one quote from Welch about how you get an entire organization to adopt a new set of behaviors, like Six Sigma. Paraphrasing, he's been quoted as saying, "You have to tell them about the new thing. Then tell them again and again, until it sticks." "Communicate, communicate, communicate" was the message. And the context around that message was powerful enough that most people reading it take it to heart.

But Welch's message was a lot deeper than that single word. It was surrounded by all the other elements of the Support Systems infrastructure for the continuous improvement processes, including Six Sigma, at GE. The communications elements just happened to be most prominent because they were always at the interface point of all the working relationships involved in making CI work at GE. But the success of Six Sigma/CI and Jack Welch at GE had to be the result of managed Support Systems that provided clear, consistent direction for the entire workforce, top to bottom.

11.3.6   Hope Is Not a Strategy

That's the title of Rick Page's savvy little book on "The 6 Keys to Winning the Complex Sale" (McGraw-Hill).[*] In it he clearly states the critical nature

---

[*]Rick Page, *Hope Is Not a Strategy;* New York: McGraw-Hill, 2001.

of planning and working the details of a process to overcome the many obstacles to sale of a complex product, system, or service package to prospective customers who are preoccupied with sinking in quicksand that the sale might help save them from.

The book's title is about what you have if you don't work the details. Just stating the targeted end results does not make it so. In fact it may even lead to a step backward if a lack of detailed plans leads to failure, disappointment, and an erosion of commitment. In "Hope...," Page is focused on the specific sales process steps for a complex sale, but throughout the discussion are examples of the Support Systems pieces that need to be in place to ensure successful follow-through. In fact, the sixth key is about communications to engage everyone involved in the strategy and tactical processes. Again, it's about the details.

11.3.7   Strength Used to Excess = Weakness

A *bias for action* has been an obvious strength of twentieth-century business cultures operating in capitalist economies. It paid off handsomely for companies that got there first to serve rapid-growing communities after the two world wars. So it seemed logical that *keeping up the pace* would continue to be a winning strategy, and that was reflected in consultant-recommended business practices, business school curriculums, and so forth.

Unfortunately, the action bias had a downside. It caused us to overlook business culture fundamentals that were necessary to drive continuous improvement in business performance. In fact, when ignored those business culture fundamentals easily became barriers to improvement that stymied even the most aggressive improvement efforts. Even when they had initial success it was frequently unsustainable.

So the action bias strength can became a de facto weakness when it's overused to the exclusion of a more balanced approach.

11.3.8   The Silver Bullet Syndrome

Another business paradigm was an accidental barrier to CI efforts in the last 30 years of the twentieth century. That was the advent of large-scale centralized *enterprise requirements planning* (ERP) systems.

ERP systems and their many IT variants had unwittingly become an impediment as they were often acquired by business leaders hoping that a "silver bullet" ERP system would magically solve a host of organizational performance problems that seemed to be holding the company back. While varied and situation dependent, the drivers behind such decisions can often be explained in the context of the Support Systems concepts described in the previous chapter. But the bottom line was that decisions to rely on an IT silver bullet solution usually resulted in a further erosion of business process effectiveness as the IT implementation diverted attention away from the business process performance issues that may have driven consideration of it in the first place.

Ironically, the ERP decisions weren't all wrong. Several Support Systems include information technology elements that are important to their effectiveness and efficiency. But putting ERP at the forefront was like putting the cart before the horse. It's truly unfortunate that many companies stumbled badly due to untimely ERP implementations that could have been quite successful if they had only understood how to use ERP as a tool *within* the organizational Support Systems (including the CI process) instead of as a driver of them.

11.3.9 A Missing Link

Two topics discussed in earlier chapters offer clues to a missing link in conventional management thinking about continuous improvement in business. Jim Collins' *Good to Great* is still the best current testimonial to how important management fundamentals can be. Much of that research demonstrated that mundane, foundational elements of a business are essential precursors to exceptional business performance and continuous improvement. And the Support Systems block in the Business Process Model (Exhibit 11.1) is a key to sustained continuous improvement (CI) in any business.

But why is this not universally understood and practiced in all organizations? Why is it not part of every company's strategic and tactical management plans?

Definitive answers to these questions will have to wait for future research. For now, for whatever reasons, management teams usually address the Support Systems issues only sporadically, when a current business condition seems to point to a need for improvement or enhancement of one of the Support Systems. Rarely is routine management of the Support Systems included in the overt business strategy or tactics.

The Support Systems thus appear to be a missing link in management thinking. At least, there seems to be a lack of understanding about Support

Systems in a strategic sense; that they should be used as a strategic tool rather than a maintenance afterthought.

The missing link point is particularly interesting when thinking of the management role within an organization. That role is primarily about providing the support necessary for the operating teams to get their work done effectively. That is all about the Support Systems block in the Business Process Model. In other words, following the steps in the model, the *voice of the customer* (VOC) is reflected in the product and service requirements (A), and the *voice of the business* (VOB) is reflected in the value-adding core process design (B). Then, the Support Systems (C) are needed to maintain the standards set in A and B, and to cause the workforce to continuously search for and implement improvement opportunities. That is a primary management role that should play out in use of the Support Systems.

11.3.10   A Mental Model

Ideally, every manager should operate with a mental model that jogs his or her thinking when confronted with a business operating problem or opportunity. That model should cause a rapid, conditioned thought pattern that looks like this:

Xxxxx Xx Xxxxxxxxxx (= the problem or opportunity I'm facing right now)

So, using the steps in the Business Process Model...

   A. Product or service outputs? OK or not? Are the output requirements clear and agreed with both supplier and customer? What might be done to improve the customer/supplier working relationship?
   B. Core process? OK or not? Are the process steps focused on value-added work relative to the customer requirements for the product or service outputs? Are there a minimum of nonvalue steps in the process? Have the value-adding steps been streamlined and standardized for consistent performance? Has economical automation been applied where justified?
   C. Support Systems? Are the process doers getting what they need from the Support Systems? What enhancements could be done in the Support Systems to make core process operations more effective and/or efficient?

That's a checklist for a quick A-B-C assessment of a situation from the viewpoint of the key management stakeholder—the person who has the most to gain or lose from how the situation is resolved. It's in a logical sequence so the customer and company interests are addressed first. And it ends with the Support Systems that are the primary responsibility of the manager—simple and quick, yet comprehensive.

11.3.11 Influence on Management Practices

Think about what day-to-day management practices often look like in our hustling world. Someone approaches the boss with a statement like: "The _____ [functions] are acting up again, and we're having trouble satisfying the _____ [customers]." The boss responds with: "Not that again! That's the fifth time this quarter [but the problem looks different each time]. Get help from _____ to get through this crunch." They do it, get through the crunch, and vow to fix the root cause as soon as they figure out what it is.

This type of behavior is common in business cultures where "action-oriented" styles are overvalued and analytical styles are undervalued. The lack of balance ends up looking like "Ready, Fire, Aim!" with frequent shots in the foot or other body parts. In any case, the participants are short-changing themselves with actions that don't make full use of information that may be right in front of them if they had a way to see and use it quickly. From the process management view, this is like jumping into the middle of the problem with conditioned reactions about possible causes. The objective is speed, not effectiveness.

Six Sigma methods are an effective way out of the "do loop" just described. So, if Six Sigma eventually becomes standard practice, then recurring situations like that should resolve themselves. But why not look for a simpler solution?

Now think about what collective management behaviors would look like if everyone practiced the A-B-C routine from several paragraphs back. The natural response would be to do a quick but methodical A-B-C assessment that starts at the customer requirements for the outputs, works inward from there through the core process issues and finally to the Support Systems. How deep to go in each area would be dictated by conclusions drawn from the initial findings. That's a much more productive approach to operational problem-solving than jumping into the middle of the problem with conditioned reactions that may or may not be correct. And a lot less dangerous than Ready, Fire, Aim!

11.3.12   A Reason Why It's Missing

One reason for the inconsistent management view of Support Systems may have to do with how we learn about them in the business schools. It's a piecemeal process with topics examined in isolation due to time constraints. So there is little time devoted to how they all fit together in the enterprise infrastructure. And to top it off, the complexity of drawing ROI cause-and-effect linkages between Support Systems and business performance makes it as difficult to get "support" for the integrated topic in business school as it is in the executive suite.

11.3.13   A Key to the Missing Link

Stop a minute and think about how that A-B-C checklist could play out routinely. What kinds of indicators would a manager be using for his/her quick status assessment of the A-B-C blocks in the Business Process Model? Process metrics should come to mind right away, because they are like the gauges on the instrument panel in your car. A quick look at the gauges is the first place to assess a car's operating health, especially while negotiating a course through traffic. An overheated condition might mean it's time to pull over and refill the cooling system.

Business operating processes present a similar situation. Shutting them down to check their health is impractical, so the various process metrics offer a way to assess opportunities for corrective or improvement action while on the fly.

The point here is that *process measurements* are a key to filling the missing link in management practices relative to continuous improvement. And that brings us back to the purpose of this book—to present an approach for making business metrics effective in tracking business process improvements over time and in clearly displaying the linkages between upstream process metrics and downstream financial results.

11.3.14   A Caveat

While holistic approaches to Support Systems management are rarely in evidence, there are many examples of how portions of the Support Systems realm are incorporated in day-to-day business operations. Unfortunately, many of them end up looking like overblown independent empires trying to compete for company resources, rather than helping the core processes use resources more effectively. Information systems and human resources functions often lapse into that mode. But when that does happen it's not necessarily their fault. Rather, it's lack of management understanding how those functions fit within the Support Systems infrastructure and of how they are crucial for sustained continuous improvement.

11.3.15   What's Been in the Way?

So why have we not made Support Systems management a mainstream discipline? It seems to be a key to organizational effectiveness, including the ability to continuously improve business performance. Why is it not a core track in the business schools? Even more to the point, why is it not an automatic part of every initiative aimed at business process improvement, including Lean and Six Sigma? Because the follow-through sustainability of all of them is dependent on Support Systems that are aligned with the core process and encourage employee participation in that direction. If not, then things will soon go back to the way they were before the new process was introduced.

The complete answer may be far more complex than we can deal with here; but we can venture a few conclusions based on 70 years of business practice observations:

- Ready, Fire, Aim! runs deep in modern business culture. We tend to believe that it's far more important to "just do it" than to plan the details of how best to do it. Solutions described in the popular business press have a tendency to make things sound simpler than they really are. Prescriptive and strategic solutions can sound very compelling until someone comes face to face with the practical reality of making it happen. And shorter attention spans conditioned by instant results on TV may be extending the problem in the general population.
- The strong focus on core process effectiveness has been both the strength and the weakness of initiatives like Lean and Six Sigma. They are absolutely on target in helping business people understand the basics of business process management for quality and productivity in our highly competitive new global economy. But such a huge investment in time and attention doesn't leave much energy for working Support Systems that may not seem germane at the time. It's not unusual for business teams to hurry through their process improvement project work so they can get back to their real jobs. However, if the Support Systems had been adjusted at the outset, then they would have realized that the process improvement project may be their most important real job.
- In the big business process improvement programs, the focus on streamlining the value-added steps and eliminating the off-line functions

may have caused an accidental inattention to the organizational Support Systems. In haste, they can be lumped into the nonvalue indirect category if their supporting relationship to a core process isn't clear.

These three conclusions have a common theme of a headfirst rush for business process simplicity and emphasis on value-added and waste reduction that is difficult to find fault with when viewed in isolation. Like motherhood and apple pie that focus on value-added and process simplicity has to be good, right? But is that all there is? What about the Support Systems in the lower box of Exhibit 11.1? Shouldn't we give them some attention before we dust off our hands and head off toward the next assignment?

11.3.16   The Simplicity/Complexity Paradox Again

Perhaps we're back to the paradox we mentioned in Chap. 4 (Measure) about the fact that Lean-Sigma-CI is about simplifying processes down to streamlined value added. But that requires a more complex view of business processes than the culture is used to, so there is a hurdle of temporary added complexity that has to be cleared before the organization can move beyond the dip in the "J-curve" of process performance. The new methods with Lean-Sigma-CI constitute part of that hurdle. But the Support Systems are a sometimes unnoticed part that will trip us up if we haven't put in the training to clear it comfortably.

Dealing with that paradox in a complex business world can be a daunting challenge, especially when our hopes are to simplify as soon as possible. An ancient quote from Plato sums up the importance:

> In order to seek one's own direction,
> one must simplify the mechanics of everyday life.

We're all aware of how difficult that can be for us as individuals. And it's easy to see that it becomes exponentially more difficult for groups of people.

A key is to remember the power of Gladwell's law of context while managing a minimal set of Support Systems to guide the organizational behaviors in the direction that "just feels right" to all involved.

11.4   Pulling It Together—Bridge Structure and Usage

Using the Bridge Process as a key part of the organizational Support Systems:

11.4.1   Bridge Structure Concepts

Basic concepts behind the structure and steps in the next section (Support Systems substeps):

Everyone has memories of outstanding team performances where average individuals came together to accomplish almost incredible results. The Apollo 13 recovery in the face of impossible odds, the 1980 U.S. Olympic hockey team of amateurs winning against a professional team from the U.S.S.R., and numerous disaster relief efforts around the world where disparate groups of people came together effectively under urgent and adverse circumstances to help others survive.

Most impressive is the overwhelming power of such dominant teams. As though their efforts are just destined to overcome any obstacles in the way. In some cases that might appear to be a function of the sheer number of people that "got on board." But even the smaller teams seem to have acquired an energy and effectiveness that's difficult to counter.

Often, such situations are viewed as lucky occurrences, or fortuitous alignment of the right people in the right place at the right time. To some extent that's true. But if you look below the surface you will most likely find a set of organizational Support Systems, maybe informal, that empowered the group for standout performance.

But what about the dominant power? What enabled it? Is it a process that can be replicated? Yes, it can. But we need to introduce another concept to fully explain the process.

11.4.2   Empowered Business Teams

In *The Tipping Point*, Gladwell refers to *transactive memory* as the ability of humans to learn complex routines and decision-making processes as part of their everyday jobs. He makes a couple of important points about transactive memory that help explain the fundamental nature of empowered business teams.

Transactive memory:

- Serves as a local experience roadmap/directory. Each individual role player contains a large amount of transactive memory that is called into play as others have become conditioned to rely on them for that specific set of information.

- Is difficult to replace in the short term. Loss of one individual's "transactive memory" can have serious short-term consequences as the rest of the organization develops replacement/s for that functional memory.

Those points help explain why Support Systems are so important, that is, to ensure maintenance and growth of "transactive memory" for effective and efficient business functions. Experience tells us that transactive memory is a critical navigation system for efficient local department operations, and can take a long time to replace if lost with a departing employee. A prime function of the organizational Support Systems is to ensure sustained maintenance of transactive memory.

Consider the empowered business teams diagram in Exhibit 11.2. To be self-sufficient and fully enabled for its mission, a business team needs four clear boundaries of empowerment:

- Autonomy to begin processing with the handoff from an upstream supplier
- Authority to make certain types of decisions and take certain types of actions
- Responsibility to deliver a specific product or service to a downstream customer
- Cohesiveness to act as a unit with common goals and operating norms

Any of the four boundaries can be changed at any time as business conditions and team roles change. But, all four should be clear at all times so the team has no questions about its role and responsibilities. That enables them for decisive action without time-wasting checks with the boss.

The team receives guidance and feedback from the organizational Support Systems that are specific to the team's role. The process owner, usually the team's direct supervisor, is primarily responsible for setting Support Systems that are appropriate to the team's role and responsibilities. However, it's best that Support Systems development be a collaborative process between process owner and operating team, so they are equally committed to the operating plan and behaviors intended.

The Support Systems block is shown under the team block for a reason. That is because the Support Systems are like a foundation for the team's structure and operations. If the Support Systems block is soft or unstable, then the team operations are likely to be less effective than desired.

A key point about Support Systems is that ignoring them is risky. Like some well-publicized business process reengineering failures, you can probably

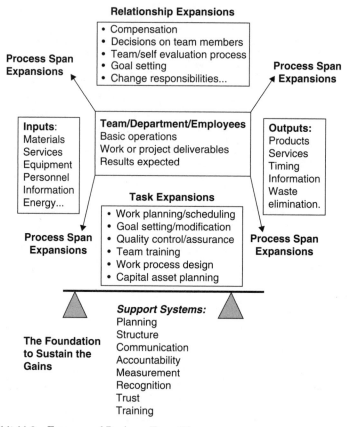

Exhibit 11.2   Empowered Business Team Diagram

think of several projects in your company's past that went well initially, but faltered in the long run. Chances are that the root cause of poor follow-through was inadequate attention to needed Support Systems adjustments in line with the new business process design.

In contrast, business teams like one at a nationally known meat processor have overcome nagging obstacles and made huge changes successfully by giving attention to the Support Systems before attempting a redesigned process implementation. In that company, there had been strong resistance for years to operating changes that included more production time utilization of the physical plant, even though they knew that competitive cost pressures were pushing them more in that direction.

Their production process redesign project had been a significant effort for the team assigned by the executive process owner. And they were having trouble reaching consensus on the final process design before going into the implementation phase. Some of the team members thought it would not be accepted by the production teams, and might potentially fail. They were used to succeeding.

Their last process design step was an assessment and modification of the Support Systems for the production process. This included rich dialogs with the production teams about what they needed to make the new process design successful. The feedback from the teams was neutral enough to convince the project team and process owner that there wasn't sufficient reason not to try the new process as a pilot in one part of the plant under controlled conditions. Three weeks later the production team said they didn't want to return to the old process, and the rest of the plant was converted soon after to increase throughput and reduce operating costs by $20 million per year.

The lesson was that a business process redesign has to include all three steps (ABC), through confirmation that appropriate Support Systems will be in place to sustain the operating team in their efforts to implement the new process and continually improve it from there. It's in the details. No way around it.

11.4.3   Key Performance Indicators and Bridge Process

Business process metrics are a key part of the Support Systems. The Bridge Process described in the earlier chapters provides a strategy for organizing the Measurement Support Systems so they are as simple as possible (easy to maintain), yet are comprehensive enough to feed ongoing management, control, and continuous improvement efforts.

The Metrics Library chapter contains a variety of business process metrics examples that may be useful for planning Measurement Support Systems.

11.4.4   Streamlining Business Support Systems

The Support Systems are just that—support. They are generally not instrumental in adding value to the products or services that your customers are willing to pay for. Therefore, Support Systems have to be viewed as a necessary evil, important to the business operations, but more in the category of resource waste than value added. So from that perspective, management is confronted with the conflicting objectives of simultaneously ensuring that the Support Systems do a good job of supporting the core business processes, but do it at the least possible cost so they don't consume resources that could be better utilized in value-adding functions.

Unfortunately, Support Systems development and rationalization are messy projects. While none of the pieces is very complicated (not rocket science), the sheer number of pieces makes the work cumbersome.

Consider the ValueLink process diagram in Exhibit 11.3. Even a simple illustration of the range of components involved in a Support Systems review and revamp can look daunting. However, you can feel more confident about tackling such a project if you think in terms of "eating the elephant a bite at a time." Once you have broken it down to the few core processes to be supported, and defined the few Support Systems issues needing immediate attention, then the individual tasks and overall project begin to feel practical and less risky.

11.4.5 New Concepts from Complex Adaptive Systems Theory

A concept from *complex adaptive systems* (CAS) theory can help make the elephant bites even more manageable. The Support Systems are somewhat like the "agent rules" for autonomous agents in CAS-based systems. The Support Systems can be cut down to a manageable size when they are viewed as the few key "rules" needed by anyone or any operating team to be fully empowered for their role. The CAS rules concept helps keep it simple.

The CAS concepts offer new insights into how business teams can be most effective. They will be discussed in more detail in the CI Process chapter (next).

11.4.6 Support Systems Substeps Using Bridge Process

The routine steps in the Bridge Process are fair game for inclusion in the Measurement and Review Support Systems. The Process Outlines chapter includes an overview of the routine process steps and the Measure and Analysis chapters discuss these steps in more detail.

ValueLink Process

For a Business Operations Rationalization Project

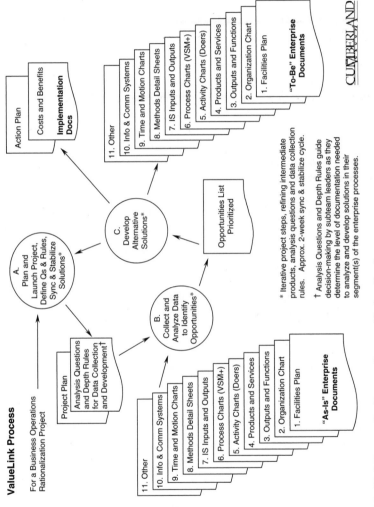

* Iterative project steps, refining intermediate products, analysis questions and data collection rules. Approx. 2-week sync & stabilize cycle.

† Analysis Questions and Depth Rules guide decision-making by subteam leaders as they determine the level of documentation needed to analyze and develop solutions in their segment(s) of the enterprise processes.

CUMBERLAND

Exhibit 11.3 ValueLink Process for Support Systems Rationalization

369

11.5   Tools for Doing It

Examples and methods for implementing Bridge Process Support Systems in your company:

The Process Outlines chapter includes a view of the main implementation steps for a Bridge Process that could serve key Measurement Support System functions.

If you are faced with an enterprise-wide cleanup of poorly maintained Support Systems, then you will want to use an umbrella methodology that organizes that large-scale effort to be efficient, comfortably paced, comprehensive, and controlled risk. Cumberland has a ValueLink process that compares the Support System *requirements* to the current Support Systems in place and facilitates decision making about how to reconfigure the Support Systems to economically meet the real requirements without the costly build-up of overhead from years of band-aid fixes to temporary problems.

11.6   What Can Go Wrong

Accidental misalignment of Support Systems with the core process served is a common pitfall. The root cause is usually some variant of not taking enough time or methodical analysis of Support Systems needs. The tollgate questions given in the next section will help head off those problems.

11.7   Tollgate Questions

To ensure adequate Support Systems for any business process, you can start with a few questions that will help determine if planning has been adequate to sustain the operating team over the long haul:

1. Have we done an assessment of the Support Systems currently in place to determine which are adequate for the new process, and which are in need of adjustment?
2. Is there a work plan with leadership and task responsibilities for development of any needed Support Systems changes?
3. Have all the stakeholders been involved in the Support Systems redesign work, so the needs of all participants are met?
4. Do we have a good plan for the Support Systems interface points with all the users? In other words, will the screens, forms, and reference documents be comprehensive and also configured for ease of use?

Chapter

12

Continuous Improvement Processes

*Good judgment comes from experience, and
often experience comes from bad judgment.*
RITA MAY BROWN

12.1 Purpose

This chapter describes the role that business process metrics play in
continuous improvement (CI) business cultures, outlines how to institutionalize the four major segments of a typical CI process for accelerated
enterprise-wide CI, and describes how the Bridge Process can provide much of
what is needed in the CI measurement subprocess of a company-wide CI process.

12.2 Introduction

Business process measurement is a key to CI process implementations that
are successfully sustained in the long run. Unfortunately, it also seems to be
an Achilles' heel for many such implementations as companies embark on
ambitious initiatives to embed a CI process in their business culture but are
not prepared for the more rigorous approach to business process measurement that is needed to support their CI project efforts. Some do per-
functory efforts to create appropriate measurement systems, but fall short of
what's needed and the entire CI process suffers for lack of effective process
measures and project tracking measures.

Robust CI processes use business process metrics as a springboard to their
continuous improvement efforts. In fact, process metrics are fundamental to
the CI process itself as they serve as mileposts in the improvement process
by making status versus target visible to everyone so they can continuously
look for ways to help improve the process toward the goal.

The four main subprocesses in a CI process are relatively easy to define and prepare for implementation. However, CI measurement is often a tricky hurdle to get over. It demands more root cause analysis and attention to detail than expected in business cultures that are used to succeeding with a "just-do-it" behavior style. The Bridge Process can simplify development of the CI measurement subprocess, and ensure effective measurement of CI process results.

12.3   Overview and Background

The slow evolution of CI process from "enigma" to "predictable standard practice."

The 1981 NBC TV documentary *If Japan Can, Why Can't We?* was a wake-up call to management teams everywhere, not just in America. For the first time in the twentieth century it focused attention on the fundamentals of business that are necessary to satisfy increasingly demanding customers in an increasingly competitive global marketplace. In the previous 30 years, businesses had been blissfully isolated in their local markets as increasing demand had provided plenty of business growth even if they squandered company resources on excess nonvalue overhead functions and were slow to improve the quality of products, services, and operating processes.

A few years later, as a senior executive with a consulting firm was helping American companies adopt "Japanese manufacturing techniques." He complained that America had a "TCE" attitude that hindered efforts to improve quality and productivity. His acronym stood for "That's close enough." He was pointing at a cultural problem that had emerged during the 1960s and 1970s when American companies could sell all they could make, even if nagging quality problems alienated many buyers. And, into the 1980s, it rang true with people who were buying more Japanese cars in reaction to the still-lagging quality from Detroit. Chrysler even used it in a commercial with a little girl who asked something like, "If everyone was satisfied with 'good enough,' would anything ever be good enough?"

But TCE described only part of the problem. While American culture in general was slipping into a lackadaisical attitude toward quality, American managers were adopting a dangerous reliance on "elegant, but inert" computer solutions to business management. Advances in computing power made it ever easier to point to "silver bullet" computer solutions "just around the corner," so it seemed like a waste of time to look at the details of business processes that might be automated soon. But "soon" never really happened, and the silver bullets often just added a shroud of mystery around the business processes, so diagnostic and improvement efforts became more difficult.

In the 1990s, the Internet and business globalization turned up the heat on businesses to accomplish better, faster, cheaper results—and accomplish them at a much faster rate, continuously, from here on. Those that don't will not survive.

In the twenty-first century, many companies are launching or relaunching efforts to achieve accelerated continuous improvement business culture performance, because they no longer doubt that it's necessary. But their collective success rate is mediocre at best. In fact, studies still indicate that the majority of company-wide business performance improvement efforts fail after a few years. That's in spite of the urgency and seriousness of the global competition that clearly has everyone's attention. So what's the problem?

12.3.1 Lean Sigma Fads?

The Lean and Six Sigma movements have made *process management* concepts more accessible to business teams. The differences between them tend to be complementary, so practitioners are finding that a blend of both makes sense. Which one to emphasize might depend on your current situation. If your cross-functional business processes have become convoluted and bloated with years of temporary fixes, then Lean might be the initial emphasis to focus attention on getting the waste steps out and streamlining the value-add steps that are left. Alternately, if the processes are reasonably "clean" but the results are too variable, then Six Sigma statistical methods might be emphasized to dig deeper in the process, find the root causes of variability, fix them, and establish on-going controls.

Those concepts should be familiar from earlier discussions in this book. But the fact that Lean-Sigma methods have gained broad acceptance doesn't help explain why the success rate of such initiatives is so low. We're all optimistic that Lean-Sigma will be different, more sustainable, because they do appear to be more fundamental. But even fundamental methods won't be sustained without disciplined practice of them. If other issues take precedence for a while, and Lean-Sigma work is put on the shelf, then it's likely that the business team, at some point, may look up and ask, "What else should we be doing to be more competitive? Lean-Sigma? Been there; done that. What's new out there that we haven't already tried?"

So, what *is* the problem? Why do business cultures tend to be "serial fad tryers" with a disappointing history of poor follow-through?

An answer is in the fundamentals of those current cultures. In other words, some features of existing business cultures amount to *gaps* in the cultural processes needed to sustain ongoing practice of proven methods like Lean, Six Sigma, BPR, TQM, and so forth. Before we look at those gaps, let's consider what a sustained continuous-improvement business culture does look like.

12.3.2   Continuous Improvement Business Culture

Business team effectiveness is a core expertise at Cumberland. So, while most of the projects clients ask us to support are variations on the "business process improvement" theme, we are happy to have many clients who appreciate the business team methods we bring to help the technical projects be more successful. Some of them have said, after the fact, that they "didn't appreciate the team-based methods during the start-up phase," but they're convinced that "those methods improved the project results and may be more important to the company in the long run than the technical project itself." Several clients are well-known companies with reputations for industry leadership, with team-based CI cultures.

One client is an especially good example for this discussion about CI business culture. Nascote Industries is a key player in the first-tier automotive supplier market. They make the molded plastic "fascia" assembly that constitutes the front end of your car: grill, bumper, headlamp housing, horn mounting, air bag sensor, and various other components. The OEM automakers order the fascia assembly in as complete a condition as possible, so it's ready to install as a unit on the designated vehicle when it arrives at the assembly plant. That includes the finished paint, so you can imagine the cosmetic quality issues Nascote deals with every day.

Nascote is a good subject for the CI discussion because they have one of the most natural team-based CI cultures we have encountered. That is not to say that they haven't worked to make CI more systemic, because they have been doing more, especially as global competition has heated up, to find ways to make their CI efforts more effective at improving their already leading-edge business processes. But, their overt CI process enhancements have always built on a solid CI culture that has been in place for a long time. In any case, Nascote exhibits all the key features of a CI culture.

Fundamentals of High-Performance Business Operations

Nascote practices the fundamentals of high-performance business operations:

- Customer-supplier partnership
- Conformance to requirements
- Prevention
- Doing it right the first time
- Measurement
- Involvement
- Continuous improvement

In fact, the company would score fairly high on any of the assessment surveys that measure business culture (such as Baldridge, ISO, and Shingo).

True CI business cultures practice all the fundamentals, not just some of them. The weakest link concept applies here, in that if any one of the fundamentals is inadequately practiced, then the business culture as a whole is unlikely to perform at a consistently high level, and will not exhibit sustained CI practices. Look at those seven fundamentals again. Can you take out any one of them and still have a sustained high-performance business culture?

Role of Measurement in Driving Improvement

Of the fundamentals, measurement may be the most fundamental:

- Measurement is the springboard to improvement.
- People do what the boss measures.
- You get what you measure.
- If you don't measure it, you are not likely to improve it.

You can probably think of several more well-known sayings that would reinforce the importance of measurement in the fundamentals.

At Nascote, measurement has always been just enough to help people focus on what's important. So, for the most part, the big issues get ongoing attention that has kept them working on business process improvements to keep them at the front of the pack in their industry group. If anything, they have placed more emphasis on development of better measurement tools in recent years as they are digging deeper in process improvement opportunities using Lean and Six Sigma methods. They saw the "process data void" that occurred during the MRP/ERP silver-bullet years and began rebuilding the manufacturing process database so it could be tapped more effectively for CI search for opportunities efforts as well as to support routine product introduction and engineering change activities. Process measurement is a common thread through all of it.

Workforce Involvement in CI

There is an "all in the same boat" atmosphere at Nascote. People and work teams naturally pitch in to help each other. It's routine to see a flood of people from the office join the production line teams when a temporary crunch has to be handled in order to meet a shipping commitment to an auto maker.

That level of involvement extends to how Nascote engages the entire workforce in CI activities. Over the years, they have used a variety of mechanisms to harvest ideas for business improvement from the workforce. Several of those subsystems have existed simultaneously as they have focused extra attention on specific areas. The consistent theme has been that the company should do as much as possible to tap the talents of the entire workforce, not just the apparent leadership group.

Team-Based Methods

Team-based methods are a staple at Nascote, as they believe that $1 + 1 = 3$ is always possible and worth a little extra investment in personnel time on the front end, because there is likely to be a good payoff on that effort at the back end. Actually, the teaming behaviors at Nascote may have preceded the institutional inclination. In project team situations they seem more comfortable than most organizations with giving up individual ownership when a committed team response is needed. They will engage in lively debate about a knotty problem, consider alternate solutions, pick one, and then commit to team-based follow-through. Even completely new concepts get thorough team consideration that often sounds like, "That's different. It might work. Let's try it." The confidence of such responses seems to come from conditioned team-based successes over the years.

It's in the Walls

Continuous improvement, the last of the seven fundamentals is a strongly held expectation of everyone at Nascote. That's probably caused somewhat by the aggressive market they serve. Any company that cannot continuously improve its internal operations will not survive for long. Even so, their business culture exhibits a remarkable integration of CI process practices in concert with mainstream business operations. Most discussions about current operations include comments about CI issues.

CI Process Evolution

Finally, a CI business culture applies that trait also to the CI process itself. In Nascote's case that is expressed by visible management actions to continuously search for ways to enhance the CI process for better, faster, cheaper results. That hasn't always looked like formal CI process developments. More often, it has been more like added pushes on the "flywheel", as Collins called it in *Good to Great*. In recent years, it has been adoption of practices from Lean and Six Sigma. But the bottom line here is that there is consistent, visible leadership by management to continuously improve their CI efforts. Any other behavior would not meet their cultural expectations.

12.3.3   Business Culture Gaps

It's possible to pick out the keys to CI business culture when comparing average companies to standouts like Nascote. Some of the more obvious gaps are:

* No measurement of CI process practices to improve them.
* No active management of Support Systems, including CI process.
* Management culture bias toward destinations instead of an ongoing journey.

Those look simplistic, but let's take a look at what they mean in terms of defining how to build a CI business culture.

No measurement of CI Process practices to improve them: This seems obvious after the previous discussions (Measure chapter) about the "causality" of well-balanced business process metrics. In other words, if an organization does no routine measurement of the things it should be doing to foster a continuous improvement culture, then it's unlikely that those things will happen, except accidentally.

No active management of Support Systems, including CI process: A CI process is part of the organizational Support Systems discussed in the previous chapter. They are primary drivers of a business culture in that the workforce is guided by the cues they get from the Support Systems (routine planning, communications, involvement, accountability, measurement and review, recognition and reward). If the leadership team doesn't manage the Support Systems, then workforce direction may be as variable as their interpretations of the organizational direction indicated in informal communications.

Management culture bias toward destinations instead of an ongoing journey: This amounts to "not walking the talk," by trying to adopt process management practices, but not yet committing to permanent "practice" of process management. This is attempting to identify a root cause of why a management team would fail to manage their organizational Support Systems when that is a key to organizational performance. There may be many other causes (e.g., lack of education, lack of experience, and lack of motivation), but the end result may be the same; good intentions that stall without committed, ongoing follow-through. Most attempts to adopt a CI process will be short lived unless management views it as a permanent journey instead of a short-term task to be completed and checked off the list.

You might notice that those three gaps were addressed in an "onion peeling" sequence with the one that might be seen in a records audit appearing first, and the others appearing in the sequence they might be found when asking "Why?" a few times. The point is that the gaps between high-performance business cultures and the also-rans can be expressed in a few key issues. However, they are not simplistic issues, and determining the scope and details of the gaps will take more than a few quick questions and answers.

But, to fill the gaps, a CI process should not be an overcomplicated chunk of added overhead. It should be as simple as possible to facilitate the kind of business culture features that are natural at companies like Nascote.

The CI process overview in the following section is focused on the Bridge Process metrics in it.

12.4   Pulling It Together—Bridge Structure and CI Process

Using the Bridge Process to feed the continuous improvement process

- *What does a continuous improvement business culture look like?*
- *How can you change a business culture to accelerate the CI rate?*
- *What constitutes a sustainable, closed-loop CI process?*
- *Why would the Bridge Process be important as part of a CI process?*

Before considering the elements of a CI Process, remember the Business Process Model (Exhibit 12.1). The Support Systems block (C) is where the CI Process resides, sharing activities in the various functions of the Support Systems. But if you have ever looked at the Support Systems as elements of CI, you probably generated more questions than answers about "what constitutes a sustainable, accelerating CI Process in our business?" In other words, the eclectic nature of the Support Systems made it difficult to discern a defined CI Process that could be managed for achieving an accelerated rate of continuous improvement in business performance.

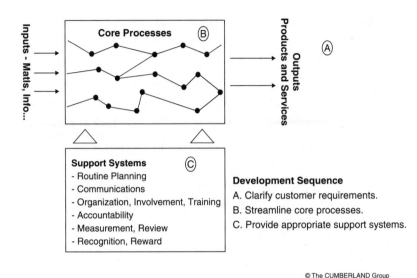

Development Sequence
A. Clarify customer requirements.
B. Streamline core processes.
C. Provide appropriate support systems.

Exhibit 12.1   Business Process Model

A key to making CI a sustainable attribute of the business culture is to establish a discrete, closed-loop structure for the CI Process, so it feeds itself. That closed-loop structure should include all the Support Systems to provide a comprehensive, stable (sustainable) foundation for the company's CI efforts. Such a process is described in the next section.

12.4.1 CI Process Concepts

You will need a frame of reference to find answers to the questions just posed. To keep it simple, consider the CI process diagram in Exhibit 12.2.

As shown in Exhibit 12.2, a basic CI process requires four subprocesses to make continuous improvement a sustainable part of a business culture:

- *Measurement* (Msmt) to constantly compare current status versus an ideal
- *Education* (Ed) about quality and productivity issues
- *Search for opportunities* (SFO) to find the best current opportunities
- *Improvement action* (IA) to mobilize appropriate resources for IA results

If any one of the subprocesses is missing or ineffective, then it's unlikely that the CI process will be sustainable in the local business culture.

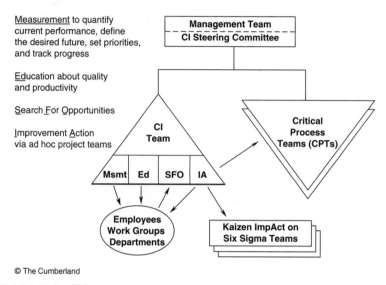

Measurement to quantify
current performance, define
the desired future, set priorities,
and track progress

Management Team
CI Steering Committee

Education about quality
and productivity

Search For Opportunities

Improvement Action
via ad hoc project teams

CI
Team

Critical
Process
Teams (CPTs)

Msmt | Ed | SFO | IA

Employees
Work Groups
Departments

Kaizen ImpAct on
Six Sigma Teams

© The Cumberland

Exhibit 12.2   CI Process

12.4.2   Bridge Structure

This is actually what this whole book is about. Initially, the view was from the financial perspective, looking for the cause-and-effect relationships and period-to-period linkages that would help evaluate business-process improvement opportunities and track progress toward them. That view naturally leads to the broadest view of an enterprise where there should also be defined linkages all the way upstream to the causal factors behind the business culture. In other words, an effective business-process metrics system would support a closed-loop CI process.

Of the four CI subprocesses, measurement is the one where the Bridge Process first comes into play. As has been proven many times in business research, it's painfully obvious that measurement is a key—maybe the most important key—to business performance improvement. "You get what you measure." "Measurement is the springboard to improvement."

Also, of the four CI subprocesses measurement may be the trickiest one because there are a lot of potential measures in a business, but only a few good measures for guiding business performance. Sorting the few useful ones from the many distracting ones can be a daunting task.

Simplifying metrics selection, the Bridge Process provides a structure for rationalizing the metrics that can be critical to CI process sustainability.

Remember the cause-and-effect structure of the Bridge Model. That is especially important for CI process effectiveness since the metrics lead the way in the search for opportunities. If we're watching unimportant metrics, then we will find unimportant opportunities. If we're watching the high-leverage causal-factors metrics, then we are likely to see many incremental opportunities that, taken together, can be a quantum-leap performance improvement ahead of the competitors.

This is somewhat like theories on creativity. Generally, having a richer initial knowledge base is a significant advantage when looking for creative new ideas. The detailed metrics of a Bridge Process can be just such a contributor to the flow of creative juices that a CI process is designed to facilitate. Detailed process metrics in the logical presentation of a Bridge Process can jog a lot of new ideas that lay just below the surface until a variety of information pieces trigger the new thoughts.

12.4.3   A CI Example

A capital equipment manufacturer discovered the power of process metrics a few years ago. Several key manufacturing staff members were looking for ways to dramatically reduce their quoted order turnaround time to customers. And along the way they hoped to improve productivity and cut production costs.

The initial conceptual discussions were less than inspiring. Opinions flew, but facts were in short supply.

To add factual data to the discussions they decided to make a video tape record of the process activities on the shop floor, then document the steps and times for analysis. That opened the floodgates for identification of improvement opportunities in the process. The process time data allowed them to easily see where the waste to be eliminated was in the process, and which steps added value and should be retained and streamlined. Eventually, they had a detailed set of "process characteristics" data that also included changeover times, production batch quantities, inventory levels, and floor space for work-in-process (WIP) queues.

The point is that their initial CI efforts were slow and unfocused—until they had real process data in front of them. Process measures were clearly the springboard to improvement for them.

12.4.4   Key Dimensions for CI Metrics

Notice that the Bridge Process (Exhibit 12.3) includes both a time dimension and a causality dimension. It simplifies the tracking of improvement project results from period to period, and correlates the subresults of individual projects to overall enterprise results on the key business goals. Those improvement-project tracking facilities are a common constraint on CI process operations when they are poorly defined as a CI process is picking up speed. Without a good tracking process it becomes difficult to maintain momentum.

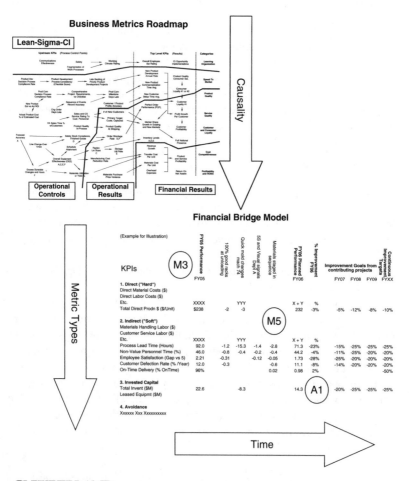

Exhibit 12.3   Building a Financial Bridge Model

12.4.5   Managing for CI (MCI) Concepts

In most organizations, successful CI processes are very dependent on leadership and involvement of the mid-management tier. If they are not engaged from the outset, then it's unlikely that a CI process can be implemented and sustained. That is because the mid-managers have operational control of the employee resource pool, and if they don't see the CI process results as a benefit, then they will not allocate adequate personnel time to make the CI process effective.

Several features are needed in a CI process to support management for CI. Not coincidentally, they tend to have metrics themes that can be linked and communicated in a Bridge Process. They are:

- Goals for continuous improvement of the primary cross-functional business processes. And clear ownership of the goals by managers who take responsibility for CI so that they will view the CI process as a useful tool instead of an off-line overhead function.
- Structured and well-publicized status reports that focus attention on the CI goals. Publicity encourages ownership and invites ideas for improvement opportunities that sometimes need CI process facilitation to find the person or department that can make use of them.
- Rigorous CI process auditing of customer requirements and zero-base values that will help the workforce (and managers) become committed to aggressive waste-reduction efforts as a way to keep ahead of the competition and grab more business.
- CI process steps that cause a proactive partnership between the mid-management group and the CI process team to *jointly search for opportunities* to close the gap between actual performance and zero-base value-added performance.

Notice that the first three items above are metrics issues. The Bridge Process adds logic and organization to developing them.

12.5   Tools for Doing It

Considering methods for using a Financial Bridge Process as a key element in your company's CI process …

> *The question is not:* To have a CI process, or not? Every surviving company does enough continuous improvement work to at least keep up with the pack. They have a de facto CI process, even if it's not a formal one that's recognized as such by the workforce.

The question is: Should you have a robust CI process that is used by the entire workforce to make performance improvements faster than the competitors so your company grows faster and more profitably for all involved?

If the answer to that question is "yes," then you are embarking on a long-term *journey* to develop a sustained CI process that enables the organization for accelerating continuous improvement. As one of the four CI sub-processes, measurement will be an important part of the journey.

12.5.1   Steps for CI Process Development

The structure and details of the CI journey can fill several books, so this will be just a brief overview to provide context for how the Bridge metrics would be positioned for use in a CI process. Keep in mind that the purpose of a formal CI process is to enhance and accelerate the continuous improvement activities already happening in a company, and to make that a permanent characteristic of the overall business culture. In other words, enable the entire workforce to produce better, faster, cheaper results every day by working smarter, not harder.

Key elements in CI process development include:

- Executive actions
  - Clarify the company vision in operational terms.
  - Define the few key goals to achieve the vision.
  - Define the mission of the CI process.
  - Allocate resources and establish leadership for the CI process.
  - Charter one or more *critical process teams* (CPTs) for immediate results.
  - Provide ongoing support and guidance.
- Critical process team(s)
  - Focused on a core process that is critical to goals achievement.
  - Empowered to develop quantum-leap process improvements.
  - Sponsored by an executive with authority to make change.
  - Have heavy-weight cross-functional membership.
  - Use DMAIC or similar methods for comprehensive process redesign.
  - Provide implementation follow-through support.
- CI process management
  - Focused on acceleration of CI in the business culture.
  - Customization of a CI process design appropriate for the company.
  - Assignment of resources and leadership for CI process functions.
  - Ongoing management leadership, involvement, and material support.

A few words of explanation: As with all important business initiatives, executive leadership is essential to the success of an enterprise-wide CI process. GE, Motorola, Hewlett-Packard, and many others have been cited in earlier chapters as examples of how a robust CI process strategy plays out in companies that intend to lead their markets. In all those cases, leadership used the CI process (whatever it was called) as a powerful lever for achieving the company goals.

The executive actions listed above reflect the DMAIC process: define what is important, measure current versus target, analyze opportunities, apply resources to take improvement action, and control the process with ongoing support. That's basic process management as applied by executive teams every day. In the leading companies, the CI process has equal priority with the current strategic initiatives.

CI process implementations usually include two coordinated paths:

- *Critical process team(s):* For the few major cross-functional projects
- *CI process management:* For broad workforce involvement in CI efforts

A *critical process team* is charted by the executive team to develop improvements in a core process that is critical to achievement of the current strategic goals, usually reflecting the voice of the customer and voice of the business in urgent, fundamental terms. Such ad hoc teams are sponsored by a senior manager, populated with respected cross-functional members, and tasked to get results quickly. CPTs are at the leading edge of a CI implementation because they produce tangible results that send a strong message about management commitment to the CI process mission.

The *CI process management* functions are typically developed behind the leading-edge CPT projects. The leg work for CI process development includes business culture assessment, Support Systems analysis, CI process design, and organization design. Those are detail-oriented foundation-building steps that are necessary to ensure CI process sustainability. However, early successes from the CPT projects provide confidence to stay the course through the detailed CI process development. Alternatives often look like succumbing to "Ready, Fire, Aim!" shortcuts that are doomed to failure.

12.5.2   Where Bridge Metrics Fit in a CI Process Development

CI measurement is the system by which data about improvement projects are turned into meaningful information to show an organization how improvements are progressing.

Ideally, the management team will have already established something like the Bridge Process to focus attention on the key business metrics, and to track improvement progress from the array of improvement initiatives, big and small. However, a CI process launch can be an excellent time to introduce a Bridge Process, since it can provide a sharper focus on the metrics that need more attention from everyone as they begin the CI journey.

Bridge metrics for a CI process come into play in two ways:

- In CI projects, to correlate results with key business improvement goals
- In CI process functions, to evaluate opportunities and prioritize actions

In CI projects, the management team begins the chartering process with a set of project goals for measurable *process improvement* (PI). The Bridge Process is a useful tool for correlating the PI goals with the corporate strategy goals, so the line of sight from project to strategy is clear enough to confirm the project priority. As the project rolls out, the Bridge metrics are useful for tracking progress and confirming the flow-through of results to the strategic goals.

In CI process functions, the Bridge Process provides a logical reference framework for guiding the entire workforce in their search for opportunities efforts. If a CI process does not include clearly defined CI goals and appropriate tracking metrics, then it's likely to fail in the long run. Process metrics are that fundamental to the continuous improvement process.

Next is a list of "lessons learned" from various CI teams about measurement of business process improvements:

1. *Measurement is critical in tracking improvement and assessing success.* People involved in the improvement effort need reinforcement that the process is working. Project measurement is an effective tool to give stakeholders feedback on how things are progressing.
2. *Work hard to understand what current data are telling you.* It often leads to goals, desired outcomes and improvement indicators.
3. *Project measurement is an effective tool to determine the effectiveness and efficiency of ImpAct Team activity.*
4. *Don't look only at dollar savings as a measurement of improvement.* Create a measurement system which is flexible and adapts to particular opportunities. Other types of measurements should focus on meeting customer requirements, timeliness, accuracy, responsiveness, and so forth.
5. *The CI measurement function must take responsibility for follow-up.* After the implementation of the solution and the disbanding of the

ImpAct Team, project measurement must provide indications that the implemented solution stays effective.

6. *CI measurement should not spend a lot of time measuring obvious benefits.* Projects should not be held up while CI measurement tries to come up with meaningful measurements. Be aware that the cost of establishing measures can exceed the cost savings for some projects.

7. *The project report form should be broad enough to allow reporting of nonfinancial benefits of the project.*

8. *CI measurement should be ready to assist the ImpAct Team at any stage of the improvement process.* If an ImpAct Team appears to be stagnating, they must be willing, in partnership with management, to help get the team back on track.

9. *ImpAct Teams are more effective when they start with an Initial Benefit Analysis and with direct involvement from management.*

It's not in the list, but a fundamental truth about measurement is probably a common cause behind several of them: "What gets measured gets done." So make sure you have the right measures. The Bridge Process will help identify them.

There are some added dimensions to CI measurement which must be addressed by a CI team. These dimensions involve taking an internal look at how your team is progressing against your action plan and measuring the effectiveness of the systems you have put in place.

Progress against Action Plan

As your team begins to accept responsibility for partnering with management, it is extremely important to answer the question: "How are we doing?" as it concerns your relationship with all involved parties. This implies setting short- and long-term goals which are measurable.

In this important audit function, the CI measurement function must view the quality systems, the process improvement effort and CI education as "projects" which must be measured.

Effectiveness of your CI systems

Your CI team needs to give some thought to establishing a few measures that will indicate the effectiveness of the systems you have created. The CI measurement function is to track these measures for the team so that you can make any needed adjustments during the improvement process.

Some CI process effectiveness measures your team can consider are:

- Level of work unit participation in the SFO system.
- Percentage of employees who have participated in the effort by working on an ImpAct Team.
- Percentage of accepted solutions versus number of problems worked and the average turnaround time.
- Feedback received from employees about their level of satisfaction with the quality systems.
- Number of SFOs submitted in each of three categories of improvement: product/service, process, and relationships. Percentage of problems worked with tangible cost/$ savings.
- Specific feedback from managers on the partnering relationship on process improvement.

12.5.3   Complex Adaptive Systems for Leading-Edge CI

Complex adaptive systems (CAS) concepts in concert with Support Systems for work-group behaviors are equal to empowered business teams. This can

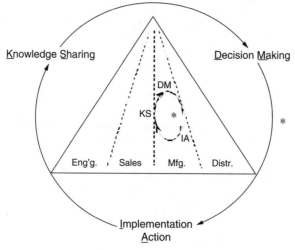

A Learning Organization

With fractals* enabling learning behaviors in a complex, adaptive organization structure

CUMBERLAND

Exhibit 12.4   CAS View of Teams Empowered for CI

be an enlightening concept for people suffering from "central program fatigue" where the previous lack of effective Support Systems have forced them to do double duty with overly elaborate project management routines just to get modest new projects moving. Showing them how to manage the Support Systems to empower work teams for more effective CI efforts could give them a lot of relief and renewed willingness to continue on with improvements in their own work areas (see Exhibit 12.4.)

12.6   What Can Go Wrong

Poor alignment between the upstream causal metrics and the downstream results is a most likely thing that can go wrong with Bridge metrics for CI process uses. In other words, the upstream causal metrics may not be as closely correlated with downstream results as needed for dependable outcomes.

A root cause of such a failure is a lack of attention to the details of cause-and-effect analysis during the metrics development phase. Plan for ample resource time and project support to ensure successful identification of upstream metrics that are tightly correlated with the targeted downstream results.

12.7   Tollgate Questions

Inadequate answers to these questions may require more work to develop Bridge Process metrics for effective support of your CI process:

1. Do we have an analysis of how well the proposed upstream metrics are correlated to our downstream results goals for business process performance improvement?
2. In the CI process, are the process metrics communicated to the process teams and owners on a timely basis?
3. For improvement projects, are there tracking processes in place to monitor progress versus the process improvement goals?

13

Multipurpose and Next-Gen Tools

*You can't hold a man down without staying
down with him.*
BOOKER T. WASHINGTON

The following tools have broad application for cross-functional process-improvement work, and generally overlap several of the DMAIC chapters (especially Measure, Analyze, and Improve).

Also, two of them are relatively new applications of complex adaptive systems (CAS) theory that offer powerful new ways to analyze and manage the extreme complexity that occurs in production processes for mass customization.

13.1   Value-Stream Mapping

Inside the plant, there are finite capacities for both materials storage and processing that need to be balanced for optimum use in satisfying typical customer demand scenarios. The Bridge metrics need views that help explain the interplay of those capacities so they can be managed for best operating and financial results. The Value-Stream Mapping (VSM) technique has become a common tool for that purpose because its usefulness "bridges" the Measure, Analyze, and Improve phases of DMAIC. And, like MRP at the macro level, VSM provides realistic views of time and space variables that are fundamental to understanding how upstream operating variables flow into the downstream financial statements.

The lead time common thread through a VSM is a key to designing manufacturing processes that fit comfortably in the space and processing capacity provided.

The following describes the basics of Value-Stream Mapping methods. For more information check one of the popular handbooks on the subject.

13.2 Value-Stream Mapping Methods

It's all about making the "value" visual, so it's easier to optimize the process around it.

The methods for Lean, Six Sigma, and continuous improvement (CI) have survived beyond the half-life of many of the business fads that came before. That shouldn't be a surprise when we take a broad view of the business landscape and see that Lean, Six Sigma, and CI are fundamental to the goals faced by most companies competing in a new global marketplace that is clearly here to stay. That's refreshing because that takes us back to operating fundamentals that had been given too little attention in the latter half of the twentieth century—but have been again proven to be essential to business success from now on.

Visual methods have played a prominent role in Lean processes that were clearly focused on the "value." Once the value was obvious it was possible to see the waste, eliminate it, and streamline what's left.

Value-Stream Mapping methods were a natural evolution of Lean development practices where visual methods work very well inside operating processes. And the visual methods of VSM make Lean development activities more effective and efficient. VSM makes communication of process improvement ideas easier, faster, and more complete.

13.2.1 Lead Time—The Common Thread

Some early Lean practitioners adopted a time-based view of the world that had a significant influence on the Value-Stream Mapping methods that eventually emerged. By the early 1990s, our friends at Motorola had concluded that if they had focused on a single process metric during the previous 25 years, then they would probably have arrived at the same point without trying a new program every couple years (SPC, JIT, TQM, and so forth) that eventually became the umbrella process now called Six Sigma. That metric was process span time, or lead time. Their conclusion came from the realization that a focus on lead time causes us to examine every element of a process, drive out the nonvalue waste, and streamline what's left. With that view we would then choose whatever tools were appropriate for the analysis or process design work at hand.

In our own work we have found that lead time is literally the "common thread" that ties all the process elements together. That has been especially evident when projects have required a Process Characteristics Chart (PCC) to display more data than can be shown on a Value-Stream Map. The lead time common thread is always important in the spreadsheet PCC views since it is a bottom-line indicator of process development progress toward the Lean vision.

About now you might be thinking something like: "OK, I sort of see why a long overall process time would indicate waste inside it. But how can I define the parts and relate them to the whole well enough to work on them easily? Or at least make some decisions about which parts to work first?" Those are key questions for the mental model we use to make practical tasks of "eating the elephant a bite at a time." To help build your model, a basic description of the lead time components will be useful.

In Exhibit 13.1, notice the "production line" of materials and equipment along the bottom, labels above them, and the overall process lead time at the top. In between are process time notes:

- Fabrication, assembly, and pack and ship are the only value-adding steps in the process, and from this macrolevel view we can't tell how much work inside them may also be waste that could be targeted for elimination.
- The transport times are necessary evils of the current plant layout.

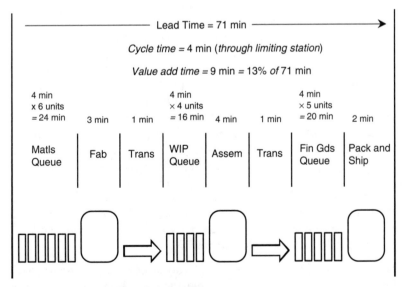

Exhibit 13.1   Process Time Relationships

- The process cycle time (CT = 4 minutes) appears to be paced by the assembly station. (This may be a line-balancing opportunity.)
- Each unit in the queues (materials, work in process, finished goods) is indexing forward at the cycle time rate (4 minutes each), so some units are waiting up to 24 minutes for their turn through the next station. (Are the queues necessary?)
- The overall process lead time (71 minutes) is the sum of the times one unit will spend in each of the steps in the process.
- The value-add portion of the overall lead time is only 13 percent. The customer told us the packing has value in their internal handling, so it has value too, although we might be otherwise inclined to discount it since it does nothing to the form, fit, or function of the product.

13.2.2   A "Bridge Span": Business Process Fundamentals

Exhibit 13.1 is a basic view of how the pieces in a process all add up to the overall total process lead time. Digging deeper in the details is needed to understand "why" each of the pieces is what it is. But you can see several fundamentals of Lean process design that lead to the bottom line even from this high-level view.

- *Lead time is the common thread.* Everything that happens in a process shows up in the overall lead time. So there is considerable power in using lead time as a key process performance indicator (KPI) since it can be an effective "continuous education tool" as the entire workforce looks for ways to remove waste from it to improve customer service and operating efficiency.
- *Inventories are a big red flag.* As the example illustrates, inventories in queue between workstations are geometric contributors to overall process lead time. That is because each unit extends lead time by one cycle time increment (multiplied by CT), so it's not unusual for "unlean" processes to have a very small percent of value-add time within a much longer overall lead time. That fact is an origin of the "Lean" label. It has been useful in helping people recognize process improvement opportunities since the physical existence of materials between operations is a clear indicator that a process is "not lean" and almost certainly has significant opportunities for improvement.
- *Any nonvalue time is waste.* This seems too obvious to be worth mentioning. But the complexity of business processes often makes it difficult to distinguish between the VA and waste steps. The VSM methods organize and simplify that work.

The natural next phase (digging deeper) is to analyze the process and pieces for improvement opportunities. Avoid the temptation to rely only on "creative, out-of-box brainstorming" in the *search for opportunities* (SFO) stage because the project team "doesn't know what it doesn't know" and could accidentally squander precious time in known territories, while the best opportunities are in the uncharted ones. Because of the wide range of process details and design possibilities it's helpful to use the typical checklists for in-process wastes and Lean process design concepts so the SFO work is both efficient and comprehensive.

To further illustrate the lead time common thread, consider Exhibit 13.2. Notice that there are several process elements that contribute to the common thread, and that having a consolidated view of them in-context could be important to fully understanding their impacts on overall process performance.

13.2.3 Value-Stream Map Examples

A Chicago region AME member company did the maps shown in Exhibits 13.3 and 13.4 as part of a kaizen project to make a key production process leaner, more efficient, and more responsive at serving customer demand changes quickly.

In the "Before" map, notice that "at a glance" you can see several Lean opportunities.

- Lead time = 16 days; customer response time slower than possible
- Lots of "push"-type production controls and overhead expenses

Then look at the contrasting "After" map in Exhibit 13.4.

In the "After" map, notice that the visual clarity of the Value-Stream Map provides an effective communication—"at a glance"—so you can easily see how the redesigned process has taken advantage of the Lean opportunities seen in the "Before" map.

- Lead time = 30 minutes; customer response time faster than expectations
- Use of "pull"-type production controls reduced WIP and overhead expenses

The focus in VSM is on the core value stream of work that converts materials, information, and energy into a product or service that the customer is willing to pay for. But, VSM also makes it easier to see nonvalue overhead functions that can be eliminated along with the in-process waste, so that should be a deliberate part of any VSM project step.

13.2.4 VSM Reference Sources

Several good reference books are available to help project teams learn the basics of Value-Stream Mapping. *Learning to See*, by Rother and Shook has good graphics and a story line around the metrics involved.

Lead Time: The "Common Thread"

Process Characteristics

Process: Airplane Factory

Model Used On	#	Work Step or Item Description	ID	Value Add X	Quality Base %	Quality Oppty %	Frequency Base U/Occur	Frequency Oppty U/Occur	Time/Occur Base Sec	Time/Occur Oppty Sec	Setup Time Base Sec	Setup Time Oppty Sec	Lead Time Base Sec	Lead Time Oppty Sec	Capacity Base U/Hr	Capacity Oppty U/Hr	Avg Inventory Base Pcs	Avg Inventory Oppty Pcs	Space Base SqFt	Space Oppty SqFt
II	1a	Set-up to run model II	#1				1000	1000	36		36		0.0	0.0						
II	1b	Get materials from stock	#1				10	100	17	17			1.7	0.2						
II	1c	Blue 16-pin blocks	BI6	X			1	1	8	8			8.0	8.0			10	300	0.1	2.1
II	1d	Assemble primary wing/airframe	#1					500		20				0.04					3.0	3.0
II	1e	Get materials from stock	#1	X																
II	1f	Blue 8-pin blocks	BO8											4.0				750		2.1
II	1g	Add nose section	#1	X			5	1	25	4			5.0	1.0						
II	1h	Deliver to #2 and return	#1										15	13	244	272			3.1	7.2
II	1i	S.T. #1											BI8	20			18	1	1.5	0.0
II	1j	WIP queue at #2														CT				
II	2a	Set-up to run model II	#2				1000	1000	51	2	51	2	0.1	0.0						
II	2b	Get materials from stock	#2				10	125	20	20			2.0	0.2					0.1	2.1
II	2c	Blue 8-pin blocks	BO8	X											144	210	25	750	3.0	3.0
II	2d	Assemble nose & wing sections	#2				1	1	19	16			19.0	16.0						
II	2e	Deliver to #3 and return	#2				5	1	20				4.0	1.0					3.1	5.1
II		S.T. #2											25	17						
II	2f	WIP queue at #3											545	20			12	1	1.5	0.0

Base = Phase 1
Oppty = Phase 4 (Opportunity)

CT: Cycle Time
LT: Lead Time

CUMBERLAND

Exhibit 13.2 Lead Time Common Thread through VSM

Process Characteristics

Process: _Airplane Factory_

Model Used On	#	Step or Item Description	ID	Value Add	Quality Base %	Quality Oppty %	Frequency Base U/Occur	Frequency Oppty U/Occur	Time/Occur. Base Sec	Time/Occur. Oppty Sec	Setup Time Base Sec	Setup Time Oppty Sec	Lead Time Base Sec	Lead Time Oppty Sec	Capacity Base U/Hr	Capacity Oppty U/Hr	Avg Inventory Base Pcs	Avg Inventory Oppty Pcs	Space Base SqFt	Space Oppty SqFt
11	3a	Set-up to run model 11	#3	X			1000	1000	46	7	46	7	0.0	0.0						
11	3b	Get materials from stock	#3				17	167	20	20			12	0.1						
11	3c	Blue 8-pin blocks	BOB														25	750	0.1	2.1
11	3d	Assemble large section of tail	#3	X			1	1	15	15			15.0	15.0					3.0	3.0
11	3e	Get materials from stock	#3					500	23	23				0.0						
11	3f	Blue 4-pin blocks	BO4															750		2.1
11	3g	Assemble cockpit	#3	X			1	1	15	4			30	4.0						
11	3h	Deliver to #4 and return	#3				5	1	15	1			9	1.0	187	20			3.1	5.1
11		5, T, #3													178					
11	3i	WIP queue at #4											636	20			14	1	1.5	0.0
11	4a	Set-up to run model 11	#4				1000	1000	50	5	50	5	0.1	0.0						
11	4b	Get materials from stock	#4				17	33.3	23	23			14	0.1						
11	4c	Blue 4-pin blocks	BO4														50	1500	0.1	2.1
11	4d	Asm nose, fusely, ckpt, tail, whls	#4	X			1	1	40	15			40.0	15.0					3.0	3.0
11	4e	Deliver to #5 and return	#4				5	1	20	1			40	1.0		224			3.1	5.1
11		5, T, #4											451	16	79					
11	4f	WIP queue at #5											136	20			3	1	0.5	0.0

LT → 636

LC → 79

LC: Limiting Capacity

Exhibit 13.2 (_Continued_)

Process Characteristics

Process: _Airplane Factory_

Model Used On	#	Step or Item Description	Value Add X	Quality Base %	Quality Oppty %	Frequency Base W/Occur	Frequency Oppty W/Occur	Time/Occur. Base Sec.	Time/Occur. Oppty Sec.	Setup Time Base Sec.	Setup Time Oppty Sec.	Lead Time Base Sec.	Lead Time Oppty Sec.	Capacity Base U/Hr.	Capacity Oppty U/Hr.	Avg. Inventory Base Pcs.	Avg. Inventory Oppty Pcs.	Space Base Sq Ft.	Space Oppty Sq Ft.
11	5a	Set-up to run model 11	#5			1000	1000	23	0	23	0	2.0	0.0						
11	5b	Inspect finished units	#5	61%	100%	1	1	11	8			1.0	8.0					3.0	3.0
11	5c	Deliver to #6 and return	#5			5	1	25	1			16.0	9.0	225	400			3.0	3.0
		S.T. #5																	
11	5d	WIP queue at #6										192	20			4	1	0.5	0.0
11	6a	Set-up to run model 11	#6																
11	6b	Tear down finished units	#6					NA	NA			NA	NA					3.0	3.0
11	6c	Return materials to stock	#6					NA	NA			NA	NA					3.0	3.0
		S.T. #6																	

Exhibit 13.2 (_Continued_)

Improvement Goals and Progress

Process: _Airplane Factory_

U/M:	Quality Base %	Quality Oppty %	Setup Time Base Sec.	Setup Time Oppty Sec.	Process Time Base Sec.	Process Time Oppty Sec.	Capacity Base U/Hr.	Capacity Oppty U/Hr.	Walking Dist Base Ft./U.	Walking Dist Oppty Ft./U.	Transport Dist Base Ft./U.	Transport Dist Oppty Ft./U.	Avg. Inventory Base Pcs.	Avg. Inventory Oppty Pcs.	Space Base SqFt.	Space Oppty SqFt.
Totals (from sheet above)	61%	100%	51	7	120	76	48	178	0	0	18	4	161	4805	24.0	28.5
Target	99.9%		15		70		180					4	3000		24	
Status 6 / 15 / 97																
Status 9 / 30 / 97																
Status 12 / 31 / 97																

U/M:	Lead Time Base Sec.	Lead Time Oppty Sec.	Cycle Time Base Sec.	Cycle Time Oppty Sec.	Takt Time Base Sec.	Takt Time Oppty Sec.	Productivity Base U/L.Hr.	Productivity Oppty U/L.Hr.
Overall Process	2,437	176	45	20	54	14	10	45
Target	150		18		14		40	
Status 6 / 15 / 97								
Status 9 / 30 / 97								
Status 12 / 31 / 97								

Base	Oppty	
5	4	= Crew Members

Base	Oppty	
7.5	7.5	= Net Avail. Prodn. Hrs. / Day

Base	Oppty	
500	2,000	= Planned Daily Output

Output Unit Description:
High-tech reconnaissance airplane

CUMBERLAND

Exhibit 13.2 (Continued)

400

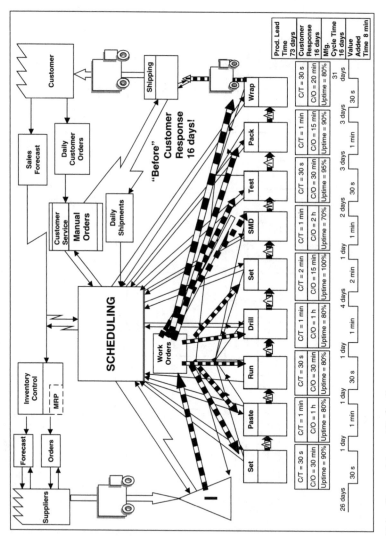

Exhibit 13.3 Value-Stream Map—"Before"

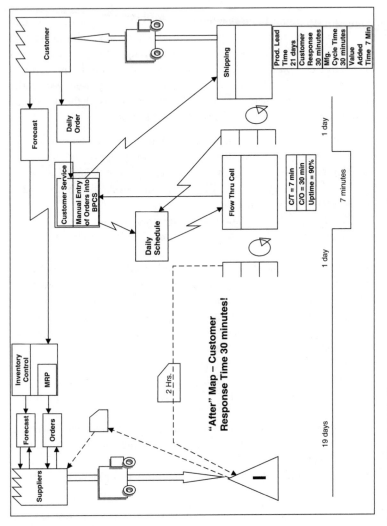

Exhibit 13.4 Value-Stream Map—"After"

The following sections summarize enough of the VSM technique mechanics
to help explain how it can come into play in the Bridge Process.

13.2.5 Typical Process Data Items

Value-Stream Mapping focuses attention first on the few most important
process metrics, so the analysis work is always in context with the overall
process objectives. That's important because the range of significant process
characteristics can be overwhelming when viewed in total, and can bog
down your initial data collection efforts. For example, you may consider
capturing all of the following as you begin observations of the individual
steps within a process, but the * items should get priority.

1. Each process step = do something and deliver to next station
   a. *Inventory (IN) = inventory created by this process step
   b. Number of SKUs = number of unique parts (stock keeping units)
   c. Every part every _____ (EPE) = indicates production batch size
   d. Number of operators (OP)
   e. *Cycle time (CT) = station operating time per unit
   f. Value-added (VA) = work the customer is willing to pay for
   g. Up time % (UT)
   h. Changeover time (CO) = to first good piece of the new product
   i. Working time (WT) = scheduled line time less planned downtime
2. Overall process = convert material/parts/energy to products/services
   a. *Cycle time (CT) = operating time per unit at limiting station
   b. *Takt time = production demand rate = available line operation time
      ÷ customer demand per day
   c. *Lead time (LT) = first thru last step, including queue times
   d. Value-added % (VA) = value-added of total operator time
   e. Line productivity (U/H) = units per total line hour (including
      downtime)
   f. Line productivity (H/U) = total line time per unit (including downtime)
   g. Crew productivity (H/U) = total crew time per unit (including
      "indirects")
   h. Working time (WT) = scheduled line time less planned downtime

---

*These items are essential. To "keep it simple" (KIS) and focused, concentrate first on col-
lecting the *-marked items. They are fundamental process measures and will be important in
maintaining a "line of sight" between the overall process objectives (customer and business
requirements) and the process details that come to light during the process analysis and
improvement phases.

13.2.6   Symbols for Value-Stream Maps

The symbols used on Value-Stream Maps are as varied as the types of industries they are used in. Administrative processes and manufacturing processes can have symbols specific to the business at hand. In any case, communication of ideas is the goal, so you might need a few specialized symbols that are especially meaningful to the local folks involved. Don't be afraid to be creative, but try to use the common conventions whenever possible to aid communications with outsiders.

As a starting point, some symbols have become common in VSM practices:

Symbol	Description
$\triangle I$	**Inventory Storage** Make note of number of SKUs and quantities. Whether random or dedicated storage may also be noted.
Avionics Assembly $\langle O \rangle$ = 2′ × 3′ = 6	**WorkStation ID/Description Box** Include any information that might be useful for analysis or process design work later, e.g., number of operators, work area square footage, equipment speeds, and tools.
CT = 420 CO = 30 UT = 90% WT = 900	**Process Data Box** Include at least the *-marked items in the previous section. Use a Process Characteristics Chart if much more data are needed for complex process designs.
■■■■▶	**Movement "Pushed"** Materials pushed to next station before needed; by schedule or production procedures.
⇨	**Movement "Pulled"** Materials pulled to next station just in time; usually by a visual signal from the "customer" station. It's often helpful to indicate "indirect" personnel as well as "direct" operators. Lean is concerned with the whole crew.

⊂O⊃	**Operator**
⌐⌐⌐⌐	**Supermarket** Indicates a materials supply area designed for quick picking of supplies to a production station.
▯▯▯	**Safety Stock Inventory** Indicates that an additional "buffer" quantity is included as a precaution for variable demands.
▱	**Document** e.g., schedule and work instructions
⟶	**Electronic Information Flow**
⟶	**Manual Information Flow**
⤏	**Kanban Signal Path**
P = 15	**Kanban Signal** Card, container, or other visual signal device Make note of kanban type. For example: W: Withdrawal, one card per container quantity P: Production, one card per container quantity B: Batch quantity, triggered by an order point

13.2.7 Step by Step VSM

A checklist for the basic Value-Stream Mapping steps:

1. Sketch and label a *next-process work-station box* for the next step *after* the end of the subject process. For example, "shipping" may be the next step after the finished goods inventory at the end of a final assembly production line. This acts like a placeholder to clarify the "out-of-scope" boundary for the subject process, and sometimes offers clues to process improvements to better serve that next, "customer" process.
2. Sketch and label an *inventory triangle* to indicate the queue or storage area created from the output of the previous step in the process. For each SKU found there, make notes for:
   - SKU # or description
   - Approximate quantities of each one
   - Material handling unit load quantity

Also note any characteristics of the inventory that may be an indication of "supplier" station operating constraints, such as outsized replenishment lot sizes that may be a clue to setup problems. That begins an analysis path with the usual fact that the replenishment lot-size portion of an inventory is owned by the supplier station, because if it could make single units immediately on demand, then a costly inventory storage point would not be needed.

3. Sketch and label a *workstation ID box* for the step that created the inventory described in #2. In the ID box, include any product or workstation information that may be useful later especially:
    - Basic machine speeds
    - Fixture batch capacities
    - Handling container capacities
4. Sketch and label a *workstation data box* for the step identified in #3. In the data box, note at least:
    - Number of operators (OP) =
    - Cycle time (CT) = station operating time per unit
    - Changeover time (CO) =
    - Working time (WT) = 820 minutes = 2 shifts $\times$ (480 – 30 – 30 – 10) $\times$ 60

Plus, any of the *typical process data items* listed in the earlier VSM Overview section. Especially note changeover issues that may affect batch sizes and the following inventory that's owned by this station.

5. *Repeat steps 2 through 4* for the upstream workstations to the beginning of the line.
6. Determine the *line cycle time* (line production rate) for the overall process. One simple way is to identify the cycle time through the limiting station. That's realistic if the operators can't help each other and there are few interruptions in the process cycle at each station. But that may overstate the throughput rate if production interruptions and other constraints are more prevalent, so station cycle times may have to be discounted by downtime expectations (changeovers, work problems, and so forth). Try to develop reasonable estimates without lapsing into "analysis paralysis."

Note: As production mix complexity increases, it can become very difficult to determine a net cycle time at individual stations or overall line due to the non-linear interplay of multiple variables. Specialized analysis tools may be necessary, especially for mixed-model and customer-configured production. See Flow-Ware in References.

7. Calculate the production *takt time* (TT) based on the customer demand rate (takt time = available work time ÷ demand). It presents production

demand from a customer perspective that is fundamental to the production plan.

8. At each workstation, post the *processing lead time* (LT) per unit on the lower level of a two-level timeline.

9. At each inventory point, calculate the queue lead time (QT) resulting from the average inventory quantity = IN × TT.

10. Calculate the total processing value-add time (VAT) from the lower-level bars of the timeline.

11. Calculate the overall process total process lead time from the upper-level bars of the timeline, plus the total processing value-add time from step 10.

These steps are enough to create a basic Value-Stream Map. However, you may have noticed that some of the steps will naturally collect other data that are relevant to the detailed process analysis work to be done inside the major process steps in it. To organize that detailed data, a Process Characteristics Chart spreadsheet may be also be needed.

13.2.8 Process Analysis and Improvement

At this point, stand back and look at the whole map. Several key process metrics should be obvious, and several analysis steps should happen naturally.

1. *Capacity* to meet expected customer demand. Compare the line cycle time to takt time. If Line CT ÷ TT > 1, then the line has inadequate capacity for the current demand level. Corrective actions might include more line working hours, increased crewing on the bottleneck station, or other solutions.

2. *Line balance* to deploy the crew resources efficiently. Check the value-added percent (VA%) of all the line stations. If some are poorly used, then there may be opportunities to adjust the overall line crew assignments for better balance for the products to be run.

3. *Overall process* **value-add time versus lead time**. If the value-add time is much less than the lead time, then there are probably good opportunities for either improving the processing steps themselves, or for reducing the batch sizes produced by them that end up in the WIP inventory queues after them.

4. *Total process lead time:* Excessive process lead time is usually an indicator of process improvement opportunities often seen when viewed through a Lean lens. That is, visually obvious inventories are usually an indicator of excess process time standing in the way of better customer service and lower operating costs. In other words,

inventories are a physical indicator of process inefficiencies that need to be worked out in order to achieve the lean agility that can meet world-class business process expectations.

13.2.9   A Bridge Span: VSM to Identify Upstream Process Metrics

The summarized process analysis steps described in the previous section should give you an idea why the Value-Stream Mapping tool can be important in the Bridge Process. Many business processes are just complex enough that managers and process teams need a common language for understanding the fundamental characteristics of their process before they can communicate about opportunities to improve it. VSM is a good framework for that common language. And the primary metrics in a VSM may be key "upstream process indicators" that build solid "bridge spans" to the "downstream financial statement."

13.3   MRP for Logistics and Supply Chain Management

We are acquiring ever more powerful IT systems to manipulate the data about the business world—how basic resources are converted into products or services and delivered to customers—at electronic speed. But the laws of physics, time, and space still apply as real value creation still happens at human speed. Those contrasting realities are a reminder that Bridge metrics need to include views of what is practical. When loaded with realistic metrics about the extended supply chain, manufacturing resources planning (MRP) continues to be an appropriate tool for managing longer lead-time supply processes.

MRP has been maligned by some of the Lean-Sigma promoters. They argue that truly Lean processes no longer need MRP because the "pull" methods and single-unit lot sizes in Lean eliminate the need for long-range materials supply planning. Flexibility to meet real-time demands makes MRP obsolete, they claim.

That may be true in the distant future. But during the transition years there will certainly be a need for MRP management of some material supplies.

The following article lays out our rationale for how MRP fits with Lean-Sigma processes and how MRP metrics would fit in a Bridge Model.

Hey! Do We Still Need MRP with Lean Manufacturing?

How do we make the decision?

How can we get maximum support from MRP for Lean Flow Mfg?

American industry has made great strides toward the Lean Flow Manufacturing vision in recent years. And it shows in vastly reduced work-in-process inventories, much shorter order lead times, and increased manufacturing productivity. No question, it's working.

Meanwhile, the role of MRP systems has become less clear. That's certainly not for lack of investment or implementation effort, particularly with thousands of new installations triggered by Y2K compliance fears. But the folks moving quickly toward the Lean ideal have generally found conventional MRP practices to be of limited value in the fast-moving Lean world. Notice we used the word "practices" rather than "systems" because the issue is one of application practices more than the basic MRP/ERP information processors themselves.

The following discussion outlines the issues and approaches involved in aligning MRP functions for best support of Lean Flow Manufacturing.

A Brief History   "Common sense" might be a good description for the Lean Flow Manufacturing principles. In fact, none of them are new, having been commonly used in production systems for a century. So you might ask, Why they are now being "discovered" by industries where you would think they should have been automatic by now?

The short answer is this: During the 1950s through 1970s companies all over the world became distracted with computer technologies that enabled much more detailed "inventory control" called *manufacturing resources planning*. With a myopic focus on individual inventory transactions that new strength became an unintended weakness.

Meanwhile, some companies in the United States, and especially in Japan, had refined the production methods to "optimize the production flow." By the time the contrasting results were noticed in the 1980s, the companies with a "production flow" mentality (*dynamic*) were about to drive many companies with the "inventory control" mentality (*static*) out of business.

In the 1990s, some of the survivors, including founding members of the Association for Manufacturing Excellence (AME), coined the terms Lean and Flow to describe the efficient production methods that were being "rediscovered." The literature is sometimes imprecise, but you can generally use "Lean" to indicate the process design attributes needed to achieve highly efficient "Flow" manufacturing—Lean to achieve Flow. So now, Lean Flow has become a strongly held expectation for competitive manufacturers.

Unfortunately, at the same time, the role of MRP in manufacturing has become less understood. Perhaps because many of the Lean practitioners haven't taken time to figure out how to use it in support of Lean. Perhaps because some of the Lean "gurus" have carelessly advocated the elimination of MRP systems altogether.

The relative roles of MRP and Lean Flow methods are clear:

- MRP is an appropriate tool for managing long lead-time material supplies, especially if predictable demand spikes overlay smaller routine demands. (Exhibit 13.5)
- Lean methods use visual controls in manufacturing processes that Flow too quickly to benefit from MRP methods.

Common Issues   More than ever, executives and managers are asking,

The MRP system burns a lot of overhead cost. Do we really need it?

Lean Flow Manufacturing has reduced the MRP role. Is it obsolete?

What would happen if we eliminated MRP?

Is MRP still needed for some planning functions?

How can we align MRP for best support of the Lean Flow vision?

High demand variability, long lead time

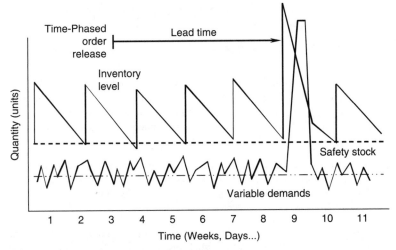

Exhibit 13.5   When MRP is Needed to Support Lean

It's unfortunate that MRP/ERP systems are so often used ineffectively. Part of the problem may be traceable to two aspects of MRP:

1. MRP is not complicated, although the way it is presented for implementation often makes it appear complicated so key operating concepts are often lost in the forest of procedural trees.
2. But MRP becomes complex (not complicated) because of the sheer number of component parts, work centers, operators, inventory control points, and minute-to-minute transactions that have to be accounted for.

The conclusion is that for an MRP implementation to be successful the users must dedicate enough effort to master both the forest and the trees. Process gaps in any level or area of MRP destroys the integrity of the entire system.

Our American culture itself may be part of the problem. We're an action-oriented culture that feels especially good about the speed and directness of the Lean Flow methods. And naturally, we're less interested in the detailed, procedural disciplines of MRP where the cause-and-effect relationships in the system are hidden inside and not visible like the real-time actions and results in Lean Flow Manufacturing operations.

Where to Start Resolving the Lean MRP issues is usually a daunting challenge since the factions involved often seem to be at odds with each other.

- The Lean manufacturing staff thinks they have "moved beyond" MRP.
- The materials staff continues to be frustrated by the lack of respect they get from manufacturing, and is convinced that it was manufacturing's inaccurate transactions that kept MRP from fulfilling its promise.
- The support departments have no interest in the MRP/ERP functions, believing it's an "operations thing" even though they seem to be working more in unison with manufacturing every day to handle the customer order and supply chain flows.

But still, getting everyone together is still the first step toward making Lean MRP a satisfying reality.

Lean MRP Is Not Another Dose of MRP Procedures Training A common "failure to communicate" occurs when MRP procedures training is mistaken for operational process management. It's not. And will alienate the manufacturing and materials staffs if done prior to carefully examining the operating issues to be resolved with Lean MRP.

Lean MRP Project Launch Work Session An effective way to engage the entire operations staff in the Lean MRP/ERP development is to begin with a session that, more than anything else, is a heart-to-heart discussion between all the participants in operations affected by MRP/ERP.

This work session provides training for anyone in the company who can be involved in using elements of the MRP system to achieve Lean Flow in your business operations.

It provides the basic concepts that you need to *know* about Lean Flow Manufacturing principles and MRP in order to participate in related activities in your own work areas.

It also provides suggestions for what you can *do* to contribute to the continual improvement of manufacturing operations. Knowledge of continual improvement (CI) processes, Lean Flow, and related methods will be useful in your ongoing roles to improve your own local area operations.

Lean MRP Workshop Objectives   The overall workshop objective is to identify ways to improve how MRP is used to support business operations.

Workshop objectives include:

* Understand the basics of the Lean Flow Manufacturing principles
* Understand the basics of MRP
* Identify problems in using MRP effectively
* Develop action plans to eliminate the most serious MRP usage problems

Typical Lean MRP Workshop Content   Primary work session modules include:

Lean flow manufacturing concepts overview

Purpose: To confirm consensus on the basic Lean Flow principles.
* Lean Flow concepts summary list
* Functional versus process layouts
* Set-up time impacts on inventory levels
* Production synchronization
* MRP versus kanbans
* 5Ss of organized workplace
* Spaghetti diagrams and standard methods
* Production linearity

Lean MRP concepts overview

Purpose: To confirm consensus about basic MRP concepts and functions.
* Example MRP display w/ calcs for typical items
* Lead time and other determinants of control methods
  ○ Cycle time from limiting station
  ○ Lead time including waste time in queues (like car wash)
  ○ MRP for long lead time, sporadic items
  ○ Kanban for short lead time, routine items
* Safety Stock calculations for MRP or Kanban
* Forecasted Demands
* Inventory Transactions and Record Accuracy
* Order Sizes, Economics, Inventory Levels

MRP demonstration and discussion

Purpose: To examine how MRP really works at your company.

Diagnosis of MRP opportunities

Purpose: To identify the most serious current obstacles to effective MRP functions at your company.

Improvement action planning

Purpose: To plan the implementation steps for improvements in the MRP functions at your company.

Visionary Collaboration is Key   Notice that the work session modules focus on the roles that everyone plays in the business, and how those roles can best contribute to the Lean Flow vision that is becoming a global business imperative. The process is best described as a collaboration of the process team members involved.

13.3.1   A Bridge Span: MRP Process Metrics That Reflect Reality

For Bridge Process purposes, the key issue in MRP usage is to keep it from becoming an inert "black box" that is not an accurate reflection of the business processes it is supposed to be supporting. The collaborative methods outlined above are designed to engage everyone involved in operating MRP or using its outputs in a dialog that culminates with clear agreements on how the system should reflect reality, and who is responsible for maintaining the database elements required.

If the MRP/ERP system is used as a feeder to the accounting system, then it must be configured and maintained so that the operating process data it provides are an accurate reflection of the actual manufacturing systems.

13.4   Operations Planning Models

After the individual process capacities are internally balanced with VSM-style tools, some of their aggregated totals need to be compared to capacities of key plant segments. For example, totaled loads from all lines should be compared to any central processing or storage functions to ensure that there is adequate capacity throughout the operating schedule. Inventory space overloads can be especially unpleasant surprises since the chaos they cause can easily break down fundamental shop floor disciplines like kanban supply routines. Operations plan views with a "whole enterprise data view" can be high-leverage tools, even in simple spreadsheet formats in lieu of specialized IT systems.

13.4.1   A Bridge Span: Identifying Process Constraints to Financial Results

For Bridge purposes, operations models can help identify process constraints that may not be visible in the individual Value-Stream Maps or process layouts. An example came from a global contract electronics manufacturer having trouble adopting basic Lean kanban "pull" methods in their plants. That seemed odd because there was no shortage of high-quality engineering, logistics, and manufacturing talent in the company.

When asked why they thought the kanban methods had failed, the quick answer was that "our shop floor people aren't disciplined enough to maintain a manual kanban process. It just gets out of whack very quickly." So a solution they thought might get around the problem was to install an "electronic kanban" system. That seemed like a major step backward toward more nonvalue off-line overhead, but they were frustrated and wanted to "solve" the problem so they could "move on" with their Lean Sigma initiative.

Interestingly, separate discussions had uncovered some related issues in other practices in the company. A fuzzy answer came back when asked about how the materials supply plans were aligned with the production line operating plans. The expected response was that the available on-line storage capacities and materials usage rates were calculated into the stocking policies for on-line parts supplies. The reality was that the stocking policies were not that closely linked to the physical constraints, and in fact it was common for replenishment supplies to not even fit in the designated storage space, so when delivered they had to sit in an aisle until space opened up.

Soon after, the learnings from both discussions came together in another one, and the root cause of the kanban failure became clear. That was, for kanban to work the materials containers must always fit in the physical spaces designated. If they don't, then the process breaks down almost immediately. Simple, but not obvious in organizations that have lost sight of that fundamental equation.

Unfortunately, a lot of companies lost that level of operational understanding as they went through the "materials management age" of the 1960s through 1980s with a focus on silver bullet "materials control" solutions with black-box MRP/ERP systems. Their attention was consumed in "keeping track of things." Meanwhile, the Lean practitioners were perfecting the methods to "move things through faster"—a vastly different perspective.

In another situation, an operations VP once faced a dip in on-time shipping performance. (Haven't we heard something like this before?) He had a financial background, so tended to view business problems from that perspective, having found that people could usually be "pushed" to discover operational solutions to financial goals. Plus, basic concepts like "not being able to sell from an empty wagon" were not lost on him.

In this case, he reacted with a knee-jerk edict: "Double all the safety stocks so we're always in stock when orders have to be picked." The production staff squirmed in their seats, but didn't question the edict. Later, someone else asked the production manager how it could be possible to double safety stocks across the board when the warehouse appeared to be too close to 100 percent full already. The production manager said it wasn't possible, but they would figure out some way to fudge the orders, schedule, or whatever to appear to follow the edict while doing *something* to address the late shipments problem. So the shop floor didn't get any more chaotic than it already was, but a couple more people found themselves in "expediter" roles to guide more of the hot replenishment orders toward the shipping service problem.

13.4.2   A Bridge Span: Operating Plans to Fit within the Real Capacities

The point is that the operating parameters for the intertwined processes involved in manufacturing have to be configured to fit the capacities involved. If they don't, then the shop floor disciplines are not maintainable and people will fall back on whatever stop-gap methods will get them through the day with the least hassle. The planners might be hoping for smooth, closed-loop operations, but frequent disconnects and overloads are more likely if the operations plan doesn't fit within the physical capacities.

If the ERP system doesn't have routines for finite capacity planning, then simple spreadsheets can fill the gap. Actually, there is often some advantage in doing that type of operations planning outside the black box, so it's visible to everyone who needs to understand what's involved. It makes it easier to ask "Why?" five or more times when it's important to know that the plan is practical.

- *Do we have a game plan for routine replenishment of the XYZ supplies?*
- *Is the supplier ready with enough capacity?*
- *Are the stocking policies appropriate for the demand rates?*
- *Does the inventory created fit within our working capital budget?*
- *Will the turns be low enough to keep the CFO off our backs?*
- *Oh, by the way, will the inventory created fit in the stockroom?*

That last one is a "forest" question. Sometimes so much time is spent working on the trees that everyone forgets to check if they still fit in the forest. In that same vein are questions about overall workload versus crew capacity, equipment capacity, and so forth. If the plan details aren't rolled up somewhere to make sure they fit in total, then there is a good chance they won't and people will be wondering why the plan isn't working and they are all working harder but still not maintaining control of the process.

Exhibits 13.6 and 13.7 contain examples of the types of issues that might be handled in simple operations models. When building a new one, remember to first decide what questions it needs to answer. Then, include the minimum information required to answer those questions so the model is as simple as possible.

The main objective is to know that the totals fit orderly in the available capacities. If they don't, send up a big red flag!

13.5   Optimizing Customer-Configured, Mixed-Model Manufacturing

Traditional tools and systems (e.g., spreadsheets and sequential-equations software like ERP) cannot "see" the unit-to-unit variations in mass-customization process flows. There is simply too much happening in such processes for conventional tools to build a realistic picture for process management purposes. So planning for mixed-model flows has been limited to "averaging" techniques that mask important intraprocess interactions that could be better configured for dynamic process balance.

13.5.1   Limited Metrics for Mass Customization

From the Bridge perspective, the conventional tools provide limited help in understanding the improvement opportunities in mass customization operations. The averaged data in them hide the opportunities for more efficient work patterns between the "agents" in a process that's handling the complexity of customer-configured everyone-unique products. So those complex interactions usually frustrate attempts to measure them and develop predictable solutions for taking the benefits to the bottom line.

Flow software applications make those interactions visible to operations planners so they can diagnose opportunities and develop improvements in otherwise unmanageable process dynamics. To create realistic dynamic process views for process analysis and operations planning, Flow software combines the normal process segment times with the rules that govern process-agent interactions.

Operations Planning Issues

Considering Process Change-Over and Storage Space Constraints

Typical Inventory Carrying Costs

Carrying costs vary by product according to their unique storage density, unit cost, annual volume, damage rate, etc.

An average carrying cost factor is often applied across a range of product families if their characteristics are similar. For example:

> 7.00% = Cost of capital tied up in inventory
>
> 12.00% = Floor space cost, for example ((64 SF/rack × $6/SF) ÷ (20 U/rack × 4 tiers)) + $40/U
>
> 5.00% = Insurance
>
> 2.00% = Obsolesence
>
> 3.00% = Damage
>
> 7.00% = Other
>
> --------
>
> 36.00%   = Total Average Inventory Carrying Cost

Economic Order Quantity (EOQ) Formula

Used to calculate an Order Quantity (Batch Quantity) that will yield the least total of Changeover Costs and Inventory Carrying Costs.

$$= \text{Square Root of } ((2 \times \text{ChangeOver Cost} \times \text{Ann. Volume}) / (\text{Unit Cost} \times \text{Carrying \%}))$$

Caution: EOQs, by themselves, do not consider capacity constraints. See following sheets for typical scenarios.

Note: Inventory Carrying Costs in following scenarios include Safety Stocks, so are slightly more than the Changeover Costs.

A. Traditional Compromise Production Batches

1. Batches established by trial-and-error, compromises between inventory producers and inventory storers.
2. Dedicated storage spaces arranged to suit typical Maximum Inventories produced.
3. Many Batches/Year, and Change-Over Costs much higher than Carrying Costs.
4. Low Inventory Carrying Costs, limited by available storage space.
5. Workable defacto compromises, but high overall Inventory Maintenance Costs due to high Change-Over Costs.

Item	Qty/Yr	Qty /Hr	Batch Qty ①	Batch Inv	Safety Stock Hrs	Safety Stock Qty	Avg Inv	Max Inv	Storage % Used	Capacity Qty	Batches Per Yr	ChgOvr Cost	ChangeOver Cost/Yr	Unit Cost	Ann Inv CarryCost
A	400,000	100	800	400	4	400	800	1,200	100%	1,200	500	$900	$450,000	$30	$8,640
B	200,000	50	400	200	4	200	400	600	100%	600	500	900	450,000	$30	4,320
C	200,000	50	400	200	4	200	400	600	100%	600	500	900	450,000	$100	14,400
D	60,000	15	200	100	4	60	160	260	100%	260	300	900	270,000	$30	1,728
E	50,000	13	200	100	4	50	150	250	100%	250	250	900	225,000	$30	1,620
F	40,000	10	100	50	4	40	90	140	100%	140	400	900	360,000	$30	972
G	40,000	10	100	50	4	40	90	140	100%	140	400	900	360,000	$100	3,240
	990,000 Total						2,090	3,190 ②	100%	3,190 ②	2,850 ③		$2,565,000 ③		$34,920 ④

2 Shifts

40 Hours per week

50 Weeks per year

4000 Hours per year

36% Annual Inventory Carrying Cost ⑤

Total Inventory Maintenance Costs = $2,599,920 ⑤

Exhibit 13.6   Operations Planning Model

B. Economic Batch Quantities, Ignoring Space Limitations

1. Batches established by EOQ formula.
2. Large Batch Inventories exceed available Storage Capacity.
3. Batches/Year and Change-Over Costs are hoped to be much lower.
4. Inventory Carrying Costs would be higher, due to larger Batches.
5. Unworkable. Rather than lower costs, results would be glutted storage areas, container shortages, trucking chaos and line stoppages.

Item	Qty Qty/Yr	Batch /Hr	Batch Qty (1)	Inv	Safety Stock Hrs	Qty	Avg Inv	Max Inv	Storage Capacity % Used	Qty	Batches Per Yr	ChgOvr Cost	ChangeOver Cost/Yr	Unit Cost	Ann Inv CarryCost
A	400,000	100	8,165	4,082	4	400	4,482	8,565	714%	1,200	49	$900	$44,091	$30	$48,411
B	200,000	50	5,774	2,887	4	200	3,087	5,974	996%	600	35	900	31,177	$30	33,337
C	200,000	50	3,162	1,581	4	200	1,781	3,362	560%	600	63	900	56,921	$100	64,121
D	60,000	15	3,162	1,581	4	60	1,641	3,222	1239%	260	19	900	17,076	$30	17,724
E	50,000	13	2,887	1,443	4	50	1,493	2,937	1175%	250	17	900	15,588	$30	16,128
F	40,000	10	2,582	1,291	4	40	1,331	2,622	1873%	140	15	900	13,943	$30	14,375
G	40,000	10	1,414	707	4	40	747	1,454	1039%	140	28	900	25,456	$100	26,896
	990,000 Total						14,563 (2)	28,136 (5)	882% (2)	3,190 (2)	227 (3)		$204,252 (3)		$220,992 (4)

2 Shifts
40 Hours per week
50 Weeks per year
4000 Hours per year

Total Inventory Maintenance Costs = $425,244

36% Annual Inventory Carrying Cost

C. Economic Batch Quantities, Adjusted to Fit Limited Space

1. Batches established by EOQ formula, and adjusted to fit available Storage Capacity.
2. Batch Inventories fit in available Storage Capacity.
3. Slight reduction in Batches/Year and Change-Over Costs.
4. Inventory Carrying Costs limited by available Storage Capacity.
5. Workable plan with Batches that fit the space. Nominal overall Inventory Maintenance Cost reduction versus original scenario A.

#	Qty Qty/Yr	Batch /Hr	Batch Qty (1)	Inv	Safety Stock Hrs	Qty	Avg Inv	Max Inv	Storage Capacity % Used	Qty	Batches Per Yr	ChgOvr Cost	ChangeOver Cost/Yr	Unit Cost	Ann Inv CarryCost
A	400,000	100	653	327	4	400	727	1,053	97%	1,081	612	$900	$551,135	$30	$7,847
B	200,000	50	462	231	4	200	431	662	100%	662	433	900	389,711	$30	4,654
C	200,000	50	253	126	4	200	326	453	100%	453	791	900	711,512	$100	11,754
D	60,000	15	253	126	4	60	186	313	100%	313	237	900	213,454	$30	2,014
E	50,000	13	231	115	4	50	165	281	100%	281	217	900	194,856	$30	1,787
F	40,000	10	207	103	4	40	143	247	100%	247	194	900	174,284	$30	1,547
G	40,000	10	113	57	4	40	97	153	100%	153	354	900	318,198	$100	3,476
	990,000 Total						2,076 (2)	3,162 (2)	99%	3,190 (2)	2,837 (3)		$2,553,151 (3)		$33,080 (4)

2 Shifts
40 Hours per week
50 Weeks per year
4000 Hours per year

0.080 Space Limit Adjuster (1)

36% Annual Inventory Carrying Cost

Total Inventory Maintenance Costs = $2,586,231 (5)

Exhibit 13.6 *(Continued)*

D. Economic Batch Quantities, in Optimum Storage Space, Dedicated Locations

1. Batches established by EOQ formula.
2. Storage Capacity increased to accommodate Economic Batch quantities (EOQs).
3. Low Batches/Year and resulting Change-Over Costs.
4. Higher Inventory Carrying Costs than previous space-constrained scenarios, due to increased Storage Capacity and Average Inventory.
5. Balanced operating scenario between Change-Over and Carrying Costs. Low overall Inventory Maintenance Costs.

#	Qty/Yr	Qty /Hr	Batch Qty (1)	Batch Inv	Safety Stock Hrs	Safety Stock Qty	Avg Inv	Max Inv	Storage Capacity % Used	Storage Capacity Qty	Batches Per Yr	ChgOvr Cost	ChangeOver Cost/Yr	Unit Cost	Ann Inv CarryCost
A	400,000	100	8,165	4,082	4	400	4,482	8,565	100%	8,565	49	$900	$44,091	$30	$48,411
B	200,000	50	5,774	2,887	4	200	3,087	5,974	100%	5,974	35	900	31,177	$30	33,337
C	200,000	50	3,162	1,581	4	200	1,781	3,362	100%	3,362	63	900	56,921	$100	64,121
D	60,000	15	3,162	1,581	4	60	1,641	3,222	100%	3,222	19	900	17,076	$30	17,724
E	50,000	13	2,887	1,443	4	50	1,493	2,937	100%	2,937	17	900	15,588	$30	16,128
F	40,000	10	2,582	1,291	4	40	1,331	2,622	100%	2,622	15	900	13,943	$30	14,375
G	40,000	10	1,414	707	4	40	747	1,454	100%	1,454	28	900	25,456	$100	26,896
	990,000 Total						14,563	28,136	100%	28,136	227		$204,252		$220,992

2 Shifts
40 Hours per week   1.000 Space Limit Adjuster   Total Inventory Maintenance Costs = $425,244
50 Weeks per year
4000 Hours per year   36% Annual Inventory Carrying Cost

E. Economic Batch Quantities, in Optimum Storage Space, Random Locations

1. Batches established by EOQ formula.
2. Storage Capacity optimized with random storage pattern (Avg Inv) instead of dedicated SKU locations (Max Inv).
3. Minimum Change-Over Costs, within storage capacity.
4. Lower Inventory Carrying Costs (vs. Scenario D), due to more efficient storage method.
5. Optimized operating scenario. Minimal overall Inventory Maintenance Costs.

#	Qty/Yr	Qty /Hr	Batch Qty (1)	Batch Inv	Safety Stock Hrs	Safety Stock Qty	Avg Inv (2)	Max Inv	Storage Capacity % Used	Storage Capacity Qty	Batches Per Yr	ChgOvr Cost	ChangeOver Cost/Yr	Unit Cost	Ann Inv CarryCost
A	400,000	100	8,944	4,472	4	400	4,872	9,344	100%	4,872	45	$900	$40,249	$30	$43,849
B	200,000	50	6,325	3,162	4	200	3,362	6,525	100%	3,362	32	900	28,460	$30	30,260
C	200,000	50	3,464	1,732	4	200	1,932	3,664	100%	1,932	58	900	51,962	$100	57,962
D	60,000	15	3,464	1,732	4	60	1,792	3,524	100%	1,792	17	900	15,588	$30	16,128
E	50,000	13	3,162	1,581	4	50	1,631	3,212	100%	1,631	16	900	14,230	$30	14,680
F	40,000	10	2,828	1,414	4	40	1,454	2,868	100%	1,454	14	900	12,728	$30	13,088
G	40,000	10	1,549	775	4	40	815	1,589	100%	815	26	900	23,238	$100	24,438
	990,000 Total						15,858	30,727	100%	15,858	207		$186,456		$200,406

2 Shifts
40 Hours per week   1.000 Space Limit Adjuster   Total Inventory Maintenance Costs = $386,862
50 Weeks per year
4000 Hours per year   30% Annual Inventory Carrying Cost

Exhibit 13.6   *(Continued)*

SKU	Average Demand Per Week	Standard Deviation of Demand	Target Demand Coverage	Lead Time (Weeks)	Safety Stock Inventory	Change-Over Cost	SKU Unit Cost	Inventory Carrying Cost %	Replen Order Quantity	Average Inventory Level	Change-Over Time Per Week	Production Time Per Week	Total Line Time Per Week
XXXX1	719	144	3	1.28	552	$400	$0.680	27%	12,518	6,811	XXXXX	XXXXX	XXXXX
XXXX2	XXXXX	XXXXX	4	XXX	XXXXX	XXXXX	XXXXX	XXXXX	XXXXX	XXXXX	XXXXX	XXXXX	XXXXX
XXXX3	XXXXX	XXXXX	3	XXX	XXXXX	XXXXX	XXXXX	XXXXX	XXXXX	XXXXX	XXXXX	XXXXX	XXXXX
XXXXX	XXXXX	XXXXX	3	XXX	XXXXX	XXXXX	XXXXX	XXXXX	XXXXX	XXXXX	XXXXX	XXXXX	XXXXX
XXXXX	XXXXX	XXXXX	3	XXX	XXXXX	XXXXX	XXXXX	XXXXX	XXXXX	XXXXX	XXXXX	XXXXX	XXXXX
XXXXX	XXXXX	XXXXX	4	XXX	XXXXX	XXXXX	XXXXX	XXXXX	XXXXX	XXXXX	XXXXX	XXXXX	XXXXX
XXXXX	XXXXX	XXXXX	3	XXX	XXXXX	XXXXX	XXXXX	XXXXX	XXXXX	XXXXX	XXXXX	XXXXX	XXXXX
XXXXX	XXXXX	XXXXX	3	XXX	XXXXX	XXXXX	XXXXX	XXXXX	XXXXX	XXXXX	XXXXX	XXXXX	XXXXX
XXXXX	XXXXX	XXXXX	3	XXX	XXXXX	XXXXX	XXXXX	XXXXX	XXXXX	XXXXX	XXXXX	XXXXX	XXXXX
XXXXX	XXXXX	XXXXX	3	XXX	XXXXX	XXXXX	XXXXX	XXXXX	XXXXX	XXXXX	XXXXX	XXXXX	XXXXX
XXXXX	XXXXX	XXXXX	4	XXX	XXXXX	XXXXX	XXXXX	XXXXX	XXXXX	XXXXX	XXXXX	XXXXX	XXXXX
XXXXX	XXXXX	XXXXX	3	XXX	XXXXX	XXXXX	XXXXX	XXXXX	XXXXX	XXXXX	XXXXX	XXXXX	XXXXX
XXXXX	XXXXX	XXXXX	3	XXX	XXXXX	XXXXX	XXXXX	XXXXX	XXXXX	XXXXX	XXXXX	XXXXX	XXXXX
			A3		*1	A1, B2		A2	*2	6,811			XXXXX

For simple make-to-stock situations where the demand rate for each SKU is much less than the production rate:

1 Safety Stock = X Std. Devs. of Demand (A3) in excess of the recent average demand during the normal replenishment lead time. More sophisticated versions would also consider supply variability and other variables.

2 Replen Order Qty = Economic Order Quantity (EOQ), based on set-up costs, inventory carrying costs, and relatively consistent demand. Seasonal, promotional or other large demand variations require additional planning steps (MRP, etc.).

A1. Temporarily Increase Changeover Std. Costs to Reduce Replenishment Lot Sizes?

A2. Temporarily increase Carrying Costs Std. to Reduce Replenishment Lot Sizes?

A3. Temporarily Reduce the Demand Coverage Target?

A4. Other Options?

Comfortably Fits within Storage Space Capacity?

No →

Yes → OK

B1. Add Production Capacity Resources?

B2. Temporarily Increase Changeover Costs to Increase Inventory Replenishment Quantities? (Short Term)

B3. Other Options?

Comfortably Fits within Production Capacity?

No →

Yes → OK

Exhibit 13.7 Inventory Planning Within Physical Capacities

419

The following overview describes the background behind flow software applications, and outlines what the future may look like for process management (Lean-Sigma-CI) and optimization of mass-customization operations.

13.5.2   Background—Lean Sustainability and Mass Customization

Lean-Sigma manufacturing methods are recognized worldwide. And tools made popular by Lean practitioners (e.g., kaizen blitz, Value-Stream Mapping, and kanban visual signals) have made initial Lean-Sigma efforts more understandable and team oriented. But sustainability has been elusive, and Lean practitioners have commented that:

We don't need more Lean education...
...We do need tools to make Lean sustainable.

They are frustrated and discouraged with current levels of success that are below their expectations. Asking "Why?" five or more times uncovers two key barriers to those expectations.

One emerged as we approached the twenty-first century with communications that promised "infinite variety" to consumers and resulted in complex mixed-model production flows that overwhelm traditional manufacturing planning tools. The activities in mixed-model production are too variable (nonlinear) to be "seen" with conventional systems, so they offer no advantage over manual spreadsheet methods for process optimization, especially when factoring in the inherently high-maintenance overhead of such systems.

The other has been here all along—but surprisingly unrecognized by Lean-Sigma proponents—in the form of clumsy process-data files. That problem has become painful as *leaner* staffs are faced with mind-numbing workloads of product-process changes to keep up with increasing "infinite variety" customer demands.

The challenge is to eliminate the barriers, smooth the path to Lean-Sigma-CI, and enable the operating teams with practical tools for the work involved in making *mass customization* efficient and flexible = agile.

13.5.3   Flow Software Functions

Flow software addresses the barriers to Lean-Sigma-CI with an integrated set of process-improvement tools that accomplish two key functions:

1. Organizes complex process data to make Lean-Sigma-CI efforts practical, efficient, and sustainable.

2. Makes complex process behaviors *visible*…to simplify process optimization efforts…including complex mixed-model manufacturing.

Organizing Complex Process Data—So It's Useful!

Flow software methods organize the large amount of line-process data records required for comprehensive Lean-Sigma-CI efforts. At the same time it provides ready access to process data for routine line changes triggered by ECNs, customer order changes, and so forth.

The capture and maintenance of manufacturing process data is part and parcel of a line-designer's normal daily activities. There are no separate system maintenance functions that are invariably fragmented and unmanageable. Instead, the Flow software database items (such as process steps, WIP queues, storage layouts, equipment characteristics, operators, and handling equipment) are automatically maintained as part of the routine line-design work.

Flow software data processing functions typically include:

Process Database. Process database provides an evolving "process data picture" as changes (such as line layout, equipment, and operators) are evaluated for implementation. This capability *makes process complexity useful* for line-design engineers, organizing what has often been a troublesome task.

Kanban Process Integrity. Kanban process integrity includes a feedback loop to ensure that there is an adequate place for everything online without incurring wasted space. The feedback loop empowers line planners to quickly adjust (maintain) online kanban storage assignment parameters and eliminates a pitfall that has been a frequent source of kanban system failures.

Off-Line Activities. Off-line activities such as line changeovers and materials handling can be critical to overall line optimization, especially in mixed-model operations. When that comprehensive process view is needed, off-line activities are included in the process database for use in the process simulator and diagnostics (below).

Exhibit 13.8 illustrates the data displays and automated analysis steps in a Flow software manufacturing process design routine. They are convenient, high-leverage process design tools (not the usual inert data forms that only feed the ERP system).

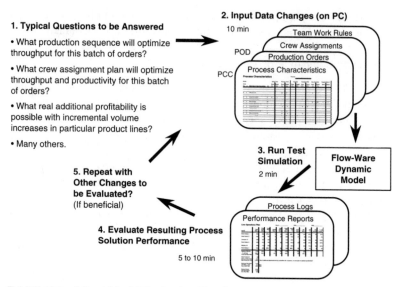

1. Typical Questions to be Answered

• What production sequence will optimize throughput for this batch of orders?

• What crew assignment plan will optimize throughput and productivity for this batch of orders?

• What real additional profitability is possible with incremental volume increases in particular product lines?

• Many others.

5. Repeat with Other Changes to be Evaluated?
(If beneficial)

4. Evaluate Resulting Process Solution Performance

5 to 10 min

2. Input Data Changes (on PC)

10 min

Team Work Rules
Crew Assignments
POD
Production Orders
PCC   Process Characteristics

3. Run Test Simulation

2 min

Flow-Ware Dynamic Model

Process Logs
Performance Reports

Exhibit 13.8   Mixed-Model Production Planning

Making Complex Process Behaviors Visible

The ability to analyze complex dynamic process activities is made possible by an engine that uses a parallel computing process to translate the large amount of process data in a mixed-model manufacturing process into a clear "operating process view." The beauty of this approach is that it is easy to see and understand the emergent patterns of line operations based on the realistic behaviors of all the "agents" involved in the process.

That realistic "operating process view" is a powerful diagnostic tool for optimizing overall line performance, especially in mixed-model manufacturing. Typical functions for mixed-model planning include:

"Real Time" Simulation.   A second-by-second floor analysis of the behavior of all the process "agents" (i.e., operators, machines, conveyors, lift trucks, and so forth) is a "real world, granular process view" and pre-production diagnostic method that saves process design time as it identifies "dynamic bottlenecks" and displays them on-screen—even before evaluating performance reports.

Process Diagnostics.   The outputs and results of mixed-model simulation can be used for diagnostics and process improvement. Customized reports from a Flow software simulation can display process performance details that cannot be displayed graphically. If you want to dig deeper, the simulation log itself can answer questions about second-by-second activities for any individual agent.

Realistic Process Times. Realistic process times are determined based on the nonlinear activities (not formulaic averages) of mixed-model production to generate a "schedule we can trust." This approach, in which *realistic performance data* replace averages (such as takt time, cycle time, lead time, and workload), provides a realistic view of intraline behaviors as well as overall operating results.

Exhibit 13.9 illustrates a detailed view of "agent" interactions in a mixed-model production process. That granular view is necessary to see and manage the agent interaction patterns for optimum productivity.

13.5.4   Cross-Functional Applications

Flow software methods can be used by a broad range of user groups involved in applying Lean, Six Sigma, and other continuous improvement methods for business agility and competitive advantage. For example:

- Line process design, analysis, and improvement
- Production management, operations planning, and scheduling
- Line crew development, assignment planning, and in-process coaching
- Strategic planning for plant assets allocation
- Business culture development to adopt Lean, Six Sigma, CI, and so forth
- Activity-based costing

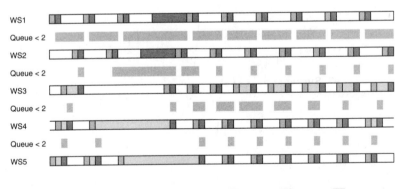

Exhibit 13.9   Granular View of In-Process Interactions

13.5.5   Benefits for Tracking in the Bridge Process

The Bridge Process would track a number of potential benefits from the process database and mixed-model optimization capabilities of Flow software methods:

1. Agile, efficient reactions to market demand changes
   a. Process data records are comprehensive, facilitating easier control of customer-required changes.
   b. Process planning is readily understood and more rapidly implemented.
   c. Participants realize a greater sense of satisfaction with less stress.
2. Least-cost mass-customization operations
   a. Mixed-model operations plans are realistic and dependable.
   b. Line and crew productivity can be optimized for specific product mix.
3. Accelerated continual improvement rate
   a. Fills a business process metrics gap in mixed-model operations.
   b. Facilitates communications between sales, operations, and finance.
   c. Provides a flexible process demonstration tool for training functions.
   d. Facilitates adoption of Lean-Sigma-CI practices and business culture.
   e. Facilitates operations team work.
   f. Focuses operations team attention to outdistance the competitors.

Exhibit 13.10 illustrates the value of unused production capacity in unoptimized mixed-model production. Flow software methods are aimed at controlling the process variations so that excess capacity is converted to productive throughput.

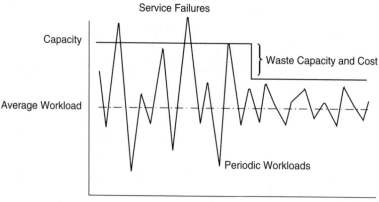

Exhibit 13.10   Managed Variations in Mass Customization

13.5.6   Practical Metrics for Mass Customization

As part of the Bridge process, Flow software methods provide a practical way to analyze the potential benefits from optimized mass customization. And, they offer solutions for routine management of such processes so the upstream control points are clear enough to ensure dependable results that should be easily tracked in the Bridge views.

Exhibit 13.11, process performance test metrics, shows the types of overall process performance data available with Flow software. This example is highlighting the difference between two different production mixtures so some of the data are left out to cut distraction, but you can see that several production configuration scenarios were tested with progressively better overall results. Four things are remarkable about the Flow software approach:

1. Scenario setups are from a line supervisor's view. That is, a scenario change looks like an operating plan change that a line supervisor might make when he decides that a lead qualified operator is needed in station 2, or the work rules for station 3 need to include an "up and back" option for today's production mix. That's a contrast to conventional systems that typically involve formulaic adjustments not generally part of frontline operations management routines. So Flow software can be useful to line managers and supervisors as well as production planners and line designers.
2. Alternate scenarios can be set up and run relatively quickly (Exhibit 13.11), so operations planners or supervisors can test "what if" options on short notice. That makes Flow software closer to a real-time operations management tool, although it seems that the higher-quality operations plans from it would generally eliminate the need for corrective-action replanning during the actual production run.
3. Pretested production performance metrics are based on the realistic behaviors of all agents in the line as they deal with the specific model mix fed through it.
4. Highly credible production schedules are possible with realistic tested production performance metrics. Exhibit 13.12 illustrates how a minute-to-minute schedule can be generated from the test run of a particular model mix through a specific line and crew configuration.

13.5.7   A Bridge Span: Performance Predictability for Mass Customization

Clearly the traditional tools cannot be effective with the complexity of customer-configured, mixed-model production. So Flow software offers a

Airplane Factory Performance — Flow-Ware Simulation

Model Mix Scenarios and Production Methods	Crew Time (Minutes)						Batch Size	Scenario Conditions		
	WIP Inventory	Starved	Blocked	Assembly (Value Add)	Total Time	Time/Unit		Normal Operator Assignment	Model Mix Sequence Control	Exceptional Conditions (See Notes Below)
E. 11-Loaded Mix										
4. As-Received Sequence	7.1	41.8	31.7	126.4	246.1	2.59	1	Fixed	Man.*2	
5. Smoothed Sequence						2.51	1	Fixed	FW*3	
6. Smoothing + Balancing						1.99	1	Fixed	FW*3	WS4 100% and Float
9. Optimum Flow						1.04	1	Float	FW*3	
G. 21-Loaded Mix										
4. As-Received Sequence	6.1	88.9	4.7	140.2	281.8	3.23	1	Fixed	Man.*2	
5. Smoothed Sequence						2.88	1	Fixed	FW*3	
6. Smoothing + Balancing						2.75	1	Fixed	FW*3	WS3 100% and Float
7. Smoothing + Balancing						2.39	1	Fixed	FW*3	WS2 100% and Float
9. Optimum Flow						1.18	1	Float	FW*3	

*Notes:
1. WIP queues max. = 1, unless otherwise noted
2. Manual smoothing.
3. Takt time smoothing algorithm in FW.

Exhibit 13.11 Process Performance Test Metrics

Work Station Schedule

Job#	Model	Compl. Time	WIP	Starved	Thinking	Setup	Mat Hdlg	Assembly	Delivery	Blocked
1	12	7:08 AM	1	0	0	0	0	35120	1040	0
2	12	7:15 AM	1	0	0	0	0	35120	1040	0
3	11	7:19 AM	0	0	0	0	0	15040	1040	0
4	12	7:27 AM	1	3500	0	0	0	35120	1040	0
5	12	7:34 AM	1	0	0	0	0	35120	1040	0
6	12	7:43 AM	1	0	0	0	0	35120	1040	0
7	12	7:50 AM	1	0	0	0	0	35120	1040	0
8	11	7:53 AM	0	0	0	0	0	15040	1040	7800
9	12	8:02 AM	1	3500	0	0	0	35120	1040	0
10	12	8:10 AM	1	0	0	0	0	35120	1040	0
11	12	8:17 AM	1	0	0	0	0	35120	1040	0
12	11	8:21 AM	0	0	0	0	0	15040	1040	0
13	12	8:29 AM	1	3500	0	0	0	35120	1040	0
14	21	8:32 AM	0	0	0	900	0	15040	1040	0
15	12	8:41 AM	1	3500	0	900	0	35120	1040	0
16	12	8:48 AM	1	0	700	0	0	35120	1040	0
17	11	8:52 AM	0	0	0	0	0	15040	1040	0

Conditions and special notes for this run:

1. WS4 is the bottleneck for this production mix. Lead operator will float from WS5 to help out.
2. Parts for model 12s are in short supply. Notify material supply operator if close to "out."

Exhibit 13.12　Schedule Based on Realistic Line Behaviors

view of the future as far as the planning tools for mass customization are concerned.

We have debated how to describe the Flow software solution for dynamic process management. On one hand, it's not a deterministic solution as typically used in scheduling software, so it's hard to call it a "scheduler." But on the other hand, its ability to simulate the behaviors of complex products through complex processes indicates that it can produce better-quality process performance data that easily translate to credible production schedules.

For Bridge Process purposes, Flow software is likely to be the eventual tool of choice for managers and project teams concerned with developing efficient new operations for mass customization—and for establishing upstream operations plans that flow dependably into the downstream financial statements.

13.6   Real-Time Analysis of Complex Process Variability Causes

Often, it's not possible, practical, or economical to capture multivariable data from inside a fast-moving process, so process metrics data may not be available for the Six Sigma statistical correlation analysis that would be used to determine the significant cause-and-effect relationships. However, another new software application based on loosely coupled sets (LCS) mathematics offers a solution to that problem. The LCS solution uses real-time data from a variety of in-equipment sensors to analyze the various independent variables in that data relative to the process outputs. Those with the closest correlation to the outputs would be the next subjects for analysis and possible improvement developments.

Gregg Ekberg, one of our favorite colloborators, wrote the white paper below to describe the future of complex real-time process diagnostic systems. We think his at the leading edge of upstream process analytics that should eventually flow through The Bridge model.

Reducing Process Variations and Related Costs...

...With Loosely Coupled Sets (LCS) Technology*

---

*Gregg Ekberg, Highline Controls, Inc., 586-530-5887, gregg@highlinecontrols.com.

This white paper introduces an innovative concept for process monitoring and control that promises to dramatically improve many operating situations that have historically been too complex for practical real-time controls. It uses the power of low-cost computing to make significant process variable relationships visible for practical control actions.

Several types of potential applications are described next. A case study is also included which describes a press monitoring project implemented to identify and monitor product quality in an automated metal-forming process.

Loosely coupled sets is a technology developed by Dick Morley and Larry Hill. They founded Invisitech Corporation in 1997 to own the resulting patents and to promote LCS applications. (For techno-history buffs, you might recognize Morley as the inventor of the ubiquitous programmable logic controller, or PLC, used in most automated equipment.)

LCS is a mathematical approach to identifying people and things, which has a variety of applications. One of the most important applications is manufacturing quality control, where the "things" it identifies are unacceptable process variations.

Although the mathematics is complex, the basic idea is very simple. If you take a lot of different measurements, which are statistically independent of one another, no one measurement by itself needs to be very accurate in order to achieve a very accurate result.

The accuracy with which you can select goes up exponentially with the number of independent measurements, and only linearly with the accuracy of an individual measurement.

This is contradictory to "conventional" thinking, where one invests money and process time in making a very accurate measurement of the one or more physical parameters that are deemed important. But generally, the cost of increasing accuracy is very high—a 1 percent error may cost $1, a 0.1 percent error $100, and a 0.001 percent error may be unachievable in a real environment (Exhibit 13.13).

On the other hand, if you make gross measurements, say to the nearest quartile or 25 percent accuracy, of five different parameters that are truly independent of each other, you achieve 0.1 percent selectivity. This is often

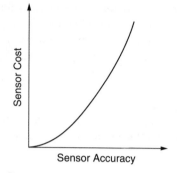

Exhibit 13.13   Sensor Cost

more reliable, more robust, and easier to maintain than the single, more precise measurement (Exhibit 13.14).

Applications of the Technology

Practical LCS applications are easy to find. Read on...

Signature Recognition

A good example of how this works is a study conducted by Invisitech of signature recognition. That is, using this approach to identify forged signatures on credit card vouchers. There is a sophisticated body of knowledge and patents relating to this problem, using sophisticated pattern-matching methods, high-resolution images, and substantial amounts of memory and processing power. The state of the art, by such methods, is as good as most humans inspecting a potentially forged versus a set of real signatures.

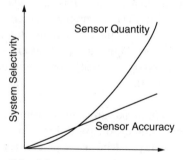

Exhibit 13.14   System Selectivity

We made three very simple measurements, all capable of very inexpensive realization:

1. The time duration of the signature, to 0.1 second
2. The maximum pressure exerted by the signer's pen on the paper
3. The "density" of the signature, defined as the areas of the smallest rectangle completely covering the signature, divided by the number of letters in the name.

The issue with signature checking, as with many tests, is the relationship of false negatives to false positives, or, in medical terms, selectivity versus specificity. You do not want to reject "honest" signatures often, but the more forgiving you are, the more forgeries will sneak through. Invisitech made actual measurements of signatures by 10 people, and of forgeries of each name by another of the group. The resulting performance was better, in terms of false negative versus false positive contour, than the compute-intensive approach. Specifically, the data collected showed 90 percent accuracy in catching forgeries, if the false positive tolerance was set so that, if you sign once a day, you will be unfairly rejected once in 27 years. Although 90 percent is not impressive by manufacturing standards, in the case of retailing, this would reduce forgeries *tenfold.*

Building Security. Systems typically involve a card or a key (an object possessed by the person, which could be stolen), a password (something the individual knows, which he or she might have revealed inadvertently or under duress) and, in high security or expensive systems, a biometric measurement, such as a voice print or a retinal scan.

By measuring several different variables grossly, such as light/medium/heavy, gait (time between steps, dominant acoustic voice frequency, delay in getting key into door after standing in front of it, and so forth, favorable accuracy can be achieved. This is like the sort of pattern your dog uses, when he realizes you, and not a stranger, are walking up your front steps, even though the dog cannot yet see or smell you.

Retail Traffic Analysis. This is the same problem, but a different application: how much of a store's floor traffic is repeat business? What is the "yield" of the traffic in terms of actual purchases?

Intelligent Toys. The method allows an inexpensive doll ($39.95 retail) to recognize and speak a dozen or so words each, to recognize favorite and unfavorite people, and to learn habits and patterns with the intelligence of a dumb but unexceptional puppy.

Food Processing.   The sugar coating on a certain candy is made according to a carefully controlled process. But sometimes the sugar coating has better or worse mechanical properties and sometimes it tastes better, or worse. Controlling the process is hard because the variations in input, which are small, compared to what can be reliably measured, amplify to become grossly observable, quality issues at the process output.

Minesweeping.   There are a variety of military applications of the technology.

Press Monitoring.   Highline Controls used the LCS approach to help Falcon Cold Forming develop a process monitoring system for one of their automated presses. Falcon wanted a system to monitor product quality, warn of drift, and shut down the process if the part was out of tolerance. Typically a vision system would be used to check the parts; however, vibration, part presentation tooling, lighting, speed, lubrication, smoke, and other process variables made vision systems expensive and unreliable. Highline proposed to use the LCS approach to monitor many independent variables and from those variables identify good from bad parts.

Highline installed acoustic sensors throughout the press with the idea we could "hear" when a bad part was made. The following sensors were installed and/or monitored:

- Main drive shaft acoustic sensor to identify load and jerk
- Intermediate drive shaft acoustic sensor
- Punch retainer ring acoustic sensor to hear side loading and metal forming
- Die retainer acoustic sensor to hear side loading and metal forming
- Knockout punch acoustic sensor to hear knockout load
- Press tonnage meter sensors monitoring loading on all 4 corners
- Main drive motor load
- Part in die and eject sensors to monitor part timing through process

The process was monitored for days and the data were analyzed for correlations between sensor readings and part quality. It was expected there would be excellent correlation with the punch and die acoustic sensors that picked up strain on the punch and die and also picked up the metal flow during the forming process.

Unintuitively, the best correlation turned out to be the knockout sensor. If a bad part was formed, it would stick to the punch and the knockout pin would never make contact. As a result, Falcon was able to install a very simple, low cost, easy-to-maintain sensor to check to be sure the knockout ejects the part from the die, or the part is bad.

13.7   In Closing—A Bridge Span: In-Process Analysis of Variation Causes

This seems like a good topic to end with. Most of this book has been focused on conventional methods and tools for predicting and tracking business process improvements into the financial statements.

The previous section on Flow software began to look to the future of tools more suited to the mass customization world that's rapidly becoming an expected norm. From that perspective, it was focused on practical methods for Lean operations even when every unit moving through a process is somewhat unique.

This last topic on applications of loosely coupled sets theory is also looking to the future, but like Six Sigma statistical process management methods, LCS offers a "deep" view of operating processes. LCS promises automation of variations analysis work that now can be quite laborious due to the data collection and analysis routines involved. LCS may be an accurate and practical shortcut in many such situations.

For Bridge Process purposes, LCS applications may make it possible to quickly develop process control routines for new production facilities that would take weeks or months today. And the predictability of those efforts will be such that the upstream-downstream causal relationships are readily definable for tracking via the Bridge Process. Maybe the typical in-line LCS system will begin to function like a "Black Belt in a box."

14

Bridge Process Outlines

Think for yourselves and let others enjoy the
privilege to do so, too.
VOLTAIRE

The Bridge Process is focused on using business process metrics as a powerful, unifying lever for a company's multifaceted continuous performance improvement efforts. To that end, it provides:

- Clarity for the linkages between the upstream control factors and the downstream business results.
- Clarity for the period-to-period changes that will be apparent in the financial statement, *if* they have been correctly accounted for in the implementation plans of improvement projects.

The following sections contain two operational checklists for the people involved.

- Routine Bridge Functions
- Bridge Implementation steps

Both outlines (routine process and implementation) follow the Six Sigma DMAIC steps to ensure comprehensive follow-through.

14.1 Routine Bridge Functions: Day-to-Day Use of a Bridge System by Process Operators and Owners

These process steps are the power of the Bridge Process in daily operations. They enable operating teams and process owners to easily monitor the few key metrics needed to ensure predictable cause-and-effect results in their business processes that show up in the financial statement as expected. Key steps in the Bridge routines are:

- Define or redefine the process metrics roadmap, so cause-and-effect relations are clear (at least quarterly).
- 100 percent performance of the analysis and diagnostic steps, as scheduled (real time, hourly, daily, weekly, quarterly...).
- Active management of the support systems to cause everyone to consistently play their role in the Lean-Sigma-CI business culture. The Bridge metrics and diagnostic steps are the "springboard to an accelerating Lean-Sigma-CI culture." The support systems must be structured appropriately to engage everyone in the process.

This checklist answers the question: What do we need to do in day-to-day business operations to get maximum value from the Bridge Process and metrics?

Note: The Bridge functional steps can be viewed as an elaboration of the *search for opportunities* (SFO) and *Measurement* (Msmt) phases of the Lean-Sigma-CI processes for company-wide *continuous improvement* (CI). Therefore, the Bridge Process includes steps that begin to feel as though it has segued into the broader CI process. To keep your bearings, you may have to occasionally remind yourself of the core concept behind Bridge. That is, the Bridge Process organizes the business performance metrics system to accurately reflect CI results, and to be a robust enabling component of the company's overall performance improvement efforts.

Define

1. Clarify key business goals; VOC and VOB.
2. Define scope of business processes to be improved and tracked with Bridge.
3. Assign process owners of Bridge metrics.
4. Clarify process output requirements and operating performance goals in collaboration with customer(s) and management team, annual or with new project(s).

Measure

1. Adjust or establish "upstream" causal process metrics, working backward from the process outputs or the key business performance goals. Organize new process metrics in Bridge categories. Establish routine measurement procedures.
   a. Convert VOC and VOB to critical voice of the process metrics (typically outputs).
   b. Identify the Big Y and Little X process metrics.
   c. Create or edit Process Metrics Roadmap.

   d. Determine appropriate upper and lower limits for reporting.

   e. Create an "Operational Definition" of metrics and data to be collected.

2. Adjust the reporting procedures to communicate to process operators and owners; highlight the "exceptions" outside upper and lower control limits in "discovery sequence" for Analyze steps below.

Analyze

1. Metrics status reporting in discovery sequence. For example:

   a. Financial results in cost records, P&L statement, and balance sheet

   b. Market demand versus competitive capacities

   c. Product and service quality levels

   d. Process output performance levels; the Big "Ys" from a, b, and c above

   e. Upstream metrics that indicate status of the causal "X" factors

2. Analyze the out-of-bounds values for "root causes." Tools options:

   a. The process diagnostics manual (for the specific process)

   b. Visual/graphic analysis tools and checklists

     • Cause-and-effect diagrams

     • Force field analysis

     • Relationship matrices

     • Failure modes and effects analysis (FMEA)

     • Process analysis

     • Function analysis

     • Process waste checklist

     • Fundamentals of high-performance processes

   c. Statistical correlations analysis (PC software)

3. Identify the best opportunities (priorities) for operational improvements.

     • Pareto-type methods; focus on the "vital few"

4. Update the process diagnostics reference manual for improved use in Analyze.

Improve

1. Search and brainstorm for solutions. Also check the Process Diagnostics Manual.

2. Test alternate solutions with Bridge "What if?" computations. Select best.

3. Forward opportunities and potential solution(s) to their appropriate local process operators or owners for improvement action or to the closed-loop CI Process for follow-through action (pass to appropriate owner in another part of the company, charter a high-level critical process team, and so forth).

Control

1. Adjust the support systems as needed to make best use of the Bridge Process and data from it, for a core business process or whole enterprise.
2. Are any of the current learnings transferable across the business? Is an action plan for spreading the best practice appropriate?

14.2 Bridge Implementation Steps

These process steps are performed by a project team chartered to develop and implement a new Bridge Process in your company.

This checklist answers the question: What steps do we need to take as part of a project to customize and install a Bridge Process and metrics for use in our company?

Define

1. Clarify purpose and key goals to be accomplished with Bridge implementation.
2. Define initial scope of business processes to be tracked with Bridge.
3. Establish Bridge project ownership and team resources.
   a. Do you have open minded, creative people as part of the team?
   b. Do you have adequate resources to complete the project?

Measure

1. Identify the results gaps, i.e., results that were expected from recent improvement projects but were not reflected in the current measurement system. In other words, what types of results have not been showing up as expected in the current performance reports?
2. Identify possible causal metrics that are needed for upstream process control that will yield dependable downstream results in line with the key process performance goals. (Note: A YX matrix may be helpful for sorting the few high-correlation causal metrics from the many possibles.)
3. Collect data and establish current performance baselines for initial process/es to be tracked in the Bridge Process.
4. Determine appropriate upper and lower control limits for exceptions reporting.
5. Establish formats and procedures for reporting to process owners and operating teams.

Analyze

1. From the results gaps identified above (Measure #1), identify the ones that should have shown the largest benefits in the financial statement (i.e., the priority results gaps).

Improve

1. Starting with the priority results gaps (above), work through the DMAIC steps of the Routine Bridge Functions (previous section) and develop a draft Bridge Process design that is customized for your business. (Note: This Bridge system implementation step addresses all the steps in the routine bridge process functions above from Define through Control, including the support systems for the ongoing Bridge Process operations.)
2. Test the Bridge Process with varying data to see how well it would represent the results that had not been tracking to the financial statement before.
3. Repeat 1 and 2, adjusting the Bridge Process model to suit your business through several successive tests to resolve the results gaps.
4. Develop procedures, organization structure changes, software modifications, other support systems, and so forth to be installed for operation of routine bridge functions.
5. Plan and run a Bridge pilot. Adjust Bridge Process design.
6. Plan and run the Bridge system implementation.

Control

1. Produce deliverables to control this Bridge implementation project.
   a. Pilot evaluation plan
   b. Implementation and execution
   c. Implementation rollout plan
   d. Clarified roles and responsibilities (accountabilities)
   e. Project performance control metrics
   f. Financial assessment plan
   g. Project leadership governance
2. Check and adjust until running as desired. Identify follow-on opportunities that should be handed off to others.
3. Review results and handoff recommendations with management team.

INDEX

ABOUT THE AUTHORS

Michael Bremer is President of The Cumberland Group—
Chicago, as well as adjunct senior consultant for Motorola
University. He is a nationally recognized speaker on process
improvement, leadership, and management team effectiveness.
He is a board member of the Association for Manufacturing
Excellence—Midwest Region.

Brian McKibben is a Co–Chief Executive Officer of
Flow-Works, Inc., and a Vice President of The Cumberland
Group—Chicago. He is a board member of the association for
Manufacturing Excellence—Midwest Region, and is past
president of the Chicago chapter of the Institute of Industrial
Engineers.

Thomas McCarty is Executive Vice President and Six Sigma
Practice Leader at Jones Lang LaSalle Americas, Inc.,
responsible for improving the business performance of
suppliers, partners, and customers through consulting on
performance, process, and continuous improvement.